Currier's Price Guide to AMERICAN ARTISTS at AUCTION

Current Price Ranges on the Original Art
of Nearly 8000 American Artists at Auction

D0067696

SIXTH EDITION

Revised and Updated to Include New Artists

Written and Compiled by William T. Currier

CURRIER PUBLICATIONS

ISBN   0-935277-16-1 Softcover
Library of Congress
Catalog Card Number 94-70935

Printed in the United States of America

COVER PHOTO:

Venice Canal, **Jane Petersen,** oil on canvas, 40" x 30", Sold for $28,600 at Kaminski auction, Stoneham, MA, 1/22/93, photo courtesy of Private Collection.

Additional copies of this book may be obtained from bookstores and selected antique dealers. To order directly from the publisher, remit $18.95 per copy, plus $3.00 shipping(book rate) and handling, or $4.25(first class). Massachusetts addresses add 5% sales tax. For bulk order discounts (6 or more copies) please write, or call, for details to:

CURRIER PUBLICATIONS
241 Main Street
Stoneham, MA 02180
(800) 344-0760

[Make check or money order payable to CURRIER PUBLICATIONS]
(U.S. dollars only, please)

ACKNOWLEDGEMENTS

Many thanks for assistance with this new edition go out to:

Cynthia Tukis, for her expertise and valuable assistance in editing and proofreading everything I do.

James R. Bakker Antiques, Inc., Cambridge, MA, and Skinner, Inc., Bolton, MA, for providing many of the photographs in this *Guide*.

Walt Reed of the Illustration House, Inc., New York, NY, for contributing photographs for this *Guide*.

Green River Gallery, Millerton, NY, Jay Johnson America's Folk Heritage Gallery, New York, NY, and James B. McCloskey, for providing photos in this *Guide*.

Keith Kelman, K. Nathan Gallery, La Jolla, CA, for taking the time, over and over again, to forward additions, and/or corrections, of artist, price, and subject matter information in this *Guide*.

Each and every one of the individuals who took time during the past three years to send in corrections and additions of which we would, otherwise, have never been aware. Their contributions helped to make this *Guide* more accurate and ultimately more useful.

Edward LaBlue, frame dealer and consultant, for his important essay on how period frames are affecting the value of paintings.

Lowy, New York, NY, and Eli Wilner & Co., New York, NY, for contributing photos for our chapter on period frames.

Lowy, New York, NY, for their essay on the the importance of the frame as an aesthetic statement.

My parents, Lillian and William, for their encouragement and support - as always.

My wife, Donna, her mother, Lorraine, my daughter, Danielle, and my son, Christopher, who sacrificed so much month after month, to make each new edition possible. I thank you especially, with love.

William T. Currier

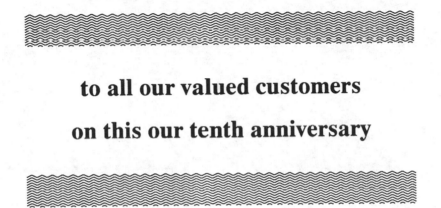

to all our valued customers

on this our tenth anniversary

About the Author

William T. Currier

William T. Currier, a graduate of Boston University, was an educator with the Boston Public Schools for over fifteen years. Although his knowledge of art history was not acquired through a "formal" education in art history, he spent thousands of hours during the past twenty years in intense independent study of both art history and the art market. Mr.Currier has been a guest speaker at adult education classes, lecturing on identifying original prints and paintings, and has attended many lectures and professional seminars on art history and art investment. He is presently director of Currier Fine Art, a member of The New England Appraisers Association, and also works privately as an agent, market liaison,and consultant.

TABLE OF CONTENTS

CHAPTER ONE: Determining Value

CHAPTER TWO: Using This Guide

CHAPTER THREE: Period Frames

American Artists at Auction

Record Prices

Appendix

PREFACE

Until the publication of our *Guide* there was no other practical reference available in an inexpensive, compact, concise and portable format that could help quickly assess the probable worth of fine examples of American art from the 18th , 19th, and 20th centuries. It is invaluable to: antique dealers, auctioneers, art collectors, estate lawyers, bank trust officers, art consultants, appraisers, and art dealers. *Currier's Price Guide to American Artists at Auction* may well be the most profitable investment that anyone, who has occasion to buy and sell American art, could ever make.

You will find that you have purchased the most practical price guide to 300 years of American art [artists born 1645-1945] available today. The compilation of data here will be useful to even the most seasoned veteran of the American art marketplace:

▶ Accurate spellings of artists' names.

▶ Accurate birth and death dates not easily found elsewhere.

▶ A "mnemonic" (meaning to assist the memory) list of subjects typical for each artist "value prioritized" - the most sought-after subjects for each artist are listed first.

▶ Current, accurate price ranges (compiled from thousands of auction results) for America's most sought-after artists.

As accurate as the Fifth Edition was, this new Sixth Edition is even more accurate:

• New Artists have been added.

• Over 1500 changes were made in this Sixth Edition. The updated price ranges reflect sales results from hundreds of auction houses, both here and abroad, thru September 1993.

- We corrected some misspelled names, added birth and death dates where there were none, and added, or made changes to, the *typical subjects* of numerous artists.

- The *Record Prices* section has been completely revised so that it is current.

- For the second time in our history, we have added advertising to the *Appendix* section of the book.

Since the publication of our first edition, we have received hundreds of calls and letters from people from all parts of the country. Without exception, all comments regarding the book's usefulness have been positive ones. With each new edition, each trade review that we receive is a positive one. Art collectors, art dealers, appraisers, and many others have found our *Guide* continually useful for *quickly* checking the auction record of the many American artists they encounter each month.

Many auctioneers use the price ranges to help establish a starting bid on works of artists with whom they are unfamiliar, or help screen items for possible consignment.

Art collectors find the *Guide* extremely interesting and especially helpful when hunting for artists whose work falls only within certain price ranges (e.g., $400-$7,500) and/or who specialize in certain subjects (e.g., marines, landscapes, still life, etc.). Many collectors report that they would keep a copy with them as they frequent yard sales, flea markets, thrift shops, or country auctions. Not infrequently, many "sleepers" are uncovered.

Appraisers use the *Guide* to quickly find what the highest price realized at auction had been on a particular artist's work. They use this information as a starting point, then proceed to do further research on the actual auction results. For appraisers, knowing the highest price realized at auction for the work of a particular artist will help avoid the chance of being penalized by the IRS for overvaluation.

Estate lawyers working with appraisers find it beneficial to know the *least* amount certain works by a particular artist have sold for, so they can justify a low valuation for estate tax purposes.

Because of information gleaned from our *Guide*, many estate executors have pursued a professional appraisal on certain works of art. It would not be unusual for someone running an estate "tag sale" to price something well below its true market value.

Antique dealers, who have occasion to buy and sell American art, but who have very little knowledge of the art market have found our *Guide* to be one of the most important references books in their library. The *Guide* helps many dealers to avoid the problem of buying too high or selling too low. And helps them to *quickly* assess the *potential* value of American artwork in many situations: house calls, estate sales, etc. Dealers can quickly determine if a recent purchase needs more research before pricing it for resale. Obviously, if a dealer purchased a large landscape, signed David Johnson, at a yard sale for $100, and he found in our *Guide* that the highest price realized for the artist's work exceeds $165,000, he'd want to have it examined by an "expert"(more on that in Chapter One.)

One financial consultant for a major Boston firm forwarded a letter stating that our *Guide* would "prove to be very helpful in my efforts to help my clients fulfill their financial goals" and added, "a person could have a fortune in artwork and not even realize it. A quick look in your *Guide* and one can tell if there is a need for further investigation."

One important dealer in American paintings,Henry B. Holt, forwarded to us the following letter which sums up quite well the *Guide's* purpose and usefulness.

> *I recently realized how very valuable I have found "Currier's Guide" and felt compelled to write to you. I keep a copy in each of my offices and ordinarily carry one in my car. This weekend, I was called out to look at some paintings and found that I didn't have my "Currier's" with me. Because a few of the artists were somewhat obscure, the Guide really would have come in handy. I have found "Currier's Guide"to be indispensable in such cases. Compact, concise, accurate, dependable! I can't imagine any collector, appraiser, or dealer's library would be complete without "Currier's Guide", since it provides a valuable insight on the price range based on auction records of so many artists, as well as many other useful and informative sidelights. My compliments on a job well done.*

Add to the list, the many thrift shop owners, pickers, museum personnel, art framers, and yard sale and flea market fanatics who find our *Guide* useful; and you can only agree that *Currier's Price Guide to American Artists at Auction* is the *first* place to look for values on the works by American artists.

One final note: You are welcome and encouraged to comment, make note of errors, and feel free to suggest changes or additions which will improve this *Guide*. Please write or call:

CURRIER PUBLICATIONS
241 Main Street
Stoneham, MA 02180
(800) 344-0760

DISCLAIMER

Although every attempt, within reason, has been made to keep the price ranges herein as accurate as possible, there may be mistakes, both typographical and in content. Therefore, this guide should be used only as a general guide, not as the final or ultimate source of the only prices which may be realized at auction by any particular artist.

Special care must be exercised when examining the prices of contemporary artists. Because of the "dynamic" nature of the market as a whole, prices can rise and fall quickly. With living artists, it is best to check with those galleries that represent them for the "final" word on current values. Prices charged in the galleries for the works of living artists can be many times those realized at auction.

Also, the compilation of conservators, and dealers in the *Appendix* is only a representative sampling of the hundreds of conservators, and dealers houses which I am sure may be of equal distinction.

The author and *Currier Publications* shall have neither liability nor responsibility to any person with respect to any loss or damage caused or alleged to be caused directly or indirectly by the information contained in this book.

CHAPTER ONE

Determining Value

Please Note: **Two assumptions are made throughout this Guide: that you are a novice in the art marketplace, and that we will always be talking about prices at fair market value (i.e., auction results).**

Until your work of art is sold, it has no real value (unlike stocks); only a subjective value based on many factors. No one can guarantee that your piece will bring a specified dollar amount at some future date. Factors influencing the price of a work of art may vary and, for that reason, you can expect a different price at each new auction. Let's look briefly at some of the direct factors and outside influences which, the author feels, most dramatically affect price.

Seven Important Factors

ARTIST   The most important factor. When we can prove who the artist is, whether or not the piece is signed, it will most directly influence the price realized. Almost without exception, the first question you will get from any major auction house, or dealer, when you call them to look for price information, will be: "Who is the artist?" Once the name is known, everything else follows: "What's the subject matter?", "What's the condition?", etc.

If you buy a piece which is unsigned, but you have been told by the seller that it was painted by a well-known artist, obtaining a letter from an authority, which states without question that it is the particular artist the seller said it was, will help immensely in increasing its desirability and value.

Most would consider the signature to be exceedingly important. The truth is that it is of the very least value, until it can be proved without question that it is indeed the signature of the artist who painted the particular work.

Signatures can be added to an oil painting by anyone feeling it will increase its value. If you have a magnifying glass of at least 10-30x, examine the signature to be sure that "old" cracks running through the signature do indeed run through - that they are not filled with paint from a "recent" signature. If you suspect a forged signature, another way to check is to rub the signature gently with a little turpentine on a soft cloth - it will usually wash out a recent signature.

An authentic signature with a date is more desirable than one without.

MEDIUM There are many good books available which explain the peculiarities of the various mediums. The novice to the art market should endeavor to familiarize him/herself with several.

The most popular medium overall today is still oils. It should be mentioned that, in the case of many contemporary artists, mixed media is extremely popular - much to the chagrin of today's conservator. Also, with contemporary artists, it is their mixed media work which often brings the highest prices.

Try to remember, that the price ranges in this *Guide* which begin with an asterisk (*) denote: mixed media, watercolors, gouaches, pastels, and/or pencil and ink drawings. With such a variety of mediums, you can expect a price range often to start in the hundreds (for drawings) and end in the hundreds of thousands of dollars (for contemporary mixed media.) Don't be mislead, though, in thinking all drawings will be of least value - *there are exceptions*. A drawing which is a preparatory study for a painting, which today is historically important, can have great value. For example, an ink and watercolor drawing by Benjamin West, a study for the painting, *The Death of General Wolfe*, sold at Sotheby's (5/84) for $165,000.

QUALITY Without question, the most exceptional pieces, regarding quality, in any medium, by any artist, will bring exceptionally high prices. Every dealer will tell you that he has no problem quickly moving the pieces of the highest quality.

The work of a much sought-after artist will only bring a meager price, if it is of meager quality. Artists are human, of course, and have their good and bad days.

During an artist's lifetime, his/her work could have evolved through several style changes, and within each style change works of varying quality can be found. The months or years which represent a particular style change are called "periods." It may happen that a small work of great quality, from a much sought-after earlier,or later period, will be of more value than a much larger work from some other "period" which is not highly sought after.

At the end of the alphabetical listings in this *Guide*, is a separate section entitled: *Record Prices*. Those prices represent values realized for works which were considered of exceptional quality. They had to be isolated, because the prices were well above the high end of all other works by that artist, and to include them would have distorted a "true" picture of the normal price range of that artist's work.

There are many factors which the novice can consider in determining a "probable" value of a fine painting, but judging quality, style, and period is best left up to the "expert": university scholar, museum curator, art dealer, certain art consultants, qualified appraiser, or some independent author or connoisseur.

SUBJECT In a broad sense, this is the main theme of a work of art. In a narrower vein, it is the "subject matter" within the subject that can affect value. As an example, the subject of a painting might be a still life, but its "subject matter" might be dead game birds. The subject of another painting might be marine, and the "subject matter," a coastal harbor scene.

Most artists have one or two subjects for which they are best known. These particular subjects are the ones most sought after and bring the highest prices (see the section on Typical Subjects in Chapter 2 for a list with an explanation.) Robert Spear Dunning is best known for his still life; John George Brown is best known as a painter of genre, etc. Knowing the subject(s) most sought after for any particular artist is very important for you in determining the *potential* value of a piece. I have done most of that work for you in this *Guide* - more on that in Chapter 2.

After attending a number of art auctions, you will begin to

note which subjects and subject matter are most and least desirable. In general, collectors today want bright colorful, non-offensive pieces for their walls. Let's look more closely at our subjects:

Figures: Studio portraits, with the exception of early folk portraits (see Primitives below), and historical figures, hold very little interest among collectors, unless done by a well-known artist. The most desirable figure paintings are those in a non-studio setting, e.g., groups of people in an interior or outdoor setting. Collectors often prefer women and children over men in both portraits and figure studies. Religious figures are not very popular, unless they are old master paintings. To certain collectors, the nude figure is desirable.

Genre: Themes which can be considered genre probably number in the thousands. Some of the more popular themes might be: a public fete, a friendly conversation, the comedies of the household, or the little dramas of private life.

Illustrations: Because of the endless variety of both subjects and mediums in the field of illustration, it is very difficult to point out a most and least popular subject. If you have any questions about American illustrators it is best to talk to someone who specializes in American illustration.

Landscapes: Collectors today prefer bright, colorful landscapes with identifiable landmarks - especially if the landmarks have local interest. Of the four seasons, winter scenes seem to draw the most attention. Landscapes with a "luminous" quality are popular - especially those of the Hudson River school of artist. American scenes are usually more desirable than European scenes by the same artist.

Marines: Collectors of marine subjects can be very particular about their ship portraits. The rigging, the position of the sails, the flags that are being flown, and many other details can affect the desirability of a marine painting. American vessels, flying American flags, are always more desirable than a foreign equivalent. From my own observations, the old side-wheelers and clipper ships under full sail enjoy considerable popularity. As with landscapes, collectors prefer coastal scenes in which there is an identifiable landmark - such as, a familiar lighthouse. Again, local interest increases value.

Primitives: Very little of the early folk art is undesirable; nearly all examples are eagerly collected. However, pieces in very poor condition, or poorly restored are an exception and attract little interest. With primitives, it is best to sell them "as is," rather than having them restored. Collectors usually have their own conservator to whom they entrust their new acquisitions, and prefer no previous restoration.

Still Life: All types of still life are collected, from our earliest primitives to today's paintings of photographic realism. Floral pieces today are enjoying popularity, as are elaborate fruit and vegetable compositions. The "grander" the composition, the greater the value. When objects which are not essential to it are introduced into a composition, they are known as accessories and can often add interest and value to a still life. As an example, a still life painting of fruit may be more interesting, and more valuable, if it includes objects such as a compote, basket, knife, flowers, table cloth, colorful screen, vase, etc..

Wildlife: Scenes with an abundance of blood will be least desirable and farm yard fowl don't enjoy much popularity. Of all the animals around the farm, horses are the most popular with collectors. Deer are always popular, if not shown being shot, and most hunting and fishing scenes will attract buyers if there is no blood and gore.

STYLE Sir Joshua Reynolds (1723-1792) said, "In painting, style is the same as in writing: some are grand, others plain; some florid and others simple." Styles can be peculiar to a "school," or a master, in design, composition, coloring, expression, and execution, but not necessarily peculiar to the artist. In many instances, artists have changed their personal styles several times during their lifetime. As stated earlier, each new style change is considered a new period. Some periods, or styles, are more sought after than others because of a greater appeal. Leading the list would be the work of the American Impressionists.

When you're assessing the "probable" value of a painting, it may be necessary to let an "expert" determine the style of the work (see "Quality" above.)

CONDITION Although "condition" seems a long way down on our list of "factors determining value," it is really the one variable to which we must pay the most attention. No matter who the artist is, a painting in very poor condition, or one that has been heavily restored, will have very little value - at best, a fraction of the worth of a similar painting in pristine condition.

Before you buy a painting on canvas in need of conservation, consider the following:

- After you spend anywhere from $100-$1500 for the cost of restoration, will you be able to realize a profit?

- Are you willing to tie that painting up for what may take as long as six months?

- If there is paint loss, is any of it in critical areas which will affect value? For instance, you do not want the paint to be falling away from the faces and bodies of people in a figure painting.

- Is the overall paint loss greater than 25% ? If so, unless the painting is extremely valuable, pass on it!

- Besides restoration, will the painting need an appropriate frame to make it saleable - another expense?

- Is the painting covered with a very dark layer of dirt and varnish? Only a professional conservator will be able to ascertain if that painting will "clean up." If she/he says definitely not, you may never see a profit.

- Has the painting already had any "bad" restoration?

- The cost of restoration can be very high if the conservator has to do a relining and extensive *inpainting* in addition to a cleaning. Relinings are often necessary when the canvas is extremely wrinkled, torn, abraded, or too loose and floppy. *Inpainting* is an expensive and involved process of repainting damaged areas to their original condition.

Remember. Though cleaning may be useful to restore the original brilliance of an old painting - though relining is sometimes needed to save it from imminent destruction - to let it be attempted by a non-professional is a sacrilege. *Always make sure that the conservator has an impeccable reputation for quality work.* Also, *never* use water to clean a painting - leave it alone until an expert can look at it.

To assist you in finding a conservator, I have compiled a representative list from around the country and abroad and have included it in the *Appendix* of this *Guide.* Your best source for a reputable conservator is the recommendation of an art museum or prestigious art gallery.

For those of you who are only vaguely familiar with the use of a blacklight for assistance in finding previous restorations, added signatures, etc., and wish to become more "expert" in its use, there is information available. Recently, Karl Gabosh, assembled a guide, complete with samples and text, entitled: *The Collector's Blacklight Guide.* It is an important tool for the serious art dealer, collector, and others.

To obtain more information on the *The Collector's Blacklight Guide*, please write to:

Peter Falk
Sound View Press
170 Boston Post Road
Madison, CT 06443
(203) 245-2246

SIZE All it will take is one afternoon at an art auction to see that there is a definite correlation between size and price. This relation holds true only among paintings by the same artist, and among paintings that are similar in subject matter, period, quality, and style.

You may never hear of a painting that is too small to be desirable, but you will likely hear of a painting being too big to be desirable. When a painting is larger than sofa size, you will find that your buying audience has shrunk considerably. Of course, there could be exceptions to this, in cases where the artist is an eminent American master.

Outside Influences on Value

As discussed above, when you purchase a painting for resale, there are inherent factors (e.g., artist, size, medium, condition, quality, subject, style) which can be quickly ascertained for determining an approximate value. There are other outside influences (e.g., historical importance, provenance, time and location of sale, competitive bidding, publicity and fads) which can have a positive or negative affect on value. Let's take a brief look at each.

HISTORICAL IMPORTANCE All preparatory studies (drawings, watercolors, oil sketches, etc.) for any major historical American painting can be valuable. If you find, while researching your artist, that he/she painted many historically important paintings, check your piece or have an "expert" check your piece, to determine if it could be an important preparatory study. The likelihood of finding an actual canvas which is a major historical painting is slim. Most are either in museums, historical societies, or private corporate collections. Don't expect to find one in someone's attic next month.

PROVENANCE Provenance is simply a list of previous owners, analogous to a pedigree. It can be important to some collectors; not so important to others. Provenance works in reverse, for example, the present owner is listed first, the previous owner is listed second, and so on, until we are back, ideally, to the artist himself. This line of ownership can make the piece very desirable, particularly if the list has some important names on it. But there can be a problem since we sometimes have no way of checking the authenticity of a particular document. Most of the people on the list may be deceased, and therefore, not available to vouch for their prior ownership of the piece in question.

A provenance is not at all necessary to transact a sale, but if you have supportable evidence that the provenance is unquestionably genuine, then it can be even more important than the signature on the piece.

Sometimes, you will find that names have been filled in to complete a gap in its provenance. Be careful. Always try to judge the piece first on its own merit as a fine work of art. If it turns out later that all the documentation included with it is authentic, then the value of the piece will increase immeasurably.

The topic of Provenance is closely related to a discussion of authentication. If you feel you have just bought an "important" painting and would like to have it properly authenticated, see the *Appendix* under "Appraisal Organizations" for a list of authentication services.

SELLING: TIME AND LOCATION OF SALE Some auction houses do better than others, selling the works of certain artists. It is valuable information to know at which auction house an artist continually commands the highest prices. Information of this type is not easily obtainable, unless you have been closely following the market all over the country. If you have a "potentially" valuable painting, I might suggest that you contact some art consultants in your area, to see if they provide that service. If they do not, the author can help you. Please call or write to William Currier, *Currier Fine Art*, P.O.Box 2098, Brockton, MA 02405,(508) 588-4509, fax:(508) 588-4227.

The worst months of the year in which to sell at auction are July and August; the best months are March, April, May, October, November, December.

If you plan to send your art to auction then keep two things in mind:

> **1.** From the day you send your piece to a *major* auction house until the day of the actual sale, two to five months may pass. Auction officials need that time to research all the paintings, determine estimates, do the presale advertising, and photograph most of the paintings in the sale for placement in a catalog, which goes out (at a price) to the patrons of the sale. A sale at a smaller auction house may be preferable!

2.Many of the *major* auction houses do not send
you your money (less commission) until 35-40 days
after the sale.They wait for buyers' checks to clear
and returns of merchandise purchased.

Be aware that the work of certain artists may only sell at
high price if there is a large concentration of collectors in the clos
geographical area of that artist.

Many of the artists who sell in the $500-10,000 range will far
better at auctions in regions where they spent most of their live:
painting. The "home-town artist" will do best near his home-town;
the big name artist will sell everywhere.

Before you ship your piece to auction, check the offers of
dealers who specialize in work by your artist - you may get an offer
you can't refuse.

COMPETITIVE BIDDING At almost every major auction
there are a number of fine paintings which sell well above the estimates - much to the delight of the consignor. Competitive bidding can
drive the price up well above estimate. All that is needed are two or
more people who want that piece desperately enough, that it seems
money is no object. In June of 1981, a Charles Sprague Pearce painting sold (with a pre-sale estimate of $10-15,000) for $247,500. Can
you imagine how happy that consignor was!

PUBLICITY AND FADS The resale value of your work of
art will leap, if it has appeared as an illustration in one or more pieces
of literature. If the work of art also has a well-documented exhibition
record, that will increase its desirability.

Someone once said, "As New York goes,so goes the country." It often seems that what starts out popular and fashionable in
New York, catches on elsewhere. If you get a chance to follow the
market more closely each year, you'll be able to stay on top of what is
currently "fashionable."

CHAPTER TWO

Using This Guide

An Overview

In the process of compiling the nearly 8,000 names of artists, it was found that in many instances, the spelling of names was incorrect, or incomplete, with only initials and a surname, as they appeared in many of the auction house catalogs nationally. This was due in part, understandably, to the haste with which many of these artists were researched and then recorded in the catalog in time for the pre-sale promotion. The full and correct spelling of names was determined as accurately as possible by checking more than one dictionary of artists for each name. If no dates were available, the century during which that artist is known to have worked was placed next to the name.

The birth and death dates, when available, were researched for accuracy and recorded next to the name. In many instances, birth and death dates which could not be easily found elsewhere were recorded.

Price ranges and typical subject(s), "value prioritized" and listed, using mnemonic letters, were established by studying the sales record of each individual artist. Vast amounts of biographical data, from my own reference library and sources outside, were carefully reviewed, in an attempt to establish those subjects most typical for each artist in question. From that point, we ascertained as accurately as possible which subject(s) consistently brought the highest prices - the most sought-after subjects by the collectors. After carefully recording all of the auction prices for each artist for the past ten years, it was possible then to record a price range which reflected the "practical" low and high for that particular artist. Any dollar amount which was well above the average high end, and which did not obviously fit into the typical price range for that artist, was recorded alphabetically on a separate list entitled, *Record Prices* - found on page 343.

Let's Keep It Simple

The names and dates need no more explanation than presented above. It will be the "price ranges" and the "typical subjects" that need clarification.

PRICE RANGES: You have to remember five things:

1. Most of the price ranges are simply low and high dollar amounts, indicating the range within which you would expect the artist's oils, acrylics, and/or tempera paintings to sell.

Example:

ARTIST	PRICES	SUBJECT
CAPP, AL (20TH C)	2500-18000	A

2. A small number of the price ranges will be preceded by an asterisk (*), indicating a price range for that artist's drawings, watercolors, gouaches, pastels, and/or mixed media. If an artist's name was listed twice, he/she was prolific enough in all mediums to have two separate price ranges. When a name is listed twice, the "typical subject" follows the second price range and the birth and death dates also follow the second listing of the name.

Example:

ARTIST	PRICES	SUBJCT
BROWNE, MATILDA	*150-2000	
BROWNE, MATILDA (1896-1953)	350-4400+	S,L

3. The plus "+" simply indicates that that artist has a *record price* which you will find in the section entitled *Record Prices*, found on page 343. In the above example, the record selling price for a painting by Matilda Browne is $30,800. Obviously, to have said that Ms. Browne's price range is $350-$12,000 would have distorted the true range within which 99% of her work falls. In all instances where one price was *well* above all others realized at auction, it was included in the *Record Prices* section.

4. Four question marks (????) will indicate an American artist whose work has not appeared at auction for the past 10 years, but whose work would sell for hundreds of thousands of dollars, or higher, if it appeared at auction today.

5. A *single* price may be found recorded for an artist in instances where a recent sale was significant enough to report, and happened to be the *only* recorded sale of a work by that artist in the past 10 years.

Typical Subjects: "Mnemonic" Letters

"Mnemonic" (pronounced "ni-monic") means *assisting or designed to assist the memory*. In that respect, you will find after each artist, if the information was available, single letters corresponding to the subjects most typical for the artist, arranged "value prioritized" (see below.) Each letter matches the following subjects:

A	Avant-Garde
F	Figures
G	Genre
I	Illustrations
L	Landscapes
M	Marines
P	Primitives
S	Still Life
W	Wildlife
X	Unknown

In the section which follows, for the benefit of the novice, we will briefly explain, with photo examples, each of the subject areas.

"Value Prioritized" simply means that you will find the subjects arranged in descending order according to value. Those subjects by a particular artist, which *generally* bring the highest prices, are listed first, and so on. Please keep in mind that no such list can be compiled with the certainty of "death and taxes" - the author has made a sincere effort to keep the list as accurate as possible. If you are aware of an error and can substantiate it, please bring it to my attention. I will make the correction in the next edition, for the benefit of everyone.

Let's take a closer look at each subject area, with examples:

TYPICAL SUBJECTS

AVANT-GARDE / A

For our purposes,"Avant-Garde" will refer to all the art works which do not easily fit into any of the other categories herein because of their unconventional styles. Such works might typically include the "experimental" works or "fads" of the 20th century - such as, Cubism, Dadaism, Surrealism, Abstract Expressionism, Minimal Art, Photorealism, and Pop Art.

Please Note: It is important to repeat here a statement made earlier in the "Disclaimer." When examining the prices of Contemporary artists (over 300 in this *Guide*),care must be exercised. Because of the "dynamic" nature of the contemporary market as a whole, prices rise and fall quickly. With regard to living artists,it is *always* best to check with those galleries that represent them for the "final" word on current values.

The best reference for finding those Galleries which represent many of the contemporary artists listed here is Paul Cumming's book, *Dictionary of Contemporary American Artists*, St. Martin's Press, New York (ISBN 0-312-20097-8, $50.00). There are no prices, but it contains plenty of biographical material covering over 900 contemporary artists.

In Gloucester Harbor
by Elizabeth Miller Lobingier, oil on canvas, 25" x 30"
(Courtesy of Skinner, Inc., Bolton, MA)

Top Hat and Rainbow
by Steven Trefonides, pastel, 39" x 30"
(Courtesy of James R. Bakker Antiques, Inc., Cambridge, MA)

Magnolia
by Dorothy Loeb, oil on canvas, 24" x 20"
(Courtesy of James R. Bakker Antiques, Inc., Cambridge, MA)

FIGURES / F

Most typically under this category are works which depict adults and/or children in various studio and non-studio settings. These figure studies may include: portraits (single and/or group), miniatures, historical figures, and people from all walks of life in settings typical of the period and location. Many "experts" will argue, with good reason , that many non-studio figure paintings are genre.

In figure painting, the artist usually is more interested in depicting the character of the individual, not so much the human situation, as in genre (see next topic.)

Religious, historical, and allegorical subjects will also be included in this category for our purposes.

Cinderella
by James Wells Champney, oil on panel, 11" x 9"
(Courtesy of a Private Collection)

Lighting Up
by William McGregor Paxton, oil on canvas
(Courtesy of James R. Bakker Antiques, Inc., Cambridge, MA)

Ballet Dancer
by Louis Kronberg, oil on canvas
(Courtesy of James R. Bakker Antiques, Inc., Cambridge, MA)

GENRE / G

Genre refers to people of all ages engaged in everyday activities typical for the period and location. Genre differs from figure studies in that usually the activity in the composition is the main theme. Typical compositions might include: western, sporting, city, country, seafaring, or domestic subjects.

Of particular note are the genre, or American scene paintings of the late 1920's, 30's, and 40's. The scenes were generally a preoccupation with the political and social realities of the day: contemporary morals and manners, the "beauty" found in the drabness and decay of our cities, studies of the poor and underprivileged, studies of the blue-collar worker of the farm and mine - a literal protest against the "pretty" pictures of the 19th century.

The Fortune Teller
by Harry Roseland, oil on canvas, 20" x 30"
(Courtesy of James R. Bakker Antiques, Inc., Cambridge, MA)

Christmas Preparations
by Carl H. Nordstrom, oil on canvas, 20" x 16"
(Courtesy of James R. Bakker Antiques, Inc., Cambridge, MA)

The Seamstress
by Frank Hector Tompkins, oil on canvas, 32" x 26"
(Courtesy of William T. Currier)

ILLUSTRATIONS / I

This is a broad category which typically involves works which were executed for the purpose of reinforcing an idea or theme of a publication and/or advertisement. In this category, you will find the greatest variety of mediums and subject matter.

Gag Cartoon (New Yorker)
by Peter Arno, brush & ink, 15" x 11"
(Courtesy of The Illustration House, New York, NY)

The Puritan Girl, from *The Courtship of Miles Standish*
by Howard Chandler Christy, oil on canvas, 63" x 44"
(Courtesy of Judy Goffman Fine Art, New York, NY)

Caricature
by Charles A. Hughes, colored pencil, 23" x 19"
(Courtesy of The Illustration House, New York, NY)

Story Illustration
by Ralph Pallen Coleman, oil on canvas, 29" x 21"
(Courtesy of The Illustration House, New York, NY)

LANDSCAPES / L

In this category, you may find compositions which depict natural scenery, and which may or may not include figures and/or man-made objects. All seasons and all times of the day may be depicted, and views might include any of the following: scenes west or east of the Mississippi, seascapes (shoreline views), and scenes outside the United States. *Genre* may often be combined with a landscape composition.

Study for Butterfly Chaser
by Thomas Hart Benton, oil on board, 8" x 6"
(Courtesy of Skinner, Inc., Bolton, MA)

Landscape with House and Pond
by Vivian Milner Akers, oil on canvasboard, 24" x 20"
(Courtesy of James R. Bakker Antiques, Inc., Cambridge, MA)

Figures on a Village Street
by Margaret Jordan Patterson, oil on canvas, 18" x 15"
(Courtesy of James R. Bakker Antiques, Inc., Cambridge, MA)

MARINES / M

This category will be used in instances where the artist's major output was nautical compositions, such as, drawings and/or paintings of vessels of all descriptions and sizes, sea scenes, and coastal or harbor scenes.

Venetian Canal
by Margaret Jordan Patterson, gouache, 17" x 14"
(Courtesy of James R. Bakker Antiques, Inc., Cambridge, MA)

Sailing About The Harbor
by Charles Henry Gifford, oil on canvas, 24" x 18"
(Courtesy of Skinner, Inc., Bolton, MA)

A Light Breeze
by Orlando Rouland, oil on canvas, 16" x 12"
(Courtesy of James R. Bakker Antiques, Inc., Cambridge, MA)

PRIMITIVES / P

The term "primitive" may be used interchangeably with two other terms: "folk art" and "naive art." For our purposes here,"primitive" will refer to all those compositions done by "non-professional" artists - typically referred to as "limners."

Primitive compositions may depict subjects from any of the other categories listed herein (e.g., portraits, landscapes, genre, etc.). Typically, a primitive painting may appear two-dimensional, lack a source of light, and be characterized by an undeveloped spatial sense.

The price ranges of the American folk artists found in this *Guide* were edited by Frank J. Miele, Frank J. Miele Gallery, New York, NY. His has helped countless collectors with questions concerning Folk Art. Whether buying, selling, or researching American folk art, you may want to get in touch with Mr. Miele. An address and telephone can be found in the *Appendix*.

One of Each
by James B. McCloskey, oil on canvas
(Courtesy of the Artist)

Portrait of Herbert J. Wright (one of a pair),
by William M. Prior, oil on board, 23" x 16"
(Courtesy of Skinner, Inc., Bolton, MA)

Romaine and Charlotte
by Antoinette Schwob, oil on canvas, 24" x 30"
(Courtesy of Jay Johnson America's Folk Heritage Gallery, New York, NY)

STILL LIFE / S

These are most often paintings of inanimate objects characterized by their beauty of color, line, or arrangement. During the 19th and 20th centuries these compositions were almost always set indoors and most typically depicted the following: fruit and/or vegetables, flowers, or objects found around the home or farm.

When objects are introduced into a composition to add interest and color, they are usually called accessories.

Dark Red Chrysanthemums
by Edward Barnard Lintott, oil on canvas, 24" x 20"
(Courtesy of James R. Bakker Antiques, Inc., Cambridge, MA)

Flowers on a Lattice Fence
by William Fuller Curtis, oil on panel, 30" x 24"
(Courtesy of James R. Bakker Antiques, Inc., Cambridge, MA)

Still Life, Oriental Statue with Vases
by Harry Willson Watrous, oil on canvas, 20" x 16"
(Courtesy of James R. Bakker Antiques, Inc., Cambridge, MA)

WILDLIFE/ W

    Many artists made a career of drawing and painting wildlife subjects (animals, fish, and/or birds) set in their natural habitat. These subjects will be included in this category along with animal subjects in a domestic or farm setting - such as, horse portraits, family pets, farmyard animals and fowl.

Taking the Bait
by Arnoud Wydeveld, oil on canvas, 24" x 18"
(Courtesy of Skinner, Inc., Bolton, MA)

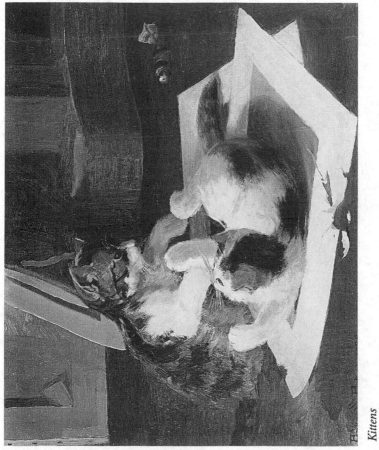

Kittens
by Parker Perkins, oil on canvas
(Courtesy of James R. Bakker Antiques, Inc., Cambridge, MA)

Call of the Wild
by Carl Rungius, oil on canvas, 35" x 64"
(Courtesy of James R. Bakker Antiques, Inc., Cambridge, MA)

UNKNOWN / X

An "X" was used when sufficient data were not available at the time, to determine the type of subject "most" typical for this artist. If the "X" is followed by any of the letters "A" thru "W" in parentheses, then that artist is known to have executed *some* works in that particular category. If you have verifiable information regarding prices or subject for any artists listed here with an "X", please send it along to the address at the front of this *Guide*.

Expert or Sleuth?

Now that you are familiar with the use of this *Guide*, what next? When you want to quickly estimate the *potential* value of a certain work of art, you'll want to use this *Guide* first. After determining that you may have a very valuable painting, and before you sell (privately, to a dealer, on consignment, through advertisement, or in your shop, etc.), you will want to determine more accurately what the painting may be worth (i.e., fair market value). You have two choices. Either you consult with an "expert" (e.g., art appraiser, qualified auctioneer, art dealer, art consultant), or you try to research it yourself.

One last comment. If you are a complete novice to the art market, I would recommend seeking the help of an expert. Only an expert will have the trained eye and the references on hand to make the most accurate estimate of the value of your piece. It is also helpful, and may eliminate later heartache, to keep in mind that you should consult with more than one expert if you feel your piece is very important!

CHAPTER THREE

Period Frames

The Frame: An Aesthetic Statement

The following essay was kindly contributed by **LOWY***, New York, New York.* **LOWY** *has served the art community around the world for many years with a complete line of fine art services, including: sales of antique frames from all periods, 20th century American frames, and complete conservation and restoration services for antique frames and furniture.*

At no time in the history of America has the awareness of the frame's importance been so great... both as an art object and as a vehicle for aesthetically and historically enhancing a work of art. Antique picture frames, while providing us with a wonderfully detailed and historical account of style and prevailing tastes, also dramatically illustrate the incredible craftsmanship and creativity called upon in the art of frame- making through the centuries.

In Europe there has been an awareness, appreciation, and even passion for antique picture frames for some time. More recently however, that same awareness, appreciation, and passion has captured the sensibility of the American collector and dealer as well. It is now common to find both European and American art connoisseurs vying for the same antique frames in the salesrooms of Paris, London, and now even occasionally in New York City. Indeed, many great European period frames now adorn paintings in most significant Old Master,

Impressionist, and Modern Master collections, whether abroad or in the United States.

A more uniquely American phenomenon however, is the most recent interest in and demand for 19th and 20th century American picture frames. Frames in particular demand from this era are those from the Arts and Crafts period.

American frame-making in the Arts and Crafts period of the late 19th and early 20th centuries was a period of extraordinary creativity. The aesthetic climate of the times signaled a move away from the more traditional ornate and complex cast frame styles being produced in the last half of the 19th century. This was a period of experimentation recalling earlier hand-crafted motifs with a greater collaborative effort between painter, sculptor, craftsman, and architect, resulting in an exuberant fusion of elements.

Artists of this era, such as James McNeill Whistler, Thomas Wilmer Dewing, Elihu Vedder, and Abbot Thayer frequently designed or worked with framers and architects to design their picture frames. These frames were often intended to be an integral part of their work. Frame-making firms of this era, such as Carrig-Rohane, Foster Brothers, Thulin, the Newcomb-Macklin Company, and Albert Mitch, among others, produced many such frames, thus developing a whole new vocabulary of framing styles and a new "American look".

Frames from the Arts and Crafts period not only represent a significant piece of frame history, but are frames which were very closely tied to the particular works of art for which they were designed and made. The specific relationship of frame to art work perhaps reached its height during this era.

The values of antique frames are bound to virtually the same set of criteria that govern the value of other antiquities, such as rarity, quality, historical significance, and condition. Although many antique picture frames can certainly be considered works of art unto themselves, and often are, their greatest value will always be realized when paired with the appropriate work of art to make an aesthetic and historical statement. This marriage of frame to art is the single consideration which will forever dominate the antique frame's utility, significance, and ultimately its value.

New York, New York, 1991
LOWY
(212) 861-8585

How Period Frames Are Affecting the Value of Paintings!

The following essay was kindly contributed by Edward P. LaBlue, of Duxbury, Massachusetts. Mr. LaBlue is a private frame dealer, consultant, and authority on period American and European frames.

Though the antique frame market has been with us for some time, the increased demand for period frames has been sparked by the keen interest and vision of art dealers and museum curators. Due to the heightened awareness of the value of quality period frames the number of establishments dealing exclusively in antique frames has also increased. Specialized exhibitions of antique frames around the United States and Europe have encouraged the development of a new sector for speculation in the field of art - that of frame collector and frame investors.

There seems to be a buyer for every type, size, color and shape frame, whether at a frame auction in London or a flea market in a small country town. The craze runs the gamut from the right frame for a painting to an interesting frame for a print or family photograph. The demand for a good frame is increasing, the supply diminishing and the prices skyrocketing.

Where does one locate antique frames? There are numerous frame dealers in America and abroad. Specialized frame sales occur at Bonham's in London two or three times a season. Antique dealers and art dealers occasionally have frames for purchase. Antique shows, particularly the large outdoor summer extravaganzas, can be a good source. Auctions, yard sales, flea markets, and attics, as well, can yield valuable frames.

Years ago, I began noting how period frames affected the price realized at auction on a number of paintings by obscure or little known American and European artists. Price estimates on these works ranged from a low of $200 up to $1,500. Many of the frames on these works were art objects in their own right, aesthetic statements, much in demand by frame dealers, art dealers, decorators, and frame collectors. Because of the demand for these quality period frames, the prices realized at auction for the work of many obscure artists were much higher than one would expect - sometimes two to three times the projected estimates.

The frame, an object which can have separate and substantial value, can compound the task of researching and assessing what a painting is worth. It is essential for buyers and sellers to be aware of what part the artwork and what part the frame play in determining price.

To acquire a valuable period frame I've sometimes paid premium prices for works by minor artists - surpassing private, dealer and auction records for those artists. As many others may have, on one occasion I drove over three hundred miles to bid on a painting. The 7' x 5' painting, a partially clad woman of french origin, rendered without too much anatomical consideration, was at best a piece of old unlined canvas. The frame, however, was a splendid French 1850's, 8 1/2" serpentine fluted cove, torus with imbricated egg and dart motif in a flawless French gold water gilt finish. The auction estimate for the painting was $500-$700; the price realized was $7,500.

That $7,500 price will be recorded as a new high for the artist when actually a substantial portion of the price realized was for the value of the frame - *all that glitters is gold*. Because of this sale a misleading price range for this artist may be established. In spite of this newly established high end of the range, at a later date this work of art could resurface at another auction stripped of its frame only to sell at a price substantially below $7,500.

Thus far, frame dealers have no firm guidelines for the purchase or selling price of period frames. You should be aware that most antique frames you're likely to encounter do not have a value exceeding several hundred dollars. How, then, do you price frames for purchase or resale? This is not an easy question to answer and several factors are important to consider:

Historical Significance	Is the frame, whether American or European, important in the history of the decorative arts?
Attribution	Was the frame produced by a specific firm or artisan whose work is much sought after by frame collectors and frame dealers?
Condition and Size	Does the frame require conservation which is time consuming and expensive? Value can be affected by restoration and necessary alterations of size.

To be able to recognize the more valuable frames requires considerable study. If you intend to become familiar with the more valuable antique frames you should plan on studying frame history, go to several frame exhibitions, and visit frequently with a knowledgeable antique frame dealer. Please consult the *Appendix* for source information regarding antique frame dealers and books pertaining to frame history.

Illustrations of a few representative frames will follow. Retail values for these frames can range from $500 to $35,000 dependent on size, historical importance, attribution to a famous firm or artisan, and condition.

A statement by Edward P. LaBlue: *I would like to express my gratitude to William Currier for the opportunity herein and hope that his readers will become more aware of how period frames can affect the value of paintings.*

Duxbury, Massachusetts, 1991
Edward P. LaBlue
(617) 834-0392

Carrig-Rohane (Boston)
carved and gilt, (Ca 1915-1920)
(Courtesy of Lowy, New York, NY)

Cove (American)
gilt composition, (19th C.)
(Courtesy of Lowy, New York, NY)

Foster Brothers (Boston)
carved and gilt, (Ca 1900-1910)
(Courtesy of Lowy, New York, NY)

Stanford White Frame (American)
gilt composition, (19th C.)
(Courtesy of Lowy, New York, NY)

Stanford White Frame (American)
gilt composition, (19th C.)
(Courtesy of Lowy, New York, NY)

Fluted Cove (American)
gilt composition, (19th C.)
(Courtesy of Lowy, New York, NY)

Original Hassam Frame (American)
carved and gilt, (Ca 1910-1915)
(Courtesy of Lowy, New York, NY)

Albert Milch Frame (New York)
carved and gilt, (Ca 1900-1905)
(Courtesy of Lowy, New York, NY)

Albert Milch Frame (New York)
gilt composition, (Ca 1890-1895)
(Courtesy of Lowy, New York, NY)

Whistler Frame (American)
carved and gilt, (Ca 1870-1875)
(Courtesy of Lowy, New York, NY)

Greek Revival (American)
(from the Boston Firm of Jordan & Harberg)
gilt with applied carved corners, (Ca 1830)
(Courtesy of Lowy, New York, NY)

Arts and Crafts (American)
carved and gilt, (turn of the century)
(Courtesy of Lowy, New York, NY)

Dutch Ripple Frame (European)
carved and ebonized, (mid-17th C.)
(Courtesy of Lowy, New York, NY)

Dutch Ripple Frame (European)
carved and ebonized (mid-17th C.)
(Courtesy of Lowy, New York, NY)

Spanish
carved and gilded, (17th C.)
(Courtesy of Lowy, New York, NY)

Reverse Profile Frame (Spanish)
gilt and polychrome, (early 17th C.)
(Courtesy of Lowy, New York, NY)

Florentine (European)
carved and gilt, (17th C.)
(Courtesy of Lowy, New York, NY)

Sansovino Frame (Italian)
carved and gilt, (late 16th to early 17th C.)
(Courtesy of Lowy, New York, NY)

Cassetta Frame (Italian)
carved, gilt, and polychrome (early 17th C.)
(Courtesy of Lowy, New York, NY)

Tuscan (European)
carved and gilt, (mid/late 16th C.)
(Courtesy of Lowy, New York, NY)

Louis XIV (French)
carved and gilt, (Ca 1720)
(Courtesy of Lowy, New York, NY)

Regence (French)
carved and gilt, (Ca 1725-1730)
(Courtesy of Lowy, New York, NY)

Louis XV (French)
carved and gilt, (mid-18th C.)
(Courtesy of Lowy, New York, NY)

Art Nouveau (French)
(from the Atelier of Georges de Feure)
gilt composition, (Ca 1900)
(Courtesy of Lowy, New York, NY)

Carrig-Rohane (Boston)
carved and gilt, (1915)
(Courtesy of Lowy, New York, NY)

Foster Brothers (Boston)
carved and gilt, (1907)
(Courtesy of Lowy, New York, NY)

Fluted Cove (American)
gilt composition, (19th C.)
(Courtesy of Lowy, New York, NY)

Composition (American)
gilt composition, (19th C.)
(Courtesy of Lowy, New York, NY)

Foster Brothers (Boston)
carved and gilt, (Ca 1910-1915)
(Courtesy of Lowy, New York, NY)

Denis Dinan (American)
cast and gilded, (Ca 1890)
(Courtesy of Eli Wilner & Co., New York, NY)

Yates (American)
carved and gilded, (Ca 1910)
(Courtesy of Eli Wilner & Co., New York, NY)

Harer (American)
carved, incised, gilded (Ca 1915)
(Courtesy of Eli Wilner & Co., New York, NY)

Foster Brothers (American)
carved and gilded, (Ca 1900)
(Courtesy of Eli Wilner & Co., New York, NY)

TB 11-22-97

Newcomb-Macklin (American)
carved and gilded, (Ca 1910)
(Courtesy of Eli Wilner & Co., New York, NY)

Harer (American)
carved and gilded, (Ca 1910)
(Courtesy of Eli Wilner & Co., New York, NY)

Newcomb-Macklin (American)
carved and gilded (Ca 1910)
(Courtesy of Eli Wilner & Co., New York, NY)

Key to Subjects

A   Avant-Garde

F   Figures

G   Genre

I   Illustrations

L   Landscapes

M   Marines

S   Still Life

P   Primitives

W   Wildlife

X   Unknown

AMERICAN ARTISTS AT AUCTION

Artist	Prices	Subject
A'BECKET, MARIA (- 1904)	150-1100	L
AARON, MABEL (19TH C)	*100-700	X (L)
AARONSON, DAVID (1923 -)	150-1000	F,G
ABARE, CONSTANCE (20TH C)	100-400	X (L)
ABASCAL, MARY (20TH C)	100-800	F
ABBATT, AGNES DEAN (1847 - 1917)	*100-2000	S
ABBETT, BOB K.	*100-650	
ABBETT, BOB K. (1926 -)	100-8400	G,F
ABBEY, EDWIN AUSTIN	*350-19000	
ABBEY, EDWIN AUSTIN (1852 - 1911)	2000-35000	I,G,F
ABBOTT, CATHERINE G. (20TH C)	100-600	X (F)
ABBOTT, ELENORE PLAISTED (1875 - 1935)	100-1000	F,L
ABBOTT, HAZEL NEWHAM (1894 -)	*100-500	L
ABBOTT, JACOB B. (- 1950)	*100-750	I
ABBOTT, LENA H. (20TH C)	200-2000	L
ABBOTT, SAMUEL NELSON	*100-1000	
ABBOTT, SAMUEL NELSON (1874 - 1955)	800-25000	I
ABBOTT, YARNALL (1870 - 1938)	100-1800	M,G,F
ABBRESCIA, JOE (20TH C)	100-800	G
ABDY, ROWENA MEEKS	*150-1500	
ABDY, ROWENA MEEKS (1887 - 1945)	1000-15000	L,G,I
ABEEL, ETHEL M. (- 1969)	100-900	X
ABEL, FRANK (19TH-20TH C)	500-1500	X (L)
ABEL, KEVIN (20TH C)	150-500	F
ABEL, MYER (1904 - 1948)	100-750	F,G
ABERCROMBIE, GERTRUDE (1909 -)	200-2200	A,L,S
ABERNATHY, JOHN (20TH C)	*100-400	X (M)
ABIETA, JAMES (20TH C)	2640	F
ABRACHEFF, NICOLAI (1897 -)	200-2500	L

ABRAHAM, CAROL SCHMIDT (20TH C)	100-900	X
ABRAMOFSKY, ISRAEL (1888 - 1934)	100-1800	L,F
ABRAMOVITZ, ALBERT (1879 - 1963)	400-2500	L,F
ABRAMS, HERBERT E. (20TH C)	100-600	X (S)
ABRAMS, LUCIEN (1870 - 1941)	300-3200	F,L
ABRIL, BEN (1923 -)	100-1000	F,L
ACEVES, JOSE (1909 -)	200-1800	L
ACHEFF, WILLIAM (1947 -)	2000-65000	G,F
ACHERT, FRED (20TH C)	200-800	X (L)
ACHESON, ALICE S. (1895 -)	200-1800	X(F)
ACHESON, GEORGINA ELLIOT (19TH-20TH C)	*100-600	X (F,S)
ACHILLI, I. (20TH C)	100-600	L
ACKERMANN, FRANK EDWARD (1933 -)	*100-750	L,I
ACKERSON, FLOYD (1889 -)	50-800	L
ACKERSON, LLYOD G. (1835 -)	50-350	L
ACORES, AUGUSTO (20TH C)	*100-400	L
ADAM, JOHN (19TH-20TH C)	100-800	G,L
ADAM, RICHARD B. (20TH C)	200-600	X (G)
ADAM, WILBUR G. (1898 -)	250-2000	L
ADAM, WILLIAM	*100-600	
ADAM, WILLIAM (1846 - 1931)	200-1200	L,M
ADAMS, CATHERINE LONGHORNE (20TH C)	600-3000	L
ADAMS, CHARLES PARTRIDGE	*350-3000	
ADAMS, CHARLES PARTRIDGE (1858 - 1942)	500-9000	L,M
ADAMS, CHAUNCEY (1895 -)	50-900	L
ADAMS, CHRISTOPHER (19TH C)	200-1000	F
ADAMS, F.W. (20TH C)	100-750	L
ADAMS, GEORGE E. (1814 - 1885)	300-3500	L,F
ADAMS, HERBERT (1858 - 1945)	200-1200	X (F)
ADAMS, J. HOWARD (19TH C)	200-1800	X (M)
ADAMS, JOANNE (20TH C?)	*100 -600	X (I,F)
ADAMS, JOHN OTTIS (1851 - 1927)	600-33000	L
ADAMS, JOSEPH ALEXANDER (1803 - 1880)	300-1000	X (L)
ADAMS, KENNETH M. (1897 - 1966)	50-900	L
ADAMS, M.B.(early 19TH C)	300-1000	F

* Denotes watercolors, pastels, drawings, and/or mixed media

ADAMS, PHILIP (1881 -)	100-800	L,F
ADAMS, WAYMAN (1883 - 1959)	400-4200	F,W,L
ADAMS, WILLIAM ALTHROPE (1797 - 1878)	200-2400	L,F
ADAMS, WILLIS SEAVER (1844 - 1921)	300-3000	G,L
ADDY, ALFRED	*100-400	
ADDY, ALFRED (19TH-20TH C)	100-800	L
ADELA, ELIZABETH (20TH C)	*100-600	X (I,F)
ADICKES, DAVID (20TH C)	100-660	X
ADLER, OSCAR F. (19TH-20TH C)	200-2000	L
ADOLPHE, ALBERT JEAN (1865 - 1940)	150-3500	L,F,G,S
ADOLPHE, VIRGINIA (1880 -)	100-900	X (S)
ADOMEIT, GEORGE G. (1879 - 1967)	100-950	L,M
ADRIANCE, M. HORTON (- 1941)	150-1500	L
ADRIANI, CAMILLE (19TH-20TH C)	200-2400	L,M
AFSARY, CYRUS (1940 -)	200-12000	L
AGATE, ALFRED THOMAS (1812 - 1846)	200-2500	M,F,W
AGATE, MISS H. (19TH C)	200-1200	L
AGNEW, WILLIAM (19TH-20TH C)	50-500	M,L
AGOSTINI, TONY (1916 -)	300-3200	A
AHL, HENRY CURTIS (1905 -)	100-400	M,L,S
AHL, HENRY HAMMOND (1869 - 1953)	100-2500+	L,I
AHLBORN, EMIL (early 20TH C)	100-500	X (L)
AHLROTH, ARTHUR (20TH C)	100-800	X (F)
AID, GEORGE CHARLES (1872 - 1938)	200-23000	X (M)
AIKEN, CHARLES AVERY	*100-850	
AIKEN, CHARLES AVERY (1872 - 1965)	200-1800	I,S
AIKEN, CHARLES G. (20TH C)	100-350	X
AIKEN, MARY HOOVER (1907 -)	50-1200	X (F)
AILKEN, J. (19TH C)	50-900	X (F)
AINSLEY, DENNIS (1880-1952)	100-900	L
AITKEN, HARRY C. (19TH-20TH C)	100-500	L
AITKEN, JAMES (early 19TH C)	200-3500	X (F)
AKELEY, CARL ETHAN (1864 - 1926)	1000-19000	W
AKERS, VIVIAN MILNER (1886 - 1966)	500-15000	L,F
AKIN, LOUIS B. (1868 - 1913)	350-4500	L,G,I

ALAJALOV, CONSTANTIN (1900 - 1987)	*200-6000	I,F,S
ALBEE, PERCY F.	*100-750	
ALBEE, PERCY F. (1883 - 1959)	100-1500	G,F
ALBERS, JOSEF	*500-9800	
ALBERS, JOSEF (1888 - 1976)	2100-320000	A
ALBERT, ARTHUR (1919 - 1987)	*200-2400	X
ALBERT, E. MAXWELL (1890 -)	100-12000	L
ALBERT, ERNEST (1857 - 1946)	500-20000	L
ALBRECHT, KURT (20TH C)	100-10000	L
ALBRICH, W. (early 20th c)	100-200	X (L)
ALBRIGHT, ADAM EMORY (1862 - 1957)	500-19000+	G,F
ALBRIGHT, DANIEL K. (19TH C)	200-2000	L
ALBRIGHT, HENRY JAMES (1887 - 1951)	200-2800	L,F,S
ALBRIGHT, HERMAN OLIVER (1876 - 1944)	*100-1200	X (L)
ALBRIGHT, IVAN LE LORRAINE	*700-4800	
ALBRIGHT, IVAN LE LORRAINE (1897 - 1983)	1500-20000	A,F,S
ALBRIZIO, CONRAD (1894 -)	100-600	L
ALBRO, MAXINE (1903 - 1966)	200-2000	F
ALDEN, REBECCA B. (early 19TH C)	*100-400	X (S)
ALDERMAN, GEORGE P.B. (1862 - 1942)	*200-850	I
ALDRICH, GEORGE AMES (1872 - 1941)	300-8300	L,F
ALDRIDGE, J.F. (20TH C)	*100-600	M
ALDRIDGE, WILLIAM JOSEPH (19TH C)	*800-3000	F
ALDRIN, ANDERS G. (1889 - 1970)	250-5000	L
ALEX, KOSTA (1925 -)	400-2500	F
ALEXANDER, CLIFFORD GREAR (1870 - 1954)	100-5000	L,I
ALEXANDER, ESTHER FRANCES (19TH C)	*200-800	X (F)
ALEXANDER, FRANCESCA (1837 - 1917)	400-6000	F
ALEXANDER, FRANCIS	*200-900	
ALEXANDER, FRANCIS (1800 - 1881)	400-8000	F
ALEXANDER, GEORGIA (20TH C)	100-900	F
ALEXANDER, HELEN DOUGLAS (1897 - 1984)	*200-900	X (I)
ALEXANDER, HENRY (1860 - 1895)	1000-14000	X (F,G)
ALEXANDER, JOHN WHITE	*250-25000	
ALEXANDER, JOHN WHITE (1856 - 1915)	1500-300000+	F,I

* Denotes watercolors, pastels, drawings, and/or mixed media

ALEXANDER, MICHAEL (19TH C)	100-900	F
ALF, MARTHA (1930 -)	1000-3000	X
ALKE, ELIZABETH (1877 - 1938)	100-900	L
ALLCHIN, HARRY (19TH-20TH C)	100-1000	L
ALLEN, CHARLES CURTIS (1886 - 1950)	100-3500	L
ALLEN, COURTNEY (1896 - 1969)	200-1400	I
ALLEN, DOUGLAS (20TH C)	500-5000	W
ALLEN, FREDERICK B. (19TH-20TH C)	*100-250	L
ALLEN, GRETA (1881 -)	50-5500	F
ALLEN, HOWARD (19TH-20TH C)	100-850	X (G)
ALLEN, J.D. (1851 - 1947)	400-3000	X (G)
ALLEN, JASPER VAN (20TH C)	100-1000	X
ALLEN, JOEL KNOTT (1755 - 1825)	300-3000	F
ALLEN, JOHN H. (1866 - 1935)	75-700	L
ALLEN, JOHN WILLIAM (19TH C)	*100-600	L,W
ALLEN, JUNIUS (1898 - 1962)	300-4000	L,G
ALLEN, MARION BOYD (1862 - 1941)	200-8500	F,L
ALLEN, PEARL WRIGHT (1880 -)	250-1800	X (L)
ALLEN, THOMAS (1849 - 1924)	300-7500	L,G
ALLIS, C. HARRY (1880 - 1938)	150-2400	L
ALLISON, J. S. (20TH C)	200-900	X
ALLSTON, WASHINGTON (1779 - 1843)	5000-???? +	F,G,L,M
ALTEN, MATHAIS JOSEPH	*100-400	
ALTEN, MATHIAS JOSEPH (1871 - 1938)	300-4000	F,L
ALTOON, JOHN (1925 - 1969)	*300-5000	A
ALVAREZ, MABEL	*100-750	
ALVAREZ, MABEL (1891-1985)	300-4300	S,L
ALVERSON, MARGARET BLAKE (20TH C)	100-850	X (S)
AMANS, JACQUES (1801 - 1888)	500-8500	F
AMES, DANIEL F. (active 1840-55)	300-3500	F
AMES, EZRA (1768 - 1836)	1000-50000 +	F,L
AMES, MAY (D. 1946)	100-400	L
AMICK, ROBERT WESLEY	*250-2500	
AMICK, ROBERT WESLEY (1879 - 1969)	2500-18000	G,I,M
AMIE, F.L. (20TH C)	50-500	X (S)

AMSDEN, WILLIAM KING (20TH C)	150-2000	L
AMSEL, RICHARD (1947 - 1985)	*4000-16000	I
ANA, CHIARA (20TH C)	*100-600	X (S)
ANDERSON, ALEXANDER (1775 - 1870)	600-3000	F,G
ANDERSON, C. STEPHEN (1896 -)	300-2500	X (S)
ANDERSON, CLARENCE WILLIAM (1891 -)	*100-1700	I
ANDERSON, DORIS (20TH C)	*50-700	L
ANDERSON, DOROTHY VISYU (20TH C)	100-1200	L
ANDERSON, FRED (early 20TH C)	100-300	X (G)
ANDERSON, FREDERIC A. (19TH-20TH C)	500-1200	X (G)
ANDERSON, G.W. (20TH C)	200-2500	X (L)
ANDERSON, HAROLD EDGERLY (1899 -)	100-400	X (G)
ANDERSON, HAROLD N.(1894 -)	500-4000	I
ANDERSON, HARRY (1906 -)	*200-1900	I
ANDERSON, J.B. (20TH C)	100-1200	X (F)
ANDERSON, KARL (1874 - 1956)	500-6500	F,G,I
ANDERSON, LENNART (1928 -)	500-1500	X (L)
ANDERSON, M.J.(19TH-20TH C)	100-300	X (F,S)
ANDERSON, MARTINUS (1878 -)	200-1600	L
ANDERSON, OSCAR (1873 -)	100-3500	M
ANDERSON, PETER (19TH C)	*200-1800	M,L
ANDERSON, RONALD	*100-400	
ANDERSON, RONALD (1886 - 1926)	300-2000	X (F,S)
ANDERSON, RUTH A.(1884 - 1939)	150-2000	F,L
ANDERSON, VICTOR COLEMAN	*100-850	
ANDERSON, VICTOR COLEMAN (1882 - 1937)	500-7500	G,L,I
ANDERSON, WALTER (1903 - 1965)	*200-3000	X (L)
ANDRADE, MARY FRATZ (early 20TH C)	200-1000	X (L,G)
ANDREW, INEZ LANGDEN (late 19TH C)	100-400	L
ANDREW, RICHARD (1869 - 1934)	200-4000	L,F,M
ANDREWS, AMBROSE (1824 - 1858)	300-8000	L,F
ANDREWS, BENNY (1930 -)	100-4500	X
ANDREWS, G. (20TH C)	50-600	L
ANDREWS, JAMES (19TH C)	*200-1000	S
ANDY, JOHN BABTIST (19TH C)	200-1500	F

110   * Denotes watercolors, pastels, drawings, and/or mixed media

ANGAROLA, ANTHONY (1893 - 1929)	400-3500	X
ANGEL, RIFKA (1899 -)	100-850	X (G)
ANGELL, LOUISE M. 19TH - 20TH C)	100-600	X (L)
ANGULO, CHAPPIE (1928 -)	150-1000	I
ANISFELD, BORIS (1879 - 1973)	400-2000	X (F,I)
ANNAN, ABEL H. (20TH C)	*100-900	X (F)
ANNES, HECTOR L. (20TH C)	100-250	L
ANNOT, JACOBI (1894 -)	300-3000	X (I,G)
ANSHUTZ, THOMAS POLLOCK	*500-25000 +	
ANSHUTZ, THOMAS POLLOCK (1851 - 1912)	5000-125000 +	F,L,G,M
ANSON, WILLIAM (19TH C)	200-1600	F
ANTHONY, CAROL (1943 -)	*300-4000	A
ANTHONY, RENEST EDWIN (1894 -)	100-800	X (L)
ANUSZKIEWICZ, RICHARD (1930 -)	700-20000	A
APPEL, CHARLES P. (1857 -)	500-5200 +	L,F
APPLETON, GEORGE WASHINGTON (1805 - 1831)	1500-12000 +	F
APT, CHARLES (1933 -)	250-3000	X (F,M)
ARCANGELO, ALLAN D'(1930 -)	500-18500	A
ARCENZA, NICOLA D' (19TH C)	*100-300	X (L)
ARDLEY, A.A.(19TH C)	100-300	X (S)
ARENO, JOSEPH R. (20TH C)	2750	L
ARENTZ, JOSEF M. (1903 - 1969)	100-1500	M,F,G,L
ARIOLA, FORTUNATO (1827 - 1872)	800-10000 +	L,M
ARKWRIGHT, R.V. (20TH C)	*100-900	X (M)
ARMER, LAURA ADAMS (1874 - 1963)	300-9000	F,L,I
ARMFIELD, MAXWELL ASHBY (1881 - 1972)	19800	F
ARMIN, EMIL (1895 - 1983)	*100-1000	L
ARMOR, CHARLES (1844 -)	100-2400	L,G
ARMS, JESSIE (1883 -)	100-450	X (F,G)
ARMS, JOHN TAYLOR (1887 - 1953)	*50-1200	X (L)
ARMSRONG, ROLF (1881 - 1960)	*500-10000	I
ARMSTRONG, DAVID MAITLAND	*200-4200	
ARMSTRONG, DAVID MAITLAND (1836 - 1918)	400-4500	G,F,M
ARMSTRONG, WILLIAM G. (1823 - 1890)	800-4800	L
ARMSTRONG, WILLIAM W. (1822 - 1914)	400-3200	L,F

ARNAUTOFF, VICTOR MIKHAIL (1896 - 1979)	200-2500	M,L
ARNDT, PAUL WESLEY (1881 -)	150-950	L
ARNEST, BERNARD (20TH C)	50-400	L
ARNING, EDDIE (1898 -)	*800-3500	P
ARNO, PETER (1904 - 1968)	*300-2500	I
ARNOLD, CLARA MAXFIELD (1879 - 1959)	*200-3500	S
ARNOLD, JAMES (20TH C)	100-1200	X (M)
ARNOLD, JAY (19TH-20TH C)	100-900	M
ARNOLD, JOHN (20TH C)	100-1000	M,L
ARNOLD, SAMUEL (20TH C)	*100-500	L
ARNOLDI, CHARLES (1946 -)	1000-25000	A
ARONSON, BORIS (1900 -)	*300-2500	X (I)
ARONSON, DAVID (1923 -)	*100-2500	F
ARRANTS, SHIRLEY	*100-1500	
ARRANTS, SHIRLEY (20TH C)	200-3500	F
ARSTE, KARL (1899 - 1942)	200-1200	L
ARTER, JOHN CHARLES (1860 - 1923)	150-3800	F
ARTHURS, G. (20TH C)	100-900	L
ARTHURS, STANLEY MASSEY (1877 - 1950)	300-10000	I
ARTIGES, EMILE (20TH C)	100-1000	L
ARTSCHWAGER, RICHARD	*700-20900	
ARTSCHWAGER, RICHARD (1923 -)	5000-180000 +	A
ARUFFT, LUIS (20TH C)	300-6500	M,L
ARY, HENRY (1802 - 1859)	1000-6500	L
ASCENZO, NICOLA D'(1871 -)	*200-800	I,L
ASHBROOK, PAUL (1867 -)	200-1500	F,L
ASHE, EDMUND M. (20TH)	*250-900	X (F,I,L)
ASHLEY, ANITA (19TH-20TH C)	*200-1500	F
ASHLEY, CLIFFORD WARREN (1881 - 1947)	500-9000	L,M,I
ASHLEY, FRANK N.	*150-4000	
ASHLEY, FRANK N. (1920 -)	300-1500	G,F
ASHTON, THOMAS B. (19TH C)	350-4500	G,L
ASKENAZY, MAURICE MISCHA (1888 - 1961)	500-11000	M,F,L
ASPLUND, TORE (20TH C)	150-1100	G
ATCKISON, JOSEPH ANTHONY (1895 -)	*100-300	X (M,L)

ATHERTON, JOHN C. (1900 - 1952)	200-3000	L,I
ATKEN, JAMES (19TH C)	500-3000	G,L
ATKINSON, LEO F. (1896 -)	200-1800	L
ATWOOD, GILBERT (19TH C)	75-900	L
ATWOOD, HELEN (1878 -)	100-800	X (W)
ATWOOD, ROBERT (1892 -)	300-4000	L
ATWOOD, WILLIAM E. (19TH-20TH C)	250-2200	L
AUBRY, EARL (20TH C)	300-3500	X (L)
AUBRY, OLIVER P. (20TH C)	100-600	X
AUDUBON, JOHN JAMES (1780/85 - 1851)	*2500-275000	W
AUDUBON, VICTOR GIFFORD (1809 - 1862)	1000-5000	L
AUERBACH-LEVY, WILLIAM (1889 - 1964)	200-1500	F
AULISIO, JOSEPH (1910 - 1974)	2000-25000	P,L
AULMANN, THEODORA (1882 -)	100-300	L
AULT, GEORGE COPELAND	*300-7000	
AULT, GEORGE COPELAND (1891 - 1948)	500-68000	A,L
AUREL, BERNATH (19TH C)	*150-800	X (L)
AUSTEN, EDWARD J. (1850 - 1930)	100-750	L
AUSTIN, ARTHUR E. JR. (20TH C)	1500-8000	A
AUSTIN, CHARLES PERCY (1883 - 1948)	500-15500	X (G,L)
AUSTIN, DARREL	*100-900	
AUSTIN, DARREL (1907 -)	500-4800	F
AUSTIN, EDWARD C.(20TH C)	*100-300	X (M)
AUSTRIAN, BEN (1870 - 1921)	200-15000	W,L
AVEDISIAN, EDWARD	*100-550	
AVEDISIAN, EDWARD (1936 -)	150-6500	A
AVERY, ADDISON E. (19TH C)	*100-300	S
AVERY, KENNETH N. (1883 -)	400-7500	F,G
AVERY, MILTON	*500-105000	
AVERY, MILTON (1885 - 1965)	1000-352000	A
AVERY, RALPH (1906 - 1976)	*100-300	L
AVINOFF, ANDRE (1884 - 1949)	*200-850	X (L)
AVISON, GEORGE (1885 -)	300-3500	I
AYARS, MARGARET T. (19TH-20TH C)	100-800	L
AYERS, H. MERVIN (1902 - 1975)	*100-300	X (F)

AYLWARD, WILLIAM JAMES (1875 - 1956)	400-1500	G,M,I
AZADIGIAN, MUNUEL (19TH-20TH C)	200-1200	X (S)

B

Artist	Prices	Subject
BABBIDGE, JAMES GARDNER (1844 - 1919)	2000-6500	M
BABCOCK, R. LLOYD (1897 - 1981)	100-700	L
BABCOCK, WILLIAM P.(1826 - 1899)	300-5000	S,G,L
BABER, ALICE (1928 -1982)	500-6500	A
BACH, BERTA (19TH C)	400-3500	X (S)
BACH, ESTHER E.(20TH)	*150-350	X (W)
BACH, FLORENCE JULIA (1887 - 1978)	100-1200	X (F)
BACHELDER, JOHN B. (1825 - 1894)	200-1200	L
BACHER, OTTO HENRY (1856 - 1909)	1500-50000	L,S,I,M
BACK, JOE W. (1899 -)	*100-400	X (W)
BACON, C.E. (19TH C)	100-600	L
BACON, CHARLES ROSWELL (1868 - 1913)	250-5000	L
BACON, FRANCIS (1909 -)	20000-6300000	A
BACON, FRANK A. (1803 - 1887)	500-3000	L
BACON, HENRY	*200-2500	
BACON, HENRY (1839 - 1912)	600-44000	F,G,L
BACON, I. LEWIS (1853 - 1910)	400-2500	S
BACON, IRVING R. (1875 - 1962)	*150-800	L,G
BACON, PEGGY B.	*100-2000	
BACON, PEGGY B.(1895 - 1987)	500-4500	F,G,I
BADGER, C.H. (20TH C)	50-600	X (W,L)
BADGER, FRANCIS (19TH-20TH C)	500-1500	X (G)
BADGER, JAMES W. (19TH C)	200-1500	S,F
BADGER, JOHN C. (1822 -)	*200-1000	F
BADGER, JOSEPH (1708 - 1765)	1500-6000	P
BADGER, SAMUEL F.M. (19TH-20TH C)	1000-16500	M
BADGER, THOMAS (1792 - 1868)	250-850	F

* Denotes watercolors, pastels, drawings, and/or mixed media

BAECHLER, DONALD	*100-5000	
BAECHLER, DONALD (20TH C)	1000-55000	A
BAEDER, JOHN (1938 -)	3500-35000	A
BAER, GEORGE (1895 -)	100-600	X (F)
BAER, JO (1929 -)	4000-72000	A
BAER, MARTIN (1894 - 1961)	200-2500	A
BAER, NORMAN (20TH C)	*100-900	I
BAER, WILLIAM JACOB (1860 - 1941)	400-3500	F,G,S
BAGG, HENRY HOWARD (1852 - 1928)	100-1650	L
BAGLEY, RALPH L. (1913 -)	50-700	L
BAILEY, JAMES G. (1870 -)	200-850	I,L
BAILEY, S.S. (19TH C)	*100-350	L
BAILEY, S.T. (LATE 19TH C)	300-3000	X (S)
BAILEY, T. (19TH-20TH C)	50-1200	M,L
BAILEY, VERNON HOWE (20TH C)	*100-700	I
BAILEY, WALTER ALEXANDER (1894 -)	200-2500	L
BAILEY, WILLIAM H.	*1000-31000	
BAILEY, WILLIAM H. (1930 -)	5000-255000	A
BAILY, C. (1866 - 1951)	*50-500	M,L
BAIRD, WILLIAM BABTISTE (1847 - 1899)	500-8500	L,W,M
BAKER, A.Z.(19TH-20TH C)	100-900	X (I)
BAKER, CHARLES (1844 - 1906)	*100-800	L,M
BAKER, ELISHA TAYLOR (1827 - 1890)	900-15000	M
BAKER, ELIZABETH GOWDY (1860 - 1927)	*100-900	F
BAKER, ELLEN KENDALL (- 1912)	200-1500	F,G
BAKER, ERNEST (19TH C)	300-2800	M
BAKER, FREDERICK VAN V. (1876 -)	50-600	L
BAKER, G.A. (19TH-20TH C)	800-9000	M
BAKER, GEORGE A. (1821 - 1880)	200-3000	F
BAKER, GEORGE HERBERT (1878 - 1943)	200-4800	G,F,L,M
BAKER, GLADYS (1821 - 1880)	100-10000	X
BAKER, J. ELDER (19TH C)	*100-3500	G,S
BAKER, O.F. (19TH C)	150-1000	M
BAKER, RALPH (1908 - 1976)	*100-900	X (F,L)
BAKER, SAMUEL BURTIS (1882 - 1967)	100-1200	L,F,S

BAKER, T.E. (19TH-20TH C)	1000-6500	M
BAKER, W.C. (19TH C)	100-700	L
BAKER, WILLIAM BLISS (1859 - 1887)	600-6500 +	M,L
BAKER, WILLIAM H. (1824 - 1875)	350-4000	L
BALAGH, BELA (20TH C)	200-1500	X (S)
BALCH, EUGENIA MCFARLANE (20TH C)	*100-500	F
BALCOM, LOWELL L. (1887 - 1938)	400-3500	X (F,I)
BALDAUGH, ANNI (1881-1953)	6325	L,F
BALDWIN, ALBERTUS H.(1865 -)	*100-350	X (M)
BALDWIN, CLIFFORD PARK (1889 - 1961)	200-2500	L,I
BALDWIN, G.B. (19TH C)	300-1500	F
BALFOUR, HELEN JOHNSON (1857 - 1925)	*100-1200	L
BALINK, HENRY C.(1882 - 1963)	3000-20000	L,F
BALL, ALICE WORTHINGTON (- 1929)	200-1200	M,S
BALL, BARGE (20TH C)	100-400	X (W)
BALL, L. CLARENCE	*200-750	
BALL, L. CLARENCE (1858 - 1915)	300-3000	L,W,S
BALL, STANLEY CRITTENDEN (1885 -)	200-1800	L
BALL, THOMAS WATSON (1863 - 1934)	75-600	M
BALLAINE, JERROLD (20TH C)	250-1500	X (F)
BALLIN, HUGO (1879 - 1956)	300-2000	F
BALLINGER, HARRY (1892 -)	200-2500	I,M
BALLOU, ADDIE L. (1837 - 1916)	200-1800	F
BALLOWE, MARCIA (20TH C)	300-2000	L
BAMA, JAMES ELLIOTT	*4000-20000	
BAMA, JAMES ELLIOTT (1926 -)	8000-38000	G,F,S
BAND, MAX (1900 - 1974)	300-5200	A,F
BANDALL, NAL (20TH C)	100-400	L
BANKS, RICHARD (1929 -)	300-3500	X (F)
BANKSON, GLEN (1890 -)	100-900	L
BANNARD, (WALTER) DARBY (1934 -)	200-20000	A
BANNISTER, EDWARD MITCHELL (1833 - 1901)	1000-20000	L,F
BANNISTER, J. (1821 - 1901)	500-2000	M,S
BANNISTER, PATTI (20TH C)	150-900	M,L
BANNON, JOHN (20TH C)	100-400	X

* Denotes watercolors, pastels, drawings, and/or mixed media

BANTA, WEART (19TH C)	100-1800	L,F
BARBER, JOHN (1898 - 1965)	500-6000	G,L
BARBER, JOHN WARNER (1798 - 1885)	*150-400	I
BARBER, JOSEPH (1915 -)	*100-300	M
BARBIER, GEORGES (1882 - 1932)	*500-4500+	F
BARCHUS, ELIZA R. (1857 - 1959)	200-3800	L
BARCLAY, MCCLELLAND	*100-750	
BARCLAY, MCCLELLAND (1891 - 1943)	400-6600	I,G,S
BARD, JAMES (and JOHN) (1815 - 1897)	35000-135000	M
BARDAZZI, PETER (1943 -)	500-3000	A
BARFUSS, INA (20TH C)	*300-2500	X (L)
BARILE, XAVIER J. (1891 - 1981)	100-3600	X (A,L)
BARKER, ALBERT W. (1874 - 1947)	*100-800	X (I,L)
BARKER, GEORGE (1882 - 1965)	100-3100	L
BARLOW, JOHN NOBLE (1861 - 1924)	400-6500	L,F
BARLOW, MYRON (1873 - 1937)	800-15000+	G,F
BARNARD, EDWARD HERBERT (1855 - 1909)	500-15400	M,L,S
BARNES, ERNEST HARRISON (1873 -)	100-3000	L
BARNES, GERTRUDE (1865 -)	300-4200	L
BARNES, J.T. (19TH-20TH C)	100-400	L
BARNES, JOHN PIERCE (1893 -)	400-4800	L
BARNES, MATTHEW (1880 - 1951)	1870	M
BARNES, PENELOPE BIRCH (early 19TH C)	*300-800	S
BARNES, WILL R. (20TH C)	*100-750	X (L)
BARNET, WILL (1911 -)	1000-26000	F,A
BARNETT, BJORN (JR) (1887 -)	300-1200	L
BARNETT, HERBERT (1910 - 1972)	500-3000	A,L
BARNETT, ISA	*50-400	
BARNETT, ISA (1924 -)	50-900	X (F)
BARNETT, LES (20TH C)	50-850	X (L)
BARNETT, RITA WOLFE (20TH C)	150-400	X (L,S)
BARNETT, THOMAS P.(1870 - 1929)	100-2000	L,M
BARNETT, WILLIAM (20TH C)	100-800	A
BARNEY, FRANK A. (1862 -)	100-3000	L
BARNITZ, A.M. (19TH C)	150-400	X (L)

BARONE, ANTONIO (1889 - 1971)	500-25000	F
BARONE, ANTONIO (1889 - 1971)	500-22000	F,L
BARR, WILLIAM (1867 - 1933)	300-5600	L,G
BARRATT, GEORGE W. (20TH C)	200-2000	I
BARRAUD, ALFRED T. (1849 - 1925)	*100-500	L
BARRETT, ELIZABETH HUNT (1863 -)	200-2400	L
BARRETT, MARY E. (19TH C)	*500-3000	L
BARRETT, OLIVER GLEN (20TH C)	100-600	L,M
BARRETT, WILLIAM S.	*100-1000	
BARRETT, WILLIAM S. (1854 - 1927)	400-3000	L,M
BARRIE, ERWIN S. (1886 -)	100-900	L
BARRITT, ROBERT C. (1898 -)	100-900	X (L)
BARRON, GRACE (1903 -)	*100-500	X (F,L)
BARRON, ROS (1933 -)	300-900	X (A)
BARROW, EDITH ISABEL(20TH C)	*50-670	S
BARROW, JOHN DOBSON (1827 - 1907)	220-2900	L
BARRY, CHARLES A. (1830 - 1892)	300-4500	X (G)
BARRY, EDITH CLEAVES (early 20TH C)	150-500	L
BARSE, GEORGE RANDOLPH (JR)	*200-4000	
BARSE, GEORGE RANDOLPH (JR) (1861 - 1938)	500-17600	L
BARSTON, S.M. (19TH C)	500-3500	L
BARSTOW, G.M. (19TH C)	50-800	L
BARTH, CARL E. (1896 - 1976)	300-4800	X (F,S)
BARTH, ELIZABETH PIUTTI (20TH C)	100-500	X
BARTHOLOMEW, TRUMAN (19TH C)	300-3500	L
BARTHOLOMEW, WILLIAM N.(1822 - 1898)	*100-500	L
BARTLE, SARA N. (20TH C)	100-800	M
BARTLETT, JENNIFER (1941 -)	20000-132000	A
BARTLETT, DANA (1878 - 1957)	400-6600	L,M,S
BARTLETT, FREDERIC CLAY (1873 - 1951)	400-3500	G,F
BARTLETT, FREDERICK EUGENE (1852 - 1911)	*100-200	X (M,L)
BARTLETT, GRAY (1885 - 1951)	500-7000	L,F
BARTLETT, JONATHAN ADAMS (1817 - 1902)	3000-10000	P
BARTLETT, PAUL WAYLAND (1865 - 1925)	400-2000	L
BARTOLL, WILLIAM THOMPSON (1817 - 1859)	250-2500	P

* Denotes watercolors, pastels, drawings, and/or mixed media

BARTON, DONALD BLAGGE (1903 - 1990)	200-2000	L,M
BARTON, HARRY (20TH C)	100-1200	X (L,F)
BARTON, LOREN R.	*300-800	
BARTON, LOREN R. (1893 - 1975)	500-2000	L,G,M
BARTON, MATTHEW (18TH-19TH C)	*150-850	L
BARTON, MINETTE (1889 - 1976)	600-6000	X (G)
BARTON, RALPH (1891 - 1931)	*200-800	S,I
BARTOO, CATHERINE R. (1876 - 1949)	100-300	X
BASCOM, ANDREW J. (19TH C)	100-1500	F
BASCOM, RUTH HENSHAW (1772 - 1848)	*3000-18000+	P
BASHFIELD, EDWIN HOWLAND (1848 - 1936)	800-4800	F
BASING, CHARLES (1865 - 1933)	200-4000	M,L
BASKERVILLE, CHARLES JR. (1896 -)	220-3000	X (F,G)
BASKIN, LEONARD (1922 -)	*200-4800	A
BASSETT, RAVEAU (1897 - 1981)	500-7000	W
BASSFORD, FRANKLYN (19TH C)	2000-25000	M
BASSFORD, WALLACE (1900 -)	200-3000	M
BATCHELLER, FREDERICK S. (1837 - 1889)	600-7000	S,L
BATES, BERTHA CORSON DAY (1875 -)	100-1200	L
BATES, DEWEY (1851 - 1899)	100-2000	F
BATES, KENNETH (1904 -)	100-1500	L,S,W
BATTLES, BLAKE D. (1887 - 1972)	*50-500	L
BATTY, ROLAND W. (20TH C)	300-4500	X (F)
BAUCHMANN, C.(late 19TH C)	100-500	L
BAUER, WILLIAM (1888 -)	150-1000	L
BAUM, CARL (1812 - 1877)	500-8000	S,L
BAUM, CHARLES (1812 - 1877)	800-10000+	S,L
BAUM, JOSEPH (19TH C)	400-1500	X (S)
BAUM, WALTER EMERSON	*100-3300	
BAUM, WALTER EMERSON (1884 - 1956)	400-44000	L,I,F
BAUMAN, KARL HERMAN (1911 - 1984)	100-10450	L,I
BAUMANN, GUSTAVE (1881 - 1971)	400-10500	L
BAUMGARTNER, J. JAY (1885 - 1946)	*100-1800	X (F,W)
BAUMGARTNER, WARREN (1894 - 1963)	*110-3500	I
BAUMGRAS, PETER (1827 - 1904)	220-3500	L,S,F

BAUMHOFFER, WALTER M. (1904 - 1986)	200-7000	I
BAURGENIS, J.A. (19TH C)	*50-400	L,F
BAXTER, BERTHA E. (19TH C)	50-600	M,L
BAXTER, ELIJAH (JR) (1849 - 1939)	150-1600	L,S
BAYARD, CLIFFORD ADAMS (1892 - 1934)	150-3000	L
BAYER, HERBERT	*200-900	
BAYER, HERBERT (1900 - 1985)	1000-6000	X (A)
BAYHA, EDWIN F. (19TH/20TH C)	500-38000	G,F
BAYLIES, WILLIAM (- 1934)	100-1500	X (L)
BAYLINSON, ABRAHAM S. (1882 - 1950)	300-7000	F,S
BAZIOTES, WILLIAM A.	*1300-75000	
BAZIOTES, WILLIAM A. (1912 - 1963)	5000-275000 +	A
BEAL, GIFFORD	*100-4800	
BEAL, GIFFORD (1879 - 1956)	600-80000	L,G
BEAL, JACK (1931 -)	1500-30000	X (A)
BEAL, REYNOLDS	*120-7000	
BEAL, REYNOLDS (1867 - 1951)	1000-41000	L,G,M
BEALES, ISAAC B. (1866 -)	*50-400	X (S)
BEALL, CECIL CALVERT	*100-2000	
BEALL, CECIL CALVERT (1892 - 1967)	100-900	I,F
BEAMAN, GAMALIEL WALDO (1852 - 1937)	250-2500	L
BEAMAN, WILLIAM (19TH-20TH C)	100-600	L
BEAME, W. (19TH C)	150-800	L
BEAN, CAROLINE VAN HOOK (1880 - 1980)	*100-3000	L,G
BEAN, HANNAH (early 19TH C)	*250-800	P
BEAR, JESSIE DREW (20TH C)	200-3600	X
BEARD, ADELIA BELLE (- 1920)	400-2500	L,F,I
BEARD, ALICE (19TH-20TH C)	300-2600	X (G)
BEARD, DANIEL CARTER (1850 - 1941)	*400-2500	I
BEARD, FRANK (1842 - 1905)	400-3500	X (L)
BEARD, HARRY (19TH C)	250-1200	X (W,S)
BEARD, JAMES CARTER (1837 - 1913)	*200-1200	X (F)
BEARD, JAMES HENRY (1812 - 1893)	1200-25000	F,G,L,W
BEARD, WILLIAM HOLBROOK	100-10400	
BEARD, WILLIAM HOLBROOK (1824 - 1900)	700-79500	F,G,L,W

* Denotes watercolors, pastels, drawings, and/or mixed media

BEARDEN, ROMARE (1914 - 1988)	*1000-71300	A
BEARS, ORLANDO HAND (1811 - 1851)	3000-77000	P (F)
BEATON, CECIL (1904 - 1980)	*300-6000	X (I,S)
BEATTIE, ALEXANDER (20TH C)	100-400	X
BEATTY, FRANK T. (1899 -)	*100-3600	M
BEATTY, JOHN WESLEY (1850 - 1924)	200-2400	X (F)
BEATTY, JOHN WILLIAM (1869 - 1941)	400-5500	L
BEAUCHAMP, ROBERT (1923 -)	300-4000	A
BEAUFORT, JOHN (19TH C)	800-9500	L
BEAUGUREAU, FRANCIS H.	*100-1700	
BEAUGUREAU, FRANCIS H. (1920 -)	800-3500	G,F,L
BEAUMONT, ARTHUR E. (1890 - 1978)	*400-1800	X (M)
BEAUMONT, ARTHUR J. (1877 - 1956)	150-2000	M,L,F
BEAUMONT, LILLIAN ADELE (1880 - 1922)	150-3500	G,F
BEAUREGARD, C.G.(19TH C)	250-1500	X (G)
BEAUX, CECILIA	*500-5000	
BEAUX, CECILIA (1855 - 1942)	1000-80000+	F,L
BEAVER, FRED (1911 -)	100-900	X
BEBIE, HENRY (1824 - 1888)	800-4500	L,F
BECHER, ARTHUR ERNST (1877 - 1960)	300-7500	I,W,L,G
BECHTLE, ROBERT	*900-9000	
BECHTLE, ROBERT (1932 -)	5000-60500	A
BECK, AUGUSTUS (19TH C)	200-1800	F,W
BECK, BERNARD (20TH C)	400-3000	A
BECK, FREIDRICH (1873 - 1921)	200-2000	L
BECK, RAPHAEL (- 1947)	100-1200	L
BECKER, FREDERICK W. (1888 - 1953)	200-2500	L
BECKER, J. (19TH C)	500-30000	S
BECKET, MARIE A. (- 1904)	100-1200	F,L
BECKETT, CHARLES E. (1814 - 1956)	200-6500	L,M
BECKHOFF, HARRY (1901 - 1979)	*100-2500	I
BECKINGHAM, ARTHUR (19TH C)	300-1200	G,F
BECKMANN, MAX	*600-110000	
BECKMANN, MAX (1884 - 1950)	3500-1600000	A
BECKWITH, ARTHUR (1860 - 1930)	250-2500	L,M

BECKWITH, JAMES CARROLL (1852 - 1917)	250-60000	F,G
BEELER, JOE NEIL	*1500-15000	
BEELER, JOE NEIL (1931 -)	3000-35000	L,G
BEERS, JULIE HART (1835 - 1913)	800-3000	L,W
BEEST, ALBERTUS VAN (1820 - 1860)	300-18000	M
BEET, CORNELIUS DE (1772 - 1840)	900-13200	S
BEGAY, HARRISON (1917 -)	100-1000	X
BEHRE, FREDERIC JOHN (19TH-20TH C)	400-2000	X (S)
BEIHLE, AUGUST (1885 - 1979)	*100-600	L
BELARSKI, RUDOLPH (20TH C)	100-600	X
BELCHER, HILDA (1881 - 1963)	*100-800	X (F)
BELKNAP, ZEDEKIAH (1781 - 1858)	650-35000+	P
BELL, CAROLINE (20TH C)	100-700	M
BELL, CECIL C.	*100-2000	
BELL, CECIL C. (1906 - 1970)	100-11000	L,F
BELL, CHARLES (1876 - 1935)	4000-187000	A
BELL, EDWARD A. (1862 - 1953)	1500-14000	F
BELL, EDWARD AUGUSTE (1862 - 1953)	600-13500+	F
BELL, GEORGE C. (19TH-20TH C)	*100-1500	M,L
BELL, LARRY	*100-2500	
BELL, LARRY (1939 -)	500-3500	A
BELLINGER, MARGARET T. (1899 -)	100-900	X (L)
BELLIS, DAISY MAUDE (1887 -)	100-800	X (S)
BELLOWS, ALBERT FITCH	*400-19800	
BELLOWS, ALBERT FITCH (1829 - 1883)	800-46500	L,G
BELLOWS, GEORGE WESLEY	*400-24000+	
BELLOWS, GEORGE WESLEY (1882 - 1925)	8500-425000+	G,F,L
BEMELMANS, LUDWIG (1898 - 1962)	*800-4000	I
BEMISH, R. HILLS (19TH-20TH C)	*100-300	L
BEN-ZION, (1897 - 1987)	100-10500	A
BENBRIDGE, HENRY (1744 - 1812)	2000-12000	F
BENDA, WLADYSLAW T. (1873 - 1948)	*150-1400	I
BENDER, BILL (1920 -)	300-3000	X (A)
BENDLE, ROBERT (1867 -)	150-900	X (L)
BENEDICT, A.C.(19TH-20TH C)	800-3500	L

* Denotes watercolors, pastels, drawings, and/or mixed media

BENEDICT, ENELLA (20TH C)	100-900	L
BENEDUCE, ANTIMO (1900 -)	*100-800	L,S
BENEKER, GERRIT ALBERTUS (1882 - 1934)	100-23000	I,G,F,M
BENGLIS, LYNDA (1941 -)	*1000-22000	A
BENGSTON, BILLY AL	*100-2200	
BENGSTON, BILLY AL (1934 -)	500-13500	A
BENJAMIN, KARL (1925 -)	500-3000	A
BENJAMIN, NORA (1899 -)	*100-900	X (I)
BENJAMIN, SAMUEL G.W. (1837 - 1914)	350-2000	M
BENN, BEN	*200-2500	
BENN, BEN (1884 - 1983)	200-4500	F,L,S
BENNETT, DOROTHY E. (20TH C)	*50-400	X (M)
BENNETT, EMILY (19TH-20TH C)	100-500	X (S)
BENNETT, JOSEPH (1899 -)	1650	M
BENNETT, LYLE HATCHER (1903 -)	400-3000	A
BENNETT, RAINEY (1904 -)	*100-400	L
BENNETT, WILLIAM JAMES (1787 - 1844)	*900-42000	L
BENSELL, GEORGE FREDERICK (1837 - 1879)	500-8000	F,G,L
BENSON, EUGENE (1839 - 1908)	500-9000+	F,L
BENSON, FRANK WESTON	*800-35000	
BENSON, FRANK WESTON (1862 - 1951)	600-165000+	F,W,L,S
BENSON, JOHN P.(1865 - 1947)	200-4200	M
BENSON, LESLIE LANGILLE (1885 -)	200-1500	G,I
BENSON, TRESSA EMERSON	*100-1400	
BENSON, TRESSA EMERSON (1896 -)	200-3200	L,F,S
BENTLEY, JOHN WILLIAM (1880 - 1951)	350-15000	L
BENTLEY, LESTER W. (1908 -)	400-2500	X (M,L)
BENTON, DWIGHT (1834 -)	250-2500	L
BENTON, THOMAS HART	*100-176000	
BENTON, THOMAS HART (1889 - 1975)	1650-550000+	G,F,L,I
BERDANIER, PAUL F. SR. (1879 -)	100-6500	L,I
BERGER, NICHOLAS (20TH C)	*50-700	M,L
BERKE, ERNEST (1921 -)	800-18000	F,L
BERKMAN, AARON (1900 -)	*50-600	L
BERKOWITZ, LEON (20TH C)	1000-5000	A

BERMAN, EUGENE	*200-10300	
BERMAN, EUGENE (1899 - 1972)	300-14000	I,F
BERMAN, HARRY G. (20TH C)	400-6000	L
BERMAN, LEONID (1896 - 1976)	400-11000	A,F,L
BERMAN, SAUL (1899 -)	800-7200	G,L
BERMAN, W.E. (19TH C)	300-3000	X (W)
BERMAN, WALLACE (1926 - 1976)	400-7000	A
BERNEKER, LOUIS FREDERICK (1872 - 1937)	150-4500 +	F,L
BERNINGER, JOHN E. (20TH C)	100-950	X (S)
BERNINGHAUS, J. CHARLES (1905 - 1988)	250-1800	L
BERNINGHAUS, OSCAR EDMUND	*1300-30000	
BERNINGHAUS, OSCAR EDMUND (1874 - 1952)	1200-225000	G,L,I
BERNSTEIN, RICHARD (1930 -)	400-3200	X
BERNSTEIN, THERESA F.(1895 -)	600-26400	F,L,S
BERRY, CARROLL THAYER (1886 - 1978)	100-1500	M,L
BERRY, PATRICK VINCENT (1852 - 1922)	350-5000	L,W
BERS, JULIE HART (1835 - 1913)	500-3000	L
BERTHELSEN, JOHANN	*350-1500	
BERTHELSEN, JOHANN (1883 - 1969)	300-8000	L,M
BERTHOT, JAKE	*300-2500	
BERTHOT, JAKE (1939 -)	500-18000	A
BERTRAM, H.C. (19TH C)	*100-400	G
BERZEVIZY, JULIUS (1875 -)	100-1000	L,M
BESS, FORREST CLEMENGER (1911 - 1977)	3000-22000	A
BESSANGER, FREDERIC H. (1886 - 1975)	200-700	A,F,L
BESSER, ARNE (1935 -)	100-2400	X
BESSIRE, DALE PHILLIP (1891 - 1974)	250-3000	L
BEST, ALICE (19TH C)	100-1500	L
BEST, ARTHUR WILLIAM (1865 - 1935)	100-4000	L,M,F
BEST, HARRY CASSIE (1863 - 1936)	250-2500	L,F
BEST, WILLARD SEWELL (19TH-20TH C)	100-600	X
BETHERS, RAY (1902 -)	100-1400	M,L
BETTINGER, HOYLAND B. (1890 - 1950)	300-3200	L
BETTS, ANNA WHELAN (19TH-20TH C)	500-6000	F
BETTS, HAROLD HARRINGTON (1881 -)	100-4500	F,L

* Denotes watercolors, pastels, drawings, and/or mixed media

BETTS, LOUIS (1873 - 1961)	150-30000	F,G,S
BETTS, VIRGINIA BATTLE (20TH C)	150-700	L,S
BEWICK, WILLIAM (1795 - 1866)	600-1200	X (G)
BEWLEY, MURRAY PERCIVAL (1884 - 1964)	600-7000	F
BEYER, M.O. (19TH C)	100-900	X (S)
BEYER, WILLIAM E. (1929 -)	*200-800	L,M
BEYET, H. (20TH C)	200-2500	X (F)
BIANCHI, A. (20TH C)	100-350	X (S)
BIBERSTEIN, FRANZ (1850 - 1930)	50-800	L
BICKERSTAFF, GEORGE (1893 - 1954)	100-2000	L
BICKFORD, NELSON NORRIS (1846 - 1943)	600-5200	X
BICKFORD, SID (1862 - 1947)	400-5000	W
BICKNELL, ALBION HARRIS (1837 - 1915)	200-8000	F,G,S
BICKNELL, E. (19TH-20TH C)	*150-400	X (L)
BICKNELL, EVELYN M.	*100-800	
BICKNELL, EVELYN M. (1857 - 1936)	250-2800	F,M
BICKNELL, FRANK ALFRED (1866 - 1943)	400-5000+	L
BICKNELL, WILLIAM H.W. (1860 - 1947)	400-13000	X (G)
BIDDLE, GEORGE (1885 - 1973)	500-7800	G,I,L
BIDWELL, A.(19TH C)	100-400	X (G)
BIEDERMANN, H.(19TH-20TH C)	*400-4500	L
BIEHLE, AUGUST F. (1885 - 1979)	200-5500	X
BIEL, JOSEPH (1891 - 1943)	200-1800	X (L,G)
BIELEFELD, OTTO (20TH C)	50-350	L
BIERSTADT, ALBERT	*1000-45000	
BIERSTADT, ALBERT (1830 - 1902)	2500-1900000+	L,M
BIGELOW, CHARLES C. (1891 -)	100-500	F,L
BIGELOW, DANIEL FOLGER (1823 - 1910)	100-2500	L,M,S
BIGELOW, THOMAS (1849 - 1924)	600-3000	L
BIGGS, GEOFFREY (1908 -)	*100-800	I
BIGGS, ROBERT OLDHAM (1920 -)	500-1800	L,G
BIGGS, WALTER (1886 - 1968)	200-13000	I
BIGOT, ALPHONSE (1828 - 1873)	400-5800	L
BILLING, FREDERICK W. (1835 - 1914)	250-2500	X (G)
BILLINGS, EDWIN T. (1824 - 1893)	300-1500	X (F)

BILLINGS, HENRY (1901 -)	*800-4500	I
BILLINGS, MOSES (1809 - 1884)	500-4000	G,F
BILLMEYER, JAMES IRWIN (1897 -)	*100-900	I
BINDER, JOHN (20TH C)	50-600	M,L
BINFORD, JULIEN (1908 -)	400-5250	X (G,F)
BINGHAM, GEORGE CALEB (1811 - 1879)	2500-4000	G,F,L
BINKS, REUBEN WARD (20TH C)	400-5000	W
BINNEY, H.N. (19TH C)	*250-800	X (M)
BINTONI, ROLLIN (19TH C)	100-350	L
BIORN, EMIL (1864 -)	50-600	M,L
BIPSHAM, HENRY COLLINS (20TH C)	100-1000	X (W)
BIRCH, REGINALD BATHURST (1856 - 1943)	*50-900	I,G
BIRCH, THOMAS (1779 - 1851)	1150-180000	L,M,F
BIRCH, WILLIAM (1755 - 1834)	*500-8000	L,G
BIRCHALL, WILLIAM MINSHAL (1884 -)	*100-3000	M
BIRDSALL, BRYON (20TH C)	*400-3500	L
BIRDSALL JR, AMOS (1865 - 1938)	200-6000	M
BIRMELIN, ROBERT (1933 -)	200-800	A,M
BIRNEY, WILLIAM VIERPLANCK (1858 - 1909)	550-12000+	F,G
BIRREN, JOSEPH P. (1864 - 1933)	350-7000	L,M
BISBING, HENRY SINGLEWOOD (1849 - 1933)	600-4000	L,W
BISCHOFF, FRANZ ALBERT (1864 - 1929)	500-66000	L,M
BISHOP, ALBERT F. (1855 -)	800-5000	L,M
BISHOP, BROOKE (20TH C)	100-1200	X
BISHOP, ISABEL	*300-4000	
BISHOP, ISABEL (1902 - 1988)	1000-11550	G,F
BISHOP, RICHARD EVETT (1887 - 1975)	250-7150+	W
BISPHAM, HENRY COLLINS (1841 - 1882)	250-6800+	L,W
BISSELL, EDGAR JULIAN (1856 -)	100-1000	L
BISSELL, KATE (19TH C?)	400-4500	X (S)
BISTTRAM, EMIL J.	*300-7500	
BISTTRAM, EMIL J.(1895 - 1976)	750-23000+	A,F,L
BITTINGER, CHARLES (1879 - 1970)	300-4500	L
BIXBEE, WILLIAM JOHNSON	*200-2500	
BIXBEE, WILLIAM JOHNSON (1850 - 1921)	100-3000	L

* Denotes watercolors, pastels, drawings, and/or mixed media

BLACK, LAVERNE NELSON (1887 - 1938)	1000-60000	F,G
BLACK, MARY C. W. (- 1943)	200-1200	X (S)
BLACK, OLIVE PARKER (1868 - 1948)	100-5500 +	L
BLACKBURN, JOSEPH (1750 - 1774)	800-45000	P
BLACKBURN, MORRIS A.	*100-950	
BLACKBURN, MORRIS A. (1902 - 1979)	100-1200	M,L,F
BLACKMAN, WALTER (1847 - 1928)	100-8000	G,L,F
BLACKMORE, ARTHUR EDWARD (1854 - 1921)	100-3500	L,M
BLACKTON, JAMES STUART (1875 - 1941)	250-6500	L,M
BLACKWELL, TOM (1938 -)	3000-25000	A
BLAIKLEY, ALEXANDER (19TH C)	*800-8500	G,L
BLAINE, NELL (1922 -)	100-3000	S,L
BLAIR, STREETER (1888 - 1966)	200-12000	L
BLAKE, LEO B. (1887 - 1976)	150-4000	L
BLAKELOCK, MARION (1880 -)	200-1800	L
BLAKELOCK, RALPH ALBERT (1847 - 1919)	250-76750	L
BLAKELY, DUDLEY (1902 -)	200-1500	L
BLANCH, ARNOLD (1896 - 1968)	250-5000	F,S,I
BLANEY, DWIGHT	*100-3800	
BLANEY, DWIGHT (1865 - 1944)	100-2000	L,M
BLANKENSHIP, ROY (1943 -)	*300-1200	L
BLASHFIELD, EDWIN HOWLAND (1848 - 1936)	500-40000	G,F
BLASS, CHARLOTTE L.(1908 - 1982)	100-2500	S,F,L
BLASS, RICO (20TH C)	50-350	X (F)
BLATAS, ARBIT (1908 -)	200-6000	A,L,S,F
BLAUVELT, CHARLES F. (1824 - 1900)	800-6500	G,F
BLECKNER, ROSS	*700-60000	
BLECKNER, ROSS (B. 1949)	2000-187000	A
BLEIMAN, MAX (19TH-20TH C)	200-1000	L
BLENNER, CARLE JOHN (1864 - 1952)	100-17000	M,F,S,L
BLEUMNER, OSCAR FLORIANUS (1867 - 1938)	*1100-7500	X
BLISS, ROBERT R. (1925 -)	100-1200	F,L,M
BLOCH, ALBERT	*100-22000	
BLOCH, ALBERT (1882 - 1961)	900-27500	A
BLOCH, JULIUS T. (1888 - 1966)	200-4800	F

* Denotes watercolors, pastels, drawings, and/or mixed media   127

BLOCH, JULIUS T. (1888 - 1966)	200-4800	F
BLOMFIELD, C. (19TH C)	250-1000	L
BLOODGOOD, MORRIS S. (1845 - 1920)	250-3500	L
BLOOM, HYMAN (1913 -)	1000-12000	A
BLOOMER, HIRAM REYNOLDS (1845 - 1911)	100-4800	L
BLOSSOM, EARL (1891 - 1970)	*100-600	I
BLOWER, DAVID H. (1901 - 1976)	*100-1500	G,L,F
BLUEMNER, OSCAR F.	*150-24500	
BLUEMNER, OSCAR F. (1867 - 1938)	5000-290000 +	A,L
BLUHM, NORMAN	*200-7200	
BLUHM, NORMAN (1920 -)	1200-22000 +	A
BLUM, JEROME (1884 - 1956)	250-1500	A,L
BLUM, ROBERT FREDERICK	*1000-77000 +	
BLUM, ROBERT FREDERICK (1857 - 1903)	2500-220000 +	L,F,I
BLUMBERG, YULI (1894 - 1964)	100-850	L
BLUME, PETER	*300-5000	
BLUME, PETER (1906 -)	1000-30000	A
BLUMENSCHEIN, ERNEST L.	*500-8000	
BLUMENSCHEIN, ERNEST L. (1874 - 1960)	1500-80000	A,F,I,L
BLUMENSCHEIN, HELEN GREENE (1909 -)	600-3000	X (L)
BLUMENSCHEIN, MARY SHEPHARD (1869 -)	1000-12000	F,G
BLUNT, JOHN S. (1798 - 1835)	1000-23000	P (M)
BLYTHE, DAVID GILMOUR (1815 - 1865)	3500-80000	G,F
BOARDMAN, WILLIAM G. (1815 - 1865)	350-6000	L
BOBIER, MICHAEL (20TH C)	*50-200	X (F)
BOCHERO, PETER CHARLIE (1895 - 1962)	700-6000	P
BOCHNER, MEL	*1000-10000	
BOCHNER, MEL (1940 -)	8000-32000	A
BOCK, FREDERICK WILLIAM (1876 -)	100-2500	L
BODWELL, A.V. (early 20TH C)	100-600	L
BOEHM, HENRY (- 1914)	300-1500	L
BOESE, HENRY (active 1845-65)	400-15500	L,W
BOGDANOVE, ABRAHAM JACOBI (1888 - 1946)	300-5200	X (L)
BOGERT, GEORGE HENRY (1864 - 1944)	200-4500	L,F
BOGGS, FRANK MEYERS	*500-4500	

BOGGS, FRANK MEYERS (1855 - 1926)	1000-50000	L,M
BOHAN, RUTH HARRIS (1891 - 1981)	250-1000	X
BOHDE, GEORGE W. (19TH C)	200-1500	G,F
BOHLER, HANS (20TH C)	100-450	L
BOHM, C. CURRY (1894 - 1971)	100-2500	L,M
BOHM, MAX (1868 - 1923)	300-44000	G,F
BOHROD, AARON	*200-6600	
BOHROD, AARON (1907 - 1992)	600-10000	G,L,S
BOICE, BRUCE (1941 -)	500-5000	A
BOILEAU, PHILIP	*300-2500	
BOILEAU, PHILIP (1864 - 1917)	400-4500	F,I
BOIS, GUY PENE DU (1884 - 1958)	3000-75000	G,F
BOIS, YVONNE PENE DU (20TH C)	100-900	X (L)
BOISSEAU, ALFRED (1823 - 1903)	350-3500	X (G,F)
BOIT, EDWARD DARLEY (1840 - 1916)	*350-8500	L
BOIZARD, C.U. (19TH-20TH C)	300-3200	G,F
BOLANDER, KARL S. (1893 -)	150-1800	X (L)
BOLEGARD, JOSEPH (20TH C)	*500-3500	I
BOLINGER, FRANZ J. (20TH C)	50-2500	L
BOLLENDONK, WALTER (19TH C)	100-900	M
BOLLES, REGINALD FAIRFAX (20TH C)	150-1200	I
BOLMER, M. DEFOREST (1854 - 1910)	200-1200	L
BOLOTOWSKY, ILYA (1907 - 1981)	1500-30000	A
BOLSTER, JANETTE WHEELER (1821 - 1883)	200-900	X (L)
BOMBERGER, BRUCE (1918 - 1980)	*100-700	I
BONAR, LESTER M. (20TH C)	100-500	X (L)
BONFIELD, GEORGE R. (1802 - 1898)	500-6000	L,M
BONFIELD, WILLIAM VAN DE VELDE (19TH C)	400-4800	L,M
BONGART, SERGEI R. (1918 - 1985)	300-7700	L,S
BONHAM, HORACE (1835 - 1892)	600-5000+	G
BONIN, R. (20TH C)	600-3000	X
BONNAR, JAMES KING	*100-1500	
BONNAR, JAMES KING (1885 - 1961)	300-4000	M,L
BONNET, LEON (19TH-20TH C)	400-2000	L
BONTECOU, LEE (1931 -)	*500-5500	A

BOOG, CARLE MICHEL	*100-4000	
BOOG, CARLE MICHEL (1877 -)	200-9500	X (G)
BOOTH, FRANKLIN (1874 - 1948)	*200-8200	I
BOOTH, HERB (20TH C)	*1000-4500	X
BORACK, STAN	*100-4500	
BORACK, STAN (1927 -)	50-1200	X (F)
BORBINO, J. (1905 - 1964)	800-4800	L,M
BOREIN, EDWARD (1872 - 1945)	*250-42000	G,L
BOREN, JAMES	*1000-25000	
BOREN, JAMES (1921 - 1990)	5000-40000	G,L
BORG, CARL OSCAR (1879 - 1947)	700-14000+	L,I
BORGLUM, JOHN GUTZON (1867 - 1941)	400-3500	X (L)
BORGO, LOUIS (1867 -)	*100-500	I
BORGORD, MARTIN (1869 - 1935)	600-3000	F,G,L,S
BORIE, ADOLPHE (1877 - 1934)	500-15000	F,G
BORMAN, LEONARD (20TH C)	100-400	L
BORNEGAR, PHILIP (19TH-20TH C)	100-600	X (L,F)
BOROFSKY, JONATHAN (1942 -)	*4000-55000	A
BORONDA, LESTER D.(1886 - 1951)	100-2000	L,G
BORRIS, ALBERT (LATE 19TH C)	100-1500	L
BOSA, LOUIS	*100-2100	
BOSA, LOUIS (1905 - 1981)	200-3000	L,G
BOSKERCK, ROBERT WARD VAN (1855 - 1932)	300-7500	L
BOSLEY, FREDERICK A.(1881 - 1941)	500-38000	F
BOSMAN, RICHARD (1944 -)	800-16500	X
BOSS, HENRY WOLCOTT (1820 - 1916)	400-5400	M
BOSS, HOMER (1820 - 1916)	250-1500	L
BOSTELLE, THOMAS (1921 -)	*100-500	L
BOSTON, F.D. (20TH C)	200-900	L
BOSTON, FREDERICK JAMES (1855 - 1932)	200-4500	F,L,S
BOSTON, JOSEPH H.(1860 - 1954)	150-41000+	F,L
BOTKE, CORNELIS (1887 - 1954)	300-5500	L,M,S
BOTKE, JESSIE ARMS (1883 - 1971)	500-28000	W,I
BOTT, E.F.E.V. (19TH C)	400-1500	L,G
BOTTO, OTTO (1903 -)	50-650	F

* Denotes watercolors, pastels, drawings, and/or mixed media

BOTTON, JEAN DE (1901 - 1978)	250-2500	X
BOTTOS, PETER D. (1935 -)	50-300	F,L
BOUCHE, LOUIS (1896 - 1969)	600-18000	L,G,I
BOUGHTON, GEORGE HENRY (1834 - 1905)	300-33000	L,G,F
BOUGUEREAU, ELIZABETH G.(1851 - 1922)	1200-35000+	F
BOUNDEY, BURTON SHEPARD (1879 - 1962)	300-7700	L,S
BOURGEOIS, LOUISE	*7500-13000	
BOURGEOIS, LOUISE (1911 - 1957)	400-26500	X (F)
BOURNE, GERTRUDE BEALS (1897 - 1962)	*150-1900	X (L)
BOUTELLE, DEWITT CLINTON (1820 - 1884)	250-31000	L,G,F
BOUVE, ROSAMOND SMITH (20TH C)	500-15000	F
BOVEE, I.A. (19TH-20TH C)	100-400	L
BOWDOIN, HARRIETTE (- 1947)	200-1200	G,I
BOWEN, BENJAMIN JAMES (1859 - 1930)	200-3200	M
BOWER, ALEXANDER	*100-1000	
BOWER, ALEXANDER (1875 - 1952)	150-13500	M,L
BOWER, MAURICE (1889 - 1980)	*300-3200	I
BOWERS, GEORGE NEWALL (1849 - 1909)	300-3000	X (F)
BOWES, BETTY W. (20TH C)	*50-300	F
BOWIE, FRANK LOUVILLE (1857 - 1936)	100-3500	L,M
BOWMAN, ADRIANUS M.(19TH C)	200-900	S
BOWYER, ALAN (19TH-20TH C)	100-600	X (G)
BOXER, STANLEY ROBERT (1926 -)	2000-10000	A
BOYD, RUTHERFORD	*100-23000	
BOYD, RUTHERFORD (1884 - 1951)	100-7000	G,F,I
BOYDEN, DWIGHT FREDERICK (1860 - 1933)	200-3200	L
BOYENHART, C. (19TH C)	100-400	X (F)
BOYER, RALPH LUDWIG (1879 - 1952)	200-1000	F,I
BOYES, G.E. (19TH C)	500-5000	F
BOYLE, CHARLES WELLINGTON (1861 - 1925)	600-4500	L
BOYLE, FERDINAND THOMAS LEE (1820 - 1906)	400-3500	F
BOYLE, JAMES N. (1931 -)	*50-500	X (L)
BOYLE, JOHN J. (1852 - 1917)	600-4500	S,F
BOYLE, NEIL (20TH C)	1000-3000	X (I)
BOYLE, W.W. (19TH C)	250-2500	X (L)

BOYNTON, RAYMOND (1864-1929)	*50-450	L
BRAAM, G. (19TH C)	*100-500	P
BRACE, REEVES (19TH-20TH C)	500-2000	L
BRACH, PAUL (1924 -)	800-5000	A
BRACKER, M. LEONE (1885 - 1937)	*100-1000	I
BRACKETT, A. LORING (19TH-20TH C)	500-3000	X (W)
BRACKETT, SIDNEY LAWRENCE (1852 - 1910)	300-3200	G,W,L
BRACKETT, WALTER M. (1823 - 1919)	400-8000	W,S
BRACKMAN, ROBERT	*200-3500	
BRACKMAN, ROBERT (1898 - 1980)	300-24000	F,S
BRACY, A.E. (20TH C)	50-1200	M,L
BRADBURY, BENNETT (20TH C)	50-1500	M,L
BRADBURY, GIDEON ELDEN (1837 - 1904)	500-4000	X (S)
BRADER, F.A. (19TH C)	*1500-12000	P
BRADFORD, WILLIAM	*400-6000	
BRADFORD, WILLIAM (1823 - 1892)	100-100000	M,L
BRADISH, ALVA (1806 - 1901)	500-3000	P
BRADLEY, ANNE CARY (1884 -)	300-4200	X (L)
BRADLEY, JOHN (- 1874)	18000-50000	P
BRADLEY, PETER (1940 -)	500-1500	A
BRADSHAW, GEORGE A. (1880 -)	50-700	L
BRADSTREET, JULIA E. (19TH C)	200-1500	S,L
BRADY, MATTHEW (1823 - 1892)	*500-2500	F
BRAGG, CHARLES (20TH C)	500-2000	X (G)
BRAINARD, ANN ELIZABETH (19TH C)	100-800	L
BRALEY, CLARENCE E. (19TH-20TH C)	*100-2500	M,L,S
BRANCHARD, EMILE PIERRE (1881 - 1938)	200-3000	L
BRANDIEN, CARL W. (20TH C)	100-1500	X
BRANDNER, KARL C. (1898 - 1961)	100-2700	L
BRANDRETT, ANTHONY (20TH C)	400-2500	M
BRANDRIFF, GEORGE KENNEDY (1890 - 1936)	200-15000	L
BRANDT, CARL LUDWIG (1831 - 1905)	250-8000	L,F
BRANDT, HENRY (1862 -)	300-1800	L
BRANDT, REX (1914 -)	400-2800	L
BRANDT, WARREN (1918 -)	100-1200	X (S)

* Denotes watercolors, pastels, drawings, and/or mixed media

BRANNAN, WILLIAM PENN (- 1866)	300-3500	X (F)
BRANSOM, PAUL	*100-1500	
BRANSOM, PAUL (1885 - 1979)	300-4000	I,W
BRASZ, ARNOLD F. (1888 - 1966)	50-850	F,G
BRAUN, MAURICE	*250-2000	
BRAUN, MAURICE (1877 -1941)	450-55000	L,M,S
BRAUNER, OLAF (1869 - 1947)	200-1200	X
BRAY, ARNOLD (1892 - 1972)	100-1400	M,L,F
BRAZINGTON, WILLIAM CAREY (1865 - 1914)	*400-1200	F
BRECHER, SAMUEL (1897 -)	500-9100	X (M,G)
BRECK, J.H. (20TH C)	150-1200	X (M,L)
BRECK, JOHN LESLIE (1861 - 1899)	126500	L
BRECKENRIDGE, HUGH HENRY (1870 - 1937)	500-7500+	S,L,F
BREDIN, RAE SLOAN (1881 - 1933)	1000-22000+	L,F
BREEM, PAUL (19TH)	300-3500	M
BREENE, ALEXANDER (20TH C)	100-350	M
BREHM, GEORGE (1878 - 1966)	*200-1400	I
BREHM, WORTH (1883- 1928)	*50-1000	X (F)
BREMER, ANNE (1872 - 1923)	150-3200	L,F
BRENEISER, STANLEY (1890 -)	*150-800	L
BRENNER, CARL CHRISTIAN (1838 - 1888)	400-7200	L
BRENNER, F.H. (19TH C)	200-1000	L
BRENNER, F.S. (20TH C)	50-700	G,F
BRENNERMAN, GEORGE W. (1856 - 1906)	500-5000	L,W,I
BRETT, DOROTHY EUGENIE (1883 - 1977)	700-11000	A
BRETT, HAROLD MATHEWS (1880 - 1955)	100-5000	I,G,F
BREUER, HENRY JOSEPH (1860 - 1932)	200-3500	L,M
BREUER, N.R. (20TH C)	100-1500	F
BREUER, THEODORE A. (19TH-20TH C)	500-12000	F
BREULL, HUGO (1854 - 1910)	300-3500	F,G
BREVITT, GEORGE (1854 -)	700-5500	L
BREVOORT, JAMES RENWICK (1832 - 1918)	500-10000	L
BREWER, ADRIAN LEWIS (1891 - 1956)	100-1700	X (L)
BREWER, NICHOLAS RICHARD (1857 - 1949)	150-5000	F,L
BREWERTON, GEORGE DOUGLAS	*100-3200	

BREWERTON, GEORGE DOUGLAS (1820 - 1901)	450-5000	L,M
BREWSTER, ANNA RICHARDS (1870 - 1952)	100-4500	L,I
BREWSTER, JULIA (20TH C)	*50-300	F,L
BREWSTER JR., JOHN (1766 - 1854)	4900-160000+	P
BROTMAN, LISA (20TH C)	*50-350	X
BRICE, WILLIAM (1921 -)	5000-20000	A
BRICHER, ALFRED THOMPSON	*100-65000+	
BRICHER, ALFRED THOMPSON (1837 - 1908)	550-110000+	M,L,G,F
BRIDGE, WILLIAM B. (20TH C)	100-1200	F
BRIDGEMAN, R. (19TH C)	100-500	P
BRIDGES, CHARLES (active 1730-45)	2500-8000	P
BRIDGES, FEDILIA	*250-10000	
BRIDGES, FIDELIA (1835 - 1923)	1000-13200	L,W,M
BRIDGMAN, FREDERICK ARTHUR (1847 - 1928)	800-180000	F,L,G
BRIDPORT, HUGH (1794-1868)	500-6500	L,F
BRIGANTE, NICHOLAS P. (1895 - 1989)	100-15000	L,F
BRIGGS, AUSTIN (1909 - 1973)	300-3000	F
BRIGGS, LAMAR (20TH C)	*100-1200	X
BRIGGS, LUCIUS A. (1852 - 1931)	*250-2000	M
BRIGGS, WARREN C. (1867 - 1903)	250-1800	L
BRIGHAM, R. JORDAN (19TH C)	200-3500	F
BRIGHAM, WILLIAM COLE (1870 -)	300-2500	L
BRIGHTWELL, WALTER (1914 -)	200-2000	I
BRILL, GEORGE REITER (1867 - 1918)	100-400	F
BRINDLE, E. MELBOURNE (1904 -)	*600-5000	I
BRINKLEY, NELL (- 1944)	*100-1200	I
BRINLEY, DANIEL PUTNAM (1879 - 1963)	400-5000	L,F
BRISCOE, DANIEL (1826 - 1883)	250-800	X (M)
BRISCOE, FRANKLIN DULLIN (1844 - 1903)	400-8300	M,L,G
BRISTOL, JOHN BUNYON (1826 - 1909)	400-15000	L
BRITTON, ARMA S. (20TH C)	1000-5000	A
BRITTON, C.W. (19TH C)	100-1000	X
BROAD, A.H. (20TH C)	100-300	L
BROCKMAN, ANN (1899 - 1943)	250-3000	X (F)
BRODERSON, MORRIS GAYLORD (1928 -)	500-5000	A

* Denotes watercolors, pastels, drawings, and/or mixed media

BRODHEAD, GEORGE H. (1860 -)	*50-400	M,L
BRODIE, GANDY (1924 - 1975)	200-3500	X (A)
BROE, VERN (1930 -)	400-2400	F,G,M
BROMLEY, FRANK C.(1860 - 1890)	200-4200	L
BROMLEY, J.W. (19TH C)	400-1500	F
BROOK, ALEXANDER	*150-850	
BROOK, ALEXANDER (1898 - 1980)	200-6500	F,L
BROOKE, RICHARD NORRIS (1847 - 1920)	250-12500	L,G
BROOKES, SAMUEL MARSDEN (1816 - 1892)	3500-50000	S
BROOKS, ADELE R. (1873 -)	100-700	L
BROOKS, ALDEN FINNEY (1840 - 1938)	150-4800	S,F,G
BROOKS, AMY (19TH-20TH C)	*100-600	X (G)
BROOKS, CORA SMALLEY (- 1930)	100-2000	L
BROOKS, HENRY HOWARD (1898 -)	100-3500	X (L,S)
BROOKS, JAMES	*100-2200	
BROOKS, JAMES (1906 - 1992)	2500-41500	A
BROOKS, NICHOLAS ALDEN (1849 - 1905)	1000-265000	S
BROUGIER, ADOLF (1870 - 1926)	300-1500	X (L)
BROWERE, ALBERTIS DEL ORIENT (1814 - 1887)	700-18000	G,L,S
BROWN, ANNA M. (19TH-20TH C)	300-4000	X
BROWN, ANNA WOOD (20TH C)	200-5000	F
BROWN, ARTHUR W. (1881 - 1966)	*100-2000	I
BROWN, BENJAMIN CHAMBERS (1865 - 1942)	600-6500+	L
BROWN, BOLTON (1865 - 1936)	400-2000	X (L)
BROWN, BRADFORD (20TH C)	*150-600	X
BROWN, CHARLES F. (1859 - 1920)	200-1200	L,M
BROWN, CHARLES V. (1848 -)	500-3000	X (F)
BROWN, DOUGLAS EDWIN (1904 -)	*150-500	X
BROWN, ETHELBERT (1870 -)	100-400	X (G)
BROWN, F. GRISWOLD (20TH C)	100-400	L
BROWN, FLORINNE (19TH C)	200-1800	X (S)
BROWN, FRANCIS F.(1891 - 1971)	100-1200	L
BROWN, FRANK A.(1876 -)	150-12000	F,G
BROWN, GEORGE ELMER (1871 - 1946)	250-6200	L
BROWN, GEORGE LORING	*250-3000	

BROWN, GEORGE LORING (1814 - 1889)	100-13200+	L,M
BROWN, GRAFTON TYLER (1841 - 1918)	250-15000	L
BROWN, HARLEY (20TH C)	*500-8000	F
BROWN, HARRISON BIRD (1831 - 1915)	600-21000	L,M
BROWN, HORACE (1876 - 1949)	100-900	L
BROWN, IRENE (1881 - 1934)	200-1400	M,L
BROWN, J. (active 1800-35)	5000-35000	P
BROWN, J. HENRY (1818 - 1891)	450-2000	F,L
BROWN, J. RANDOLPH (1861 -)	350-2000	X (M)
BROWN, JAMES (mid 19TH C)	700-9000	X (G)
BROWN, JAMES FRANCIS (1862 - 1935)	200-4700	F
BROWN, JOAN (1938 - 1991)	450-36000	A
BROWN, JOHN APPLETON	*275-16500	
BROWN, JOHN APPLETON (1844 - 1902)	450-16500+	L,M
BROWN, JOHN BUNYAN (1826 - 1909)	400-3500	L
BROWN, JOHN GEORGE	*100-3000	
BROWN, JOHN GEORGE (1831 - 1913)	2500-193000+	G
BROWN, MANNEVILLE E.D. (1810 - 1896)	800-9000	L,F
BROWN, MATHER (1761 - 1831)	400-7500	F
BROWN, MAURICE (1877 - 1941)	150-900	X (L)
BROWN, MCALPIN (20TH C)	100-500	F,L
BROWN, P. (19TH-20TH C)	100-400	X (M)
BROWN, PAUL (1893 - 1958)	*200-4200	I
BROWN, PAUL F. (1871 - 1944)	*200-4200	X
BROWN, ROGER (1941 -)	4650-29000	A
BROWN, ROY H. (1879 - 1956)	100-7000	L
BROWN, SAMUEL JOSEPH (1907 -)	400-3000	A,F
BROWN, W. WARREN (1853 - 1929)	300-1800	M
BROWN, W.H. (active 1875-1890)	200-750	X (L)
BROWN, WALTER FRANCIS (1853 - 1929)	400-4000	L,I
BROWN, WILLIAM ALDEN (1877 -)	100-900	L
BROWN, WILLIAM MARSHALL (1863 - 1936)	750-8400	G
BROWN, WILLIAM MASON (1828 - 1898)	300-35500+	S,L
BROWN, WILLIAM THEO (1919 -)	100-5000	X (F,G)
BROWNE, BYRON	*200-4200	

BROWNE, BYRON (1907 - 1961)	600-22000	A
BROWNE, CHARLES FRANCIS (1859 - 1920)	100-7200	L
BROWNE, GEORGE ELMER	*100-500	
BROWNE, GEORGE ELMER (1871 - 1946)	100-12000	M,L,G
BROWNE, HAROLD PUTNAM (1894 - 1931)	*150-500	X (L)
BROWNE, MARGARET FITZHUGH (1884 - 1972)	100-3500	S,F,L
BROWNE, MATILDA	*150-2000	
BROWNE, MATILDA (1896 - 1953)	350-4400 +	S,L
BROWNELL, CHARLES DE WOLF (1822 - 1909)	650-21000	L,S
BROWNELL, FRANKLIN (1857 - 1946)	50-12000	X
BROWNELL, MATILDA AUCHINLOSS (1869 -)	300-6000	L
BROWNING, COLLEEN (1927 -)	300-1800	X
BROWNSCOMBE, JENNIE	*100-6100	
BROWNSCOMBE, JENNIE (1850 - 1936)	150-32000	F
BROWNSON, WALTER C. (19TH-20TH C)	100-850	L
BROWNSWORTH, D. (19TH C)	100-750	X (F)
BRUCE, EDWARD (1879 - 1943)	100-10500	L
BRUCE, GRANVILLE (20TH C)	*200-800	X
BRUCE, JAMES CHRISTIE (19TH-20TH C)	150-1100	M
BRUCE, JOSEPHINE (19TH C)	100-300	X (S)
BRUCE, PATRICK HENRY (1881 - 1935)	2000-30000	X (S)
BRUCE, WILLIAM BLAIR (1857/59 - 1906)	350-11000	L,G
BRUCKMAN, LODEWIYK (1903 -)	400-3300	X (F,S)
BRUEL, HUGO (1854-1910)	*100-1600	L
BRUESTLE, BERTRAM G. (1902 -)	200-3500	L
BRUESTLE, GEORGE M.(1871 - 1939)	400-6700	L
BRUMBACK, LOUISE UPTON (1872 - 1929)	100-750	L
BRUMIDI, CONSTANTINO (1805 - 1880)	2000-35000	G,F
BRUNDAGE, WILLIAM TYSON (1849 - 1923)	200-2500	M
BRUNET, ADELE LAURE (1879 -)	100-250	F
BRUNNER, FREDERICK SANDS (1886 - 1954)	800-9000	I
BRUNTON, RICHARD (- 1832)	800-4800	P
BRUSH, GEORGE DE FOREST (1855 - 1941)	500-70000 +	F
BRUTON, HELEN (1898-1985)	*50-450	L
BRUTON, MARGARET (1894- 1983)	200-1800	L,F

BRUZZI, ? (19TH C)	100-500	X (W)
BRYANT, EVERETT LLOYD (1864 - 1945)	200-12000	F,S,L
BRYANT, HAROLD E.(1894 - 1950)	800-4500	X (F)
BRYANT, HENRY C.(1812 - 1881)	1000-7000	L,F
BRYANT, WALLACE (19TH-20TH C)	150-600	M,F,L
BRYERS, DUANE	*100-600	
BRYERS, DUANE (20TH C)	300-5000	I
BUCHTERKIRCH, ARMIN (1859 -)	100-900	F,L,M
BUCK, CLAUDE	*200-2000	
BUCK, CLAUDE (1890 - 1974)	300-3500	F,S,L
BUCK, WILLIAM H. (1840 - 1888)	2000-33000	L,G
BUCKLER, CHARLES E. (1869 -)	100-1500	L
BUCKLEY, JOHN MICHAEL (1891 - 1958)	100-2000	L,M
BUCKLIN, WILLIAM SAVERY	*100-1500	
BUCKLIN, WILLIAM SAVERY (1851 - 1928)	300-2500	L
BUDGEON, T. (19TH C)	500-3000	L
BUDNER, T. (20TH C)	100-400	X (G)
BUDSEY, ALFRED (20TH C)	*100-500	X (F,L)
BUEHR, G.F. (early 20TH C)	100-400	X (L)
BUEHR, KARL ALBERT (1866 - 1952)	1000-125000	L
BUELL, ALFRED (1910 -)	300-2500	I
BUFANO, BENIAMINO (1898 - 1970)	*200-1000	A
BUFF, CONRAD (1886 - 1975)	500-21000	L
BUHLER, AUGUSTUS W. (1853 - 1920)	500-2500	M,L
BULL, CHARLES LIVINGSTON (1874 - 1932)	*200-2500	I,W,M
BULLARD, OTIS A. (1816 - 1853)	800-4500	F,G,L
BUMANN, SYDNEY W. (19TH C)	150-850	X (F)
BUNCE, WILLIAM GEDNEY (1840 - 1916)	200-5000	L,M
BUNDY, GILBERT (1911 - 1955)	*100-600	I
BUNDY, HORACE (1814 - 1883)	300-5300+	P
BUNDY, JOHN ELWOOD (1853 - 1933)	300-3000	L
BUNKER, DENNIS MILLER (1861 - 1890)	1200-45000	F,L,M
BUNNER, ANDREW FISHER (1841 - 1897)	800-7500	L,M
BURBANK, ELBRIDGE AYER (1858 - 1947)	100-10000	F,S
BURCHFIELD, CHARLES EPHRAIM (1893 - 1967)	*400-150000	L,A

* Denotes watercolors, pastels, drawings, and/or mixed media

BURDICK, HORACE ROBBINS (1844 - 1942)	100-1100	L,F,S
BURGDORFF, FERDINAND	*150-3500	L
BURGDORFF, FERDINAND (1883 - 1975)	200-3500	L,M
BURGESS, GEORGE H. (1831 -)	400-8000	L
BURGESS, RUTH PAYNE (1865 - 1934)	350-3500	F,S
BURHENNE, MINNIE (19TH-20TH C)	200-3200	X (M)
BURKHARDT, EMERSON C. (1905 - 1969)	500-8400	X (L)
BURKHARDT, HANS GUSTAV (1904 -)	*200-3000	A
BURLEIGH, SIDNEY RICHMOND	*100-7500	
BURLEIGH, SIDNEY RICHMOND (1853 - 1931)	500-8500	L,F
BURLIN, HARRY PAUL (1886 - 1969)	250-5000	A
BURLINGAME, CHARLES A. (1860 - 1930)	100-2200	L
BURLIUK, DAVID	*100-1800	
BURLIUK, DAVID (1882 - 1966)	100-55000+	G,S,L,F
BURNETTE, M. (20TH C)	100-1400	L
BURNHAM, THOMAS MICKELL (1818 - 1866)	1000-30000	G,L,F
BURNS, CHARLES H. (1932 -)	200-1000	X
BURNS, MILTON JEWETT	*100-800	
BURNS, MILTON JEWETT (1853 - 1933)	600-5500	M,G,L
BURNS, PAUL C. (1910 - 1990)	*600-2000	I,L
BURNS-WILSON, ROBERT (1851 - 1916)	*50-1200	F,L
BURNSIDE, CAMERON (1887 - 1952)	*250-800	X (L)
BURPEE, WILLIAM PARTRIDGE	*200-1000	
BURPEE, WILLIAM PARTRIDGE (1846 -)	800-8500+	M,L
BURR, GEORGE BRAINERD (1876 - 1950)	700-10500	L
BURR, GEORGE ELBERT	*200-950	
BURR, GEORGE ELBERT (1859 - 1939)	600-6100	L,S
BURR, HAROLD SAXTON (1889 - 1973)	200-1800	L
BURRIDGE, WALTER WILCOX (1857 -)	*200-750	L
BURRILL JR., EDWARD (1835 -)	100-2000	G,M
BURRISS, R. HAL (20TH C)	*50-450	
BURROUGHS, BRYSON (1868 - 1934)	200-12000	F
BURT, JAMES (ac 1835 - 1849)	400-4000	L,M
BURTON, ARTHUR G. (1883 -)	300-2100	L
BURTON, CHARLES (active 1820-1832)	*5000-16000+	P

BURWASH, NAT (20TH C)	*100-600	F
BUSBY, C.A. (active 1810-30)	*1000-4000	X (P)
BUSCH, CLARENCE FRANCIS (1887 -)	350-2100	X (F)
BUSCHER, FRANZ (19TH C)	300-4000	L
BUSH, HARRY (1883 -)	200-3200	L
BUSH, JACK (1909 - 1977)	5000-66000	A
BUSH, NORTON (1834 - 1894)	400-32200	L,M
BUSSMANN, FRED J. (19TH C)	150-1200	X (S,L)
BUTEAU, W.A. (19TH C)	100-600	L
BUTLER, B.L. (19TH-20TH C)	100-400	X
BUTLER, CHARLES E. (19TH C)	800-3500	G
BUTLER, EDITH EMERSON (late 19TH C)	*100-400	L
BUTLER, GEORGE BERNARD (1838 - 1907)	700-5000	F,S
BUTLER, H.D. (early 20TH C)	250-800	L
BUTLER, HOWARD RUSSELL	*100-250	
BUTLER, HOWARD RUSSELL (1856 - 1934)	100-16100	L,M,F
BUTLER, MANLEY (20TH C)	100-1000	X (L)
BUTLER, MARY (1865 - 1946)	100-1600	L,M
BUTLER, PHILLIP A. (19TH C)	200-1700	L
BUTLER, THEODORE EARL (1861 - 1936)	800-62000	L,M,F,S
BUTMAN, FREDERICK (active 1855-70)	350-5500	L
BUTTERFIELD, A. (19TH C)	100-750	X (S)
BUTTERSWORTH, JAMES E.(1817 - 1894)	7500-187000	M
BUTTON, ALBERT PRENTICE (1872 -)	100-2300	L
BUTTON, JOHN (1929 -)	400-10000	A
BUXTON, HANNAH P. (19TH C ?)	600-3000	X (F)
BUYCK, EDWARD P. (1868 -)	50-400	L
BYE, RANULPH (1916 -)	*50-900	X
BYRUM, RUTHVEN HOLMES (1896 - 1958)	100-500	L

C

Artist	Prices	Subject
CABOT, AMY (- 1934)	200-1500	X
CABOT, EDWARD CLARKE (1818 - 1901)	*150-1500	L
CABRAL, R. (20TH C)	100-1000	M
CADENASSO, GIUSEPPE (1858 - 1918)	600-13500	L
CADMUS, PAUL	*500-10000	
CADMUS, PAUL (1904 -)	1800-99000+	G,F
CADY, EMMA JANE (19TH C)	*1500-6500	X (S)
CADY, HARRISON	*100-1700	
CADY, HARRISON (1877 - 1970)	350-7000+	I
CADY, HENRY N.	*150-650	
CADY, HENRY N. (1849 -)	200-4800	M,L
CADY, SAM (1943-)	100-700	X (L)
CAFFERTY, JAMES H. (1819 - 1869)	400-6500	G,F,S
CAHILL, WILLIAM VINCENT (1878 - 1924)	750-6100	L
CAHOON, CHARLES (1861 - 1951)	400-31000	L
CAHOON, MARTHA (1905 -)	300-7500	L,S
CAHOON, RALPH (1910 - 1982)	750-35000	P
CALCAGNO, LAWRENCE (1916 -)	200-4000	A
CALDER, ALEXANDER	*450-55000	
CALDER, ALEXANDER (1898 - 1976)	1500-75000	A
CALDER, ALEXANDER STIRLING (1870 - 1945)	*1000-28500	A
CALDWELL, ATHA HAYDOCK (19TH-20TH C)	100-1400	X (G)
CALDWELL, GEORGIA (20TH C)	50-400	L
CALIFANO, JOHN (1864 - 1924)	200-15000+	G
CALIGA, ISAAC HENRY (1857 - 1940)	500-5500	F
CALLAHAN, CAROLINE R. (1871 -)	150-1000	X (S)
CALLAHAN, JAMES (20TH C)	*100-400	L
CALLE, PAUL	*900-18000	
CALLE, PAUL (1928 -)	10000-90000	L,I
CALLOWHILL, JAMES (19TH-20TH C)	150-1200	L
CALYO, NICCOLINO VICOMTE (1799 - 1884)	800-6500	L,M
CAMERON, EDGAR SPIER (1862 - 1944)	300-3500	L
CAMERON, JOHN (1828 -)	2500-15000	L,M
CAMERON, R.A. (20TH C)	*100-1000	X

CAMERON, WILLIAM ROSS (1893 - 1971)	250-1800	L
CAMP, JOSEPH RODEFER DE (1858 - 1923)	2500-65000	L
CAMPBELL, BLENDON REED (1872 -)	300-1200	I
CAMPBELL, C.M. (active c.1900)	*600-1800	G
CAMPBELL, COLIN (1894 -)	100-600	L
CAMPBELL, GEORGE F. (20TH C ?)	400-1500	X (M)
CAMPBELL, HARRY (20TH C)	100-250	X
CAMPBELL, J.F. (20TH C)	100-700	L
CAMPBELL, LAURENCE A. (20TH C)	100-1800	X
CAMPBELL, R. (20TH C)	100-1400	G,F
CAMPBELL-PHILLIPS, JOHN (1873 -)	6400	F
CANFIELD, ABIJAH (1769 - 1830)	*2000-15000	P
CANIFF, MILTON (1907 -)	*250-850	X (F)
CANTEY, MAURINE (1901 -)	200-1000	X
CANTRALL, HARRIET M. (20TH C)	100-600	M
CAPEN, NATHANIEL (B. 1841)	500-6500	F,G
CAPLES, ROBERT (20TH C)	*200-1000	L
CAPP, AL (20TH C)	700-18000	A
CARBEE, J.C. (19TH-20TH C)	400-1200	X (F)
CARBEE, SCOTT CLIFTON (1860 - 1946)	400-3000+	F
CARBONE, CARMINE (20TH C)	100-700	F
CARDELL, MRS. FRANK HALE (1905 -)	200-900	X (S)
CARDENASSO, GIUSEPPE (1858 - 1918)	200-900	L
CARISS, HENRY T. (1840 - 1903)	400-3500+	G,L,M
CARL, EWAN B. (19TH C)	100-900	X
CARL, KATHERINE AUGUSTA (- 1938)	200-650	F
CARLES, ARTHUR BEECHER (1882 - 1952)	700-80000	A,S,F
CARLETON, ANNE (1878 - 1968)	250-2000	L,F
CARLETON, CLIFFORD (1867 - 1946)	*100-500	I
CARLEY, S.G. (late 19TH C)	100-350	X (S)
CARLIN , ANDREW B. (19TH C)	800-10000	F
CARLIN, JOHN (1813 - 1878)	500-6000	G,L,F
CARLISLE, HAROLD I. (1904 -)	100-700	X
CARLISLE, MARY HELEN	*100-700	
CARLISLE, MARY HELEN (- 1925)	100-900	X (L)

* Denotes watercolors, pastels, drawings, and/or mixed media

CARLO, GIRARDO DE (20TH C)	100-300	L
CARLSEN, DINES (1901 - 1966)	500-22000	S,L
CARLSEN, FLORA B. (1878 -)	50-400	L
CARLSEN, SOREN EMIL (1853 - 1932)	650-85000	S,L
CARLSON, JOHN FABIAN (1875 - 1947)	600-34000+	L
CARLSON, OSCAR (1895 -)	50-300	L
CARLTON, ANNE (19TH-20TH C)	250-2500	L,G
CARLTON, FREDERICK (19TH C)	100-500	L,W
CARLTON, WILLIAM TOLMAN (1816 - 1888)	750-3500	G
CARMER, H. NIMMO (20TH C)	200-3000	L,W
CARMIENCKE, JOHANN HERMANN (1810 - 1867)	300-14500	L
CARONE, NICOLAS (1917 -)	50-300	X
CARPENTER, DUDLEY (1870 -)	100-400	X
CARPENTER, ELLEN MARIA (1836 - 1909)	300-1500	L,F,S
CARPENTER, FRANCIS BICKNELL (1830-1900)	300-3500	X (F)
CARPENTER, FRED GREEN (1882 - 1965)	200-6500	L,F
CARPENTER, H.J. (20TH C)	*50-250	L
CARPENTER, KATE HOLSTON	*100-650	
CARPENTER, KATE HOLSTON (1863 - 1947)	200-2000	L,G,I,S
CARR, JOHN (- 1837)	400-4800	X (S,L)
CARR, LYELL (1857 - 1912)	650-8500	G,F
CARR, SAMUEL S. (1837 - 1908)	800-83000	G,L,W
CARROL, ROBERT (20TH C)	350-2500	X
CARROLL, BERYL (20TH C)	50-150	X (S)
CARROLL, JOHN WESLEY	*100-850	
CARROLL, JOHN WESLEY (1892 - 1959)	250-2500	F,S
CARSMAN, JON (20TH C)	400-7500	G,L
CARSON, FRANK (1881 -)	150-8000	M,L
CARSON, W.A. (early 20TH C)	100-500	L
CARSTAIRS, JAMES STEWART (19TH-20TH C)	200-900	X (L)
CARTER, CHARLES M. (1853 - 1929)	50-300	X
CARTER, CLARENCE HOLBROOK (1904 -)	500-6000+	F
CARTER, DENNIS MALONE (1827 - 1881)	400-8000	G,F
CARTER, ESTHER H. (20TH C)	100-600	X (F)
CARTER, GARY (1939 -)	1000-12000	X

CARTER, HENRY (1821 - 1880)	*100-700	X (G)
CARTER, JAMES (1817 - 1873)	350-800	F
CARTER, PRUETT A. (1891 - 1955)	300-4500	I,F
CARTER, WILLIAM SYLVESTER (1909-)	*100-1200	A
CARTWRIGHT, ISABEL BRONSON (1885 -)	300-8500	X (M,S)
CARVER, FRANKLIN H. (20TH C)	50-400	X (L)
CARY, WM.DE LA MONTAGNE (1840 - 1922)	700-65000	G,S,I
CASE, EDMUND E. (1840 - 1919)	350-8600	L
CASENELLI, VICTOR (1867 - 1961)	*400-4500	F,G
CASER, ETTORE (1880 - 1944)	400-6500	L,F,S
CASH, HERBERT (19TH-20TH C)	250-3000	S
CASHELL, V. (19TH-20TH C)	*400-1000	L
CASILEAR, JOHN WILLIAM (1811 - 1893)	1200-25000+	L
CASINELLI, VICTOR (1865 - 1961)	*100-2500	G,F,L
CASS, GEORGE NELSON (1831 - 1882)	300-3600	W,L,S
CASS, KAE DORN (1901 - 1971)	*100-450	L
CASSATT, MARY	*4500-3850000+	
CASSATT, MARY (1844 - 1926)	8500-3100000	F
CASSELLE, JEANNE (20TH C)	100-700	M
CASSIDY, IRA D. GERALD (1879 - 1934)	1000-25000	F,L,I
CASSIN, F.B. (20TH C)	300-1000	X
CASTAIGNE, JEAN ANDRE (1860 -)	100-4500	I
CASTALDO, AMAYLIA (1906 -)	50-1000	F
CASTANO, JOHN (20TH C)	500-2000	X (G)
CASTELLON, FEDERICO (1914 - 1971)	1000-10500	A
CASTER, JAMES (20TH C)	100-1000	X
CASTLE-KEITH, WILLIAM (19TH-20TH C)	200-1800	L
CATHCART, JOHN (19TH C)	100-500	X (F)
CATLIN, GEORGE	*2500-35000	
CATLIN, GEORGE (1796 - 1872)	2000-325000+	F,L,M
CAULDWELL, LESLIE GRIFFEN (1861 - 1941)	500-4500	F
CAVALLON, GIORGIO	*500-71500	
CAVALLON, GIORGIO (1904 -)	4000-72000+	A
CEDERQUIST, ARTHUR E. (1884 - 1955)	250-800	L
CHACE, HELEN B. (20TH C ?)	100-350	X (M)

* Denotes watercolors, pastels, drawings, and/or mixed media

CHADEAYNE, ROBERT O. (1897 -)	300-3500	F,L
CHADWICK, ELLEN N. (?)	100-600	X (L)
CHADWICK, WILLIAM (1879 - 1962)	1000-94000	F,L,M
CHAESE, EMILIE (18TH C)	800-8000	X (G)
CHAESE, NORA (19TH C)	250-1200	G,F
CHAFFEE, OLIVER NEWBURY (1881 - 1944)	*250-3000	X (A)
CHAFFEE, SAMUEL R. (19TH-20TH C)	*100-1200	M,L
CHALFANT, JEFFERSON DAVID	*100-26500	
CHALFANT, JEFFERSON DAVID (1856 - 1931)	6500-65000	G,F
CHALIAPIN, BORIS (20TH C)	100-700	X (F)
CHALLEE, S.R. (late 19TH C)	*100-400	X (L)
CHALONER, WALTER L. (20TH C)	600-3000	X (L,M)
CHAMBERLAIN, ELWYNN (1928 -)	5000-15000	X
CHAMBERLAIN, NORMAN STILES (1887 - 1961)	800-7000	X (L)
CHAMBERLAIN, WYNN (1929 -)	500-12200	A,F,S
CHAMBERLIN, FRANK TOLLES	*200-800	
CHAMBERLIN, FRANK TOLLES (1873 - 1961)	*250-3000	L,S
CHAMBERLIN, HELEN (20TH C)	100-1000	F,L
CHAMBERLIN, PRICE A. (19TH C)	*100-400	L
CHAMBERS, C. BOSSERON (1883 -)	250-2500	F,I
CHAMBERS, CHARLES EDWARD (1883 - 1941)	300-4500	I
CHAMBERS, JOSEPH K. (- 1916)	200-1800	L
CHAMBERS, RICHARD (1863 - 1944)	*50-1200	F,L
CHAMBERS, THOMAS (1808 - 1866)	1500-35000 +	P
CHAMPNEY, BENJAMIN (1817 - 1907)	500-26000	L,G,S
CHAMPNEY, E.G. (19TH C)	200-1200	L
CHAMPNEY, JAMES WELLS	*200-8500	
CHAMPNEY, JAMES WELLS (1843 - 1903)	500-45000	G,F,L
CHAN, GEORGE (20TH C)	200-900	L
CHANDLER, HENRY DALAND (19TH C)	*250-2500	I
CHANDLER, JOHN GREEN (1815 - 1879)	400-5400	F
CHANDLER, JOSEPH GOODHUE (1813 - 1880)	5000-35000 +	P
CHANDLER, MRS. JOSEPH G.(1820 - 1868)	100-1000	X (F,S)
CHANDLER, WILLIAM HENRY (1854 - 1928)	100-350	L,M
CHANDLER, WINTHROP (1747 - 1790)	10000-75000	P

CHANEY, LESTER JOSEPH (1907 -)	150-2000	M
CHANLER, ROBERT WINTHROP (1872 - 1930)	*600-1800	X (W)
CHAPEL, GUY MARTIN (1871 -)	200-850	L
CHAPIN, ALPHEUS (1787 - 1870)	400-1200	F
CHAPIN, BRYANT (1859 - 1927)	200-13500	S,L
CHAPIN, C.H. (active 1850-85)	500-3000	L
CHAPIN, FRANCIS (1899 - 1965)	*100-1500	G,F
CHAPIN, JAMES ORMSBEE (1887 -1975)	300-7000	X (G)
CHAPIN, JOHN R. (1823 -)	*150-1000	F,L
CHAPIN, LUCY GROSVENOR (1873 - 1939)	400-4500	F
CHAPLIN, SARAH (19TH C)	*250-650	X (S)
CHAPMAN, CARLTON THEODORE	*100-800	
CHAPMAN, CARLTON THEODORE (1860 - 1925)	300-8500 +	I,M,L
CHAPMAN, CHARLES SHEPARD (1879 - 1962)	300-5000	F,L,I
CHAPMAN, CONRAD WISE	*100-70500	
CHAPMAN, CONRAD WISE (1842 - 1910)	700-46000	G,L,M
CHAPMAN, CYRUS DURAND (1856 - 1918)	200-3000	S,L
CHAPMAN, JOHN GADSBY (1808 - 1890)	600-18000	G,L,I,M
CHAPMAN, JOHN LINTON (1839 - 1905)	1000-26000	G,L,M
CHAPMAN, MINERVA JOSEPHINE (1858 - 1947)	300-1700	G,S,L
CHAPPEL, ALONZO	*200-3000	
CHAPPEL, ALONZO (1828 - 1887)	350-7500	F,M
CHARMAN, FREDERICK MONTAGUE (1894 - 1986)	*50-900	L,F
CHARMAN, JESSIE BONE (1895 - 1986)	*200-1400	X (F,S)
CHARTRAND, ESTEBAN (1825 - 1889)	300-4200	L
CHASE, ADELAIDE COLE (1869 - 1944)	100-1200	F,S
CHASE, C.H. (19TH C)	400-3000	M
CHASE, ELSIE ROWLAND (1863 - 1937)	300-4000	X (F)
CHASE, FRANCIS (- 1955)	50-400	A
CHASE, FRANK SWIFT (1886 - 1958)	350-8400	L,M
CHASE, HENRY (HARRY) (1853 - 1889)	200-10000	M
CHASE, JESSIE K. (1879 - 1970)	200-2000	L
CHASE, JOSEPH (1878 - 1965)	50-600	X (F)
CHASE, LILA ELIZABETH (19TH-20TH C)	350-1500	X (F)
CHASE, LOUISA (1951 -)	900-18000	A

* Denotes watercolors, pastels, drawings, and/or mixed media

CHASE, RICHARD (1891 -)	150-900	L,F
CHASE, SIDNEY M. (1877 - 1957)	300-8500	F,L
CHASE, WILLIAM MERRITT	*1200-850000+	
CHASE, WILLIAM MERRITT (1849 - 1916)	5000-1100000	L,F,S
CHATTERTON, CLARENCE K. (1880 - 1973)	750-18000	I,F
CHATTIN, LOU-ELLEN (1891 - 1937)	200-1000	X (L,F)
CHECK, R.S. (19TH C)	200-600	F
CHEN, CHI (1912 -)	*350-3200	L
CHEN, GEORGE (20TH C)	100-700	X (F)
CHEN, HILO (1942 -)	1000-6500	X (F)
CHENEY, HAROLD W. (1889 - 1946)	200-3200	G,F
CHENEY, PHILIP (1897 -)	50-350	X (M)
CHENEY, RUSSELL (1881 - 1945)	100-3500	L,S
CHERNEY, MARVIN (1925 - 1967)	200-1200	A
CHERNOW, ANN (20TH C)	*300-1500	A
CHERRY, KATHRYN (1880 - 1931)	200-2500	L
CHESTER, C. (19TH C)	150-500	P
CHICHESTER, ARCHIBALD (19TH C)	*100-600	L
CHICHESTER, CECIL (1891 -)	250-3200	L,I
CHICKERING, CHARLES R. (1934 -)	250-650	X (G)
CHILD, EDWIN BURRAGE (1868 - 1937)	250-3000	F,L,I
CHILLMAN, PHILIP E. (1841 -)	100-1000	X (G,F)
CHIRIACKA, ERNEST (1920 -)	350-8500+	L,F
CHITTENDEN, ALICE BROWN (1860 - 1934)	400-17600+	S,L,F
CHRISTENSEN, DAN (1942 -)	1500-20000	A
CHRISTENSEN, RONALD J. (1923 -)	50-400	A,S
CHRISTOPHER, WILLIAM (1924 - 1973)	*300-1200	X
CHRISTY, F. EARL (1882 - 1961)	*300-1200	F,I
CHRISTY, HOWARD CHANDLER	*350-19000	
CHRISTY, HOWARD CHANDLER (1873 - 1952)	1000-48000+	I,F
CHUEY, ROBERT (20TH C)	500-2500	X(A)
CHUMLEY, JOHN WESLEY (1928 - 1984)	*400-5500	X (L,G)
CHURCH, FREDERIC EDWIN (1826 - 1900)	2500-2750000+	L,M
CHURCH, FREDERICK STUART (1842 - 1924)	250-44000	L,I
CHURCHILL, ALFRED VANCES (1864 -)	100-1000	L,S

CHURCHILL, WILLIAM WORCESTER (1858 - 1926)	600-10000	F
CICERI, ERNEST (1817 - 1866)	*150-500	X (M)
CIGE, THEO VAN (20TH C)	50-300	L
CIKOVSKY, NICOLAI (1894 - 1934)	300-3900	F,L,S,M
CIMIOTTI, GUSTAVE (1875 - 1934)	250-2000	L
CINQUEGRANA, LIVIA (1894 -)	100-1000	X (F)
CIPRICO, MARGUERITE (20TH C)	100-1200	L
CIRINO, ANTONIO (1889 - 19823)	1000-11000	M,L,I
CLAGHORN, JOSEPH C.	*150-1500	
CLAGHORN, JOSEPH C. (1869 - 1947)	500-8000	L
CLAGUE, RICHARD (1816 - 1878)	700-25000	L
CLAIR, R.A. (19TH C)	450-2500	L
CLAITON, J.(19TH-20TH C)	150-650	X (M)
CLAPP, WILLIAM HENRY (1879 - 1954)	350-22000	L,F
CLARK, ALSON SKINNER (1876 - 1949)	900-20000	F,L,I
CLARK, BENTON (1895 - 1964)	800-9500	I
CLARK, BERTRAM (20TH C)	100-600	X (F)
CLARK, C. MYRON (1858 - 1923)	100-2500	M,L
CLARK, ELIOT CANDEE (1883 - 1980)	150-9900	L
CLARK, EMERSON (19TH C)	200-850	X (G)
CLARK, FRANCIS HERBERT (1876 -)	150-2000	X (L)
CLARK, FREEMAN (19TH C)	200-750	L
CLARK, GEORGE MERRITT (- 1904)	350-1500	G
CLARK, MATT (1903 - 1972)	*50-450	
CLARK, MATT (1903 - 1972)	200-1200	I,G,F
CLARK, RENE (1886 - 1969)	*200-900	I
CLARK, ROLAND (1874 - 1957)	*50-800	W
CLARK, ROY C. (1889 -)	100-850	L
CLARK, VIRGINIA KEEP (1878 -)	100-400	F
CLARK, WALTER A. (1848 - 1917)	300-5500	M,L
CLARK, WALTER APPLETON (1876 - 1906)	200-3500 +	L,W
CLARK, WALTER LEIGHTON (1859 - 1935)	150-2800	X
CLARKE, BRANDUS J. (20TH C)	100-600	L
CLARKE, J.V. (late 19TH C)	100-600	X (L)
CLARKE, JOHN CLEM (1937 -)	500-18000	A

CLARKE, ROBERT A. (early 19TH C)	3500-25000	G
CLARKSON, EDWARD (active 1845-60)	750-3000	X (G)
CLAUS, WILLIAM A.J. (1862 -)	150-1200	F,M
CLAVE, ANTONI (1913 -)	*5000-150000 +	A
CLAY, JORDAN (20TH C)	300-2500	X
CLAY, MARY F.R. (- 1939)	250-1000	F,L
CLAYES, BERTHE DES (1877 - 1968)	*100-8600	L
CLEARY, SHIRLEY (20TH C)	*100-900	X (G)
CLEAVES, W.R. (late 19TH C)	200-800	L
CLIME, WINFIELD SCOTT (1881 - 1958)	250-6000	L,M
CLINEDINST, BENJAMIN WEST	*100-850	
CLINEDINST, BENJAMIN WEST (1887 - 1970)	350-6100	I,G,F
CLINEDINST, MAY S. (1887 - 1960)	100-700	M
CLINTON, C.F. (19TH C)	500-2000	X (F)
CLOAR, CARROLL (1913 -)	300-12000	X
CLONESSY, W. (19TH C)	100-600	X (G)
CLONNEY, JAMES GOODWYN (1812 - 1867)	25000-275000	G,F
CLOSE, CHUCK (1940 -)	*10000-231000	A
CLOSE, E. (19TH C)	100-600	L,W
CLOSSON, WILLIAM BAXTER P.(1848 - 1926)	350-5500	F,G
CLOUGH, GEORGE L. (1824 - 1901)	400-8000	L,M,F
CLOUGH, STANLEY THOMAS (1905 -)	*100-1600	L
CLOVER, LEWIS P. (1819 - 1896)	250-1500	F,G
CLURE, W.M. (19TH-20TH C)	300-1500	L
CLUSMANN, WILLIAM (1859 - 1927)	500-15000	L,F
CLYMER, EDWIN S, (20TH C)	*100-600	X (L)
CLYMER, JOHN FORD (1907 - 1989)	1000-140000	I,G
CLYNE, A.J. (20TH C)	100-500	L
COALE, GRIFFITH BAILY (1890 - 1950)	300-3500 +	I,F
COAST, OSCAR REGAN (1851 - 1931)	200-850	L
COATES, EDMOND C. (1816 - 1871)	500-19550+	L,G,M
COATES, JOHN (19TH C)	400-1500	L,G
COATS, RANDOLPH (1891 -)	200-3100	L
COB, LYMUSES E. (19TH C)	650-2000	X (F)
COBB, ALFRED F. (19TH C)	*100-500	X (L)

COBB, CYRUS (1834 - 1903)	150-650	L,F,M
COBB, DARIUS (1834 - 1919)	200-1800	L,S,F,M
COBB, HENRY IVES (1859 - 1931)	*100-700	X (F)
COBURN, FRANK (1862 - 1938)	100-7000	L,M,S,F
COBURN, FREDERICK SIMPSON	*200-3000	
COBURN, FREDERICK SIMPSON (1871 - 1960)	900-31000	L,F
COCHRAN, ALLEN DEAN (1888 - 1971)	150-8500	L,F
COCHRANE, CONSTANCE (20TH C)	150-650	L,M
COCKS, JOHN H. (1850 - 1938)	*300-1200	X (W,L)
CODMAN, CHARLES (1800 - 1842)	1000-15500	L,M
CODMAN, EDWIN E. (19TH C)	100-600	M
CODMAN, JOHN AMORY (1824 - 1886)	600-7700	L,M,F
COE, ETHEL (1880 - 1938)	*50-350	X (F)
COFFEE, WILLIAM JOHN (20TH C)	100-550	L,F
COFFIN, ELIZABETH REBECCA (1851 - 1930)	800-4800	F
COFFIN, GEORGE ALBERT (1856 - 1922)	100-850	M
COFFIN, WILLIAM ANDERSON (1855 - 1925)	200-15000	L,M,F
COFFIN, WILLIAM HASKELL	*200-2500	
COFFIN, WILLIAM HASKELL (1878 - 1941)	400-8000	M,L,F
COGGELSHALL, JOHN I.	*100-400	
COGGELSHALL, JOHN I. (1856 - 1927)	200-1500	G,L,M
COGGESHALL, K.M. (20TH C)	100-350	L
COGSWELL, WILLIAM F. (1819 - 1903)	250-6000	F
COHEN, FREDERICK (19TH C)	200-3200	L
COHEN, GEORGE (1919 -)	350-1500	X (G)
COHEN, LEWIS (1857 - 1915)	350-3200	L,F
COIT, CAROLINE (- 1934)	*150-500	M,L
COLBURN, ELEANOR RUTH (1866 - 1939)	300-3500	F,G
COLBURN, SAMUEL BOLTON (1909 -)	*100-650	L
COLBY, GEORGE E. (1859 -)	350-1800	L
COLBY, JOSEPH WOOD (1862 - 1930)	500-6000	X (F)
COLCHIDAS, GUS (20TH C)	300-4000	X (F)
COLE, ALPHAESUS PHILEMON (1876 - 1989)	300-6000	F,L
COLE, CASILEAR (1888 -)	800-7500	X (F)
COLE, CHARLES OCTAVIUS (1814 -)	600-15000	L,F

* Denotes watercolors, pastels, drawings, and/or mixed media

COLE, JOSEPH FOXCROFT (1837 - 1892)	200-6000	L,F
COLE, JOSEPH GREENLEAF (1803 - 1858)	350-1500	F
COLE, THOMAS (1801 - 1848)	3500-1045000	L
COLE, THOMAS CASILEAR (1888 - 1976)	100-85000	X (F)
COLEGROVE, M.B. (19TH C)	100-650	L
COLEMAN, BLANCHE E. (19TH C)	100-800	X (F)
COLEMAN, CHARLES CARYL	*300-7000	
COLEMAN, CHARLES CARYL (1840 - 1928)	700-100000+	L,G,F
COLEMAN, GLENN O. (1887 - 1932)	3500-25000	L
COLEMAN, HARVEY B. (1884 - 1959)	100-1000	L
COLEMAN, LORING W. (20TH C)	150-900	L
COLEMAN, MARION (20TH C)	150-650	X (F)
COLEMAN, MARY DARTER (1894 - 1956)	150-2000	L
COLEMAN, RALPH PALLEN (1892 - 1968)	100-1200	I,F
COLEMAN, SAMUEL	*100-3600	
COLEMAN, SAMUEL (1832 - 1920)	1500-35000	L,M
COLFER, JOHN (20TH C)	100-700	L
COLL, JOSEPH C. (1881 - 1921)	*100-1600	I
COLLIER, B.L. (19TH-20TH C)	100-400	L
COLLIER, WILLIAM R. (19TH C)	*300-1500	X (L)
COLLINS, AMELIA (20TH C)	*100-800	X
COLLINS, C.L. (19TH C)	50-600	L
COLLINS, EARL (1925 -)	400-4000	M,L
COLLINS, F. (19TH C)	400-3500	X (G)
COLLINS, FRANK H. (- 1935)	100-750	X (F)
COLLINS, JULIA ALICE (20TH C)	100-500	F
COLLINS, SEWELL (1876 -)	*100-500	I
COLLVER, ETHEL BLANCHARD (1875 - 1955)	750-4500	F,G
COLMAN, ROI CLARKSON (1884 - 1945)	200-3000	M,L
COLEMAN, SAMUEL	*100-3600	
COLEMAN, SAMUEL (1832 - 1920)	1500-35000	L,M
COLT, MORGAN (1876 - 1926)	450-4800	L
COLTMAN, ORA	*100-500	
COLTMAN, ORA (1860 -)	100-1000	L
COLVON, S.M. (19TH C)	100-700	X (S)

COLYAR, P.M. (19TH-20TH C)	*100-600	M,L
COLYER, VINCENT (1825 - 1888)	*150-1500	L
COMAN, CHARLOTTE BUELL (1833 - 1925)	350-3500	L
COMEGYS, GEORGE H. (early 19TH C)	350-3500	G
COMINS, ALICE R. (- 1934)	300-650	L
COMINS, EBEN F. (1875 - 1949)	100-1000	X (F)
COMPERA, ALEXIS (1856 - 1906)	400-1200	L
COMPTON, W.W. (20TH C)	50-250	M,L
COMSTOCK, ENOS BENJAMIN (1879 - 1945)	600-3000	X (I)
CONANT, ALBAN JASPER (1821 - 1915)	650-3000	F,M
CONANT, LUCY SCARSBOROUGH	*200-900	
CONANT, LUCY SCARSBOROUGH (1867 - 1921)	300-3800	L
CONARROE, GEORGE W. (1803 - 1882)	600-2500	F
CONDO, GEORGE	*600-8000	
CONDO, GEORGE (1957 -)	2000-60500	A
CONE, MARVIN D. (1891 - 1964)	700-33000	L,F
CONELY, WILLIAM B. (1830 - 1911)	300-2800	G,S,F
CONGDON, ADAIRENE VOSE (19TH C)	600-1800	X (G)
CONGDON, ANNE RAMSDELL (1873 - 1958)	*200-1500	L,M
CONGDON, THOMAS RAPHAEL	*200-750	
CONGDON, THOMAS RAPHAEL (1862 - 1917)	400-4000	X (G)
CONGER, WILLIAM (early 20TH C)	*200-850	X (G)
CONKLIN, S. (19TH-20TH C)	350-1200	X (M)
CONNAWAY, JAY HALL (1893 - 1970)	250-5500	M,L
CONNELL, EDWIN D. (1859 -)	400-3600	F,W
CONNER, ALBERT CLINTON (1848 - 1929)	150-850	L
CONNER, JOHN ANTHONY (1892 - 1971)	150-2200	L,M
CONNER, JOHN RAMSEY (1859 - 1952)	400-12000	M,L
CONNOLLY, HOWARD (1907 -)	100-3500	I,F,L
CONNORS, BRUCE G. (1909 -)	*250-800	X (L)
CONREY, LEE F. (1883 -)	*100-650	I
CONSTABLE, WILLIAM (1783 - 1861)	*100-1000	L
CONSTANT, GEORGE (1892 - 1978)	*150-1500	I
CONTENT, DANIEL (1902 - 1990)	300-4500	I
CONTI, GINO EMILIO (1900 -)	100-500	G

* Denotes watercolors, pastels, drawings, and/or mixed media

CONWAY, FREDERICK E. (1900 - 1972)	*150-850	L,M
CONWAY, JOHN S. (1852 - 1925)	300-6500	X (F)
COOK, C.M. (19TH C)	150-1200	M
COOK, CAPTAIN (19TH-20TH C)	1000-6000	P
COOK, CHARLES BAILEY (early 20TH C)	200-900	X (L)
COOK, DELIA E. (20TH C)	100-400	F,L
COOK, GLADYS EMERSON (1889 - 1976)	*50-300	X (W)
COOK, JOHN A. (1870 - 1936)	*200-850	M
COOK, MARION (19TH C ?)	300-1200	X (L)
COOK, NELSON (1817 - 1892)	300-5000	F
COOK, OTIS PIERCE (Jr.) (20TH C)	200-3000	M,L
COOK, W.B. (19TH-20TH C)	100-750	L
COOKE, GEORGE (1793 - 1849)	700-5000	L,M
COOKMAN, CHARLES EDWIN (1856 -1913)	250-2000	F
COOLEY, B. (19TH C)	400-3500	X (L)
COOLIDGE, CASSIUS MARCELLUS (1844 - 1934)	1000-17600	W
COOLIDGE, JOHN (1882 -)	100-900	X (L)
COOLIDGE, JOHN (1918 - 1984)	150-1500	X (M)
COOMANS, DIANA (19TH-20TH C)	500-6000	F
COOMBS, DELBERT DANA (1850 - 1938)	150-11000	L,M
COOPER, A.L. (19TH C)	100-1000	X (M)
COOPER, ASTLEY D. M.(1856 - 1924)	300-15000	S,L,G,F
COOPER, COLIN CAMPBELL	*250-15000	
COOPER, COLIN CAMPBELL (1856 - 1937)	500-78000	L,F,G
COOPER, EMMA LAMPERT	*400-1000	
COOPER, EMMA LAMPERT (1860 - 1920)	400-6200	L,F,G
COOPER, GEORGE (1796 - 1849)	200-1500	F
COOPER, GEORGE VICTOR (1810 - 1878)	150-650	L
COOPER, J. (18TH - 19TH C)	200-850	F
COOPER, LILLIAN (19TH-20TH C)	350-4000	G,F
COOPER, M. (19TH-20TH C)	100-1200	L
COOPER, T.S. (19TH C)	100-1000	X (W)
COPE, GEORGE (1855 - 1929)	500-35000	S,L
COPE, GORDON (1906 - 1970)	250-4000	L
COPELAND, ALFRED BRYANT (1840 - 1909)	350-14500	G,L,S

COPELAND, CHARLES (1858 - 1945)	*100-2400+	L,I,M
COPELAND, ELEANOR R. (1875 -)	*100-400	X (M)
COPELAND, JOSEPH FRANK (1872 -)	*100-850	L
COPLEY, JOHN SINGLETON (1737 - 1815)	2500-650000	F,M
COPLEY, WILLIAM (BILL) NELSON	*350-10000	
COPLEY, WILLIAM (BILL) NELSON (1919 -)	700-20000	A
COPP, WILLIAM S. (1891 -)	100-900	L
COPPEDGE, FERN ISABELL (1883/88 - 1951)	800-29000	L,M
COPPER, J. (18TH C)	5000	F
COPPERMAN, MILDRED TURNER (20TH C)	400-4000	L
COPPIN, JOHN (1904 - 1986)	50-800	X (L,F)
CORBETT, EDWARD (1919 - 1971)	*200-1000	A
CORBINO, JON (1905 - 1964)	400-5500	F,G,L
CORCOS, LUCILLE (1908 -)	*500-6000	X (L)
CORDREY, EARL SOMERS (1902 - 1977)	*150-700	I
COREY, BERNARD (20TH C)	250-800	L
CORNE, MICHEL FELICE (1752 - 1832)	*2000-25000	F,M
CORNELL, JOSEPH (1903 - 1972)	*10000-495000	A
CORNER, THOMAS (1865 - 1938)	400-4000	F
CORNETT, ROBERT FRANK (1867 -)	100-500	L
CORNOYER, PAUL (1864 - 1923)	800-88000	L
CORNWELL, DEAN (1892 - 1960)	1000-45000	I
CORSON, ALICE VINCENT (- 1915)	750-3000	X (F)
CORSON, CHARLES SCHELL (- 1921)	400-6000	L
CORWIN, CHARLES ABEL (1857 - 1938)	450-16500	M,G,L
COSTELLO, A. (20TH C)	100-500	X (M)
COSTELLO, DAVID (20TH C)	300-800	X
COSTIGAN, JOHN EDWARD	*400-3000	
COSTIGAN, JOHN EDWARD (1888 - 1972)	450-15000	L,F
COSTSANEN, J. (1888 -)	1200-6000	G
COTE, ALAN (1937 -)	500-5000	A
COTSWORTH, STAATS (1908-)	50-600	F
COTTINGHAM, ROBERT	*1000-15000	
COTTINGHAM, ROBERT (1935 -)	6500-200000	A
COTTON, JOHN (1868-1931)	200-2500	L

* Denotes watercolors, pastels, drawings, and/or mixed media

COTTON, WILLIAM H.	*200-1800	
COTTON, WILLIAM H. (1880 - 1958)	350-7500	F,I
COUGHLIN, A.T. (late 19TH C)	400-2000	L
COUGHLIN, H. (20TH C)	*100-800	I
COULON, EMMA (19TH-20TH C)	800-3500	L,G
COULON, GEORGE DAVID (1823 - 1904)	850-4500	L,F
COULON, PAULINE (19TH C)	*400-1200	X (W)
COULTER, MARY J. (20TH C)	100-700	L
COULTER, WILLIAM ALEXANDER (1849 - 1936)	900-50000	M
COUSE, EANGER IRVING	*500-25000	
COUSE, EANGER IRVING (1866 - 1936)	2000-180000	F,G
COUTER, FRANKLYN C. (19TH C)	700-2000	X (F)
COUTTS, ALICE (1880 - 1973)	400-4500	L,G
COUTTS, GORDON (1880 - 1937)	450-6000 +	F,L
COVEY, ARTHUR SINCLAIR (1877 - 1960)	*100-1000	X (M)
COWAN, SARAH EAKIN (19TH-20TH C)	*150-900	F
COWDERY, EVA (19TH-20TH C)	400-5000	G,F
COWELL, JOSEPH GROSS (19TH-20TH C)	100-700	X (L,F)
COWLARD, ALICE (1898 - 1986)	*200-950	S
COWLES, FLEUR (20TH C)	250-900	X
COX, ALBERT SCOTT (1863 - 1920)	500-3200	G,L,F,I
COX, ALLYN (1896 - 1982)	100-1500	L,F,S
COX, ARTHUR (late 19TH C)	*150-650	X (L)
COX, CHARLES BRINTON (1864 - 1905)	400-4000	X (G)
COX, KENYON	*100-2500	
COX, KENYON (1856 - 1919)	500-15000	F,I
COX, L. CARR (19TH C)	100-600	X (S)
COX, L.M. (19TH-20TH C)	100-400	X (L)
COX, LOUISE (1865 - 1945)	400-3500	F
COX, WALTER (1866 - 1930)	100-5000	X (L)
COXE, REGINALD CLEVELAND (1855 -)	300-2800	M,L
COZZENS, FREDERICK SCHILLER (1846 - 1928)	*300-8500	M,I
CRAFFT, R.B. (active 1835-65)	600-2000	F
CRAIG, CHARLES (1846 - 1931)	850-8500	L,G,F
CRAIG, FRANK (1874 - 1918)	*200-1800	I

CRAIG, ISAAC EUGENE (1830 -)	250-2000	F,L
CRAIG, J.W. (20TH C ?)	*100-400	L
CRAIG, ROBERT (19TH C)	200-1000	L
CRAIG, THOMAS BIGELOW	*150-1500	
CRAIG, THOMAS BIGELOW (1849 - 1924)	250-5000	L
CRAIG, WILLIAM (1829 - 1875)	*150-2800	L
CRAM, ALLEN GILBERT (1886 - 1947)	500-5000	M,F
CRAMER, FLORENCE BALLIN (1934 -)	100-800	X (S)
CRAMER, KONRAD (1888 - 1965)	900-24500	A
CRANCH, CHRISTOPHER PEARSE (1813 - 1892)	400-6500	L,F,S
CRANDELL, BRADSHAW (1896 - 1966)	*400-4000	I
CRANE, (ROBERT) BRUCE	*400-7000	
CRANE, (ROBERT) BRUCE (1857 - 1937)	800-43000	L
CRANE, ALAN H. (1901 -)	*50-350	G,W
CRANE, ANN (- 1948)	250-850	L
CRANE, FREDERICK (1847 - 1915)	50-600	X (F)
CRANE, JAMES (20TH C)	800-4500	P
CRANE, STANLEY WILLIAM (1905 -)	450-1800	L,S
CRANE, WILBUR (1875 -)	50-2000	L
CRASTENBURG, A.J. (19TH C)	100-800	L,M
CRATZ, BENJAMIN (1888 -)	100-1000	X (L)
CRAVEN, E. (19TH-20TH C)	300-2000	X (W)
CRAVEN, STANLEY W. (1905 -)	100-1000	X (S)
CRAWFORD, ALICE BERLE (20TH C)	*100-400	X (L)
CRAWFORD, BRENETTA H. (1876 - 1956)	100-1000	F
CRAWFORD, EARL STETSON (1877 -)	600-3500	F
CRAWFORD, JAMES W. (1832 -)	*150-7000	S,G
CRAWFORD, LANSON H. (20TH C)	*50-600	X
CRAWFORD, RALSTON	*300-15500	
CRAWFORD, RALSTON (1906 - 1978)	10000-185000	A
CRAWFORD, W. (1869 - 1944)	*100-900	I
CREE, JAMES (1867 - 1951)	*150-1400	X (L)
CREO, LEONARD (1923 -)	100-800	X (F,G)
CRESSWELL, WILLIAM NICHOL (1822 - 1888)	*100-1000	X (L,M)
CRIEFELDS, RICHARD (1853 - 1939)	400-2000	S,F

* Denotes watercolors, pastels, drawings, and/or mixed media

CRILEY, THEODORE MORROW (1880 - 1930)	400–6600	M,L,F
CRIPS, G.A. (19TH-20TH C)	150-1200	L
CRISP, ARTHUR WATKINS (1881 -)	600-3000	G,I
CRISS, FRANCIS H.(1901 - 1973)	1000-19000	A,F,L
CRITCHER, CATHERINE CARTER (1868 -)	5000-32000	F
CROCKER, JOHN DENISON (1823 - 1879)	650-6000	L,F
CROCKWELL, DOUGLAS S. (1904 -1968)	600-7500	I
CROCKWELL, SPENCER DOUGLAS (1904 - 1968)	600-6000	I
CROMPTON, EDNA L. (20TH C)	100-500	X
CROMWELL, CHARLES (1838 -)	700-3000	F
CROMWELL, JOAN (1889 - 1966)	100-1100	L
CROOKS, RON (1925 -)	400-1500	G
CROPSEY, JASPER FRANCIS	*1000-27000	
CROPSEY, JASPER FRANCIS (1823 - 1900)	2500-300000 +	L,M
CROSBY, GEORGE L. (1833 -)	300-2500	G,M
CROSBY, RAYMOND MOREAU	*150-500	
CROSBY, RAYMOND MOREAU (1875 - 1945)	150-1500	L,F,M
CROSKEY, W.H. (19TH C)	500-1500	X (G)
CROSMAN, JOHN (20TH C)	400-2500	X (S)
CROSS, AMY (1865-1939)	*50-550	L
CROSS, ANSON KENT (1862 - 1944)	150-2800	L
CROSS, HENRY H. (1837 - 1918)	500-77000	L,G,F
CROSS, WATSON (1918 -)	*100-2200	M,L
CROSSMAN, WILLIAM HENRY (1896 -)	350-1200	L,G
CROW, LOUISE (20TH C)	100-400	X (S)
CROWLEY, DAVID B. (20TH C)	100-650	X (L)
CROWLEY, J.M. (active c.1830-40)	*1200-4000	P
CROWNINGSHIELD, FREDERIC (1845 - 1918)	400-6300	L
CRUSET, SEBASTIEN (20TH C)	700-2000	X (L)
CRUTCHFIELD, WILLIAM (1932 -)	*500-1800	X
CUCARO, PASCAL (1915 -)	100-500	X
CUCCHI, ANTHONY (20TH C)	200-750	X
CUCUEL, EDWARD (1875 - 1951)	1000-44000	F,L
CULBERTSON, JOSEPHINE (1852 - 1939)	150-1800	M,L
CULLEN, MAURICE GALBRAITH (1866 - 1934)	350-4000	X (M)

CULLINGANE, A.C. (19TH C)	100-300	P
CULMER, HENRY L.A. (1854 - 1914)	800-3500	X
CULVER, CHARLES (1908 - 1967)	*100-2200	L,W,F
CULVERHOUSE, JOHANN MONGELS (1820 - 1891)	3000-23000	G,L
CUMMING, ARTHUR (19TH C)	150-1600	M,S
CUMMING, CHARLES ATHERTON (1858 - 1932)	400-4000	G,L
CUMMINGS, THOMAS SEIR (1804 - 1894)	700-5000	F
CUNEO, CYRUS C. (1878 - 1916)	150-2800	X (L,G)
CUNEO, RINALDO (RICHARD) (1877 - 1939)	250-10500	L,M,S
CUNNINGHAM, EARL (1893 - 1978)	400-7700	P
CUNNINGHAM, FERN FRANCES (1889 -)	100-650	X (L,S)
CUNNINGHAM, PATRICIA S. (1919 -)	200-1500	X (M,L)
CUNNINGHAM (SR), CHARLES C. (1841 - 1918)	800-3500	M
CUPREIN, FRANK W. (1871 - 1948)	250-9000	L,M
CURRAN, CHARLES COURTNEY (1861 - 1942)	2000-105000	F,L,S
CURRAN, J. (19TH-20TH C)	500-4000	F,L
CURRIER, CYRUS B. (1868 - 1946)	50-650	L
CURRIER, EDWARD WILSON (1857 - 1918)	100-3000	L
CURRIER, JOSEPH FRANK	*200-1500	
CURRIER, JOSEPH FRANK (1843 - 1909)	600-2500	G,L
CURRIER, WALTER BARRON (1879 - 1934)	250-1600	L
CURRY, JOHN STEWART	*500-19000	
CURRY, JOHN STEWART (1897 - 1946)	700-40000+	G,L
CURRY, ROBERT FRANZ (1872 - 1945)	500-3600	L
CURTIN, THOMAS R. (1899 - 1977)	150-900	L
CURTIS, ALICE MARION (1847 - 1911)	200-2300	L,S
CURTIS, ASA (- 1858)	100-450	M
CURTIS, C. (19TH C)	100-2800	F
CURTIS, CALVIN (1822 - 1893)	250-1200	L
CURTIS, ELIZABETH (1873 -)	100-3000	L,M
CURTIS, EMILE (20TH C)	150-600	X (F)
CURTIS, GEORGE (1826 - 1881)	300-9500	M
CURTIS, LELAND (1897 -)	200-1800	L,M
CURTIS, MARIAN (1912 -)	*100-400	L
CURTIS, PHILIP C. (20TH C)	800-10000	X

158   * Denotes watercolors, pastels, drawings, and/or mixed media

CURTIS, RALPH WORMELEY (1854 - 1922)	600-40000	F,L
CURTIS, ROGER (20TH C)	100-500	L
CUSHING, HOWARD GARDINER (1869 - 1915)	600-21000	L,F
CUSHING, J.C. (19TH C)	200-1000	X (S)
CUSHING, LILY (20TH C)	200-1200	X (S)
CUSHING, MARY A. (19TH C)	*200-600	F
CUSHING, OTHO (1871 - 1942)	*100-800	I
CUSHING, SHAILER (19TH C)	100-800	L
CUSHMAN, ALICE (1854 -)	*100-650	X (L,M)
CUSHMAN, M.H. (19TH C)	*50-400	L
CUSTER, E.A. (19TH-20TH C)	100-850	L
CUSTER, EDWARD L. (1837 - 1880)	500-4500	L,W
CUSTIS, ELEANOR PARKE (1897 - 1983)	*500-6500	L,G,F
CUTHBERT, VIRGINIA (1908 -)	300-3500	G
CUTTING, FRANCIS HARVEY (1872 - 1964)	100-850	L,M

D

Artist	Prices	Subject
D'AMICO, OSKAN (1923 -)	800-3500	A
D'ARCANGELO, ALLAN (1930 -)	3000-20000	A
DABB, RAYMOND (19TH C)	650-2000	M
DABO, LEON	*200-2500	
DABO, LEON (1868 - 1960)	250-26000 +	M,L,F,S
DABO, THEODORE SCOTT (1877 -)	150-3500	M,L
DAGGETT, GRACE E. (1867 -)	50-550	X (L)
DAGGY, RICHARD S. (1892 -)	*200-750	L
DAHLAGER, JULES (20TH C)	700-2500 +	L
DAHLGREEN, CHARLES W. (1864 - 1955)	400-2200	L
DAHLGREN, CARL CHRISTIAN (1841 - 1920)	300-5000	L
DAHLGREN, MARIUS (1844 - 1920)	400-3500	L
DAINGERFIELD, ELLIOTT (1859 - 1932)	500-8000	L,F,I
DAKIN, SIDNEY TILDEN (1876 - 1935)	100-2000	L

DALBIAC, F. (20TH C)	200-750	F
DALE, GEORGE EDWARD (1840 - 1873)	300-1500	X (G)
DALE, WILLIAM (19TH-20TH C)	500-2500	L
DALEE, JUSTUS (active 1826-1848)	*300-4000+	P
DALLAS, WILLIAM WILKINS (19TH C)	100-600	L
DALLIN, CYRUS EDWIN (1861 - 1944)	200-2000	L
DAMPIER, WILLIAM (1910-1985)	100-1200	L,F
DAMROW, CHARLES (1916 -)	350-4500	G,L
DANA, WILLIAM P.W. (1833 - 1927)	600-2000	L,G,M
DANGERS, BENHAM C. (1916 -)	500-5000	A,F,S
DANIEL, LEWIS (1901 -)	100-400	X (I)
DANIELL, WILLIAM SWIFT	*150-1000	
DANIELL, WILLIAM SWIFT (1865 - 1933)	100-1000	L,M
DANIELS, ELMER HARLAND (1905 -)	100-300	L,F
DANIELS, GEORGE F. (1821 -)	1500-25000	L
DANLON, F. (JR.) (19TH-20TH C)	600-5000	X (I,S)
DANNAT, WILLIAM TURNER (1853 - 1929)	500-3500	F,G
DANNER, SARA KOLB (1894 - 1969)	150-5500	L
DANTZIG, M. (20TH C)	100-1000	X (F)
DAPHNIS, NASSOS (1914 -)	100-5000	A
DARBY, ELIZABETH CLORINDA (- 1906)	500-2500	X (S)
DARBY, MARY (20TH C)	*100-500	X (L)
DARGE, FRED (1900 -)	100-400	G,L
DARLEY, FELIX OCTAVIUS CARR	*100-6500	
DARLEY, FELIX OCTAVIUS CARR (1822 - 1888)	700-36000	I,G
DARLING, DAVID T. (20TH C)	100-700	X (L)
DARLING, J. NORWOOD (1876 -)	300-2500	X (L)
DARLING, ROBERT (19TH C)	2500-10000	F
DARLING, WILDER M.	*100-500	
DARLING, WILDER M. (1856 - 1933)	100-1500	L
DARLING, WILLIAM S. (1882 - 1963)	100-3300	L
DARRAH, ANN SOPHIA TOWNE (1819 - 1881)	250-3000+	S,L,M
DARRAH, S.T. (1819 - 1881)	100-900	M,L
DARRO, TOM (20TH C)	300-2000	F
DART, RICHARD POUSETTE (1916 -)	2000-99000	X (F)

* Denotes watercolors, pastels, drawings, and/or mixed media

DASBURG, ANDREW MICHAEL	*500-19000	
DASBURG, ANDREW MICHAEL (1887 - 1979)	1200-125000	A,L
DASH, ROBERT (1934 -)	350-4000	L
DATZ, ABRAHAM MARK (1891 - 1969)	100-450	L
DAUGHERTY, JAMES HENRY	*350-11000	
DAUGHERTY, JAMES HENRY (1889 - 1974)	600-40000	A,I
DAUGHERTY PAUL (1877 - 1947)	700-2800	L
DAVENPORT, HENRY (1882 -)	200-3100	G,L
DAVENPORT, W.S. (19TH-20TH C)	150-900	X (L)
DAVEY, RANDALL	*1000-28000	
DAVEY, RANDALL (1887 - 1964)	1500-55000	W,F
DAVID, S.S. (DE SCOTT EVANS)(1847 - 1898)	500-30000	S,G,F
DAVIDSON, ALLAN DOUGLAS (1873 - 1932)	100-400	X (G)
DAVIDSON, CHARLES GRANT (1866 - 1945)	*150-1000	L
DAVIDSON, GEORGE (1889 - 1965)	250-1800	L,G
DAVIDSON, GRACE (20TH C)	100-850	L
DAVIDSON, JO (1883 - 1952)	*100-1500	F
DAVIDSON, MORRIS (1979 -)	*100-450	A
DAVIES, ALBERT WEBSTER (1889 - 1967)	400-3500	P
DAVIES, ARTHUR BOWEN	*400-6500	
DAVIES, ARTHUR BOWEN (1862 - 1928)	800-40000	A,F,L,
DAVIES, HAROLD CHRISTOPHER (1891 - 1976)	500-3000	X (L)
DAVIES, KEN (1925 -)	800-4500	S
DAVIES, WILLIAM S. (1826 - 1901)	*300-1800	X (L)
DAVIS, A.C. (19TH-20TH C)	100-500	X (S)
DAVIS, A.F. (20TH C ?)	150-750	L
DAVIS, ALEXANDER JACKSON (1803 - 1892)	*5000-20000	L
DAVIS, ALICE (1905 -)	200-1500	X (L,M)
DAVIS, CECIL CLARK (20TH C)	100-300	X (F)
DAVIS, CHARLES HAROLD	*100-1900	
DAVIS, CHARLES HAROLD (1856 - 1933)	600-24500	L,G
DAVIS, EMMA EARLENBAUGH (1891 -)	250-1000	X (S)
DAVIS, F. WATSON (19TH-20TH C)	*100-1500	F,G
DAVIS, FLOYD MACMILLAN (1896 - 1966)	*250-3000	I
DAVIS, GENE (1920 - 1985)	1500-29000	A

DAVIS, GLADYS ROCKMORE (1901 - 1967)	300-6600	F
DAVIS, H.A. (19TH C)	500-1800	L
DAVIS, HARRY JR. (20TH C)	350-1500	X (G)
DAVIS, J. A. (active 1830-55)	*1000-9500	P
DAVIS, JAMES EDWARD (1901 -)	900-5000	X (G)
DAVIS, JERROLD (1926 -)	100-900	X
DAVIS, JOHN STEEPLE (1844 - 1917)	300-2500	X (G)
DAVIS, JOSEPH H. (1811 - 1865)	*1500-30000	P
DAVIS, LEE E. (1910 -)	100-600	X
DAVIS, LEONARD MOORE (1864 - 1938)	300-3500	L
DAVIS, M.A. (19TH C)	200-800	X (S)
DAVIS, MARY DEFOREST (19TH C)	300-2800	L
DAVIS, O.E. (19TH C)	*100-1200	X (M)
DAVIS, RONALD (RON) WENDELL	*300-4000	
DAVIS, RONALD (RON) WENDELL (1937 -)	2500-30000	A
DAVIS, STARK	*100-25000	
DAVIS, STARK (B. 1885 -)	100-3000	X (L)
DAVIS, STUART	*1000-100000	
DAVIS, STUART (1894 - 1964)	12000-275000	A
DAVIS, THEODORE RUSSELL (1840 - 1894)	*300-3000	F,G
DAVIS, VESTIE E. (1904 - 1978)	400-8500	P
DAVIS, WARREN B.	*200-2500+	
DAVIS, WARREN B. (1865 - 1928)	400-7500+	F
DAVIS, WILL PARKER (19TH-20TH C)	*100-500	X (F)
DAVIS, WILLIAM MOORE (1829 - 1920)	500-65000	L,G,S
DAVIS, WILLIAM R. (20TH C)	800-8000	M
DAVIS, WILLIS E. (1855 - 1910)	1800	X (L)
DAVISSON, H.G. (1866 -)	*100-500	L,W
DAVOL, JOSEPH P. (1864 - 1923)	100-1100	X (M)
DAWANGYUMPTEWA, DAVID (20TH C)	100-500	X (A)
DAWES, DEXTER B. (1872 -)	*50-500	L
DAWES, EDWIN M. (1872 - 1945)	350-1500	L
DAWSON, GEORGE WALTER (1870 -)	300-1200	L,G,S
DAWSON, JOHN W. (1888 -)	*50-300	L
DAWSON, MANIERRE (1887 - 1969)	5000-58000	X (A)

* Denotes watercolors, pastels, drawings, and/or mixed media

DAWSON, MARK (19TH C)	100-600	X (L)
DAWSON-WATSON, DAWSON (1864 - 1939)	450-15000	L
DAY, JAMES FRANCIS (1863 - 1942)	500-8800	L,G,F
DAY, LARRY (20TH C)	100-1700	L,F,S
DAY, NELLIE M. (19TH C)	150-850	L,G
DAY, W. PERCY (20TH C)	500-2500	F
DAYMUDE, GENE (1925 -)	50-800	M,F
DAYNE, EDGAR ALWIN (1882 - 1947)	400-4500	L
DE BOIS, YVONNE (1913 -)	200-2000	X
DE CAMP, JOSEPH RODEFER (1858 - 1923)	650-65000	L,F
DE CAMP, RALPH EARLL (1858 - 1936)	100-1000	L
DE DIEGO, JULIO (1900 - 1979)	*100-750	X
DE ERDELY, FRANCIS (1904 - 1959)	100-14500	F,S
DE FOREST, LOCKWOOD (1850 - 1932)	400-1800	X (M)
DE LEIRIS, JEANNE W. (20TH C)	*150-900	X (S)
DE LUCE, PERCIVAL (1847 - 1914)	*200-2000	X (F)
DE NAGY, ERNEST (1906 - 1944)	100-1100	M
DE NERO, ROBERT (1922 -)	400-2000	A
DE RIBCOWSKY, DEY (1880 - 1936)	200-5000	M,L
DE SOTO, RAPHAEL (1904 - 1987)	500-4000	I
DE THULSTRUP, THURE	*250-2000	
DE THULSTRUP, THURE (1849 - 1930)	700-6500	F,M,I
DE YONG, JOE (1894 - 1975)	200-1500	L
DEAKIN, EDWIN	*200-3200	
DEAKIN, EDWIN (1838 - 1923)	350-25000	S,L
DEAN, EDWARD CLARENCE (1879 -)	*250-850	X (L)
DEAN, SOPHIA (19TH C)	800-2500	P
DEAN, WALTER LOFTHOUSE (1854 - 1912)	300-3800	M,G,L
DEARBORN, SAMUEL H. (actice 1800-25)	*200-500	F
DEARTH, HENRY GOLDEN (1864 - 1918)	900-9500	L,F
DEAS, CHARLES	*600-12000	
DEAS, CHARLES (1818 - 1867)	1000-165000	G,F
DEBLOIS, FRANCOIS B. (1829 - 1913)	400-6500	S,L
DEBONNET, MAURICE G. (1872 - 1946)	100-400	M
DECAMP, RALPH EARL (1858 - 1936)	400-3000	L

DECHAR, PETER (1942 -)	800-4500	A
DECKER, JOSEPH (1853 - 1924)	3500-225000+	S,L
DECKER, ROBERT M. (1847 -)	300-4500	L
DEFOREST, ROY (1930 -)	300-27500	A
DEFREES, T. (late 19TH C)	200-850	L
DEGREGORIO, L. (19TH-20TH C)	100-700	L
DEHAAS, M.F.H. (1832 - 1895)	1000-33000+	M
DEHAVEN, FRANKLIN (1856 - 1934)	350-7500	L
DEHN, ADOLPH ARTHUR	*350-15000	
DEHN, ADOLPH ARTHUR (1895 - 1968)	500-11000	G,L
DEKLYN, CHARLES F. (20TH C ?)	150-600	L
DELAND, CLYDE OSMER (1872 - 1947)	250-1200	X (I)
DELANEY, BEAUFORD (1902 - 1979)	250-850	X (M)
DELANEY, JOSEPH (1904 -)	300-1500	X (G)
DELANO, GERARD CURTIS (1890 - 1972)	1500-30000	L,G
DELANOY, ABRAHAM (1740 - 1786)	*750-1500	P,F
DELBOS, JULIUS	*100-850	
DELBOS, JULIUS (1879 - 1967)	200-3000	M,L
DELCOURT, HECTOR (20TH C)	*50-250	M,L
DELEROISE, C. (19TH C)	100-650	X (L)
DELLENBAUGH, FREDERICK S. (1853 - 1935)	800-25000	G,L
DELUCE, PERCIVAL (1847 - 1914)	200-5500	F
DEMEAUX, M. (20TH C)	100-300	F,L
DEMETROPOULOS, CHARLES (1912 - 1976)	*300-3000	X (L)
DEMING, EDWIN WILLARD	*450-4200	
DEMING, EDWIN WILLARD (1860 - 1942)	500-12000+	F,G,I,W
DEMPSEY, RICHARD (1919 - 1987)	1000-8000	G,L,F
DEMUTH, CHARLES	*800-310000	
DEMUTH, CHARLES (1883 - 1935)	825000	A,F,S,L
DENNIS, L. (19TH-20TH C)	100-500	L
DENNIS, ROGERS WILSON (1902 -)	150-4000	L
DENNY, GIDEON JACQUES (1830 - 1886)	400-7500	L,G,M,W
DENNY, J.C. (- 1900)	250-2000	M
DENSLOW, WILLIAM WALLACE (1856 -)	*100-500	L
DERBY, HORACE B. (19TH C)	*150-850	M

  * Denotes watercolors, pastels, drawings, and/or mixed media

DEROME, ALBERT (1885 - 1959)	300-1800	M,L
DERIJCKE, J.L. (20TH C)	100-600	X (G)
DERRICK, WILLIAM ROWELL (1858 - 1941)	350-2400	X (L)
DES PORT, A. (19TH C)	750-4500	X (G)
DESATNICK, MIKE (1943 -)	5000-18000	X
DESSAR, LOUIS PAUL (1867 - 1952)	500-25000	G,L,W
DESVARREUX-LARPENTEUR, JAMES (1847 - 1937)	400-3300	L,W
DETHLOFF, PETER HANS (1869 -)	*100-650	L
DETREVILLE, RICHARD (1864 - 1929)	450-3000	L
DETWILLER, FREDERICK K. (1882 - 1953)	200-2000	I,L
DEVLAN, F.D. (1835 - 1870)	400-2000	L
DEVOLL, FREDERICK USHER (1873 - 1941)	400-4500+	L
DEWEY, CHARLES MELVILLE (1849 - 1937)	400-7500	L
DEWEY, EDWARD H. (1850 - 1939)	500-3000	L,W
DEWEY, JAMES (19TH-20TH C)	100-1000	X (G)
DEWING, MARIA OAKEY (1857 -)	850-18000	G
DEWING, THOMAS WILMER	*650-46500	
DEWING, THOMAS WILMER (1851 - 1938)	3000-175000+	F
DEWOLFE, SARAH BINDER (- 1905)	100-750	X (S)
DI SUVERO, MARK (1933 -)	*1000-5500	I,F
DIAO, DAVID (1943 -)	350-3000	A
DICK, CECIL (1915 -)	*200-1200	X (F)
DICK, H.R. (19TH-20TH C)	300-3500	X (F)
DICK, JAMES L. (1834 - 1868)	400-5100	G,F
DICK, M.G. (19TH-20TH C)	200-750	X (S)
DICKERMAN, ALBERT (19TH-20TH C)	250-4400	L
DICKINSON, ANSON (1780 - 1852)	*300-1300	F
DICKINSON, DAROL (1942 -)	1500-4500	X (G)
DICKINSON, EDWIN W.	*100-5500	
DICKINSON, EDWIN W. (1891 - 1979)	3000-26500	A,L,F
DICKINSON, HOWARD CLINTON (20TH C)	100-700	L,M
DICKINSON, J.S. (19TH C)	150-600	X (G)
DICKINSON, PRESTON	*850-26500	
DICKINSON, PRESTON (1891 - 1930)	500-75000+	A
DICKINSON, ROSS (1903 -)	100-1000	X (L)

DICKINSON, SIDNEY EDWARD (1890 -)	450-6500	F
DICKMAN, CHARLES JOHN (1863 - 1943)	200-1800	L
DIEBENKORN, RICHARD	*5000-198000	
DIEBENKORN, RICHARD (1922 -)	150000-1760000	A
DIEGO, JULIO DE (1900 - 1979)	*100-850	X
DIEHL, ARTHUR VIDAL (1870 - 1929)	200-4100	M,L
DIELMAN, FREDERICK (1847 - 1935)	*300-8000	I,F
DIETRICH, ADELHEID (1827 -)	5000-80000	S
DIETZ, H.R. (1860 -)	600-5000	M
DIKE , PHILIP LATIMER (1906 -)	100-3300	L,M
DILLAWAY, THEODORE M. (1874 -)	100-850	L
DILLER, BURGOYNE	*2000-20000	
DILLER, BURGOYNE (1906 - 1965)	3000-150000	A
DILLON, JULIA MCENTEE (1834 - 1919)	500-9500	S,L
DILLWORTH, C. (19TH C)	100-750	L
DINE, JIM	*4500-400000+	
DINE, JIM (1935 -)	10000-300000+	A
DINKEL, GEORGE W. (early 20TH C)	100-800	L
DINNERSTEIN, HARVEY (1928 -)	*200-900	I
DIRK, NATHANIEL (1895 - 1961)	*100-1700	X (M)
DITEMAN, HALL (20TH C)	400-1800	X (L)
DITTMANN, JOHAN (- 1847)	100-850	F
DITZLER, H. (19TH C)	100-700	X (F)
DIX, CHARLES TEMPLE (1838 - 1873)	100-1000	L,M,A
DIXON, FRANCIS STILLWELL (1879 - 1967)	200-4100	L
DIXON, L. MAYNARD	*200-10000	
DIXON, L. MAYNARD (1875 - 1946)	750-63250+	L,F,I
DOBKIN, ALEXANDER (1908 - 1975)	100-850	X
DODD, LAMAR (1909 -)	400-3200	X (F)
DODD, MARK D. (1888 -)	50-12100	L
DODDS, PEGGY (1900 -)	*100-500	X (G)
DODGE, CHESTER L. (1880 -)	150-750	L
DODGE, JOHN W. (1807 - 1893)	*50-450	X
DODGE, WILLIAM DE LEFTWICH (1867 - 1935)	600-17000	L,S
DODSON, RICHARD WHATCOAT (1812 - 1867)	*350-750	F

* Denotes watercolors, pastels, drawings, and/or mixed media

DODSON, SARAH BALL (1847 - 1906)	600-6100	L,G,F
DOFFLEMEYER, ? (19TH-20TH C)	300-900	X (L)
DOHANOS, STEVAN	*400-5500	
DOHANOS, STEVAN (1907 -)	800-20000	I
DOLE, WILLIAM (1917 -)	*1000-6000	A
DOLEY, PETER (1907 -)	100-3300	L
DOLICE, LEON	*100-1000	
DOLICE, LEON LOUIS (1892 - 1960)	200-2000	L,M
DOLINSKY, NATHAN (1890 -)	100-2000	L,F
DOLPH, JOHN HENRY (1835 - 1903)	750-13000	W,G,F
DOMINIQUE, JOHN A. (1893 -)	100-1000	L
DONAGHY, JOHN (1838 - 1931)	500-4800	S,L
DONAHUE, WILLIAM HOWARD (1881 -)	300-1800	L
DONATI, ENRICO (1909 -)	800-18000	A
DONLY, EVA BROOK (1867 -)	100-850	L,M
DONNELL, JOHN (early 20TH C)	150-650	F
DONNELLY, THOMAS J. (1893 -)	100-1500	X
DONOHO, GAINES RUGER (1857 - 1916)	500-15400	L
DONSKOY, ISIDORE K. (1898 -)	100-800	M
DORAZIO, PIERO (1927 -)	2000-150000	A
DORIAN, C.S. (19TH-20TH C)	300-1200	X (G,M)
DORIANI, WILLIAM (1891 - 1966)	200-800	G
DORINZ, D. (19TH-20TH C)	*400-1000	X (I)
DORNE, ALBERT (1904 - 1965)	*250-1200	I
DOUGHERTY, PARKE CUSTIS (1867 -)	400-7500	L
DOUGHERTY, PAUL (1877 - 1947)	300-25000	M,L
DOUGHTY , THOMAS (1793 - 1856)	2000-135000	L,M
DOUGLAS, CHESTER (1902 -)	300-1500	X
DOUGLAS, LUTHER (20TH C)	100-400	X
DOUGLAS, WALTER (1868 -)	350-2000	W,L
DOVE, ARTHUR GARFIELD	*2500-150000	
DOVE, ARTHUR GARFIELD (1880 - 1946)	15000-320000 +	A,M,I
DOW, ARTHUR WESLEY (1857 - 1922)	1000-47000	L
DOW, NELL PIERCE (20TH C)	200-750	L
DOW, OLIN (19TH C ?)	*350-900	L

DOW, WILLIAM J. (1899-1973)	100-700	M,L
DOWNAN, E. NEWMAN (19TH C)	100-700	X (F,L)
DOWNES, P.S. (late 19TH C)	*600-6000	P (M)
DOWNING, THOMAS (1928 -)	250-3100	A
DOYLE, WILLIAM M.S. (1769 - 1828)	400-6500	F
DRAGO, GABRIELLE (20TH C)	100-600	X (M)
DRAKE, CHARLES E. (1865 - 1918)	200-3000	F,L
DRAKE, WILLIAM HENRY (1856 - 1926)	200-2100	W,I
DRAPER, EDITH (early 20TH C)	100-400	X (F)
DRAPER, WILLIAM FRANKLIN (1912 -)	350-1500	X (L)
DRAVER, ORRIN (20TH C)	100-650	L
DRAYTON, JOHN (1766 - 1822)	*250-800	X (I)
DREIER, KATHERINE S. (1877 - 1952)	500-14500	A
DREW, CLEMENT (1806 - 1889)	500-8000	M
DREW, GEORGE W. (1875 -)	200-3500	L
DREW BEAR, JESSIE (1877 - 1962)	100-3000	G,M,S
DREWES, WERNER (1899 - 1985)	700-28000	A
DREXEL, FRANCES MARTIN (1792 - 1863)	500-3500	X (L)
DRIGGS, ELSIE	*300-3500	
DRIGGS, ELSIE (1898 -)	1500-18000	A
DRISCOLL, ROBERT E. (20TH C)	*50-350	X (L)
DROWN, WILLIAM STAPLES (- 1915)	250-3200	L
DRURY, WILLIAM (1888 -)	100-800	X (M)
DRYDEN, HELEN (1887 -)	*500-4500	I
DRYSDALE, ALEXANDER JOHN	*150-4500	
DRYSDALE, ALEXANDER JOHN (1870 - 1934)	400-6500	L
DUBE, MATTIE (1861 -)	350-1500	G,F
DUBOIS, CHARLES EDOUARD (1847 - 1885)	200-7000	L
DUBOIS, GUY PENE (1884 - 1958)	3000-105000	G,F
DUBREUIL, VICTOR (19TH-20TH C)	1200-18000	S
DUCKETT, V.F. (20TH C)	*100-500	L
DUDLEY, FRANK VIRGIL (1868 - 1957)	250-4500	L
DUESBURY, HORACE (1851 - 1904)	200-1200	L
DUESSEL, HENRY A. (19TH-20TH C)	200-3000	L,M
DUFNER, EDWARD	*500-12000	

* Denotes watercolors, pastels, drawings, and/or mixed media

DUFNER, EDWARD (1872 - 1957)	1000-58000 +	L,F
DUGMORE, A. RADCLYFFE (20TH C)	100-400	X (W)
DUGMORE, EDWARD (1915 -)	700-3000	A
DULL, JOHN J. (1862 -)	*100-900	L
DUMLER, MARTIN GEORGE (1868 - 1934)	150-650	F,S
DUMMER, H. BOYLSTON (1878 - 1945)	100-1000	I
DUMMER, JOSEPH OWEN (?)	250-1000	L
DUMOND, FRANK VINCENT (1865 - 1951)	400-8300	I,L
DUMONT, JO (19TH-20TH C)	400-1000	G,F
DUMONT, PAUL (AC.C 1915 - 1930)	150-700	X (M)
DUNBAR, CARL (20TH C)	100-600	X(L)
DUNBAR, HAROLD (1882 - 1953)	150-2000	L,F,I,S
DUNBAR, LILI (20TH C)	450-1200	X (G)
DUNBAR, PATRICK (20TH C)	450-1500	M
DUNBIER, AUGUSTUS WILLIAM (1888 - 1977)	600-1800	L
DUNCAN, GERALDINE BIRCH (1883 - 1972)	100-1400	L
DUNCANSON, ROBERT SCOTT (1821 - 1872)	400-35500	L
DUNINGTON, A. (19TH C)	200-1400	X (M)
DUNLAP, EUGENE (AC. 1930s - 1940s)	100-2000	L
DUNLAP, MARY STEWART (20TH C)	100-450	L
DUNLAP, WILLIAM (1766 - 1839)	500-3000	F
DUNLOP, DAN (20TH C)	100-400	X (G)
DUNN, HARVEY T. (1884 - 1952)	2000-65000	I
DUNN, JULIA E. (1850 -)	*200-700	F
DUNNING, ROBERT SPEAR (1829 - 1905)	800-65000 +	S,L
DUNSMORE, JOHN WARD	*100-500	
DUNSMORE, JOHN WARD (1856 - 1945)	700-3500	G,F
DUNTON, WILLIAM HERBERT	*100-7000	
DUNTON, WILLIAM HERBERT (1878 - 1936)	2500-60000	I,F,L
DUPONT, ANNE (19TH-20TH C)	*100-700	F
DURAN, A. (late 19TH C)	20900	S
DURAN, BOB (ROBERT)(1938 -)	500-3000	A
DURAND, ASHER BROWN (1796 - 1886)	3000-140000	L
DURAND, ELIAS (19TH C)	100-3100	X (L)
DURAND, J.C. (19TH C)	150-900	L

DURAND, JOHN (18TH C)	500-3500	P
DUREAU, GEORGE (1930 -)	500-5500	F
DUREN, KARL (19TH-20TH C)	500-3000	L
DUREN, TERENCE ROMAINE (1907 - 1968)	300-6500	G
DURGIN, LYLE (19TH-20TH C)	300-2000	X (F)
DURRIE, GEORGE HENRY (1820 - 1863)	5000-265000+	L,F
DUTANT, CHARLES (1908 -)	150-900	L
DUTHEIL, E. (19TH-20TH C)	150-850	G,M
DUTTON, RAOUL (19TH C)	100-800	X (F)
DUVENECK, FRANK (1848 - 1919)	3000-85000	F,L
DUYCKINCK, GERARDUS (1695 - 1742)	8000-35000	P
DWIGHT, JULIA S. (1870 -)	800-5500	F,L
DWIGHT, MABEL (1876 - 1955)	100-3000	X (S)
DWYER, A. (19TH C)	*150-750	I,G
DYE, CHARLIE (1906 - 1973)	10000-85000	L
DYE, CLARKSON (1869 - 1955)	250-3500	L
DYER, C.L. (19TH C)	150-800	X (L)
DYER, CHARLES GIFFORD (1846 - 1912)	*300-1200	L
DYER, ELIZABETH GRIFFIN (19TH C)	100-600	L
DYER, HEZEKIAH ANTHONY	*200-1500	
DYER, HEZEKIAH ANTHONY (1872 - 1943)	200-1600	L,M
DYER, MARION (19TH-20TH C)	*100-800	F,G
DYER, NANCY A. (1903 -)	*100-850	X (I)
DYER, URIAH N. (19TH C)	350-1200+	X (S)
DYKE, SAMUEL P. (active 1855-70)	200-3500	L,G
DYNINGER, F. (20TH C)	100-400	L
DZIGURSKI, ALEXANDER (1911 -)	350-2800	M,L
DZUBAS, FRIEDEL (1915 -)	1500-27500	A

E

Artist	Prices	Subject
EAKINS, SUSAN MACDOWELL (1851 - 1938)	450-6500	F,G
EAKINS, THOMAS	*3500-575000 +	
EAKINS, THOMAS (1844 - 1916)	8000-2450000	G,F,M
EARHART, JOHN FRANKLIN (1853 - 1938)	300-1500	L
EARL, JAMES (1761 - 1796)	2000-17550	F
EARL, RALPH (1751 - 1801)	800-30000	P
EARL, RALPH E.W. (1786 - 1838)	5000-44000	P
EARLE, EYVIND (1916 -)	500-3500	L
EARLE, LAWRENCE CARMICHAEL	*250-3000	
EARLE, LAWRENCE CARMICHAEL (1845 - 1921)	400-7000	F,S
EARLY, MILES T. (1886 -)	200-750	L,G
EARNEST, ESTELLE (1870 - 1962)	100-400	X (S)
EARNIST, FLORENCE REINHOLD (20TH C)	50-750	L
EASTMAN, EMILY (1804 -)	*1000-6000	F
EASTMAN, WILLIAM JOSEPH (1888 - 1950)	100-900	L,S
EASTWOOD, RAYMOND J. (1898 -)	100-1100	L
EATON, ALFRED J. (19TH C)	100-600	L
EATON, CHARLES HARRY (1850 - 1901)	400-4500	L
EATON, CHARLES WARREN	*200-4500	
EATON, CHARLES WARREN (1857 - 1937)	500-14500	L
EATON, DOROTHY (1893 -)	200-1600	L,S
EATON, JOSEPH ORIEL (1829 - 1875)	350-4500	G,F
EATON, VALOY (1938 -)	800-8000	X (L)
EATON, WYATT (1849 - 1896)	500-7200	F
EBERT, CHARLES H. (1873 - 1959)	600-25000	L,M
EBERT, MARY ROBERTS (1873 - 1956)	*200-1200	L,M
EBY, KERR (1889 - 1946)	*200-2500	I
ECKART, CHRISTIAN (20TH C)	22000	X
EDDY, DON (1904 -)	4000-61000	A
EDDY, HENRY STEPHENS (1878 - 1944)	300-3500	L,M
EDDY, OLIVER TARBELL (1799 - 1868)	400-1500	X (F)
EDE, FREDERIC (1865 - 1907)	400-5900	G,L
EDGERLY, BEATRICE (20TH C)	100-300	X (F)
EDLICH, STEPHEN (1944 -)	*500-10000	A

* Denotes watercolors, pastels, drawings, and/or mixed media   171

EDMONDS, FRANCIS WILLIAM (1806 - 1863)	1500-75000	G,L
EDMONDSON, EDWARD (JR) (1830 - 1884)	400-8000	S,F
EDMONDSON, WILLIAM JOHN (1868 - 1966)	150-10000	F,L
EDSTROM, PETER DAVID (1873 - 1938)	100-2000	L
EDWARD, CHARLES (1797 - 1868)	200-1200	L
EDWARDS, ALICE (19TH C)	200-800	X (L)
EDWARDS, GEORGE WHARTON	*100-1000	
EDWARDS, GEORGE WHARTON (1869 - 1950)	300-12000+	G,F,L
EDWARDS, HARRY C. (1868 - 1922)	200-1500	F,I
EDWARDS, JEANETTE SLOCOMB (20TH C)	100-600	L
EDWARDS, LIONEL	*200-11000	
EDWARDS, LIONEL (1874 - 1964)	300-30000	L
EDWARDS, T.F. (20TH C ?)	200-800	X (G)
EDWARDS, THOMAS (active 1820-55)	500-2500	F,L,
EFFIE, WILLIAM (active 1835-50)	700-2000	F
EGAN, ELOISE (1874 - 1967)	300-1500	L,M,S,F
EGGENHOFER, NICK	*450-20000	
EGGENHOFER, NICK (1897 - 1985)	6000-50000	G,F,I
EGGINTON, FRANK J. (1908 - 1990)	*100-2380	L
EGGLESTON, ANNA C. (20TH C)	200-2000	X (F)
EGGLESTON, BENJAMIN OSRO (1867 - 1937)	300-7800	G,F,L,M
EGGMEYER, MAUDE KAUFMAN (1877 - 1959)	100-800	L
EGLAU (EGLAN), MAX (1825 -)	750-5000	L,S
EHNINGER, JOHN WHETTON (1827 - 1889)	300-30000	G,F
EHRIG, WILLIAM C. (1892-1969)	200-1200	L,M
EICHELBERGER, ROBERT A. (19TH C)	500-3200	G
EICHHOLTZ, JACOB (1776 - 1842)	700-25000	F
EILERS, EMMA (20TH C)	400-3500	X
EILSHEMIUS, LOUIS MICHEL	*100-1200	
EILSHEMIUS, LOUIS MICHEL (1864 - 1942)	200-6100	A,F,L
EISELE, CHARLES C. (20TH C)	200-2200	L
EISELE, CHRISTIAN (19TH-20TH C)	250-1800	L,F
EISENLOHR, EDWARD G. (1872 - 1961)	200-2000	L
EISENMAN, MICHAEL (20TH C)	100-900	F,G,L
EKMAN, STAN (20TH C)	50-700	X (A)

* Denotes watercolors, pastels, drawings, and/or mixed media

ELDER, JOHN ADAMS (1833 - 1895)	500-5000	G,F
ELDRED, LEMUEL D. (1848 - 1921)	500-20000	M
ELK, ALBERT LOOKING (20TH C)	400-3500	L
ELKINS, HENRY ARTHUR (1847 - 1884)	300-5500	L
ELLINGER, DAVID (1940 - 1980)	*150-3000	P
ELLIOT, LIDIE (19TH C)	100-450	X (F)
ELLIOTT, CHARLES LORING (1812 - 1868)	350-5000	F
ELLIS, A. (active 1830-35)	3000-45000	P
ELLIS, CLYDE GARFIELD (1879 -)	100-300	X (L)
ELLIS, FREMONT F. (1897 - 1985)	800-15000	L
ELLSWORTH, CLARENCE ARTHUR	*250-1800	
ELLSWORTH, CLARENCE ARTHUR (1885 - 1961)	700-10000	F,G
ELLSWORTH, JAMES SANFORD (1802 - 1874)	*500-6100	P (F)
ELTING, N.D. (19TH C)	350-1500	X (S)
ELVGREN, GIL (20TH C)	200-14000	I
ELWELL, D. JEROME (1857 - 1912)	400-3000	L
ELWELL, ROBERT FARRINGTON (1874 - 1962)	300-4000	G,F
ELWELL, W.H. (?)	100-500	M
EMBRY, NORRIS (1921 - 1981)	*500-2500	A
EMBURY, J.H. (19TH C)	200-1500	L
EMERSON, ARTHUR WEBSTER (1885 -)	100-1000	X (M,L)
EMERSON, CHARLES CHASE (1874 - 1922)	350-5000	I
EMERSON, WILLIAM C. (20TH C)	200-1500	F,L
EMERY, JAMES (active 1865-75)	250-5500	M
EMMET, LYDIA FIELD (1866 - 1952)	800-19500+	F,I
EMMONS, ALEXANDER HAMILTON (1816 - 1879)	300-1500	F
EMMONS, CHANSONETTA S.(1858 - 1937)	350-2500	L,F,G,S
EMMONS, DOROTHY STANLEY (1891 -)	350-4200	M,L
EMPEL, JAN VAN (20TH C)	700-2000	X
ENDERS, FRANK (20TH C)	500-2500	X (F)
ENDERS, OSCAR (19TH C ?)	100-500	L
ENGEL, NISSAN (1931 -)	500-2000	G
ENGELHARDT, EDNA P. (19TH-20TH C)	100-1100	L,S
ENGELHARDT, WALTER (1893 - 1956)	100-1000	L
ENGLE, HARRY L. (1870 -)	200-2500	L

ENGLEHART, JOSEPH J. (1867 - 1915)	100-1500	L
ENGLEHEART, JOHN C.D. (1783 - 1862)	100-650	F
ENGLISH, FRANK F.	*200-4000	
ENGLISH, FRANK F. (1854 - 1922)	300-7000	L,G
ENGLISH, JOHN A. (20TH C)	500-1800	X (M)
ENGLISH, MABEL BACON (1861 -)	150-1800	X (M)
ENNEKING, JOHN JOSEPH (1841 - 1916)	650-66000+	L
ENNEKING, JOSEPH ELIOT (1881 - 1942)	200-6500	L,M
ENNIS, GEORGE PEARCE	*250-4400	
ENNIS, GEORGE PEARCE (1884 - 1936)	300-7500	M,L
ENRIGHT, MAGINEL WRIGHT (1881 - 1966)	*400-2200	I
ENSER, JOHN F. (1898 -)	150-1000	X (L)
ENWRIGHT, J.J. (1905 -)	100-1500	M
ENWRIGHT, WALTER J. (1879 -)	100-600	M,L
EPPENS, WILLIAM H. (1885 -)	100-500	L,M
ERDELEY, FRANCIS DE	*100-700	
ERDELEY, FRANCIS DE (1904 - 1959)	200-5500	G,F
ERICSON, DAVID (1873 - 1946)	250-1800	M,L
ERNESTI, ETHEL H. (19TH-20TH C)	200-1800	F
ERNST, JIMMY	*500-4000	
ERNST, JIMMY (1920 - 1984)	800-25000	A
ERTZ, EDWARD F.	*100-750	
ERTZ, EDWARD F. (1862 - 1954)	300-6200	L,F,I
ESLEY, DONALD W. (20TH C)	*100-700	F
ESNAULT, MAURICE (20TH C)	100-400	L
ESPOY, ANGEL DE SERVICE (1879 - 1963)	350-6200	M,L
ESSIG, GEORGE EMERICK	*150-1800	
ESSIG, GEORGE EMERICK (1883 - 1926)	450-4000	M,I
ESTES, A. FOWLES (20TH C)	100-600	X (M)
ESTES, RICHARD	*900-50000	
ESTES, RICHARD (1936 -)	3000-550000	A
ETHERIDGE, C.B. (19TH C)	800-3000	X (S)
ETNIER, STEPHEN MORGAN (1903 - 1984)	400-5000	M
ETTING, EMLEN (1905 -)	200-3000	X
EUBANKS, TONY (1939 -)	1000-15500	X (F)

* Denotes watercolors, pastels, drawings, and/or mixed media

EUSTON, JACOB HOWARD (1892 -)	100-1000	L
EUWER, ANTHONY HENDERSON (1877 -)	*300-1500	X (L)
EVANS, BRUCE (20TH C)	800-3500	A
EVANS, DE SCOTT (S.S.DAVID)(1847 - 1898)	500-30000	S,G,F
EVANS, J. (active 1831-1835)	*1500-5500	P
EVANS, JAMES GUY	*750-7500	
EVANS, JAMES GUY (mid 19TH C)	5000-50000	P (M)
EVANS, JESSIE BENTON (1866 - 1954)	250-1000	L,F
EVANS, RUDULPH (1878 - 1960)	200-850	F
EVERETT, E. DEARBURN (19TH C)	*100-400	L
EVERGOOD, PHILIP	*250-16500	
EVERGOOD, PHILIP (1901 - 1973)	1800-25000+	A
EVERINGHAM, MILLARD (1912 -)	100-500	X
EVERLY, C. (20TH C)	100-600	X (S)
EVERS, JOHN (1797 - 1884)	400-3500	L,G,S
EVETT, KENNETH WARNOCK (1913 -)	100-300	X (F)
EYDEN, WILLIAM ARNOLD JR (1893 -)	*200-1200	L
EYDEN, WILLIAM T. (1859 - 1919)	100-900	L
EYLES, D.C. (- 1975)	200-2000	X (F)
EYTINGE, SOLOMON (JR) (1833 - 1905)	700-5000	X (G,I)

F

Artist	Prices	Subject
FABER, JOHN (- 1906)	100-400	L
FABER, LUDWIG E.	*100-600	
FABER, LUDWIG E. (1855 - 1913)	200-1800	L,M
FAGAN, JAMES (1864 -)	100-850	F
FAHAN, EDWARD W. (1920 -)	250-2400	X (L)
FAHNESTOCK, HENRY REIGERT (1830 - 1909)	600-3800	L
FAHNESTOCK, WALLACE WEIR (1877 -)	250-4000	L
FAIRFIELD, HANNAH T. (1808 - 1894)	15000-47000	P
FAIRMAN, JAMES (1826 -1904)	800-28000	L

FAIVRE, JUSTIN (1902 -)	100-1500	L
FALCONER, JOHN M. (1820 - 1903)	1000-6500	L
FALES, P. (late 19TH C)	100-750	X (G)
FALKNER, HENRY (20TH C)	100-700	X
FALTER, JOHN PHILIP (1910 - 1982)	300-20000	I
FANGOR, WOJCIECH (1922 -)	900-3500	A
FANNING, WILLIAM S. (1887 -)	50-800	L
FARBER, MANNY (20TH C)	50-800	X
FARETO, P. (19TH C)	150-1500	X (S)
FARIS, J.A. (late 19TH C)	*350-1200	F
FARLEY, RICHARD BLOSSOM (1875 - 1901)	500-5500	L
FARLOW, HARRY (1882 -)	300-3500	X (F)
FARNDON, WALTER (1876 - 1964)	300-5000	M,L
FARNES, W.M. (19TH C)	100-750	X (M)
FARNHAM, AMMI MERCHANT (1846 - 1922)	50-600	L,F
FARNSWORTH, ALFRED VILLIERS (1858 - 1908)	*200-3200	G,M
FARNSWORTH, ETHEL N. (1873 -)	100-3000	S
FARNSWORTH, JERRY (1895 - 1983)	300-5000	I,F
FARNUM, HERBERT CYRUS (1886 -)	500-6000	F,M
FARNY, HENRY FRANCES	*1500-230000	
FARNY, HENRY FRANCES (1847 - 1916)	2000-525000	I,G,L
FARRE, HENRI (1871 - 1934)	450-11000	L
FARRER, HENRY (1843 - 1903)	*800-19000	L
FARRINGTON, MRS ARCH (19TH-20TH C)	500-3000	G
FASONE, PHILIP A. (20TH C)	100-500	L
FASSETT, TRUMAN E. (1885 -)	200-2200 +	L
FATTON, GEORGE (19TH C)	150-650	X (F)
FAULKNER, HERBERT W. (1860 - 1940)	200-1800	L,G,I
FAURE, MARIE (19TH C)	250-1500	W,S
FAUSETT, WILLIAM DEAN (1913 -)	100-800	L
FAWCETT, ROBERT (1903 - 1967)	*250-4500	I
FAY, WILLIAM E. (1882 - 1967)	*200-900	X (G)
FAYSASH, JULIUS P. (1904 - 1977)	300-1200	L
FECHIN, NICOLAI IVANOVICH (1881 - 1955)	4500-176000	F,G
FEELEY, PAUL (1913 - 1966)	1500-9000	A

* Denotes watercolors, pastels, drawings, and/or mixed media

FEHER, JOSEPH (1908 -)	100-600	L
FEININGER, LYONEL	*600-78000	
FEININGER, LYONEL (1871 - 1956)	20000-495000+	A,I
FEININGER, THEODORE LUX (1910 -)	100-3000	A
FEINSTEIN, SAMUEL (20TH C)	*100-300	X (G)
FEITELSON, LORSER (1898 - 1978)	7700	A
FEKE, ROBERT (1724 - 1769)	800-5000	F
FELINGER, JEAN PAUL (late 19TH C)	200-900	X (F)
FELL, J.R. (20TH C)	100-400	L
FELLOWS, BYRON W. (19TH-20TH C)	100-900	X (M)
FELLOWS, FRANK WAYLAND (1833 - 1900)	200-1000	X (L)
FELLOWS, FRED (1934 -)	2000-18000	X (L)
FELTER, DURAND (19TH-20TH C)	*50-600	L
FENETTI, F.M. (19TH C)	300-1800	S
FENIMORE, T.J. (19TH C)	300-1200	X (L)
FENN, HARRY (1845 - 1911)	*250-6100	I
FENSON, R. (19TH-20TH C)	200-950	L
FENTON, CHARLES L. (1808 - 1877)	600-2000	X (F)
FENTON, HALLIE CHAMPLIN (1880 - 1935)	100-900	L
FENTON, JOHN WILLIAM (1875 -)	150-900	X (S)
FEO, CHARLES DE (1892 - 1978)	*100-500	X (F)
FERBER, HERBERT	*6000-18000	
FERBER, HERBERT (1906 - 1991)	15000-50000	A
FERGUSON, ELEANOR M. (1876 -)	100-900	X (S)
FERGUSON, HENRY AUGUSTUS (1851 - 1911)	1000-22000	L
FERRARA, JOE (20TH C)	400-3500	X (F)
FERREN, JOHN	*300-3500	
FERREN, JOHN (1905 - 1970)	600-15500	A
FERRIS, JEAN LEON GEROME (1863 - 1930)	1000-17000	G
FERY, JOHN (1865 - 1934)	400-7425+	L,W
FETHERSTONHAUGH, OLIVE J.G. (1896 - 1986)	100-1200	M,L
FETT, WILLIAM (1918 -)	100-600	X
FEUDEL, ARTHUR (1857 - 1929)	*150-900	L
FEVRET DE ST MEMIN, CHARLES (1770 - 1852)	2500-8000	F
FIEDLER, LEOPOLD (19TH C)	*100-700	X (L)

FIELD, EDWARD LOYAL (1856 - 1914)	250-2700	L
FIELD, ERASTUS SALISBURY (1807 - 1900)	1500-35000+	P
FIELD, ROBERT (1769 - 1819)	700-6000	F
FIELDING, G. (19TH C)	100-1000	X (L,M)
FIENE, ERNEST	*100-3600	
FIENE, ERNEST (1894 - 1966)	550-30000	L,S,F
FILCER, LUIS (20TH C)	100-700	A
FILLEAU, EMERY A. (active 1890-1910)	500-4500	G,L,F
FILMUS, TULLY (1903 -)	*100-4300	X (G,F)
FINCH, E.E. (active 1832-1850)	800-32000	P
FINCH, KEITH (1920 -)	150-800	A
FINCH, RUBY DEVOL (19TH C)	1000-4800	F
FINCK, HAZEL (1894 - 1977)	300-8800+	L
FINCKEN, JAMES H. (1860 - 1943)	150-650	L
FINK, DON (1923 -)	100-1000	A
FINK, FREDERICK (1817 - 1849)	500-2500	G,F
FINKELGREEN, DAVID (1888 - 1931)	650-3000	G,F
FINKERNAGEL, ERNST (19TH C)	100-600	X
FINSTER, REVEREND HOWARD (1916 -)	200-4500	P
FIRENZE, PAUL (20TH C)	*1500-3500	X
FISCHER, ANTON OTTO (1882 - 1962)	500-8500	M,G,I
FISH, CARRIE NOELLA (19TH-20TH C)	*100-450	L
FISH, GEORGE G. (1849 -)	*100-850	X (I,M)
FISH, JANET	*250-10000	
FISH, JANET (1933 -)	4000-105000	A
FISHER, ALVAN (1792 - 1863)	1500-26000	L,G,F,M
FISHER, ANNA S.	*100-750	
FISHER, ANNA S. (1873 - 1942)	400-3000	S,M,L
FISHER, D.A. (19TH C)	100-500	L,M
FISHER, ELIZA C. (1871 - 1959)	50-700	G,F
FISHER, GEORGE H. (19TH C ?)	*400-1500	L
FISHER, HARRISON (1875 - 1934)	*400-24000	I
FISHER, HUGO ANTON	*150-2500	
FISHER, HUGO ANTON (1854 - 1916)	300-5000	L,W
FISHER, HUGO MELVILLE (1876 - 1946)	100-3500	M,L

* Denotes watercolors, pastels, drawings, and/or mixed media

FISHER, MAC S. (20TH C)	*100-600	L
FISHER, MARK (WILLIAM MARK)(1841 - 1923)	500-10000	L,F
FISHER, WILLIAM	*100-1500	
FISHER, WILLIAM (1890 -)	100-8800	F,L
FISK, HARRY T. (20TH C)	500-1200	X
FISKE, GERTRUDE (1879 - 1961)	500-10500+	F,L
FITLER, WILLIAM CROTHERS	*100-3700	
FITLER, WILLIAM CROTHERS (1857 - 1915)	250-3700	L
FITZ, ALLEE C. (19TH-20TH C)	300 -1500	X (S)
FITZ, BENJAMIN RUTHERFORD (1855 - 1891)	400-2500	X (G)
FITZGERALD, EDMOND JAMES (1912 -)	150-2000	X (I)
FITZGERALD, HARRINGTON (1847 - 1930)	150-1500	M,L
FITZGERALD, JAMES (1899 - 1971)	*100-650	L
FLACK, AUDREY (1931 -)	56000-230000	X
FLAGG, H. PEABODY (1859 - 1937)	*100-750	L,M,G
FLAGG, JAMES MONTGOMERY	*150-5000	
FLAGG, JAMES MONTGOMERY (1877 - 1960)	800-10000	I
FLAGG, MONTAGUE (1842 - 1915)	400-1200	X (S)
FLAHERTY, JAMES THORP (19TH C)	300-4800	X (L)
FLAHERTY, THORPE (19TH-20TH C)	300-750	L
FLANNAGAN, JOHN BERNARD (1897 - 1942)	*450-3500	X (F)
FLANNERY, VAUGHN (20TH C)	250-1600	X (G)
FLAVELLE, GEOFF H. (19TH-20TH C)	*150-650	L,M
FLAVIN, DAN (1933 -)	*750-33000	A
FLECK, JOSEPH A. (1893 - 1977)	1000-20000	L,F
FLEISCHBEIN, FRANTZ (1804 - 1862)	350-8000	F
FLEMING, CAPEN A. (20TH C)	100-500	L
FLENEAR, J.W. (19TH C)	100-800	X (L)
FLETCHER, AARON DEAN (1817 - 1902)	300-7500	X (F)
FLETCHER, CALVIN (1882 -)	200-850	L,M
FLOCH, JOSEPH (JOSEF) (1895 - 1977)	200-10900	F
FLOETER, KENT (1937 -)	*300-700	A
FLORIAN, WALTER (1878 - 1909)	600-1500	L,F
FLORIMONT, AUSTIN (active 1775-95)	*800-1800	F
FLORSHEIM, RICHARD ABERLE (1916 - 1979)	150-650	X

* Denotes watercolors, pastels, drawings, and/or mixed media   179

FOERSTER, EMIL (1822 - 1906)	500-12000	F
FOERSTER, HERBERT (20TH C)	50-650	L,M
FOGARTY, THOMAS	*150-3500	
FOGARTY, THOMAS (1873 - 1938)	400-14000	I
FOLAWN, THOMAS JEFFERSON (1876 - 1934)	*100-900	X (F)
FOLINSBEE, JOHN FULTON (1892 - 1972)	500-20000	L,M,F
FOLLETT, FOSTER O. (1872 -)	500-1800	S
FONDA, HARRY STUART (1864 - 1942)	100-1000	L
FOOTE, JACK (20TH C)	250-900	X
FOOTE, MARY (1847 - 1931)	*300-1500	L
FOOTE, WILL HOWE (1874 - 1965)	300-10000	L,F,M
FORBES, CHARLES S. (1860 -)	100-2500	L,F,I
FORBES, EDWIN	*250-12100	
FORBES, EDWIN (1839 - 1895)	750-11000	L,W,M
FORD, ELISA (20TH C)	100-600	X (S)
FORD, HENRY CHAPMAN (1828 - 1894)	250-7700	L
FORD, LOREN (1891 - 1973)	900-31000	G
FORD, NEILSON (- 1931)	200-800	X (F)
FORDNEY, B.F. (1873 -)	400-4500	F,G
FOREST, LOCKWOOD DE (1850 - 1932)	150-7500	L,M
FOREST, ROY DE	*300-3500	
FOREST, ROY DE (1930 -)	500-7500	A
FOREST, WESNER LA (20TH C)	700-4800	F
FORESTER, ? (19TH C)	100-400	X (S)
FORESTORR, ? (20TH C)	*100-600	X (G)
FORKER, EDWIN (20TH C)	100-600	L
FORKUM, ROY (20TH C)	100-1500	A
FORRESTAL, F.J. (20TH C)	250-1200	L
FORRESTER, L. (19TH-20TH C)	100-650	L
FORSTER, GEORGE (1860 - 1880)	1000-15000	S,G
FORSYTHE, VICTOR CLYDE (1885 - 1962)	400-6000	L,G
FORTUNE, EUPHEMIA CHARLTON	*200-3000	
FORTUNE, EUPHEMIA CHARLTON (1885 - 1969)	500-15000	L,F
FOSBURGH, JAMES WHITNEY (1910 -)	100-2400	X
FOSS, HARRIEET CAMPBELL (1860 - 1938)	150-1200	X (F)

* Denotes watercolors, pastels, drawings, and/or mixed media

FOSS, OLIVIER (1920 -)	200-2700	L
FOSS, PETER OLIVER (1865 - 1932)	450-3000	P
FOSTER, AGNES (19TH-20TH C)	*100-400	F,L
FOSTER, ALAN (1892 - 1934)	700-4500	I
FOSTER, ARTHUR TURNER (1877 -)	100-750	X (L,S)
FOSTER, BEN	*200-1200	
FOSTER, BEN (1852 - 1926)	200-6000+	L,S
FOSTER, CHARLES (1850 - 1931)	300-1800	L
FOSTER, G.S. (20TH C)	200-750	L
FOSTER, H.K. (19TH C)	400-1800	L
FOSTER, HAL (1892 - 1982)	*1000-5500	I
FOSTER, JOHN (1648 - 1681)	*500-950	F,I,L
FOSTER, WILL (1882 - 1953)	150-5500	F,S
FOUJIOKA, NOBOM (20TH C)	100-600	L
FOULKE, CAPTAIN B.F. (19TH-20TH C)	100-400	X (M)
FOULKES, LLYN (1934 -)	1000-8000	A
FOUNTAIN, GRACE R. (1857 - 1942)	100-900	L
FOURNIER, ALEXIS JEAN (1865 - 1948)	500-41800	L
FOWLER, FRANK (1852 - 1910)	200-2800	F
FOWLER, O.R. (early 19TH C)	900-5000	P
FOWLER, TREVER THOMAS (1830 - 1871)	400-3100	G,F
FOX, ROBERT ATKINSON (1860 - 1927)	350-3000	L,G,I
FOY, FRANCES (1890 -)	*100-350	M,L
FRANCA, MANUEL JOACHIM DE (1808 - 1865)	450-7500	F,G
FRANCE, EURILDA LOOMIS (1865 - 1931)	200-9000	L,I
FRANCE, JESSE LEACH (1862 -)	100-1500	L,M
FRANCIS, JOHN F. (1808 - 1886)	2500-265000	S,F
FRANCIS, JOHN JESSE (1889 -)	*100-500	L
FRANCIS, MRS. JYRA (19TH C)	200-700	X (M)
FRANCIS, SAM	*10000-550000	
FRANCIS, SAM (1923 -)	8500-1870000	A
FRANCISCO, JOHN BOND (1863 - 1931)	400-4500	L,S
FRANDZEN, EUGENE M. (1893 - 1972)	100-1600	L
FRANK, CHARLES L. (19TH-20TH C)	100-1500	L
FRANK, E.C. (19TH-20TH C)	100-1000	F

FRANK, GERALD A. (1888 -)	150-2700	X (G,S)
FRANK, MARY (1933 -)	*200-1500	A
FRANKENBERG, H. (19TH C)	150-1400	G
FRANKENSTEIN, GODFREY N.(1820 - 1873)	500-5000+	L
FRANKENTHALER, HELEN	*100-9200	
FRANKENTHALER, HELEN (1928 - 1988)	4000-720000	A
FRANQUINET, EUGENE (1875 - 1940)	300-2000	G,F,M
FRANSIOLI, THOMAS ADRIAN (1906 -)	600-5500	A
FRANZEN, AUGUST	*300-2200	
FRANZEN, AUGUST (1863 - 1938)	3500-9000	G,F
FRASCONI, ANTONIO M. (1919 -)	*100-850	I
FRASER, CHARLES A. (1782 - 1860)	600-4500	L,F
FRASER, THOMAS DOUGLAS (1883 - 1955)	300-2800	L
FRAZER, WILLIAM (18TH - 19TH C)	400-1500	M
FRAZIER, JOHN ROBINSON (1889 -)	300-1800	X (L,M)
FRAZIER, KENNETH (1867 - 1949)	450-20000	L,F
FRAZIER, KENNETH (1867 - 1949)	800-21000	L
FREDERICK, FRANK FOREST (1866 -)	250-1000	L
FREDERICKS, ALFRED (19TH C)	150-800	I
FREDERICKS, ERNEST (1877 - 1927)	100-2200	L
FREEDLANDER, ARTHUR R. (1875 - 1940)	100-700	L,F
FREEDLEY, DURR (1888 - 1938)	500-5000	X (F)
FREEDMAN, MAURICE (1904 -)	300-1000	X (S)
FREELAND, ANNA C. (1837 - 1911)	100-700	F,G,S
FREEMAN, CHARLES H. (1859 - 1918)	400-3500	X
FREEMAN, DON (1908 - 1978)	500-13500	G
FREEMAN, GEORGE (1787 - 1868)	400-2800	F
FREEMAN, JAMES EDWARD (1808 - 1884)	500-2000	F,G
FREEMAN, LLOYD (20TH C)	300-1500	X (F,G)
FREEMAN, STEWART (20TH C)	100-400	X
FREEMAN, WILLIAM (1927 -)	500-2000	X (W)
FREER, FREDERICK WARREN	*250-1500	
FREER, FREDERICK WARREN (1849 - 1908)	450-9500	F,L
FREEZOR, W.H.M. (20TH C)	100-600	X (F)
FREILICHER, JANE (1924 -)	200-1000	L

FREITAG, CONRAD (1801 - 1895)	900-35000	M
FRELINGHUYSEN, SUZY (1912 -)	2500-18000	A
FRENCH, FRANK (1850 - 1933)	300-1800	A (G)
FRENCH, JARED (1905 -)	1500-65000	G,I
FRENZENY, PAUL (19TH C)	*200-1200	F
FRERICHS, WILLIAM C. A. (1829 - 1905)	600-15400+	L,M,S
FRESQUIS, PEDRO ANTONIO (active 1810-40)	100-850	X (G)
FREY, JOSEPH (1892 - 1977)	200-1500	L
FRIEDENTHAL, DAVID (20TH C)	*200-1200	X (L)
FRIEDMAN, ARNOLD (1879 - 1946)	850-12000	L,F,S
FRIEDMAN, MARTIN (1896 -)	100-400	M
FRIEND, WASHINGTON F. (1820 - 1886)	*150-2100	L
FRIES, CHARLES ARTHUR (1854 - 1940)	400-4700	L,I
FRIESEKE, FREDERICK CARL (1874 - 1939)	5000-640000+	F,L
FRIIS, FREDERICK TRAP (1865-1909)	300-15000	F,L,S
FRITZ, HENRY EUGENE (1875 -)	300-2500	G
FROHER, ROWLAND (20TH C)	*100-600	X (G)
FROMKES, MAURICE (1872 - 1931)	100-2400	F,S
FROMUTH, CHARLES HENRY (1861 - 1937)	*350-6000	L,M,S
FRONTIERO, PAUL (20TH C)	50-300	M
FROST, ARTHUR BURDETT	*400-86000	
FROST, ARTHUR BURDETT (1851 - 1928)	2000-20000	I
FROST, FRANCIS S. (late 19TH C)	300-2500	L
FROST, GEORGE ALBERT (1843 -)	400-2800	L,G
FROST, JOHN (1890 - 1937)	600-44000	L,F
FROST, JOHN ORNE (1852 - 1928)	500-18000	P,M
FROTHINGHAM, JAMES (1786 - 1864)	700-4800	F
FRY, JOHN HEMMING (1861 - 1946)	400-30000	L
FRYMIRE, JACOB (1770 - 1822)	5000-15000	P
FUCHS, ERNEST (20TH C)	100-600	X (F)
FUECHSEL, HERMANN (1833 - 1915)	700-41000	L,M
FUERTES, LOUIS AGASSIZ (1874 - 1927)	*500-19000	W
FUGLISTER, FRITZ (20TH C)	350-1500	X (F)
FUHR, ERNEST (1874 - 1933)	*200-850	I
FULDE, EDWARD (19TH-20TH C)	600-2800	X (G)

FULLER, A. (19TH C)	800-8000	L
FULLER, ARTHUR D. (1889 - 1966)	*200-1200	I
FULLER, CHARLES O. (19TH C)	200-1000	X (M)
FULLER, G.F. (19TH C)	150-700	X (L)
FULLER, GEORGE (1822 - 1884)	500-27500	M,L,F
FULLER, LEONARD (1822 - 1871)	300-1500	X
FULLER, RICHARD HENRY (1822 - 1871)	400-8000	L
FULLER, S.W. (19TH C)	100-750	L
FULLICK, E. (early 20TH C)	100-600	L,F
FULLONTON, ROBERT DUDLEY (1876 - 1933)	100-900	L
FULOP, KAROLY (1898 - 1963)	*250-3100	G,M,L
FULTON, DOROTHY (20TH C)	50-700	L
FULTON, FITCH BURT (1879 - 1955)	100-4700	L
FULTON, H.D. (20TH C)	100-600	L
FURLMAN, FREDERICK (1874 -)	100-850	L
FURLONG, CHARLES WELLINGTON (1874 -)	500-7500	I
FURSMAN, FREDERICK F. (1874 - 1943)	400-4500	F
FUSSELL, CHARLES LEWIS	*800-15000	
FUSSELL, CHARLES LEWIS (1840 - 1909)	200-3600	G,F,M

G

Artist	Prices	Subject
GAENNSLEN, OTTO ROBERT (1876 -)	150-1000	X
GAERTNER, CARL F. (1898 - 1952)	100-1200	L,F,I
GAFFNEY, LOUIS E. (20TH C)	100-500	L
GAG, WANDA HAZEL (1893 - 1946)	*200-1200	L,G,I
GAGE, GEORGE WILLIAM (1887 - 1957)	200-2500	I
GAGE, HARRY LAWRENCE (1887 -)	100-1200	M
GAGE, JANE (B. 1914)	100-1000	X (G)
GALE, GEORGE (20TH C)	*300-2800	X (M)
GALLAGHER, SEARS	*100-1800	
GALLAGHER, SEARS (1869 - 1955)	400-3500	L,M,F

* Denotes watercolors, pastels, drawings, and/or mixed media

GALLATIN, ALBERT EUGENE (1882 - 1952)	*1000-21000	A
GALLI, STANLEY (1912 -)	100-750	X (L)
GALLISON, HENRY HAMMOND (1850 - 1910)	300-4500	L
GALLO, FRANK (1933 -)	*100-900	F
GAMBIER, M. (19TH C)	100-750	L
GAMBLE, EDNA (19TH-20TH C)	*100-450	X (S)
GAMBLE, JOHN MARSHALL (1863 - 1957)	500-22000	L
GAMBLE, ROY C. (1887 - 1972)	150-1800	G,F,I
GAMMELL, ROBERT HALE IVES (1893 - 1981)	350-11000+	F,G,L
GANDELL, VICTOR (1903 - 1977)	50-600	L
GANNAM, JOHN (1907 - 1965)	*300-4000	I
GANSO, EMIL	*150-2500	
GANSO, EMIL (1895 - 1941)	400-12000	F,L,M
GARBER, DANIEL (1880 - 1958)	2500-155000	L
GARDENER, ROBERT (early 19TH C)	*1000-3000	X (L)
GARDINER, DONALD (20TH C)	150-750	X (G)
GARDNER, ARCHIBALD S. (1904 -)	200-800	M
GARDNER, SHEILA (20TH C)	*500-2000	L
GARMAN, ED (1914 -)	1000-15000	A
GARRATT, J.H.(19TH-20TH C)	*100-500	L
GARRETSON, DELLA (1860 -)	*100-600	X (L)
GARRETT, EDMUND HENRY	*150-1500	
GARRETT, EDMUND HENRY (1853 - 1929)	200-3300	I,L
GARSON, ETTA CORBETT (1898 - 1968)	200-900	L
GASKE, F.J. (19TH-20TH C)	*200-850	X (L)
GASKINS, LEE	*100-800	
GASKINS, LEE (1882 - 1935)	300-3500	X (M,W)
GASPARD, LEON SCHULMAN (1882 - 1964)	1800-231000	L,F
GASPARO, ORONZO (1903 -)	200-1550	X
GASSER, HENRY MARTIN	*150-5300	
GASSER, HENRY MARTIN (1909 - 1981)	400-7200	F,L,M
GASSETTE, GRACE (19TH-20TH C)	100-700	X (M)
GASSIM, MARY W. (19TH C)	150-750	L
GASTAVSON, LEALAND R. (1899 - 1966)	100-1500	X
GATCH, LEE	*300-3500	

GATCH, LEE (1902 - 1966)	700-15000	A
GATTER, OTTO (1892 - 1926)	400-2500	X (I,L)
GAUEN, M. (early 20TH C)	100-600	F
GAUGENGIGL, IGNAZ MARCEL (1855 - 1932)	1000-77000	F
GAUL, WILLIAM GILBERT (1855 - 1919)	600-32000	G,F,L
GAUL, ARRAH LEE (1888 - 1980)	200-2000	X (M,L)
GAULEY, ROBERT DAVID (1875 - 1943)	350-4000	F
GAULT, MARY D. (early 19TH C)	500-4750	X (L)
GAVENCKY, FRANK J. (1888 -)	250-1800	X (L)
GAW, WILLIAM A. (1891 - 1973)	100-3100	S,F,M
GAY, AUGUST (1891 - 1949)	100-13000	W,L
GAY, EDWARD B. (1837 - 1928)	500-15000+	L
GAY, GEORGE HOWELL	*100-3200	
GAY, GEORGE HOWELL (1858 - 1931)	200-4000	M,L
GAY, PATRICIA (1876 - 1965)	400-5000	L
GAY, WALTER (1856 - 1937)	500-27500+	G,L,S
GAY, WINCKWORTH ALLAN (1821 - 1910)	350-5500	L,M
GAYER, A. (19TH C)	200-1000	L
GAYLOR, SAMUEL WOOD (1883 -)	*200-5500	I
GAZE, HAROLD (20TH C)	*450-3900	I
GEARHART, FRANCES (1869 - 1958)	50-350	L,M
GECHTOFF, LEONID (20TH C)	100-2200	L,S
GEDDES, MATTHEW (1899 -)	150-1200	X (L)
GEDEOHN, PAUL (20TH C)	250-1500	X (G)
GEHRING, LOUIS H. (1900 -)	100-600	L
GEHRY, P. (19TH C)	100-700	X (S)
GEIBERICH, OSCAR (20TH C)	100-1200	L
GELLENBECK, ANN P. (19TH-20TH C)	250-1500	X (L,W)
GELWICKS, D.W. (20TH C)	100-650	L,F
GENTH, LILLIAN MATILDA (1876 - 1953)	250-12500	F,L
GEOFFROI, HARRY (19TH-20TH C)	250-1200	X
GEORGE, A. (late 19TH C)	100-500	L
GEORGE, VESPER	*200-1000	
GEORGE, VESPER (1865 - 1934)	300-6000	X (L)
GEORGES, PAUL (1923 -)	5000-35000	A

GEORGI, EDWIN A	*100-1350	
GEORGI, EDWIN A. (1896 - 1964)	150-1300	F,I
GERBI, CLAUDIO (20TH C)	100-600	X (S)
GERBINO, ROSARIO U. (19TH-20TH C)	200-900	L
GERLASH, ANTHONY (19TH C)	200-3000	L
GERRY, SAMUEL LANCASTER (1813 - 1891)	500-11500+	L
GETMAN, WILLIAM (1917 - 1972)	*100-400	X (S)
GEYER, HERMAN (19TH C)	150-2000	L
GHIZE, ELEANOR DE (1896 -)	150-1500	L,F
GIACOMO, ELSIO SAN (20TH C)	100-750	M
GIBBS, E.T. (19TH C)	*100-400	L
GIBBS, GEORGE	*500-3600	
GIBBS, GEORGE (1870 - 1942)	200-2000	I
GIBBS, H. (20TH C)	100-500	A
GIBBS, MARY ANN (19TH C)	*400-1800	F
GIBRAN, KAHIL (20TH C)	300-7000	X(F)
GIBSON, CHARLES DANA	*300-9000	
GIBSON, CHARLES DANA (1867 - 1944)	500-7500	I,F
GIBSON, GEORGE (1904 -)	*300-2200	X
GIBSON, WILLIAM ALFRED (1866 - 1931)	200-1000	L
GIBSON, WILLIAM HAMILTON (1850 - 1896)	*100-850	L,I
GIDDINGS, FRANK A. (1882 -)	*100-500	X
GIEBERICH, OSCAR H. (1886 -)	100-2500	X (L)
GIES, JOSEPH W. (1860 - 1935)	100-5000	F,L,M
GIFFORD, CHARLES HENRY	*200-8000	
GIFFORD, CHARLES HENRY (1839 - 1904)	650-25000	M,L
GIFFORD, EDWARD C. (20TH C)	100-400	L
GIFFORD, PAULINE (19TH-20TH C)	200-900	X (S)
GIFFORD, ROBERT GREGORY (1895 -)	*100-500	I
GIFFORD, ROBERT SWAIN (1840 - 1905)	450-8500+	L
GIFFORD, SANFORD ROBINSON (1823 - 1880)	1800-365000+	L
GIGNOUX, REGIS FRANCOIS (1816 - 1882)	1500-34500	L
GIHON, ALBERT DAKIN (1866 -)	200-900	L
GIHON, CLARENCE MONTFORT (1871 - 1929)	500-8400	L
GIKOW, RUTH (1913 - 1983)	200-1200	A

* Denotes watercolors, pastels, drawings, and/or mixed media 187

GILBERT, ARTHUR (1819 - 1895)	100-2400	L
GILBERT, ARTHUR HILL (1894 - 1970)	700-19000	L,M,G
GILBERT, C. IVAR (20TH C)	300-2000	L,S
GILBERT, CHARLES ALLAN (1873 - 1929)	*300-2800	F
GILCHRIST, WILLIAM WALLACE (1879 - 1926)	700-29000+	F,L
GILDER, ROBERT F. (1856 - 1946)	200-1500	L
GILE, SELDON CONNOR (1877 - 1947)	1000-47000	L
GILES, HORACE P.	*100-800	
GILES, HORACE P. (1806 -)	250-3200	L
GILES, HOWARD (1876 - 1955)	*50-350	X (L)
GILL, ANN (early 19TH C)	*100-800	X
GILL, DELANCEY W. (1859 - 1940)	200-4500	L
GILL, JAMES (1934 -)	500-2500	A,F
GILL, MARIQUITA (20TH C)	500-4800	X (L)
GILL, TOM (1899 -)	*200-900	L
GILLESPIE, GREGORY (1936 -)	700-7500	X
GILLETTE, WILLIAM B. (1864-1957)	*100-650	M
GILLIAM, SAM JR. (1933 -)	1500-15000	A
GILSON, ROGER E. (20TH C)	100-500	X (L)
GIOBBI, EDWARD (1926 -)	*200-1800	X
GIOVANNI, N. (20TH C)	100-600	L
GIRADET, KARL (1813 - 1871)	1000-65000	G,F,L
GIRARDIN, FRANCIS J. (1856 - 1945)	250-1500	L
GISEVIUS, GERHARD (20TH C)	100-600	L
GISIKE, IDA (20TH C)	150-650	X (L)
GISSON, ANDRE (1928 -)	400-4700	F,L,S
GIURGOLA, ROMALDO (19TH-20TH C)	*200-800	I
GLACKENS, LOUIS M (1866 - 1933)	*200-1800	I
GLACKENS, WILLIAM JAMES	*150-25000	
GLACKENS, WILLIAM JAMES (1870 - 1938)	2500-440000+	F,L,I
GLADDINGS, TIMOTHY A. (1818 - 1864)	400-5000	F
GLARNER, FRITZ (1899 - 1972)	2500-240000+	A
GLASER, ELIZABETH (active 1830-40)	*500-7500	P
GLASGOW, BERNO (19TH-20TH C)	200-1200	X
GLASS, F.R. (20TH C)	*100-500	X

* Denotes watercolors, pastels, drawings, and/or mixed media

GLASS, JAMES WILLIAM (1825 - 1857)	450-2500	G,F
GLAVE, C.L. (20TH C)	100-700	M
GLEASON, JOE DUNCAN (1881 - 1950)	200-4000	I
GLEITSMAN, LOUIS A. (1883 - 1970)	100-1000	F
GLEITSMAN, RAPHAEL	*100-2900	
GLEITSMAN, RAPHAEL (1910 -)	2000-33000	X
GLEW, EDWARD LEES (1817 - 1870)	1000-10000	L,F
GLINTENCAMP, HENDRIK	*100-900	
GLINTENCAMP, HENDRIK (1887 - 1946)	150-2500	I,L
GLUCKMANN, GRIGORY (1898 - 1973)	450-16000	F
GLYNDON, F. (20TH C)	200-1600	X (F)
GODARD, GABRIEL (1933 -)	100-1700	X
GODDARD, MARGARET E. (1882 -)	400-1800	S
GODFREY, E. (19TH C)	100-500	L
GODFREY, FRANK T. (1873 -)	100-600	I
GODOY, A.T. (20TH C)	100-750	M,L
GODWIN, FRANK (1889 - 1959)	*150-3000	
GOEBEL, PAUL (1877 -)	200-1200	L
GOEBEL, ROD (20TH C)	500-2800	L
GOETSCH, GUSTAV F. (1877 - 1969)	100-850	F,L
GOETZ, EDITH (19TH-20TH C)	*100-500	X
GOETZ, HENRI	*200-11000	
GOETZ, HENRI (1909 - 1989)	300-28000	A
GOETZ, RICHARD V. (20TH C)	100-1500	X (I,S)
GOINGS, F. (19TH C)	100-600	L
GOINGS,RALPH	*350-16000	
GOINGS, RALPH (1928 -)	2000-77000	A
GOLD, ALBERT (1916 - 1972)	100-3500	I
GOLDBERG, MICHAEL	*100-2200	
GOLDBERG, MICHAEL (1924 -)	750-28000	A
GOLDBERG, RUBE (1883 - 1970)	*100-2000	I
GOLDEN, ROLLAND (1931 -)	*200-1400	X (L)
GOLDING, CECIL (20TH C)	100-900	X
GOLDING, WILLIAM O. (1874 - 1943)	*600-2500	P
GOLDINGHAM, J.B. (19TH C)	100-400	L

GOLDMAN, I. (20TH C)	150-1500	L
GOLDSTEIN, HYMAN (20TH C)	*100-500	L
GOLDTHWAITE, ANNE (1869 - 1944)	*100-2500	F,L
GOLLINGS, WILLIAM ELLING	*400-7000	
GOLLINGS, WILLIAM ELLING (1878 - 1932)	700-35000	G,F
GOLUB, LEON ALBERT (1922 -)	1500-41250	A
GONSKE, WALT (20TH C)	200-1200	X (L)
GONZALES, XAVIER (1899 -)	100-900	A
GOODALL, W. (early 19TH C)	*100-1000	W
GOODE, JOE	*500-2500	
GOODE, JOE (1937 -)	600-6500	A
GOODELL, IRA CHAFFEE (1800 - 1875)	3000-20000	P (F)
GOODELL, J.C. (AC.C 1825 - 1832)	800-4000	F
GOODES, EDWARD A. (active 1855-85)	500-3000	X (M)
GOODMAN, H.K. (active 1845 - 1850)	2500-32000	P
GOODMAN, SYDNEY (1936 -)	500-5500	X (G)
GOODNOUGH, ROBERT (1917 -)	500-19000	A
GOODRIDGE, SARAH (1788 - 1853)	300-1200	F
GOODWIN, (RICHARD) LABARRE (1840 - 1910)	600-15000+	S,W,L
GOODWIN, ARTHUR CLIFTON	*400-20000	
GOODWIN, ARTHUR CLIFTON (1866 - 1929)	500-35000	L,M
GOODWIN, BELLE (19TH C)	800-3500	X (S)
GOODWIN, EDWIN WEYBURN (1800 - 1845)	5000-35000	P
GOODWIN, PHILIP RUSSELL	*100-1700	
GOODWIN, PHILIP RUSSELL (1882 - 1935)	900-21000	G,L,I
GOODYEAR, C. (19TH C)	*100-500	X (S)
GORBINO, ROSARIO (20TH C)	100-800	X
GORCHOV, RON (1930 -)	800-6000	A
GORDER, LUTHER EMERSON VAN (1861 - 1931)	150-5000	G,L
GORKY, ARSHILE	*3000-375000+	
GORKY, ARSHILE (1904 - 1948)	5000-880000	A
GORLICH, SOPHIE (1855 - 1893)	1000-9000	G
GORMAN, R.C. (1933 -)	*400-4600	X (F)
GORMON, JAMES O. (19TH C)	200-3500	M,L
GORSON, AARON HENRY (1872 - 1933)	1000-38000	L,F

* Denotes watercolors, pastels, drawings, and/or mixed media

GOSMINSKI, RICHARD (20TH C)	*50-400	X (G)
GOTHELF, LOUIS (1901 -)	50-700	L
GOTLIEB, JULES (1897 -)	200-3500	I
GOTTLIEB, ADOLPH	*1500-88000	
GOTTLIEB, ADOLPH (1903 - 1974)	8000-352000	A
GOTTLIEB, HARRY (1895 - 1992)	300-2600	X (L)
GOTTLIEB, LEOPOLD (1883 - 1933)	*350-2100	X
GOTTSCHALK, MAX (20TH C)	50-400	F
GOTTWALD, FREDERICK C. (1860 - 1941)	500-4500	G,L
GOULD, JOHN F. (1906 -)	*100-700	I
GOULD, WALTER (1829 - 1893)	4000-110000	G,F
GOURNSEY, C. (19TH C)	*250-1200	X (L)
GRABACH, JOHN R.	*300-4500	
GRABACH, JOHN R. (1886 - 1981)	1500-30000	F,G,L
GRACE, F. (19TH C)	100-900	L
GRACE, GERALD (1918 -)	100-900	X (G)
GRAECEN, EDMUND (1877 - 1949)	200-22000	X (S)
GRAF, CARL C. (1890 - 1947)	300-6000	L
GRAFTON, ROBERT W. (1876 - 1936)	900-17000	G,F,L
GRAHAM, CHARLES (1852 - 1911)	*400-6100	L,F
GRAHAM, DONALD (20TH C)	300-7000	L,M
GRAHAM, GEORGE (19TH-20TH C)	*100-400	X (G)
GRAHAM, JOHN D.	*100-800	
GRAHAM, JOHN D. (1881 - 1961)	3000-150000+	A
GRAHAM, RALPH W. (1901 -)	*100-800	G
GRAHAM, ROBERT ALEXANDER (1873 - 1946)	400-9000	F,L
GRAHAM, WILLIAM (1841 - 1910)	400-2000	L
GRAILLY, VICTOR DE (1804 - 1889)	400-10000	L,F
GRAMATKY, HARDIE (1907 - 1979)	*250-1200	I
GRAND, HENRY LE (19TH C)	600-4500	L
GRANDEE, JOE RUIZ (1929 -)	400-2800	F
GRANER Y ARUFFI, LUIS (1867 - 1929)	300-22000	F,G,L
GRANT, CHARLES HENRY	*100-2000	
GRANT, CHARLES HENRY (1866 - 1938)	250-2500	M
GRANT, CLEMENT ROLLINS (1849 - 1893)	300-8500	L,F

GRANT, DONALD (B. 1951)	150-16500	X
GRANT, DWINELL	*100-1800	
GRANT, DWINELL (1912 -)	500-3800	X (A)
GRANT, FREDERIC MILTON (1886 - 1959)	800-8500+	I,L
GRANT, GORDAN HOPE	*300-3600	
GRANT, GORDON HOPE (1875 - 1962)	500-15000	M,I
GRANT, J. JEFFREY (1883 - 1960)	300-2600	L,M
GRANT, JAMES (1924 -)	*300-1200	A
GRANT, WILLIAM (mid 19TH C)	*1000-7000	P
GRANVILLE-SMITH, WALTER	*150-8800	
GRANVILLE-SMITH, WALTER (1870 - 1938)	350-35000	L,F,I
GRAUER, WILLIAM C.	*100-350	
GRAUER, WILLIAM C. (1896 -)	300-4000	L,M
GRAVES, ABBOTT FULLER	*100-1500	
GRAVES, ABBOTT FULLER (1859 - 1936)	1500-137500	S,F,G,L
GRAVES, CAPTAIN (AC.C 1860 - 1890)	300-2200	M
GRAVES, MORRIS COLE	*600-13000	
GRAVES, MORRIS COLE (1910 -)	1000-30000	A
GRAVES, NANCY	*2000-30000	
GRAVES, NANCY (1940 -)	8000-50000	A
GRAVES, O.E.L. (1912 -)	150-2500	F,W
GRAY, HENRY PERCY	*900-47000	
GRAY, HENRY PERCY (1869 - 1934)	700-20000	L,M
GRAY, BESSIE (19TH C)	*100-750	X (L)
GRAY, CHARLES A. (1857 - 1933)	200-1400	F
GRAY, CLEVE (1918 -)	500-14000	A
GRAY, FREDERICK G. (19TH-20TH C)	100-750	X (F,G)
GRAY, HENRY PETERS (1819 - 1877)	300-10000	F
GRAY, JACK L. (1927 - 1981)	1500-34500	M,F
GRAY, JIM (20TH C)	*300-1700	X (M)
GRAY, M. MAY (20TH C)	100-350	X (F)
GRAY, MARY (20TH C)	100-1000	L
GRAY, MARY M. (20TH C)	100-500	L
GRAY, RALPH W. (1880 - 1944)	*150-800	X (F,L)
GRAY, U.L. (20TH C)	200-1200	X (L,S)

* Denotes watercolors, pastels, drawings, and/or mixed media

GRAY, URBAN (20TH C ?)	150-650	X (L)
GRAY, WILLIAM F. (1866 -)	150-750	X (M)
GRAZIA, TED DE	*250-800	
GRAZIA, TED DE (1909 -)	300-2500	W
GRAZIANI, SANTE (1920 -)	800-3000	A
GREACEN, EDMUND WILLIAM	*100-1000	
GREACEN, EDMUND WILLIAM (1877 - 1949)	2000-48000+	F,S,L
GREACEN, NAN	*300-14500	
GREACEN, NAN (1909 -)	100-2000+	L,S,M
GREASON, DONALD CARLISLE (1897 -)	100-7500	L,M
GREASON, WILLIAM (1884 -)	200-2100	L,M
GREATOREX, KATHLEEN HONORA (1851 -)	600-11000	S,I
GREAVES, HARRY E.(1854 - 1919)	100-1000	L
GREENE, ALBERT VAN NESSE (B. 1887 -)	400-4400	X (L)
GREEN, BERNARD (1887 - 1951)	200-3100	L
GREEN, CHARLES EDWIN LEWIS	*100-1500	
GREEN, CHARLES EDWIN LEWIS (1844 - 1915)	500-8800	L,M
GREEN, EDITH JACKSON (1876 - 1934)	100-850	X (L)
GREEN, FRANK RUSSELL (1856 - 1940)	350-11000	S,L
GREEN, ROLAND (1896 - 1972)	*200-2100	W,L
GREEN, ROSE (19TH C)	100-500	S
GREEN, WILLIAM BRADFORD (1871 - 1945)	100-2600	L
GREENBAUM, JOSEPH DAVID (1864 - 1940)	200-3600	L,F
GREENBERG, MAURICE (1893 -)	100-800	X (F)
GREENE, BALCOMB (1904 -)	500-5800	A
GREENE, J. BARRY (1895 - 1966)	100-1600	L,M
GREENE, STEPHEN (1918 -)	800-3500	A
GREENE, WALTER L. (19TH-20TH C)	*100-1400	L,M,I
GREENFIELD, EVAN JOHN FORREST (1866 -)	100-1500	X
GREENLEAF, JACOB I. (1887 - 1968)	100-2200	L,M
GREENWOOD, ETHAN ALLEN (1779 - 1856)	750-8500	F
GREENWOOD, JOHN	*100-1000	
GREENWOOD, JOHN (1727 - 1792)	400-2000	P
GREENWOOD, JOSEPH H. (1857 - 1927)	250-9500	L
GREENWOOD, MARION (1909 - 1970)	500-3000	G

GREER, JAMES EMERY (19TH C)	100-900	L
GREGOR, HAROLD (1929 -)	900-15000	A,L
GREGORY, ELIOT (1854 - 1915)	100-10000	F
GREIG, DONALD (20TH C)	100-1000	X (F)
GRELL, LOUIS FREDERICK (1887 -)	*100-1600	X
GREMKE, DICK (19TH-20TH C)	200-1000	L
GREMKE, HENRY DIEDRICH (1860 - 1933)	300-4200	L
GREMKE, M.D. (active 1865-1900)	400-1500	L
GRIFFIN, DELANCY (19TH C)	50-600	L
GRIFFIN, THOMAS BAILEY (AC.1860 - 1899)	300-3500	L
GRIFFIN, WALTER	*200-3000	
GRIFFIN, WALTER (1861 - 1935)	500-14500	L
GRIFFIN, WILLIAM (1861 -)	600-5000	L
GRIFFIN, WORTH DICKMAN (1892 -)	100-850	X (M)
GRIFFITH, BILL (20TH C)	*100-600	X
GRIFFITH, GRACE ALLISON (1885 - 1955)	*400-3600	L,W
GRIFFITH, JULIE SULZER (- 1945)	100-400	M
GRIFFITH, LOUIS K. (20TH C)	*100-600	X (G)
GRIFFITH, LOUIS OSCAR (1875 - 1956)	100-1700	L,F
GRIFFITH, MARIE O. (20TH C)	400-14000	S
GRIFFITH, WILLIAM A. (1866 - 1940)	400-4500	L,M,F
GRIGGS, SAMUEL W. (1827 - 1898)	200-10000	L,S
GRILLEY, ROBERT (1920 -)	200-850	X
GRILLO, JOHN (1917 -)	600-1200	A
GRIMM, PAUL (1892 - 1974)	400-12000	L
GRINNELL, GEORGE VICTOR (1878 - 1946)	100-2000	L
GRIOMARE, EDWARD T. (20TH C)	300-1200	X
GRISET, ERNEST (1844 - 1907)	*100-500	F,G
GRISWALD, CASIMIR C. (1834 - 1918)	250-2500	L
GROESBECK, DANIEL SAYRE (20TH C)	*100-1200	F
GROHE, GLENN (1912 - 1956)	50-600	X (F)
GROLL, ALBERT LOREY	*100-450	
GROLL, ALBERT LOREY (1866 - 1952)	250-8000	L
GROOMS, FRANK R. (19TH C)	100-1500	X (G)
GROOMS, MIMI (20TH C)	*100-500	X

* Denotes watercolors, pastels, drawings, and/or mixed media

GROOMS, RED	*100-12650	
GROOMS, RED (1937 -)	*1000-77000	A
GROPPER, WILLIAM	*250-5000	
GROPPER, WILLIAM (1897 - 1977)	1000-46500+	G,F,I
GROS, D. (early 19TH C)	300-1200	L
GROSE, DANIEL CHARLES (active 1865-90)	200-7500	L
GROSE, HARRIET ESTELLE (- 1914)	400-2000	X (S)
GROSS, CHAIM (1904 - 1991)	*200-3100	A,M,L
GROSS, G. (20TH C)	200-1200	G,F
GROSS, JULIET WHITE (1882 - 1934)	400-1800	X
GROSS, OSKAR (1871 - 1963)	500-5500	X (A)
GROSS, PETER ALFRED (1849 - 1914)	150-1500	L,G
GROSSENHEIDER, RICHARD PHILIP (1911 - 1975)	*800-4500	X
GROSSETE, L. (19TH C)	100-700	L
GROSSMAN, EDWIN BOOTH (1887 - 1957)	100-2100	L,M
GROSSMAN, JOSEPH (1889 -)	200-2500	L
GROSZ, GEORGE	*500-150000+	
GROSZ, GEORGE (1893 - 1959)	1000-33000	A,L,F
GROTH, JOHN (1908 - 1988)	*200-1200	I
GROVER, OLIVER DENNET (1861 - 1927)	550-10000	L,G
GRUELLE, RICHARD BUCKNER (1851 - 1915)	200-1200	L,S
GRUGER, FREDERIC RODRIGO (1871 - 1953)	*200-1200	I
GRUNER, CARL (active 1850-65)	700-2000	F
GRUNEWALD, GUSTAVUS (19TH C)	25300	L
GRUPPE, CHARLES PAUL	*100-2200	
GRUPPE, CHARLES PAUL (1860 - 1940)	700-13500	L,M
GRUPPE, EMILE ALBERT (1896 - 1978)	800-29000	L,M,F
GUE, DAVID JOHN (1836 - 1917)	300-5500	L,M,F
GUELLOW, W. (19TH C)	200-3500	X (W)
GUERELSON, A.M. (20TH C ?)	700-4000	X
GUERIN, JOSEPH (1889 -)	300-1800	L,M
GUERIN, JULES (1866 - 1946)	*400-4500	F,I
GUERRERO, JOSE	*100-5700	
GUERRERO, JOSE (1914 - 1991)	300-35000	X
GUERRERO, JULES (1914 -)	800-6500	X (A)

* Denotes watercolors, pastels, drawings, and/or mixed media   195

GUGLIELMI, O. LOUIS	*100-1600	
GUGLIELMI, O. LOUIS (1906 - 1956)	3000-46000	A
GUIFON, LEON (19TH C)	400-2000	X (L)
GUILFORD, MARGARET (19TH C)	100-600	A
GUILLAUME, L. (19TH C)	*150-750	L,F
GUION, MOLLY (1910 -)	200-1800	G,S
GUIPON, LEON (1872 - 1910)	200-1800	X (G,F)
GUISE, M.H. (19TH C)	100-800	L
GUISTO, REGINA (20TH C)	100-700	A
GULAGER, CHARLES (active 1860-80)	250-1200	X (M)
GULLAGER, CHRISTIAN (1762 - 1826)	400-14500	F
GUMPEL, HUGH (20TH C)	*100-400	L
GUNN, EDWIN H. (1876 - 1940)	*200-1500	X (M)
GUPTILL, ARTHUR L. (1891 -)	50-400	L
GURGIN, W. (19TH C)	350-1200	X (W)
GUSSOW, BERNARD (1881 - 1957)	300-6600	L,F
GUSTAVSON, HENRY (1864 - 1912)	250-900	L
GUSTEMER, G. (AC. 1840 - 1850)	4000-35750	F
GUSTON, PHILIP	*1100-71500	
GUSTON, PHILIP (1913 - 1980)	8500-550000	A
GUTHERSON, F. JEROME (20TH C)	*100-600	X (L)
GUTHERZ, CARL (1844 - 1907)	400-6600	F
GUTMANN, BERNHARD (1869 - 1936)	200-1100	X (F)
GUY, FRANCIS (1760 - 1820)	4000-60000	L
GUY, SEYMOUR JOSEPH (1824 - 1910)	3000-125000	G,F
GWATHMEY, ROBERT	*600-7200	
GWATHMEY, ROBERT (1903 - 1988)	1000-24200	A,G,F
GYBERSON, INDIANA (19TH-20TH C)	500-1800	F

H

Artist	Prices	Subject
HAAG, HY (20TH C)	200-2400	X (F)
HAAPPANEN, JOHN NICHOLS (1891 -)	300-2500	L,M
HABERLE, JOHN	*800-8500	
HABERLE, JOHN (1856 - 1933)	7500-300000+	S,F
HACKETT, MALCOLM (20TH C)	100-1000	X (L)
HADDOCK, ARTHUR (20TH C)	700-2000	L
HAELEN, JOHN A. (19TH-20TH C)	100-500	F
HAERST, G. (19TH C)	100-850	L
HAES JANVIER, FRANCES DE (1775 - 1824)	450-2000	F
HAESELER, ALICE P. SMITH (19TH-20TH C)	*200-700	M,L
HAGAMAN, JAMES (20TH C)	150-900	G,L
HAGBERG, CHARLES J. (19TH C)	100-400	M
HAGEFUL, H. (19TH-20TH C)	200-1000	X (M)
HAGERBRUNNER, DAVID (20TH C)	*400-2800	X (W)
HAGERUP, NELS (1864 - 1922)	300-3800	M
HAGNY, J. (19TH C)	100-400	P
HAGUE, MAURICE (1862 -)	100-500	L
HAHN, KARL WILHELM (1829 - 1887)	4000-60000	G
HAHN, WILLIAM (1840 - 1890)	1500-40000	G
HAIG, MABEL (1884 -)	*100-600	M,L
HAILMAN, JOHANNA K. (1871 -)	50-700	L
HAINES, RICHARD (1906 -)	100-800	X (L)
HALBERG, CHARLES EDWARD (1855 -)	100-800	M
HALE, ELLEN DAY	*100-2000	
HALE, ELLEN DAY (1855 - 1940)	1000-28000	F,L
HALE, GARDNER (1894 - 1931)	*100-500	L
HALE, GERARD VAN BARKALOO (1886 - 1958)	100-750	X (F)
HALE, LILIAN WESTCOTT (1881 - 1963)	800-48000	F
HALE, MARY POWELL HELME (1862 - 1934)	100-900	X (L)
HALE, PHILIP LESLIE	*500-10000	
HALE, PHILIP LESLIE (1865 - 1931)	1000-45000+	F
HALE, ROBERT BEVERLY (1901 -)	*100-850	X
HALEY, ROBERT DUANE (1892 - 1959)	300-3200	X
HALL, ANNE (1792 - 1863)	700-4500	F

HALL, E. W. (19TH C)	300-1200	L
HALL, FREDERICK GARRISON (1879 - 1946)	150-1000	X (G,F)
HALL, GEORGE HENRY (1825 - 1913)	600-22000 +	G,S,F
HALL, HENRY BRYAN (1808 - 1884)	500-3500	F,S
HALL, HOWARD HILL (1887 - 1933)	500-10000	X (G)
HALL, PETER (1828 - 1895)	*100-900	F
HALL, SADIE VAN PATTEN (20TH C)	100-1000	X (M)
HALL, THOMAS VICTOR (20TH C)	*100-600	X (G)
HALL, WILLIAM SMITH (19TH C)	800-4500	F
HALLETT, HENDRICKS A.	*100-1000	
HALLETT, HENDRICKS A. (1847 - 1921)	350-4500 +	M,L
HALLMAN, HENRY T. (1904 -)	50-600	X
HALLOWAY, GEORGE (20TH C)	100-600	X (L)
HALLOWELL, ANNA D. (19TH C)	*200-2000	X (M)
HALLOWELL, GEORGE HAWLEY	*100-6500	
HALLOWELL, GEORGE HAWLEY (1871 - 1926)	500-6500	L
HALLOWELL, ROBERT (1886 - 1939)	*100-2200	X (M,S)
HALLWIG, OSCAR (1858 - 1880)	300-1500	X (F)
HALOW, E.J. (19TH-20TH C)	150-1000	L
HALOWAY, EDWARD STRATTON (- 1939)	100-800	X (M)
HALPERT, SAMUEL T.	*200-1800	
HALPERT, SAMUEL T. (1884 - 1930)	350-8000	L,F,S
HALSALL, WILLIAM FORMBY (1841 - 1919)	400-5200	M,L
HALTON, MINNIE HOLLIS (20TH C)	100-750	X (G)
HAM, GORDON R. (20TH C)	100-900	X (L)
HAMBIDGE, JAY (1867 - 1924)	*200-1500	I
HAMBLEN, STURTEVANT J. (active 1835-55)	3000-45000 +	P
HAMBLETT, THEORA (1895 -)	250-1200	P
HAMBRIDGE, JAY (1867 - 1924)	350-2500	F,I,S
HAMILTON, EDGAR SCUDDER (1869 - 1903)	400-2000	X (G)
HAMILTON, EDWARD WILBUR DEAN (1862 - 1943)	500-8500	L,F
HAMILTON, HADASSAH (19TH C)	200-1500	L
HAMILTON, HAMILTON (1847 - 1928)	250-14000 +	L,F
HAMILTON, HELEN (19TH-20TH C)	300-1500	L
HAMILTON, HILDEGARD (1906 -)	100-600	L

* Denotes watercolors, pastels, drawings, and/or mixed media

HAMILTON, JAMES (1819 - 1878)	500-14500+	M,L,I
HAMILTON, JOHN MCLURE	*100-1600	
HAMILTON, JOHN MCLURE (1853 - 1936)	1500-44000	F,I,S
HAMILTON, ROBERT (1877 - 1954)	250-1500	G,L,F
HAMILTON, WILLIAM A. (1877 -)	100-1200	X (L)
HAMILTON, WILLIAM R.(1810 - 1865)	400-6500+	F
HAMMER, JOHN J. (1842 - 1906)	350-3500	G,L,M
HAMMERAS, RALPH (1939 -)	200-1500	L
HAMMERSTAD, JOHN H. (19TH C)	100-1200	X (M,L)
HAMMOND, ARTHUR J. (1875 - 1947)	150-4200	M,L,S
HAMPSON, ALBERT W. (1911 - 1990)	600-3500	I
HAMPTON, JOHN W.	*300-6000	
HAMPTON, JOHN W. (1918 - 1976)	600-11000	I,G,L,W
HANARTY, ALICE E. (late 19TH C)	100-500	X (L)
HANAU, JEAN (1899 - 1966)	*300-1000	X (I)
HANDWRIGHT, GEORGE (1873 - 1951)	*200-1000	X
HANE, ROGER (1938 - 1974)	200-1500	I
HANKINS, A.P. (20TH C)	100-400	X (F)
HANKS, JERVIS F. (1799 -)	500-2000	P
HANKS, LON (19TH-20TH C)	200-850	X (M)
HANLEY, J.B. (active 1870-85)	500-4000	G
HANLEY, SARAH E. (- 1958)	100-2000	L,F
HANNA, THOMAS KING (- 1916)	300-7800	X (I)
HANNA JR, THOMAS KING (1872 - 1957)	*200-1200	I
HANNAH, H.K. (19TH-20TH C)	200-1800	L
HANSEN, ARMIN CARL	*100-5225	
HANSEN, ARMIN CARL (1886 - 1957)	900-61000	M,L,F
HANSEN, EJNAR (1884 - 1965)	500-15000	F
HANSEN, HANS PETER (1881 - 1967)	100-1500	G,F
HANSEN, HARALD (1890 - 1967)	*100-400	L
HANSEN, HERMAN WENDELBORG	*2500-50000	
HANSEN, HERMAN WENDELBORG (1854 - 1924)	5000-66000	G,F
HANSON, D. (19TH C)	100-600	M
HANSON, R. (19TH C)	100-600	X (S)
HARBESON, GEORGIANA BROWN (1894 -)	*350-1500	G,F,I

* Denotes watercolors, pastels, drawings, and/or mixed media   199

HARDENGERGH, GERARD R.(1856 - 1915)	*100-850	L
HARDING, CHESTER (1792 - 1866)	500-9000	F
HARDING, GEORGE MATTHEWS	*250-1500	
HARDING, GEORGE MATTHEWS (1882 - 1959)	450-4000	I
HARDING, H.H. (late 19TH C)	200-1200	M
HARDING, JOHN L. (1848 - 1882)	500-3500	F
HARDWICK, MELBOURNE H.	*300-1900	
HARDWICK, MELBOURNE H. (1857 - 1916)	400-4500	M,L,G
HARDY, ANNA ELIZA (1839 - 1934)	200-2800	S,L,F
HARDY, JEREMIAH P.(1800 - 1888)	350-1500	F
HARDY, WALTER MANLEY (1877 -)	*150-900	L,I
HARDY, WILLIAM F. (19TH-20TH C)	150-900	L
HARE, JOHN C. (20TH C)	*100-750	L,M
HARE, JOHN KNOWLES	*100-1500	
HARE, JOHN KNOWLES (1884 - 1947)	200-2000	I,M,L
HARE, WILLIAM (active 1820-50)	3000-15000	M,F
HARGENS, CHARLES (1893 -)	100-3600	G
HARGRAVE, HARRY S. (20TH C)	300-1500	L
HARGREAVES, EDGAR W. (20TH C)	*200-1200	M,L
HARING, KEITH (1958 - 1990)	*5000-50000	A
HARIS, T. (20TH C)	100-750	L
HARLAND, MARY (1863 -)	100-700	L,F
HARLES, VICTOR J. (1894 - 1975)	100-3600	L
HARLOW, LOUIS KENNEY (1850 - 1930)	*50-600	L,M
HARMAN, FRED (1902 - 1982)	*200-7000	I
HARMER, ALEXANDER F.	*100-900	
HARMER, ALEXANDER F. (1857 - 1925)	400-9500	G,F
HARMON, CHARLES H. (1859 - 1936)	100-1600	L,F
HARMON, W.S. (19TH C)	400-1500	L
HARNDEN, WILLIAM (1920 - 1983)	200-1800	X (L)
HARNETT, WILLIAM MICHAEL (1848 - 1892)	1000-300000	S
HARNEY, PAUL E. (1850 - 1915)	350-2000	W,L,F
HARPER, WILLIAM ST. JOHN	*1000-53000	
HARPER, WILLIAM ST. JOHN (1851 - 1910)	600-53000	I,F,G
HARRA, M.A. (19TH C)	300-1500	X (S)

* Denotes watercolors, pastels, drawings, and/or mixed media

HARRINGTON, E. (20TH C)	100-900	L,F
HARRINGTON, GEORGE (1833 - 1911)	300-2500	L
HARRINGTON, OLIVER W. (1913 -)	100-500	X (L)
HARRINGTON, RUFUS (20TH C)	100-600	X (M)
HARRIS, C. GOODWIN (1893 - 1981)	*100-1000	X (M)
HARRIS, CHARLES GORDON (1891 -)	300-2000	L,M
HARRIS, CHARLES X. (1856 -)	700-8500	F,G
HARRIS, LAWREN STUART (1885 - 1970)	800-28000	L,I
HARRIS, MARION D. (1904 -)	*100-850	L,F
HARRIS, ROBERT GEORGE (1911 -)	400-3500	I,F
HARRIS, SAM HYDE (1889 - 1977)	200-7400	L,M
HARRIS, W. (19TH C)	100-500	L
HARRISON, (THOMAS)ALEXANDER (1833 - 1930)	450-21000	M,L
HARRISON, BIRGE (1853 - 1929)	500-38000	L
HARRISON, CHARLES (19TH-20TH C)	100-500	X (L)
HARRISON, MARK ROBERT (1819 - 1894)	500-5000	L,G
HARRISON, THOMAS ALEXANDER (1853 - 1930)	300-5560	M,L,G,F
HART, GEORGE O. ("POP" HART)(1868 - 1933)	*250-3500	L,G
HART, J. (19TH-20TH C)	300-1600	X (L)
HART, JAMES MCDOUGAL (1828 - 1901)	500-31000	L,G
HART, LETITIA BONNET (1867 -)	400-3500	F,L
HART, MARY THERESA (1872 - 1921)	300-3500	X (S)
HART, SALOMON ALEXANDER (1806 - 1881)	600-15000	G
HART, T.H. (19TH C ?)	100-850	L
HART, WILLIAM HOWARD (1863 - 1934)	400-5500	L
HART, WILLIAM M. (1823 - 1894)	800-40000 +	L,W
HARTIGAN, GRACE (1922 -)	1500-12000	A
HARTING, LLOYD (1901 - 1976)	*100-1200	F,G
HARTLEY, ELAINE (20TH C)	100-500	X
HARTLEY, MARSDEN	*500-30000	
HARTLEY, MARSDEN (1878 - 1943)	5000-550000 +	A,S
HARTLEY, RACHEL (1884 -)	300-8500	G,I
HARTMAN, C. BERTRAM	*200-4400	
HARTMAN, C. BERTRAM (1882 - 1960)	400-21000	L,S
HARTMAN, GEORGE (- 1934)	100-1700	X (F)

HARTMAN, SYDNEY K. (1863 -)	*100-450	I,L
HARTRATH, LUCIE	*100-800	
HARTRATH, LUCIE (1868 - 1962)	100-8800	L
HARTSHORNE, HOWARD MORTON (19TH-20TH C)	400-5200	X
HARTSLY, A. (19TH C)	100-700	L
HARTSON, WALTER C.	*100-1200	
HARTSON, WALTER C. (1866 - 1946)	100-1200	L
HARTWICK, HERMAN (1853 - 1926)	550-24500	L,W,F
HARTWICK, GEORGE GUNTHER (active 1845-60)	600-9400	L
HARTWIG, HEINE (1937 -)	250-3000	L
HARVEY, A.T. (19TH C)	100-1500	X (F,G)
HARVEY, ELI (1860 - 1957)	450-1800	L,F
HARVEY, EUGENE (19TH C)	200-1000	M,L
HARVEY, GEORGE	*200-5000	
HARVEY, GEORGE (1800 - 1878)	1000-65000 +	L,F
HARVEY, GEORGE W.	*100-1500	
HARVEY, GEORGE W. (1835 - 1920)	300-6500	L,F
HARVEY, GERALD (1933 -)	8000-100000	L,G
HARVEY, HENRY T. (19TH C)	250-1500	L,F
HARVEY, PAUL (1878 - 1948)	100-1800	L
HASBROUCK, DU BOIS FENELON	*100-700	
HASBROUCK, DU BOIS FENELON (1860 - 1917)	250-5000	L
HASELTINE, CHARLES FIELD (1840 -)	100-1500	L
HASELTINE, WILLIAM STANLEY	*100-2800	
HASELTINE, WILLIAM STANLEY (1835 - 1900)	450-72000	L
HASENFUS, RICHARD C. (20TH C)	500-4000	X (M)
HASKELL, ERNEST (1876 - 1925)	*250-900	L
HASKELL, IDA C. (1861 - 1932)	350-3500	G
HASKELL, JOSEPH ALLEN (1808 - 1894)	200-2500	P
HASKELL, T.R. (late 19TH C)	100-500	L
HASKINS, GAYLE PORTER (1887 - 1962)	500-3000	X (G)
HASLER, WILLIAM N. (1865 -)	200-1500	L
HASSAM, FREDERICK CHILDE	*1000-825000	
HASSAM, FREDERICK CHILDE (1859 - 1935)	4500-3190000	L,F

* Denotes watercolors, pastels, drawings, and/or mixed media

HASSAN, E. (19TH C)	100-600	X (W,L)
HASSELBUSH, LOUIS (1863 -)	600-1500	X (F)
HASSLER, CARL VON (1886 - 1969)	1000-10000	L,F
HASTINGS, HOWARD L. (20TH C)	100-850	L
HASTINGS, MATTHEW (1834 - 1919)	250-1500	F,G
HATFIELD, JOSEPH HENRY (1863 - 1928)	500-4000	F,L
HATFIELD, PAULINE (early 20TH C)	100-500	X (S)
HATHAWAY, GEORGE M.	*300-1000	
HATHAWAY, GEORGE M. (1852 - 1903)	600-3500	M,L
HATHAWAY, RUFUS (1770 - 1822)	5000-90000	P
HATHERELL, WILLIAM (20TH C)	*100-1000	I
HAUGH, N. (19TH C)	*100-800	X (S)
HAUPT, ERIK GUIDE (1891 -)	800-6500	L,F
HAUPT, THEODORE G. (1902 -)	*200-1000	A
HAUSER, JOHN	*600-18000	
HAUSER, JOHN (1858 - 1913)	1000-28000	F,L
HAUSHALTER, GEORGE M. (1862 -)	100-1000	G
HAUSMAN, CHAUNCEY (19TH C)	100-700	F
HAVARD, JAMES PICKNEY (1937 -)	1500-82500	A
HAVELL, ROBERT JR (1793 - 1878)	1500-38000	L
HAVEN, FRANKLIN DE (1856 - 1934)	450-4000 +	L
HAWES, CHARLES (20TH C)	*100-500	X (M,L)
HAWKINS, JOHN (20TH C)	200-700	X (M)
HAWKS, EDITH B. (20TH C)	100-800	X
HAWLEY, HUGHSON (1850 - 1936)	*300-7000	X (L,I)
HAWORTH, EDITH E. (20TH C)	100-700	L,F
HAWSKWORTH, E.J. (19TH C)	100-700	X (S)
HAWTHORNE, CHARLES WEBSTER (1872 - 1930)	500-95000 +	F,G,L
HAWTHORNE, E.D. (19TH C)	600-7500	G
HAYDEN, CHARLES HENRY (1856 - 1901)	300-3500	L
HAYDEN, EDWARD PARKER (- 1922)	300-2800	L
HAYDEN, ELLA FRANCES (1860 -)	*100-750	L
HAYNES, PERRY (1870 -)	100-600	L
HAYNIE, WILBUR (1929 -)	100-400	A
HAYS, BARTON STONE (1826 - 1914)	350-7800	S,L,W,F

HAYS, GEORGE A. (1854 -)	250-4000	L,W
HAYS, WILLIAM JACOB JR (1872 - 1954)	700-4500	L,G
HAYS, WILLIAM JACOB SR (1830 - 1875)	800-10000+	W,S
HAYTER, CHARLES (1761 - 1835)	*700-2000	F
HAYWARD, FRANK (1867 -)	250-1200	L
HAYWARD, PETER (1905 -)	150-1000	X (M)
HAYWARD, ROGER (1899 - 1979)	*150-650	A
HAZARD, ARTHUR MERTON (1872 - 1930)	200-4000	L,F,I
HAZARD, S. (19TH C)	150-1200	L
HAZELL, S.N. (19TH C)	400-1500	G
HAZELTON, MARY BREWSTER (1868 - 1953)	400-7000	F,L
HAZEN, BESSIE ELLA (1862 - 1946)	*100-750	X (L)
HAZLITT, JOHN (1767 - 1837)	200-1000	F
HEAD, J. (19TH C)	100-600	L
HEADE, MARTIN JOHNSON	*100-27600	
HEADE, MARTIN JOHNSON (1819 - 1904)	7500-1650000+	L,S,F
HEALY, ARTHUR K.D. (1902 -)	*100-800	F,L
HEALY, FRANCIS D. (- 1948)	50-500	L
HEALY, GEORGE PETER A. (1813 - 1894)	300-12000+	F
HEASLIP, WILLIAM JOHN (1898 - 1965)	200-1200	L
HEATH, EDDA MAXWELL (1875 - 1972)	200-1500	X (L)
HEATH, FRANK L. (1857 - 1921)	500-4500	L,M
HEATH, W.A. (late 19TH C)	150-750	X (L)
HEATON,AUGUSTUS GEORGE G. (1844 - 1931)	500-5500	F,G
HEATON OF ALBANY, JOHN (18TH C)	1000-6500	P
HEBERER, CHARLES (early 20TH C ?)	200-4000	L,M
HECHT, ZOLTAN (1890 - 1968)	100-900	L
HECKSHER, E. (19TH-20TH C)	100-500	X (S)
HEDGES, ROBERT D. (1878 -)	100-850	M
HEDINGER, ELISE (1854 -)	800-4800	X (S)
HEFFRON, M. (19TH C)	400-1800	X
HEICHER, FORD (late 19TH C)	100-900	G
HEIL, CHARLES EMILE	*150-650	
HEIL, CHARLES EMILE (1870 - 1953)	200-2800	L,I
HEINE, F.W. (1845 - 1921)	100-1500	L,W

* Denotes watercolors, pastels, drawings, and/or mixed media

HEINZE, ADOLPH (1887 -)	50-800	L
HEITER, MICHAEL M. (1883 -)	100-1200	L
HEITH, V. (20TH C ?)	100-750	L
HEITLAND, WILMAT EMERTON (1893 -)	100-1500	X (F)
HEITZEL, GEORGE (1826 - 1906)	*100-400	L
HEIZER, MICHAEL (1944 -)	2000-20000	A
HEKKING, JOSEPH ANTONIO (active 1860-80)	800-20000	L
HELCK, PETER CLARENCE (1893 - 1988)	*400-4800	I
HELD, AL	*400-27500	
HELD, AL (1928 -)	5000-320000	A
HELD, JOHN (JR) (1889 - 1958)	*300-4000	I
HELDNER, KNUTE (1877 - 1952)	400-6100	X (L,G)
HELIKER, JOHN EDWARD (1909 -)	800-6500	A,I,L
HELLER, E. (20TH C)	200-1000	L
HELLER, JOHN M. (20TH C)	350-2500	X (I)
HELLER, S. (20TH C)	100-600	X
HELMICK, HOWARD (1845 - 1907)	400-4500	I
HENDERSON, LUIS (20TH C)	100-800	W
HENDERSON, WILLIAM PENHALLOW (1877 - 1943)	*400-5300	F,G
HENDRICKS, BESSIE (1867 - 1929)	200-1500	L
HENDRICKS, DAVID (20TH C)	*100-400	X (L)
HENDRIX, JIMI (1942 - 1970)	*2500-5500	A
HENNESSEY, FRANK C. (1894 - 1941)	*300-2800	L
HENNESSY, TIMOTHY (1925 -)	200-750	A
HENNESSY, WILLIAM JOHN (1839 - 1917)	500-30000	G,L,I
HENNINGS, ERNEST MARTIN	*450-17000	
HENNINGS, ERNEST MARTIN (1886 - 1956)	1000-80000	G,F,L
HENRI, ROBERT	*350-15000	
HENRI, ROBERT (1865 - 1929)	1000-175000 +	F,G
HENRICI, JOHN H. (1839 -)	250-4000	G,F
HENRY, EDWARD LAMSOM	*400-12700	
HENRY, EDWARD LAMSON (1841 - 1919)	700-195000 +	G,L,F
HENRY, HARRY R. (1882 - 1974)	500-7000	L
HENSCHE, HENRY (1901 -)	1100-1900	X (S)
HENSHAW, GLENN COOPER (1885 - 1946)	200-2500	L,M

HERBST, FRANK C. (20TH C)	200-1500	I
HERGENRODER, EMILE (19TH-20TH C)	100-700	X (F)
HERGESHEIMER, ELLA S. (1873 - 1943)	250-1200	F,S
HERGET, HERBERT (1885 - 1950)	900-8000	F,G,L
HERING, HARRY (1887 -)	100-800	G,F
HERKOMER, HERMAN G. (1863 -)	500-3000	G,F
HERMANN, FRANK S. (1866 - 1942)	*100-1000	X
HERNANDEZ, CAESAR (20TH C)	*500-2500	M
HERRERA, VELINO SHIJE (1902 - 1973)	*250-1200	X (L)
HERRICK, C.K. (19TH C)	300-1800	X (G,F)
HERRICK, HENRY W. (1824 - 1906)	*100-1400	L,F
HERRICK, MARGARET COX	*100-1000	
HERRICK, MARGARET COX (1865 - 1950)	200-1800	L,M,F,S
HERRING, LEE (20TH C)	100-1000	X (L,F)
HERRMANN, FRANK S. (1866 - 1942)	*350-2000	L
HERRMANN, NORBERT (1891 - 1966)	100-850	L
HERSCH, LEE F. (20TH C)	500-5000	L,F
HERTER, ADELE (1869 - 1953)	400-7500	F,S
HERTER, ALBERT	*900-6600	
HERTER, ALBERT (1871 - 1950)	2000-99000	F,G,L
HERZEL, PAUL (1876 -)	100-21000	I
HERZOG, FRANS M. (19TH-20TH C)	*50-750	F,L
HERZOG, HERMANN (1832 - 1932)	2000-70000	L,M
HERZOG, LOUIS (1868 -)	150-850	L
HERZOG, MAX (19TH-20TH C)	150-1000	X (S)
HESS, J.N. (late 19TH C)	400-2000	X (G)
HESS, SARA M. (1880 - 1960)	500-3500	L
HESSE, EVA (1936 - 1970)	*2500-110000	A
HESSELIUS, JOHN (1728 - 1778)	2500-45000	F
HESTHAL, WILLIAM J. (1908 -)	150-1500	I
HETHERINGTON, ALFRED (1868 -)	*100-600	L
HETHERINGTON, CHARLES (20TH C)	100-700	M
HETZEL, GEORGE (1826 - 1899)	450-15000	S,L,F
HEUEL, BOB (20TH C)	100-500	X (F)
HEUSTIS, LOUISE LYONS (B. 1878 -)	350-1500	F

* Denotes watercolors, pastels, drawings, and/or mixed media

HEWETT, EDWARD (1874 -)	150-650	X (A)
HEWINS, AMASA (1785 - 1855)	1000-6500	G,F,L
HIBBARD, ALDRO THOMPSON (1886 - 1972)	1000-17000	L
HIBBARD, MARSH (20TH C)	300-2800	M,L
HIBBARD, MARY (19TH-20TH C)	100-600	F,G
HIBEL, EDNA (1917 -)	400-6000	F
HICKOK, CONDE WILSON (19TH-20TH C)	400-2200	L
HICKS, EDWARD (1770 - 1849)	25000-671000+	P
HICKS, GEORGE (20TH C)	200-1000	X (L)
HICKS, MORLEY (1877 - 1959)	100-500	X (L,F)
HICKS, SIDNEY S. (19TH C)	*150-750	X (M)
HICKS, THOMAS (1823 - 1890)	500-11500+	F,L,G
HIDLEY, JOSEPH H. (1830 - 1872)	5000-80000	P
HIGGINS, CARLETON (1848 - 1932)	350-1800	L,G
HIGGINS, EUGENE	*100-1500	
HIGGINS, EUGENE (1874 - 1958)	250-6600	G,F,L
HIGGINS, GEORGE FRANK (active 1855-85)	350-3200	L
HIGGINS, WILLIAM VICTOR	*500-25000	
HIGGINS, WILLIAM VICTOR (1884 - 1949)	800-40000	L,F
HIGHWOOD, CHARLES (19TH-20TH C)	500-2000	L
HIKKIMG, J.A. (19TH C)	700-4000	X (L)
HILDA, E. BAILY (19TH-20TH C)	400-1800	X
HILDEBRANDT, HOWARD LOGAN (1872 - 1958)	400-6000	F,G,S
HILDEBRANT, CORNELIA E. (20TH C)	100-600	F
HILER, HILAIRE (1898 - 1966)	100-4200	L,G
HILL, ALBERT D. (1897 - 1898)	500-6000	L
HILL, ANDREW P. (19TH C)	350-1800	L,G
HILL, ANNA GILMAN (20TH C)	350-1500	L
HILL, ARTHUR TRUMBULL (1868 -)	500-2500	L,F
HILL, BESSIE M. (19TH C?)	400-3500	X (S)
HILL, CHARLES EMIL (1870 - 1953)	100-800	L
HILL, CHARLES W. (20TH C)	100-1000	L
HILL, EDWARD (1843 - 1923)	250-3200	L
HILL, EDWARD RUFUS (1852 - 1908)	300-5000	L,G
HILL, GEORGE S. (19TH C)	100-1000	G,F

HILL, HOMER (- 1968)	100-850	L,G
HILL, HOWARD (AC. 1860 -1870)	600-8500	W
HILL, JOHN HENRY (1839 - 1922)	*600-9000	L
HILL, JOHN WILLIAM	*800-9500+	
HILL, JOHN WILLIAM (1812 - 1879)	1000-30000	L,G,S
HILL, POLLY KNIPP (1900 -)	*100-900	X (I)
HILL, THOMAS (1829 - 1908)	1500-80000	L,F,S
HILL, W.R. (19TH C)	100-500	L
HILLBOM, HENRIK (1863 - 1928)	100-700	L
HILLERN, BERTHA VON (19TH C)	150-900	X (L)
HILLIARD, F. JOHN (1886 -)	400-2000	F
HILLIARD, WILLIAM HENRY (1863 - 1905)	300-3500	L,M,F
HILLINGS, JOHN (- 1894)	5000-38500	P
HILLS, ANNA ALTHEA (1882 - 1930)	400-6600	L,F
HILLS, LAURA COOMBS (1859 - 1952)	*800-32000+	S
HILLSMITH, FANNIE (1911 -)	150-4500	L
HILLYER, WILLIAM (JR.) (early 19TH C)	500-2000	F
HILTON, JOHN WILLIAM (1904 -)	400-3500	L
HILTON, ROY (19TH-20TH C)	500-4000	X
HINCKLEY, LAWRENCE (1900 -	100-800	L
HINCKLEY, THOMAS HEWES (1813 - 1896)	350-7500+	W,L,S
HIND, WILLIAM GEORGE R.(1833 - 1888)	*100-750	L
HINES, BOB (20TH C)	*100-600	X (W,L)
HINES, PAUL (19TH-20TH C)	300-1500	L,F
HINGER, H. (19TH C)	100-800	X (S)
HINKLE, CLARENCE KEISER	*100-750	
HINKLE, CLARENCE KEISER (1880 - 1960)	500-15000	M,L,S
HINKLEY, THOMAS HEWER (1813 - 1896)	6050	F
HINMAN, CHARLES (1932 -)	1000-18000	A
HINTERMEISTER, HENRY ("HY") (1897 -)	400-8800	I
HINTON, W.H. (20TH C)	200-900	I
HIRSCH, JOSEPH	*100-1100	
HIRSCH, JOSEPH (1910 - 1981)	500-25000	A,G,F,I
HIRSCH, STEFAN (1899 - 1964)	800-40000	A
HIRSCHBERG, CARL (1854 - 1923)	200-16500	L,F,M,S

* Denotes watercolors, pastels, drawings, and/or mixed media

HIRSCHFELD, ALBERT (1903 -)	*300-5000	I
HIRSH, ALICE (1888 - 1935)	200-1500	L,M
HIRSHFIELD, MORRIS (1872 - 1946)	5000-45000	P
HIRST, CLAUDE RAGUET	*400-17000	
HIRST, CLAUDE RAGUET (1855 - 1942)	1000-44000	G,S,M
HISLOP, ANDREW (20TH C)	100-600	X (F,G)
HITCH, SAMUEL (19TH C)	600-2000	F
HITCHCOCK, DAVID HOWARD (1861 - 1943)	350-5500	L,I
HITCHCOCK, GEORGE	*250-4500	
HITCHCOCK, GEORGE (1850 - 1913)	1500-66000	F,L,M
HITCHCOCK, LUCIUS WOLCOTT (1868 - 1942)	700-18000	L,F,I
HITCHINGS, HENRY (- 1903)	*100-2800	L
HITCHINS, JOSEPH (19TH C)	400-2000	X (L)
HITTELL, CHARLES JOSEPH (1861 - 1939)	300-4200	M,L
HOBART, CLARK	*100-900	
HOBART, CLARK (1880 - 1948)	200-16000	L
HOBBS, GEORGE THOMPSON (1846 -)	300-3500+	L
HOBBS, MORRIS HENRY (1892 -)	*200-1000	X
HOCKNEY, DAVID	*2500-210000	
HOCKNEY, DAVID (1937 -)	7000-2200000	A
HODGDON, L. W. (20TH C)	100-700	M
HODGDON, SYLVESTER PHELPS (1830 - 1906)	300-3500	L,F
HODGKIN, HOWARD (1932 -)	7000-506000	A
HODGKINS, A.W. (19TH-20TH C)	*100-600	L
HODGKINS, S. (19TH-20TH C)	100-600	L
HODRIDGE, R.D. (19TH-20TH C)	200-1200	L
HOEBER, ARTHUR (1854 - 1915)	500-7500	L,F
HOEGGER, AUGUSTUS (1848 - 1908)	100-850	X (S)
HOEN, L. (20TH C)	*100-500	L
HOERMAN, CARL (1885 -)	100-850	L
HOFF, MARGO (1912 -)	*200-1200	X
HOFFBAUER, CHARLES C. J.	*200-6500+	
HOFFBAUER, CHARLES C. J. (1875 - 1957)	900-40000+	M,F,G
HOFFMAN, ARNOLD (1886 - 1966)	250-2000	L
HOFFMAN, CHARLES (1821 - 1882)	15000-80000+	P (L)

HOFFMAN, FRANK B. (1888 - 1958)	600-3500	I
HOFFMAN, GUSTAVE A. (1869 - 1945)	50-3500	L,F
HOFFMAN, IRWIN D. (1901 -)	100-1000	X (F)
HOFFMAN, RICHARD P. (1911-)	*50-300	F
HOFFMAN, RONALD (20TH C)	50-300	X
HOFMAN, EARL FRANCIS (20TH C)	100-900	X (L)
HOFMANN, HANS	*500-64000	
HOFMANN, HANS (1880 - 1966)	6500-715000	A
HOFSTETTER, WILLIAM A. (1884 -)	*100-500	L
HOGAN, JEAN (20TH C)	100-600	X (M)
HOGG, A.W. (early 20TH C)	100-700	L
HOGNER, NILS (1893 -)	300-1700	G
HOIT, ALBERT GALLATIN (1809 - 1856)	500-11000	F,L
HOKINSON, HELEN E. (1893 - 1949)	*150-700	I
HOLBERG, RICHARD A.	*100-600	
HOLBERG, RICHARD A. (1889 - 1942)	150-1800	F,M
HOLBERG, RUTH LANGLAND (1891 -)	100-2000	L
HOLBERTON, WAKEMAN (1839 - 1898)	200-1200	L
HOLBROOK, L.T. (19TH C)	200-900	L
HOLCOMB, ALICE WHITE (20TH C)	200-2000	F,S
HOLDEN, JAMES ALBERT	*200-1200	
HOLDEN, JAMES ALBERT (19TH-20TH C)	100-1100	X (F,L)
HOLDEN, SCHUYLER (19TH C)	200-3200	X (L)
HOLDENSEN, PETER (20TH C)	100-1000	X (L)
HOLDING, JOHN (late 19TH C)	*100-400	X (I)
HOLDREDGE, RANSOME G. (1836 - 1899)	350-8500	L,F
HOLL, H.H. (19TH C)	100-1000	L
HOLLAND, A. (20TH C)	100-600	X (F)
HOLLAND, FRANCIS RAYMOND (1886 - 1934)	100-11000	L
HOLLAND, TOM (1936 -)	*500-9500	A
HOLLOWAY, CHARLES (1859 - 1941)	100-1400	X
HOLLOWAY, EDWARD STRATTON (- 1939)	250-1800	L,I
HOLMAN, LOUIS A. (1866 - 1939)	100-1500	L
HOLMER, CHARLES J. (20TH C)	100-600	X (M)
HOLMES, JOHN F. (20TH C)	200-1500	X

* Denotes watercolors, pastels, drawings, and/or mixed media

HOLMES, RALPH (1876 - 1963)	250-3200	L,I
HOLMES, ROSINDA SELLERS (20TH C)	100-600	X (F)
HOLMES, WILLIAM HENRY (1846 - 1933)	*200-7700	M,L,F
HOLMGREN, R. JOHN (1897 - 1963)	*100-1400	
HOLSLAG, EDWARD J. (1870 - 1925)	100-950	X
HOLST, LAURITS B. (1848 - 1934)	200-3500	M,L
HOLT, NELL (20TH C)	*200-800	G
HOLTY, CARL ROBERT	*350-4000	
HOLTY, CARL ROBERT (1900 - 1973)	800-8000	A
HOMER, WINSLOW	*3500-770000 +	
HOMER, WINSLOW (1836 - 1910)	10000-2000000	M,G,F,L,I
HONDIUS, GERRIT (1891 - 1970)	200-1500	F,L
HONDO, K. (20TH C)	*100-400	F
HOOD, GEORGE W. (1869-1949)	50-500	L
HOOPES, FLORENCE JANE (1895 - 1984)	100-1400	F,L
HOPE, JAMES	*100-600	
HOPE, JAMES (1818 - 1892)	900-15000	L,G,F
HOPE, THOMAS H. (- 1926)	750-5500	S,L
HOPKIN, ROBERT	*100-1500	
HOPKIN, ROBERT (1832 - 1909)	300-6000	M,L
HOPKINS, A. (19TH C)	*100-500	X (G,I)
HOPKINS, BUDD (1931 -)	400-3500	A
HOPKINS, C.E. (1886 -)	*100-600	L
HOPKINS, GEORGE E. (1855 -)	*200-1800	X (L)
HOPKINS, MILTON WILLIAM (1789 - 1844)	2000-38000 +	P
HOPKINS, PETER (1911 -)	500-5500	G,F
HOPKINSON, CHARLES SYDNEY	*200-3200	
HOPKINSON, CHARLES SYDNEY (1869 - 1965)	600-18000	F,L
HOPKINSON, HAROLD (20TH C)	200-1500	L
HOPPENRATH, C. (20TH C)	100-500	L
HOPPER, EDWARD	*1000-137500	
HOPPER, EDWARD (1882 - 1967)	6000-2420000	G,L
HOPPIN, THOMAS FREDERICK (1816 - 1872)	400-3000	G,I
HORD, DONAL (1902 - 1966)	*100-850	X (L)
HORNBY, LESTER GEORGE	*75-600	

HORNBY, LESTER GEORGE (1882 - 1956)	150-2500	L,M,F
HOROWITZ, LOUISE MCMAHON (20TH C)	100-500	G,M
HORSFALL, ROBERT BRUCE (1869 -)	*100-1100	X (W)
HORSFORD, A.J. (- 1877)	100-1600	X (L,F)
HORSTMEIER, ALBERT (20TH C)	400-6500	L,F
HORTER, EARL	*300-11000	
HORTER, EARL (1881 - 1940)	400-72000	S,L
HORTON, ELIZABETH S. (1902 -)	200-1000	G,L
HORTON, WILLIAM SAMUEL	*250-12100	
HORTON, WILLIAM SAMUEL (1865 - 1936)	600-40000 +	G,L,F,S
HOSKINS, GAYLE PORTER (1887 - 1962)	400-6000	I
HOUSE, HOWARD ELMER (1877 -)	*100-500	L
HOUSTON, FRANCES C.	*200-2000	
HOUSTON, FRANCES C. (1867 - 1906)	400-4500	F
HOUSTON, WILLIAM (19TH C)	400-5000	X (M,L)
HOVENDEN, THOMAS (1840 - 1895)	1000-35000	G,F
HOVSEPIAN, LEON (1915 -)	*150-1400	X (L)
HOW, KENNETH G. (1883 -)	150-3500	L,G
HOWARD, BESSIE JEANETTE K. (1872 -)	150-3400	L
HOWARD, CHARLES (1899 -)	400-3500	A
HOWARD, HENRY MOWBRAY (1873 -)	200-18000	M,L
HOWARD, HUGH HUNTINGTON (1860 - 1927)	100-1700	L
HOWARD, JOHN LANGLEY (1902 -)	400-8300	M,L,F,A
HOWARD, MARION (1883 -)	300-3500	L
HOWARD, NELLIE C. (1855 - 1956)	150-1200	L
HOWARD, ROBERT BOARDMAN (1896 - 1983)	*100-1000	X
HOWE, E.R. (19TH C)	100-800	L
HOWE, H.H. (20TH C)	100-600	M,L
HOWE, R.O. (19TH C)	100-800	L
HOWE, WILLIAM HENRY (1846 - 1929)	250-3000	L,G
HOWELL, FELICIE WALDO	*700-18000	
HOWELL, FELICIE WALDO (1897 - 1968)	900-27500	L,F,M
HOWELL, WILLIAM H. (1860 - 1925)	400-3000	L
HOWITT, JOHN NEWTON (1885 - 1958)	300-3000	I,L
HOWLAND, ALFRED CORNELIUS (1838 - 1909)	400-5000	G,L

* Denotes watercolors, pastels, drawings, and/or mixed media

HOWLAND, GEORGE	*100-800	
HOWLAND, GEORGE (1865 - 1928)	400-3500	F,L
HOWLAND, ISABELLA (1895 -)	*100-400	X
HOWLAND, JOHN DARE (19TH-20TH C)	500-4500	W,L
HOYLE, RAPHAEL (1804 - 1838)	600-5000	L
HUBACEK, WILLIAM (1866 - 1958)	200-4300+	L,S
HUBARD, WILLIAM JAMES (1807 - 1862)	3500-18000	F
HUBBARD, CHARLES (1801 - 1876)	250-4500	M,L
HUBBARD, F.M.B. (1869 - 1930)	200-1000	X (S)
HUBBARD, LYDIA M.B. (1849 - 1911)	200-2000	X (S)
HUBBARD, RICHARD WILLIAM (1816 - 1888)	400-5000	L,M,F
HUBBARD, WHITNEY MYRON (1875 -)	100-4500	L
HUBBELL, CHARLES H. (20TH C)	100-750	X
HUBBELL, HENRY SALEM (1870 - 1949)	700-38000	F
HUDDLE, REBA E. (20TH C)	100-600	G,F,L
HUDSON, CHARLES BRADFORD (1865 -)	200-2500	X (L)
HUDSON, CHARLES WILLIAM	*150-750	
HUDSON, CHARLES WILLIAM (1871 - 1943)	150-1650	L,F
HUDSON, ERIC ELMER FOREST (1862 -)	*100-850	X (G)
HUDSON, GRACE CARPENTER (1865 - 1937)	1000-56500	F,L
HUDSON, JOHN BRADLEY JR	*100-1000	
HUDSON, JOHN BRADLEY JR (1832 - 1903)	400-4500	L,G
HUDSON, KENNETH (1904 - 1988)	50-600	A
HUFFINGTON, JOHN C. (1864 - 1929)	*200-1200	M,L
HUGE, JURGAN FREDERICK (1809 - 1878)	*10000-35000	P
HUGENTOBLEN, E. J. (20TH C)	250-1800	L
HUGGINS, M.W. (20TH C)	100-500	L,S
HUGHES, DAISY MARGUERITTE (1883 - 1968)	100-7000	L
HUGHES, GEORGE (1907 - 1990)	200-5000	I
HULBERT, CHARLES ALLEN	*100-600	
HULBERT, CHARLES ALLEN (19TH-20TH C)	100-1800	L
HULBERT, KATHERINE ALLMOND (- 1937)	200-1500	L,S
HULDAH, (20TH C)	350-5000	F
HULINGS, CLARK (1922 -)	10000-145000	G,L,F
HULISTON, J.D. (early 20TH C)	100-500	L

HULLENKREMER, ODON (20TH C)	350-1200	X
HULTBERG, JOHN (1922 -)	*100-7500	A
HUMANN, O. VICTOR (20TH C)	300-2000	X (L)
HUMMELL, ANTHONY (20TH C)	*150-1000	X
HUMPHREY, MAUD (19TH-20TH C)	*200-1000	I
HUMPHREY, RALPH	*100-1500	
HUMPHREY, RALPH (1932 - 1990)	1000-25000	A
HUMPHREY, WALTER BEACH (1892 - 1952)	150-3500	I
HUMPHREYS, CHRALES S. (19TH C)	400-7000	X
HUNLEY, KATHERINE JONES (1883 - 1964)	200-1500	L,I
HUNT, CHARLES D. (1840 - 1914)	200-2800	L,F
HUNT, ESTHER (1875 - 1951)	*400-2500	X (F)
HUNT, HENRY P. (19TH C)	500-3500	L,G
HUNT, LYNN BOGUE	*300-11000	
HUNT, LYNN BOGUE (1878 - 1960)	500-9500	W,G,I
HUNT, SAMUEL VALENTINE (1803 - 1893)	500-3500	L,S
HUNT, THOMAS L. (1882 - 1938)	600-15000+	M,L
HUNT, WILLIAM MORRIS	*500-8500	
HUNT, WILLIAM MORRIS (1824 - 1879)	800-65000	F,L
HUNTER, CLEMENTINE (1886 - 1988)	250-5000	P
HUNTER, FRANCIS TIPTON (1896 - 1957)	*150-2500	I
HUNTER, FREDEICK LEO (1862 - 1943)	100-1600	M,L
HUNTER, ISABEL (1878 - 1941)	400-4500	L
HUNTER, JOHN YOUNG (1874 - 1955)	500-12000	X (G)
HUNTER, LIZBETH CLIFTON (1868 -)	*100-750	X (S)
HUNTER, MAX (19TH - 20HT C)	100-400	L
HUNTINGTON, C. LYMAN (19TH C)	200-850	X (F)
HUNTINGTON, D.W. (19TH-20TH C)	*100-3100	W,G
HUNTINGTON, DANIEL	*300-2400	F,G
HUNTINGTON, DANIEL (1816 - 1906)	900-26400	F,G
HUNTINGTON, ELIZABETH H. T.(1878 - 1963)	150-750	L,M
HUNTINGTON, JIM (1941 -)	600-4500	A
HURD, L. FRED (19TH C)	*150-1400	X (M,L)
HURD, PETER	*400-18000	
HURD, PETER (1904 - 1984)	1000-30500	L,I,G

* Denotes watercolors, pastels, drawings, and/or mixed media

Artist	Prices	Subject
HURDLE, GEORGE LINTON (1868 - 1922)	*100-850	L
HURLEY, WILSON (1924 -)	500-25000	L
HURST, EARL O. (1895 - 1958)	*50-400	X
HURTING, J.D. (19TH-20TH C)	*100-400	L
HURTT, ARTHUR R. (1861 -)	250-1500	L,I
HUSTON, WILLIAM (late 19TH C)	500-3800	L
HUTCHENS, FRANK TOWNSEND (1869 - 1937)	350-7000+	F,L
HUTCHINS, A. (20TH C)	100-850	G,I,M
HUTCHINSON, D.C. (1869 - 1954)	100-1500	I
HUTCHISON, ELLEN WALES (1867 - 1937)	150-1500	L
HUTCHISON, FREDERICK W.(1871 - 1953)	200-4400	L
HUTT, HENRY (1875 - 1950)	*150-1200	I
HUTTY, ALFRED HEBER (1877 - 1954)	*300-4000	G,L
HUWITSIT, JESSE (20TH C)	100-800	L
HYDE, H. H. (20TH C)	100-1000	X (S)
HYDE, LELAND (20TH C)	50-600	L
HYDE, WILLIAM HENRY (1858 - 1943)	200-2600	F,L
HYND, FREDERICK S.	*100-600	
HYND, FREDERICK S. (1905 -)	200-2000	M,F
HYNEMAN, HERMAN N. (1859 - 1907)	600-6500	F,S
HYNEMAN, JULIA (19TH-20TH C)	250-1000	L

I

Artist	Prices	Subject
IDELL, MARGARET C. (20TH C)	*100-400	L,M
IGNATIEV, ALEXANDER (1913 -)	300-3600	M,L
ILIGAN, RALPH W. (20TH C)	300-2000	X (L)
ILLAWAY, H. (19TH C)	100-700	L
ILSLEY, FREDERICK JULIAN (1855 - 1933)	200-900	L,M
ILYIN, CALEB (20TH C)	100-700	X
ILYIN, PETER (1887 - 1958)	200-1100	L,M
IMHOF, JOSEPH A. (1871 - 1955)	*250-6500	F,G

INDIANA, ROBERT CLARK (1928 -)	4500-105000	A
INGALLS, WALTER J. (1805 - 1874)	250-1500	F,S,G
INGEMANN, KEITH (20TH C)	300-2500	X
INGEN, HENRY A. VAN (1833 - 1899)	500-4800	L,W
INGERLE, RUDOLPH F. (1879 - 1950)	350-2700	L,G
INGHAM, CHARLES CROMWELL (1796 - 1863)	600-2000	F
INGHAM, ELIZABETH H. (19TH-20TH C)	*200-1500	X (M)
INGHAM, WILLIAM (active 1855-1860)	700-4800	F,S
INGLIS, ANTOINETTE (1880 -)	100-1500	L
INGLIS, JOHN J. (1867 - 1946)	100-1000	X (M)
INMAN, HENRY (1801 - 1846)	350-15000	F,L,G
INMAN, JOHN O'BRIEN (1828 - 1896)	400-11000	G,F,S
INNESS, GEORGE (1825 - 1894)	1200-500000+	L
INNESS (JR), GEORGE (1853 - 1926)	300-12100	L
INSLEY, ALBERT B. (1842 - 1937)	350-6600	L
INUKAI, KYOHEI (1913 - 1985)	400-11000+	A
IPCAR, DAHLOV (1917 -)	*100-2200	X
IPSEN, ERNEST LUDWIG (1869 - 1951)	400-11000	F
IRELAND, LEROY (1889 -)	400-3000	G,S,F
IRVINE, WILSON HENRY	*200-3500	
IRVINE, WILSON HENRY (1869 - 1936)	1500-53000	F,L,M
IRVING, JOHN BEAUFAIN (1826 - 1877)	600-3500	F,G
IRWIN, BENONI (1840-1896)	250-2000	X (F)
IRWIN, ROBERT (1928 -)	5000-95000	A
IRWIN, WILLIAM HYDE (1903 -)	100-1500	X (F)
ISENBURGER, ERIC (1902 -)	150-3500	L
ISHAM, SAMUEL (1855 - 1914)	200-3000	F
ISHMAEL, WOODI (1914 -)	*100-1500	X
ISOM, GRAHAM (20TH C)	50-600	X
ISRAEL, MARVIN (20TH C)	*50-200	X
ITLEY, PAUL (20TH C)	100-500	L,M
ITO, MIYOKO (1918 -)	*100-1800	L
ITTNER, RICHARD R. (20TH C)	*100-600	X (W)
IVANOWSKI, SIGISMUND (1875 - 1944)	600-11000	F,L
IVES, FREDERICK EUGENE (1856 - 1937)	250-1000	F

* Denotes watercolors, pastels, drawings, and/or mixed media

IVES, PERCY (1864 - 1928)	250-4500	G,F

J

Artist	Prices	Subject
JACKMAN, REVA (1892 - 1966)	150-5000	X (M)
JACKMAN, WINIFRED (20TH C)	100-900	X (L)
JACKSON, ANNIE HURLBURT (1877 -)	*300-3000	S,L
JACKSON, CHARLES AKERMAN (1857 -)	100-850	L
JACKSON, CLIFFORD (1923 -)	100-700	L
JACKSON, ELBERT McGRAN (1896 - 1962)	300-4500	I
JACKSON, ELIZABETH LESLEY (1867 - 1934)	*100-600	M,L
JACKSON, HERBERT W. (19TH-20TH C)	200-900	F
JACKSON, JOHN EDWIN (1876-)	*100-800	X (M)
JACKSON, LEE (1909 -)	400-3800	G,L
JACKSON, LUCY ATKINS (19TH-20TH C)	300-1500	X (G)
JACKSON, MARIAN W. (20TH C)	*100-500	L
JACKSON, MARTIN JACOB (1871 - 1955)	100-1100	F,L
JACKSON, ROBERT (1891 -)	150-1400	X (F)
JACKSON, ROBERT L. (20TH C)	100-450	X
JACKSON, WILLIAM FRANKLIN (1850 - 1936)	300-7500	L
JACKSON, WILLIAM H. (1832 -)	*250-2500	L
JACKSON, WILLIAM HENRY (1843-1942)	9350	L
JACOB, NED	*900-4500	
JACOB, NED (1938 -)	5000-30000	G,F
JACOBS, MICHEL (1877 - 1958)	300-3500	F,S,L
JACOBS, MILNE (early 20TH C)	100-1800	L
JACOBS, TED SETH (1927 -)	200-6000	F
JACOBSEN, ANTONIO NICOLO GASPARA	*800-6000	
JACOBSEN, ANTONIO NICOLO GASPARA (1850 - 1921)	1200-45000+	M
JACOBSON, OSCAR BROUSSE (1882 - 1934)	150-1500	M,L,G
JAHAM, M.DE (20TH C)	100-600	G

JAHNKE, WILLIAM (1937 -)	100-400	X (L)
JAKOBSEN, KATHERINE (1952 -)	6000-17000	P
JAMBOR, LOUIS (1884 - 1954)	600-28000	G,F
JAMES, ALICE ARCHER SEWALL (1870 - 1955)	100-1000	X (L)
JAMES, FREDERICK (1845 - 1907)	500-6000	X (F)
JAMES, H. (19TH C)	*300-1500	X
JAMES, JOHN W. (20TH C)	100-1200	X (M,L)
JAMES, WILLIAM (19TH-20TH C)	200-1200	X (F)
JAMESON, JOHN (1842 - 1864)	500-5500	L
JAMIESON, MITCHELL (1915 -)	50-1400	L
JAMISON, PHILIP (1925 -)	*200-4000	L,S
JANSEN, LEO (20TH C)	100-400	X (F)
JANSSON, ALFRED (1863 - 1931)	300-5000	L
JARVIS, JOHN WESLEY (1780 - 1840)	600-35000+	F
JAUDON, VALERIE	*100-1100	
JAUDON, VALERIE (1945 -)	900-42000	A
JECT-KEY, D. WU (20TH C)	100-500	X (L)
JEFFERSON, JOSEPH IV (1829 - 1905)	250-2000	L
JEN, PANG (20TH C)	100-400	F
JENKINS, BURRIS (JR) (1897 - 1966)	*100-700	X
JENKINS, CHARLES WALDO (1820 -)	600-1500	F
JENKINS, GEORGE WASHINGTON (1816 - 1907)	250-35000	G,F,L,S
JENKINS, HANNAH T. (1855 - 1927)	50-750	M,L
JENKINS, J. LeBRUN (1876 - 1951)	150-850	L,G
JENKINS, JOHN ELLIOT (1868 -)	100-600	L
JENKINS, PAUL	*300-10000	
JENKINS, PAUL (1923 -)	1000-65000	A
JENNEY, NEIL (1945 -)	10000-210000	A
JENNIN, JONATHAN (active 1830-40)	*1500-5500	P
JENNINGS, RICHARD (19TH C)	800-3500	F
JENNYS, WILLIAM (active 1795-1805)	1500-20000	P
JENSEN, ALFRED J.	*100-7500	
JENSEN, ALFRED J.(1903 - 1983)	2500-80000	A
JENSEN, GEORGE (1878 -)	200-2500	L
JENSEN, HOLGER H. (1880 -)	200-2000	L

   * Denotes watercolors, pastels, drawings, and/or mixed media

JENSEN, THOMAS M. (1831 - 1916)	300-1800	X (F,M)
JERREMS, LENORE S. (20TH C)	*50-550	X (S)
JEWELL, ELIZABETH G. (1874 - 1956)	300-1500	M,S
JEWETT, WILLIAM SMITH (1812 - 1873)	2000-45000	L
JEX, GARNET W. (1895 - 1979)	150-1200	L,G
JICHA, JOE (20TH C ?)	100-500	L
JOCELYN, NATHANIEL (1796 - 1881)	150-4000	L,F,G
JOHANSEN, JEAN MCLANE (1878 - 1964)	1000-10000+	F
JOHANSEN, JOHN CHRISTIEN (1876 - 1966)	250-8700	L,G
JOHNS, CLARENCE M. (1843 - 1925)	400-4500	L
JOHNS, JASPER	*100-55000	
JOHNS, JASPER (1930 -)	*10000-15500000+	A
JOHNS, JOSEPH W.	*5000-75000	
JOHNS, JOSEPH W. (1833 - 1877)	2500-12000	L,G
JOHNSON, ARTHUR (1874 - 1954)	700-6000	F,L
JOHNSON, AVERY F. (1906 -)	*200-2000	I
JOHNSON, BEN (1902 -)	900-3000	A
JOHNSON, CAROLINE R. (19TH-20TH C)	150-1000	F
JOHNSON, CHARLES HOWARD (20TH C)	*500-1500	I
JOHNSON, CLARENCE R. (1894 - 1981)	10000-121000	L
JOHNSON, CLINTON (20TH C)	100-600	L
JOHNSON, CONTENT (- 1949)	200-1500	L,G
JOHNSON, DAVID	*100-5250	
JOHNSON, DAVID (1827 - 1908)	1000-165000	L
JOHNSON, EASTMAN	*2500-110000	
JOHNSON, EASTMAN (1824 - 1906)	750-375000	G,F
JOHNSON, EDVARD ARTHUR (1911 -)	800-5000	A
JOHNSON, FRANCIS NORTON (1878 - 1931)	200-1000	X
JOHNSON, FRANK TENNEY	*400-3500	
JOHNSON, FRANK TENNEY (1874 - 1939)	2500-140000 +	F,G,I
JOHNSON, GORDON	*100-2000	
JOHNSON, GORDON (1924 - 1989)	400-2500	I
JOHNSON, GUY (1927 -)	250-3000	A
JOHNSON, HARVEY (1920 -)	3000-28000	G
JOHNSON, HORACE (1820 - 1890)	100-950	F,G

JOHNSON, J. (19TH C)	500-2500	M
JOHNSON, J.W.A. (19TH-20TH C)	250-5500	X (W)
JOHNSON, JOSHUA (active 1800-1824)	5000-150000+	P (F)
JOHNSON, LESTER	*500-8500	
JOHNSON, LESTER (1919 -)	1000-31000	A
JOHNSON, LUCAS (1940 -)	300-1200	A
JOHNSON, MARSHALL (1850 - 1921)	800-13000	M
JOHNSON, PAUL (20TH C)	*100-600	X
JOHNSON, RAYMOND (1927 -)	5000-70000	A
JOHNSON, ROY (1890-1963)	100-700	F
JOHNSON, SAMUEL FROST (1835 -)	400-5000	X (S)
JOHNSON, WILLIAM H.	*350-15500	
JOHNSON, WILLIAM H. (1901 - 1980)	150-6600	X
JOHNSTON, DAVID C. (1797 - 1867)	400-5000	X (I)
JOHNSTON, JONATHAN EASTMAN (1824 - 1906)	400-5000+	F,L
JOHNSTON, FRANK HANS (1888-1949)	200-2600	L
JOHNSTON, FREDERIC J. (1890 -)	100-700	L
JOHNSTON, JOHN (1753 - 1818)	650-34100	F
JOHNSTON, JOHN HUMPHREYS (1857 - 1941)	400-3500	L
JOHNSTON, JOHN R. (active 1850-75)	500-4000	F,L
JOHNSTON, REUBEN LE GRANDE (1850 - 1914)	250-3200	L,W
JOHNSTON, RICHARD T. (20TH C)	100-650	L
JOHNSTON, ROBERT E. (1885 - 1933)	300-7200	I
JOHONNOT, RAPLH H. (1880 - 1940)	300-900	L
JOINER, HARVEY (1852 - 1932)	400-2800	L
JOLLEY, MARTIN GWILT (1859 -)	100-1100	X (F)
JOLLY, WADE L. (1909 -)	100-500	L
JONES, F. EASTMAN (19TH C)	350-1500	L,W
JONES, FRANCIS COATES	*100-14000	
JONES, FRANCIS COATES (1857 - 1932)	750-48000	F,G
JONES, GRACE CHURCH (20TH C)	200-1000	X (F)
JONES, HUGH BOLTON	*100-2500	
JONES, HUGH BOLTON (1848 - 1927)	800-31000	L
JONES, J. WATKINS (19TH C)	100-500	X (F)
JONES, JOE (or JOSEPH JOHN) (1909 - 1963)	1000-20000+	G,F

JONES, LEON FOSTER (1871 - 1940)	300-3500	L
JONES, MARY B. (1868 - 1924)	200-2500	L
JONES, MARY E.H. (mid 19TH C)	*300-1200	P
JONES, NORA (20TH C)	*100-600	X (F)
JONES, PAUL (1860 -)	450-2800	W,F
JONES, ROBERT (1926 -)	*50-250	X
JONES, ROBERT EDMOND (1887 -)	*400-4500	I
JONES, SETH C. (1853 - 1930)	*100-1000	I
JONES, SUSAN (1897 -)	250-1200	X (I,S)
JONES, WELL CHOATE (1879 -)	100-1200	L,F,S
JONES, WILLIAM F. (19TH C)	1200-8000	W,G
JONNEVOLD, CARL HENRIK (1856 - 1930)	250-3000	L
JONNIAUX, ALFRED (1882 -)	350-19000	F
JONSON, RAYMOND (1891 - 1982)	1000-71000	A
JONTINEL, J.H.R. (19TH C)	500-3000	X (L)
JORDAN, ANDREW (20TH C)	*50-650	X
JORDAN, GUS (19TH-20TH C)	350-1800	X (M)
JORDAN, MARGUERITE (20TH C)	*100-900	X (F)
JORDAN, SAMUEL (19TH C)	800-2800	F
JORGENSEN, CHRISTIAN	*200-5000	
JORGENSEN, CHRISTIAN (1860 - 1935)	400-4800	L,M
JORGENSON, WILLIAM (20TH C)	400-1800	X (G)
JOSEPH, RICHARD (20TH C)	800-4500	A
JOSEPHI, ISAAC (19TH-20TH C)	450-1800	L,F
JOUETT, F.S. (19TH C)	350-2500	X (M)
JOUETT, MATTHEW HARRIS (1787 - 1827)	400-10000	F
JOULLIN, AMEDEE (1862 - 1917)	350-5500	F,G
JOULLIN, LUCILLE (1876-1924)	100-800	L
JOY, ROBERT (1901 -)	300-2500	L
JOYCE, MARSHALL W. (20TH C)	150-1000	X (F)
JOYLES, C.S. (19TH C)	300-1200	X (M)
JUDD, DONALD (1928 -)	*600-5000	A
JUDSON, ALICE (- 1948)	300-3500	L,M
JUDSON, C. CHAPEL (1864 -)	100-800	L, M
JUDSON, MINNIE LEE (1865 - 1938)	100-2500	L

JUDSON, WILLIAM LEES	*200-1200	
JUDSON, WILLIAM LEES (1842 - 1928)	400-4000	L,G,F
JUERGENS, ALFRED (1866 - 1934)	200-7000	F,M,L
JULES, MERVIN (1912 -)	50-950	G,F
JULIEN, MARVIN (1894 -)	50-450	X (S)
JUNG, CARL S. (1880 -)	*50-300	M,L

K

Artist	Prices	Subject
KACERE, JOHN C. (1920 -)	5000-33000	A
KACZUROWSKI, MICHAEL (20TH C)	*100-500	L
KAELIN, CHARLES SALIS	*300-6000	
KAELIN, CHARLES SALIS (1858 - 1929)	400-13500	M,L
KAESELAU, CHARLES (1889 -)	*50-350	L,M
KAHILL, JOSEPH B. (1882 - 1957)	300-1500	F
KAHLER, CARL (1855 -)	400-18000	X (W)
KAHN, WOLF (1927 -)	1000-18000	A,L
KALBFUS, GEORGE (19TH C)	1000-6500	G,F
KALI, MRS. HENRYK WEYNEROWSKI (20TH C)	200-1200	X (F)
KALIN, VICTOR (1919 -)	250-1500	I
KALISKI, HENRY (19TH C)	300-4500	L
KALLEM, HENRY (1912 -)	100-600	X
KALMENOFF, MATTHEW (1905 -)	250-1200	L
KAMP, ANTON	*100-400	
KAMP, ANTON (20TH C)	150-1700	X (L,S)
KAMY, BERNARD (20TH C)	50-500	M,L
KANE, JOHN (1860 - 1934)	1500-28000	G,F,L
KANE, THEODORA (1906 -)	*100-500	L
KANTOR, MORRIS	*150-1000	
KANTOR, MORRIS (1896 - 1974)	200-2000	A
KAPPES, ALFRED (1850 - 1894)	500-10000	G,F
KAPPES, KARL A. (1861 - 1943)	100-1000	L

KARAWINA, ERICA (1904 -)	*75-450	X
KARFIOL, BERNARD	*100-1000	
KARFIOL, BERNARD (1886 - 1952)	500-5500	F,L,M
KAROLY-SZANTO, (20TH C?)	*100-600	X
KARRAS, SPIRO JOHN (1897 -)	200-1800	L
KARTOCHVILL, STEPHEN (1876 -)	250-2500	L
KATZ, ALEX	*4000-14500	
KATZ, ALEX (1927 -)	6000-121000	A
KATZ, RAYMOND A. (1895 - 1974)	50-450	G,F
KATZENSTEIN, IRVING (1902 -)	100-600	L
KAUFFMANN, GEORGE F. (19TH C)	*100-400	X (F)
KAUFFMANN, ROBERT (1893 -)	200-1500	I
KAUFMANN, FERDINAND (1864 - 1942)	700-13000	M,L
KAUFMANN, THEODORE (1814 - 1887/90)	5000-45000	G
KAULA, LEE LUFKIN (1865 - 1957)	500-32000	F,L
KAULA, WILLIAM JURIAN (1871 - 1953)	500-20000+	L,M
KAUMEYER, G.F. (20TH C)	100-700	L
KAUTZKY, TED	*200-1000	
KAUTZKY, TED (20TH C)	200-2200	L
KAY, GERTRUDE (20TH C)	*150-600	X (L)
KAYE, OTIS (1885 - 1974)	2000-46000	S
KAYN, HILDE BAND (1906 - 1950)	200-1200	X (G)
KAZ, NATHANIEL (1917 -)	*100-500	X
KEANE, FRANK (1876 -)	50-350	L
KEARL, STANLEY (20TH C)	100-450	X (F)
KEAST, SUSETTE SCHULTZ (1892 - 1932)	250-3000	L
KEEGAN, MARIE (1941 -)	2750	P
KEEP, A.L. (20TH C)	100-400	X (L)
KEFFER, FRANCES (1881 - 1953)	200-1000	W,L
KEIFFER, EDWIN L. (1921 -)	300-1500	X (L)
KEINHOLZ, EDWARD (1927-)	*100-2200	A
KEITH, CASTLE (1863 - 1927)	200-2200	L
KEITH, ELIZABETH (1887 -)	500-4800	X (S)
KEITH, WILLIAM (1839 - 1911)	800-32000	L,F
KELLER, ARTHUR IGNATIUS (1866 - 1925)	*200-3500	I

KELLER, CHARLES FREDERICK (19TH-20TH C)	200-1000	L
KELLER, CLYDE LEON (1872 - 1961)	200-1800	L,M
KELLER, EDGAR M. (1868 - 1932)	200-5500	L
KELLER, HENRY GEORGE	*100-1200	
KELLER, HENRY GEORGE (1869 - 1949)	300-3000	L,G,S
KELLEY, RAMON (1939 -)	*400-15000	X
KELLOGG, HARRY J. (19TH C)	300-2500	X (S)
KELLOGG, MARY KILBORNE (1814 - 1889)	150-650	X (L)
KELLOGG, NOAH J. (19TH C)	100-600	L
KELLY, CLAY (19TH-20TH C)	100-400	X (F)
KELLY, ELLSWORTH	*4000-36000	
KELLY, ELLSWORTH (1923 -)	10000-715000	A,F,S
KELLY, FRANCIS ROBERT (1927 -)	200-1500	X
KELLY, GRACE VERONICA (1884 -)	*100-750	X (F)
KELLY, J. REDDING (1868 - 1939)	150-900	F,L
KELLY, LEON	*150-1800	
KELLY, LEON (1901 -)	100-3200	F,L,M,S
KELPE, PAUL	*100-3200	
KELPE, PAUL (1902 - 1985)	4000-20000 +	A
KELSEY, C. (19TH C)	1500-5400	P (F)
KEMBLE, EDWARD WINDSOR (1861 - 1933)	*100-4700	I
KEMP, OLIVER (1887 - 1934)	400-12000	I
KEMPER, HENRY W. (19TH C)	600-4500	L,F
KEMPTON, ELMIRA (1892 -)	100-900	X
KENDALL, KATE (- 1915)	*100-900	X (M)
KENDALL, MARIE BOENING (1885 - 1953)	100-1000	L
KENDALL, WILLIAM SERGEANT (1869 - 1938)	800-8000 +	F
KENDRICK, DANIEL (20TH C)	100-500	X
KENNEDY, DAVID (1816 - 1898)	*5000-15000	P (L)
KENNEDY, EDWARD L. (20TH C)	100-900	X (M)
KENNEDY, S.J. (1877 -)	100-1000	L,F,S
KENNEDY, WILLIAM W. (1817 - 1870)	1500-12000 +	P (F)
KENNICOTT, ROBERT (1892 - 1983)	300-1500	A,F
KENNON, C.H. (19TH C)	100-600	L
KENSETT, JOHN FREDERICK	*100-1500	

KENSETT, JOHN FREDERICK (1816 - 1872)	1500-310000+	M,L
KENSIL, WILLIAM H. (19TH C)	400-1500	X (S)
KENT, H.H. (19TH C)	200-2400	L
KENT, ROCKWELL	*350-7200	
KENT, ROCKWELL (1882 - 1971)	900-65000	L,F,I
KENYON, HENRY (1861 - 1926)	250-2000	L
KEPES, GYORGY (1906 -)	400-3100	A
KEPLINGER, LONA MILLER (1876 - 1956)	*150-700	X (M)
KEPPLER, JOSEPH (1838 - 1894)	*100-850	I
KERFOOT, MARGARET (1901 -)	*100-500	X (M)
KERKAM, EARL	*100-600	
KERKAM, EARL (1890 - 1965)	150-2000	A,F
KERN, HERMAN (1839 - 1912)	400-7500	G,F
KERNAN, JOSEPH F. (1878 - 1958)	400-7000	I
KERR, H.M. (19TH C)	200-750	X (S)
KERR, VERNON (20TH C)	100-1000	M,L,S
KESTER, LENARD (1917 -)	100-850	X (L)
KESZTHEYLYI, ALEXANDER SAMUEL (1874-1953)	1430	L
KETT, EMILE (1838 - 1880)	400-3500	L,S
KEY, JOHN ROSS (1832 - 1920)	500-32000+	L
KEY, MABEL (1874 - 1926)	*400-6500	X (S)
KEYES, BERNARD M. (1898 - 1973)	300-2700	L,W
KIENBUSCH, WILLIAM A. (1914 -)	300-1000	X
KIENHOLZ, EDWARD	*200-2200	
KIENHOLZ, EDWARD (1927 -)	1500-44000	A
KIESALAK, J. (19TH C)	300-1000	X (L)
KIHN, WILLIAM LANGDON (1898 - 1957)	1500-12000	L,F
KILEY, GLENN (19TH C)	100-400	X (L)
KILLGORE, CHARLES P. (20TH C)	200-2100	L
KILM, WILFRED LANGDON (1898 -)	200-3500	F,L
KILPATRICK, AARON EDWARD (1872 - 1953)	250-5500	L
KILVERT, B. CORY (1881 - 1946)	*100-1500	I,M
KIMBALL, CHARLES FREDERICK	*100-600	
KIMBALL, CHARLES FREDERICK (1835 - 1907)	250-18700	L,M
KIMBEL, RICHARD M. (1865 - 1942)	350-3100	L,M

KING, ALBERT F. (1854 - 1945)	300-25000	S,L
KING, CHARLES BIRD	*300-5500	
KING, CHARLES BIRD (1785 - 1862)	1000-122000+	F,G,S
KING, EMMA B. (20TH C)	300-1500	X (G)
KING, GEORGE W. (1836 - 1922)	400-5000	L
KING, HAMILTON (1871 - 1952)	*100-800	I
KING, JOE (20TH C)	400-1800	F
KING, PAUL (1867 - 1947)	400-13500	L,M
KINGMAN, CHARLES R. (1895 -)	*100-500	X (L)
KINGMAN, DONG M. (1911 - 1985)	*400-27000	A,I,L
KINGSBURY, EDWARD R. (- 1940)	200-1800	L,M
KINGSTEIN, JONAH (1923 -)	100-400	X
KINGWOOD, CHARLES (20TH C)	*100-500	X (L)
KINKADE, THOMAS (1947 -)	400-5000	L
KINNARD, H. (19TH-20TH C)	100-500	X (M)
KINSELLA, JAMES (1857 - 1923)	100-850	L
KINSEY, ALBERTA (1875 - 1955)	100-5200	F
KINSTLER, EVERETT RAYMOND	*400-8800	
KINSTLER, EVERETT RAYMOND (1926 -)	1000-50000	I
KIPNESS, ROBERT (1931 -)	200-3100	X (A)
KIRK, ELIZABETH (1866 -)	100-750	L
KIRK, RICHARD (20TH C)	100-400	X
KIRKPATRICK, FRANK LE BRUN (1853 - 1917)	500-4500	F,G,I
KIRKPATRICK, WILLIAM A. (1880 -)	250-3500	F,I
KIRMSE, MARGUERITE (1885 - 1954)	*200-800	I
KIRTLEY, F.W. (19TH C)	100-700	L
KISSACK, R.A. (1878 -)	*100-500	F
KISSEL, ELEANORA (1891 - 1966)	250-4000	L,S
KITAJ, RONALD BROOKS	*27500	
KITAJ, RONALD BROOKS (1932 -)	5000-330000+	A
KITCHELL, HUDSON MINDELL (1862 - 1944)	100-2800	L,M
KITCHELL, JOSEPH GRAY (1862 -)	150-1200	L
KITCHEN, TELLA (1902 -)	4700	P
KITELL, ROBERT (20TH C)	100-400	X (I)
KITTELL, NICHOLAS BIDDLE (1822 - 1894)	200-4000	L,F

226   * Denotes watercolors, pastels, drawings, and/or mixed media

KIVETT, B. CORY (20TH C)	200-900	X
KLACKNER, C. (19TH C)	400-2500	X (G)
KLAGSTAD, ARNOLD (1898 -)	100-500	X (L)
KLEBE, GENE (1907 -)	*150-1400	G,M
KLEEMAN (KLEMANN?), RON (1937 -)	1000-22000	A
KLEIN, KATHY M. (20TH C)	*100-500	L
KLEIN, M.J. (20TH C)	100-300	X (L)
KLEINHOLTZ, FRANK (1901 -)	100-1000	X (L)
KLEITSCH, JOSEPH (1885 - 1931)	2500-78000	F,L
KLEMPNER, ERNEST S. (1867 - 1962)	500-3500	F,I
KLEY, HEINRICH (1863 - 1945)	*900-7500	I
KLINE, FRANZ	*1200-155000	
KLINE, FRANZ (1910 - 1962)	4500-2860000 +	A
KLINKER, ORPHA (1891 - 1964)	100-800	L,M
KLIREN, H.C. (20TH C)	100-400	L
KLITGAARD, GEORGINA (1893 -)	*150-2600	S,L
KLOSS, F. (20TH C)	*200-1000	X (L)
KLOTZ, EDWARD (20TH C)	100-400	L
KLUMPKE, ANNA ELISABETH (1856 - 1942)	*500-6000	F
KLUMPP, GUSTAV (1902 -1980)	1000-7500	P
KNAP, JOSEPH DAY (1875 -)	*200-1500	W,I
KNAPER, G.H. (20TH C ?)	100-500	X (L)
KNAPP, CHARLES W. (1822 - 1900)	450-27000	L
KNATHS, KARL OTTO	*100-1800	
KNATHS, KARL OTTO (1891 - 1971)	450-13500	A
KNEEDLER, J. (20TH C)	100-500	X
KNIGHT, CHARLES ROBERT (1874 - 1953)	*200-5000	W,L
KNIGHT, CLAYTON (1891 - 1969)	*100-700	I
KNIGHT, DANIEL RIDGWAY	*600-8800	
KNIGHT, DANIEL RIDGWAY (1839 - 1924)	2500-75000	F,G
KNIGHT, JOHN A. (1825 -)	100-750	M,L
KNIGHT, LOUIS ASTON (1873 - 1948)	700-31000	L
KNOBLAUCH, L.V. (20TH C)	100-500	X (S)
KNOLL, LEON (1884 - 1975)	200-1500	X (L)
KNOPF, NELLIE AUGUSTA (1875 - 1962)	100-850	M,L

* Denotes watercolors, pastels, drawings, and/or mixed media   227

KNOWLES, FARQUHAR MCGILLVRAY	*100-800	
KNOWLES, FARQUHAR MCGILLVRAY (1860 - 1932)	350-5000	M,L,I
KNOWLES, JOSEPH (20TH C)	*100-500	L,M,G
KNOWLTON, HELEN MARY (1832 - 1913)	150-1000	L
KNOX, FRANK (20TH C)	*100-600	X (L)
KNOX, JAMES (1866 -)	100-4400	X (L)
KNOX, SUSAN RICKER (1875 - 1959)	150-5400	F
KOCH, GERD (1929 -)	100-600	X (L)
KOCH, JOHN (1909 - 1978)	2500-363000	F,S,G
KOCH, PYKE (1901 -)	2500-32000	X
KOCH, SAMUEL (1887 -)	100-900	X (S)
KOCHER, FRITZ (1904 - 1973)	100-1100	M
KOCHER, MARY (20TH C)	100-500	X (L)
KOEHLER, PAUL R. (1875 - 1909)	200-2000	L
KOEHLER, ROBERT (1850 - 1917)	300-15000	F
KOENIGER, WALTER (1881 - 1945)	400-18000	L
KOERNER, HENRY (1915 -)	1000-47500+	A,F,G
KOERNER, P.K. (19TH C)	100-500	X (L)
KOERNER, WILLIAM HENRY D. (1878 - 1938)	1000-45000	I
KOHLER, WILLIAM EIFFE V.R. (19TH C)	300-1500	X (L)
KOLLNER, AUGUSTUS (1813 - 1870)	*300-2000	M,L
KOLLOCK, MARY (1840 - 1911)	500-3500	L,F,S
KOONING, ELAINE DE	*100-850	
KOONING, ELAINE DE (1920 - 1989)	600-8500	A
KOONING, WILLEM DE	*3000-800000+	
KOONING, WILLEM DE (1904 - 1988)	7500-3630000+	A
KOOPMAN, AUGUSTUS (1869 - 1914)	300-1500	X (L)
KOOPMAN, JOHN R. (1881 - 1949)	*100-600	X (L,M)
KOPF, MAXIM (20TH C)	100-500	X
KOPMAN, BENJAMIN D. (1887 - 1965)	200-2400	F,G
KOPPLEMAN, DOROTHY (1920 -)	100-500	X
KORAB, KARL (1937 -)	2500-20000	A
KORSAKOFF, S. DE (20TH C)	100-400	X (M)
KOSA (JR), EMIL JEAN	*100-9000	

* Denotes watercolors, pastels, drawings, and/or mixed media

KOSA (JR), EMIL JEAN (1903 - 1968)	400-16000	F,G,L,A
KOSKI, ? (20TH C)	*100-400	X (F)
KOST, FREDERICK WILLIAM (1865 - 1923)	200-1600	L,G
KOTIN, ALBERT (1907 - 1980)	200-1000	A
KOTZ, DANIEL (1848 - 1933)	200-2800	L
KRAFFT, CARL RUDOLPH	*100-1600	
KRAFFT, CARL RUDOLPH (1884 - 1930)	400-6500	L,G,S
KRASNER, LEE	*750-33000	
KRASNER, LEE (1912 - 1984)	4500-165000	A
KRASNOW, PETER (1890 - 1979)	500-3500	X
KREHBIEL, ARTHUR H. (1875 - 1945)	150-2400	G,L
KREPP, FRIEDRICH (19TH C)	200-700	X (F)
KRESS, FREDERICK B. (1888 - 1970)	400-4500	L
KRETZINGER, CLARA JOSEPHINE (1883 -)	200-8000	X (G)
KREUTER, WERNER (20TH C)	*100-400	X (F)
KRIEGHOFF, CORNELIUS (1812 - 1872)	1200-175000	G,F
KRIMMEL, JOHN LEWIS (1787 - 1821)	10000-150000 +	G,F
KROGH, PER LASSON (1889 -)	200-5200	F
KROLL, ABRAHAM (1919 -)	400-3200	F,G
KROLL, LEON	*200-7000	
KROLL, LEON (1884 - 1974)	1000-80000 +	F,L
KRONBERG, LOUIS	*300-4000	
KRONBERG, LOUIS (1872 - 1965)	400-10000 +	F,G
KRONENGOLD, ADOLPH (20TH C)	100-600	L
KROTTER, R. (20TH C)	100-400	L
KRUEGER, E. (19TH-20TH C)	150-750	X (G)
KRUGER, RICHARD (20TH C)	150-1100	L
KRUIF, HENRI GILBERT DE (1882 - 1944)	200-1000	X
KRUPPENDORF, FRANZ (20TH C)	100-500	L
KRUSHENICK, NICHOLAS (1929 -)	1500-13500	A
KRUSOE, WILLIAM (20TH C)	*50-500	L
KRYZANOVSKY, ROMAN (1885 - 1929)	400-3500	X (L)
KUBIK, KAMIE (20TH C)	*200-1200	X (L)
KUEHNE, MAX	*100-1300	
KUEHNE, MAX (1880 - 1968)	700-33000	L,M,S

* Denotes watercolors, pastels, drawings, and/or mixed media   229

KUENSTLER, G. (20TH C)	100-400	X (L)
KUHLMANN, G. EDWARD (1882 - 1973)	100-1000	L,F
KUHN, WALT	*600-16000	
KUHN, WALT (1880 - 1949)	2000-195000+	A,S,F,L
KULICKE, ROBERT M. (1924 -)	200-1800	X
KULLOCK, M. (19TH C)	100-500	X (L)
KUNDERT, B. (19TH-20TH C)	300-1200	L
KUNIYOSHI, YASUO	*200-57200	
KUNIYOSHI, YASUO (1893 - 1953)	5000-260000+	A,F,L
KUNSTLER, MORT (1931 -)	300-8500	I,F
KUNTZ, KARL (1770 - 1830)	350-13000	X (G)
KURILOFF, EDNA (1889 - 1979)	50-3100	X (S)
KURLANDER, H.W. (20TH C)	150-650	X (F)
KWAL, PAUL (20TH C)	100-600	L
KYLE, JOSEPH (1815 - 1863)	300-1200	F,G,S

L

Artist	Prices	Subject
L'ENGLE, LUCY (20TH C)	100-1200	F,G
L'ENGLE, WILLIAM (1884 - 1957)	100-1200	X (G)
LA CHAISE, EUGENE A. (1857 - 1925)	600-18000	F
LA CHANCE, GEORGE (1888 -)	200-1500	L,F
LA FARGE, JOHN	*750-93500	
LA FARGE, JOHN (1835 - 1910)	3000-110000	S,F
LA FARGE, JULES (19TH C)	150-850	L
LA GATTA, JOHN (1894 - 1977)	300-6500	I
LABRIE, ROSE (1916 -)	1000-5000	P
LACHAISE, GASTON (1882 - 1934)	*500-10000	F
LACHMAN, HARRY B. (1886 - 1974)	1000-14000	L,M
LACROIX, PAUL (active 1855-70)	1000-15000	S
LADD, C. (19TH-20TH C)	150-1200	L
LADD, LAURENCE (active 1870-92)	3300	P

* Denotes watercolors, pastels, drawings, and/or mixed media

LAER, ALEXANDER T. VAN	*150-1000	
LAER, ALEXANDER T. VAN (1857 - 1920)	300-3000	L,M
LAFORET, EUGENE (20TH C)	100-600	L
LAGERBERG, DON (1938 -)	400-1500	A
LAHEY, RICHARD FRANCIS (1893 - 1979)	*200-800	G,F
LAING, GERALD (20TH C)	500-4500	A
LAKEMAN, NATHANIEL (- 1823)	10450	P (F)
LAMASURE, EDWIN (1886 - 1916)	*100-1500	L
LAMB, ADRIAN (1901 -)	200-1200	X (F)
LAMB, ELLA C. (1862 - 1936)	50-400	L
LAMB, F. MORTIMER	*100-3000	
LAMB, F. MORTIMER (1861 - 1936)	300-7000	L,F,W
LAMB, KATE B. (20TH C)	100-500	X (L)
LAMB, RUBEN G. (19TH C)	500-2500	X (S)
LAMBDIN, GEORGE COCHRAN	*100-4100	
LAMBDIN, GEORGE COCHRAN (1830 - 1896)	1200-48000	S,F,G
LAMBDIN, JAMES REID (1807 - 1889)	700-15000	F
LAMBDIN, ROBERT (1886 - 1981)	*50-550	X (F)
LAMBERT, B. (20TH C)	100-700	L
LAMBERT, THEODORE (1905 - 1960)	3000-18000	X (L)
LANCASTER, MARK (1938 -)	400-3000	A
LANCKEN, FRANK VON DER (1872 - 1950)	350-3000	F,G
LAND, ERNEST ALBERT (20TH C)	150-850	X
LANDERYOU, R. (late 19TH C)	100-750	L
LANDIS, H.W. (19TH-20TH C)	150-1500	X
LANE, EMMA (late 19TH C)	100-400	X (S)
LANE, ERNEST (19TH C)	100-700	X (L)
LANE, FITZ HUGH (1804 - 1865)	20000-825000	L,M
LANE, FRANCIS (20TH C)	100-500	L
LANE, MARTELLA CONE (1875 - 1962)	100-1000	L
LANE, SUSAN MINOT (1832 - 1893)	*100-600	X (F)
LANG, LOUIS (1814 - 1893)	750-60000	F,G,L
LANGE, ERNA (1896 -)	200-1800	X (L)
LANGENBACH, CLARA EMMA (1871 -)	200-1800	X (F)
LANGERFELDT, THEODORE O. (1841 -)	*100-600	L

LANGLEY, EDWARD	*100-750	
LANGLEY, EDWARD (20TH C)	300-3500	L
LANGWORTHY, WILLIAM H. (late 19TH C)	300-1200	G,L
LANMAN, CHARLES (1819 - 1895)	350-4500	L
LANSIL, WALTER FRANKLIN (1846 - 1925)	500-9000	M,L
LANSIL, WILBUR H. (19TH-20TH C)	250-3500	L
LARENCE, R.J. (19TH-20TH C)	*100-500	L
LARIMER, BARBARA (20TH C)	100-800	L
LARMOUR, WILLIAM (1870 - 1943)	*200-1200	M
LARRAZ, JULIO (1944 -)	2000-46200	X
LARSEN, L. (19TH-20TH C)	100-800	L
LARSEN, MIKE (20TH C)	*100-700	X (F)
LARSEN, MORTEN (20TH C)	100-750	L
LARSON, EDWARD (1931 -)	1000-8500	P
LARSSON, KARL (20TH C)	*100-400	X
LARSSON, MARCUS (1825 - 1864)	500-10000	L
LASCARI, SALVATORE (1884 - 1967)	100-900	X (F)
LASKY, BESSIE MONA (1890 - 1972)	200-2000	M,L
LASSNER, N.T. (19TH C)	150-850	X (F)
LASSONDE, OMAR THOMAS (1903 - 1980)	100-950	X (A,S)
LATHROP, DOROTHY P. (1891 -)	*100-600	I
LATHROP, FRANCIS (1849 - 1909)	200-1800	X (F)
LATHROP, IDA PULIS (1859 - 1937)	200-1500	L,M,F
LATHROP, WILLIAM LANGSON (1859 - 1938)	500-13000+	L
LATIMER, F.R. (19TH-20TH C)	*100-500	X (F)
LATIMER, LORENZO PALMER	*150-1500	
LATIMER, LORENZO PALMER (1857 - 1941)	300-2500	L
LATOIX, GASPARD DE	*1000-6000	
LATOIX, GASPARD DE (1890 - 1910)	1000-12000	F
LATTARD, PHILLIP (19TH-20TH C)	300-12100	X (F)
LAUDER, S.A. (19TH C)	100-800	L
LAUDIN, MARGARET E. (19TH-20TH C)	150-1200	X (S)
LAUFFER, ERWIN (20TH C)	50-300	L
LAUFMAN, SIDNEY (1891 -)	100-2500	X (F,L)
LAUGHLIN, EDWARD (20TH C)	100-650	X

LAUGHNER, L.M. (20TH C)	100-500	X
LAURENCE, SYDNEY MORTIMER	*800-6500	
LAURENCE, SYDNEY MORTIMER (1865 - 1940)	700-75000+	L,F
LAURENT, JOHN (20TH C)	250-1000	F
LAURENT, ROBERT (1890 - 1970)	*100-950	X (W)
LAURITZ, JACK (20TH C)	100-800	L
LAURITZ, PAUL (1889 - 1975)	500-15000	L,M
LAUSSUCQ, HENRI (20TH C)	*100-400	X
LAUTERER, ARCH (20TH C)	*200-600	I
LAUX, AUGUST (1847 - 1921)	400-11000	S,W,L
LAVALLE, JOHN	*100-750	
LAVALLE, JOHN (1896 - 1971)	500-8500	G,F
LAVALLEY, JONAS JOSEPH (1858 - 1930)	500-3500	S
LAVERTY, ELIZABETH S. (1899 -)	*50-300	X
LAVIGNE, AUDREY RAE (19TH C)	*100-400	X
LAW, HARRY V. (20TH C)	100-700	L
LAWLESS, CARL E. (1896 - 1934)	300-5000	L
LAWLOR, GEORGE WARREN (1848 -)	200-6000	F,G
LAWMAN, JASPER HOLMAN (1825 - 1906)	700-7500+	L,F
LAWRENCE, EDNA W. (1898 - 1987)	*150-1000	X (M,L)
LAWRENCE, JACOB (1917 -)	*1000-44000	A
LAWRIE, ALEXANDER (1828 - 1917)	600-4000+	F,L
LAWS, ARTHUR J. (- 1960)	1000-11000	L,F
LAWSON, ERNEST (1873 - 1939)	1000-530000	L,M
LAWSON, MARK (20TH C)	650-2500	I
LAZARUS, JACOB HART (1822 - 1891)	200-1600	F
LAZZARIO, PIETRO (1898 - 1979)	*200-1000	A
LAZZELL, BLANCHE	*300-5000	
LAZZELL, BLANCHE (1878 - 1956)	600-26500	A,L,M
LEA, TOM (1907 -)	800-4800	I
LEACH, ALICE F. (1857 - 1943)	200-2500	X (L)
LEACH, FREDERICK (20TH C)	*100-500	X (F)
LEAH, K.C. (19TH C)	100-500	X (S)
LEAKE, GERALD (1885 -)	400-1800	X (F)
LEAR, JOHN (20TH C)	100-800	F

LEAR, LAVIN (20TH C)	*100-400	X (F)
LEAVITT, AGNES (1859 -)	*100-600	L
LEAVITT, EDWARD CHALMERS (1842 - 1904)	400-15000	S,L
LEAVITT, J.A. (20TH C)	*100-800	X (M)
LEAVITT, JOHN FAUNCE (1905 - 1974)	*250-2000	M
LEAVITT, R.C. (20TH C ?)	200-900	X (M)
LEAVITT, SHELDON (JR) (19TH C ?)	500-3500	X
LEBDUSKA, LAWRENCE H.	*250-5200	
LEBDUSKA, LAWRENCE H. (1894 - 1966)	300-16500	P
LEBRUN, RICO	*200-4800	
LEBRUN, RICO (1900 - 1964)	300-6000	A
LECHAY, MYRON (1898 -)	150-950	L,F
LECLEAR, THOMAS (1818 - 1882)	300-5000	G,F,M
LECOQUE, ALOIS (1891 - 1981)	200-6200	L
LEE, BERTHA STRINGER (1873 - 1937)	200-4500	L,M
LEE, BOB (1933 -)	500-10000	L
LEE, CHEE CHIN S. CHEUNG (20TH C)	100-800	X
LEE, DORIS EMRICK (1905 - 1983)	500-33000	F,G,L
LEE, HENRY CHARLES (1864 - 1930)	100-800	L
LEE, JAMES (20TH C)	100-500	X (G)
LEE, JERRY (1944 -)	100-600	X
LEE, LAURA (1867 -)	300-2400	L
LEE, MANNING DE VILENEUE (1894 -)	200-1600	X
LEE, MATTIE (19TH C)	100-600	L
LEE, SAMUEL M. (- 1841)	300-1500	L,F
LEE-SMITH, HUGHIE (1915 -)	100-2500	X (M)
LEEDY, LAURA A. (1881 -)	150-850	X (L)
LEETEG, EDGAR (20TH C)	400-3600	F
LEFEVRE, LAURA (19TH C)	300-3800	L
LEGANGER, NICOLAY TYSLAND (1832 - 1894)	250-3100	L,M
LEGRAND, HENRY (active 1855-85)	400-5000	L,F
LEHR, ADAM (1853 - 1924)	150-3000	S
LEIGH, WILLIAM ROBINSON (1866 - 1955)	2000-187000	I,F
LEIGHTON, KATHRYN W.(1876 - 1952)	800-15000	F,L
LEIGHTON, SCOTT (1849 - 1898)	900-38000	W,F,L

LEIKER, W. (19TH C)	150-600	X (L)
LEISSER, MARTIN B. (1845 - 1940)	500-3000	L
LEITCH, RICHARD PRINCIPAL (19TH C)	*100-2000	L
LEITH-ROSS, HARRY	*200-2200	
LEITH-ROSS, HARRY (1886 - 1973)	400-10000	L,S
LEITNER, LEANDER (1873 -)	100-1200	X (L)
LELAND, HENRY (1850 - 1877)	600-5000	G,F
LEMAIRE, CHARLES (20TH C)	*200-1000	X (I)
LEMBECK, JACK (1942 -)	500-15500	X
LEMMENMEYER, M. (20TH C)	100-400	X
LEMOS, PEDRO J. (1882 - 1954)	100-1200	L
LENHART, A. (20TH C)	100-600	L
LEONE, JOHN (20TH C)	800-7100	X (I)
LESLIE, ALFRED	*200-8500	
LESLIE, ALFRED (1927 -)	2500-50000	A
LESLIE, FRANK (see HENRY CARTER)		
LESLIE, G. (late 19TH C)	300-1200	L
LESSHAFFT, FRANZ (1862 -)	*100-600	L,W
LESTER, RUTH WILSON (20TH C)	300-1500	X (F)
LEU, AUGUST WILHELM (1819 - 1887)	1000-10000	L
LEUTZE, EMANUEL GOTTLIEB (1816 - 1868)	600-47000	F,G,M
LEVER, RICHARD HAYLEY	*200-15000	
LEVER, RICHARD HAYLEY (1876 - 1958)	500-41000	M,L
LEVI, JULIAN (1874 -)	250-3000	F,M,G
LEVICK, MILNES (1887-)	50-600	F,L
LEVIER, CHARLES (1920 -)	250-5500	L,M,S
LEVINE, DAVID (1926 -)	*150-5500	I,L,F
LEVINE, JACK	*400-6500	
LEVINE, JACK (1915 -)	1500-60000+	A,G,F
LEVY, ALEXANDER OSCAR (1881 - 1947)	500-9500+	L,G,F,I
LEVY, HENRY (1868 -)	50-800	F
LEVY, NAT (1896 - 1984)	*100-2500	L,M
LEVY, WILLIAM AUERBACH (1889 - 1964)	200-1500	X (F,L)
LEWAN, DENNIS (1943 -)	100-1000	X
LEWANDOWSKI, EDMUND D. (1914 -)	800-4700	X

LEWIN, JAMES MORGAN (1836 - 1877)	500-3000	X (S)
LEWIS, C.H.	*100-650	
LEWIS, C.H. (19TH C)	400-2500	F,M
LEWIS, EDMUND DARCH	*300-12000	
LEWIS, EDMUND DARCH (1835 - 1910)	1000-26000	L,M
LEWIS, EMERSON (20TH C)	*100-2100	I
LEWIS, GEORGE JEFFREY (20TH C)	150-800	X (L,F)
LEWIS, HARRY EMERSON (1892 - 1958)	100-2000	L
LEWIS, JEANETTE MAXFIELD (1894 - 1982)	300-2000	X (L)
LEWIS, JOHN CHAPMAN (1920 -)	500-2000	F
LEWIS, MARTIN (1883 - 1962)	*500-9500	G,L
LEWIS, V. (20TH C)	100-900	X (L)
LEWITT, SOL (1928 -)	*1500-165000	A
LEYDENFROST, ALEXANDER (1888 - 1965)	*400-1500	I
LEYENDECKER, FRANCIS XAVIER (1877 - 1924)	500-8500	I
LEYENDECKER, JOSEPH CHRISTIAN (1874 - 1951)	700-40000	I
LIBBY, FRANCIS ORVILLE (1884 -)	100-1000	L
LIBERMAN, ALEXANDER (1912 -)	800-10000	A
LIBERTE, JEAN (1896 - 1965)	100-500	X (L,F)
LICHTENAUER, JOSEPH M. (1876 -)	200-1200	X (F)
LICHTENBERG, MANES (20TH C)	300-2200	L
LICHTENSTEIN, ROY	*3000-575000	
LICHTENSTEIN, ROY (1923 -)	7000-6050000	A
LIE, JONAS (1880 - 1940)	650-75000	M,L
LIE, ROBERT (1899 - 1980)	200-1400	M
LILJESTROM, GUSTAVE (1882 - 1958)	200-2500	X (W,L)
LILLIE, JOHN (1867 -)	50-400	L
LIMARZI, JOSEPH (1907 -)	100-1500	X (F)
LINCOLN, EPHRAIM FRANK (?)	400-4500	M
LINDE, OSSIP L. (1871 - 1940)	300-5000	L
LINDEN, CARL (1869 - 1942)	200-2200	L
LINDEN, FRANK L. (20TH C)	*100-600	L
LINDENMUTH, TOD (1885 - 1976)	300-2700	L,G,M
LINDER, HENRY (1854 - 1910)	100-1200	L
LINDGREN, MARJORIE REED (20TH C)	300-1500	X

LINDHOLM, W. (19TH C)	300-1000	X (M)
LINDIN, CARL OLAF ERIC (1869 - 1942)	100-750	X (M)
LINDNER, E. (20TH C)	*100-500	X (L)
LINDNER, RICHARD	*1500-47000	
LINDNER, RICHARD (1901 - 1978)	3500-418000	A (F)
LINDNEUX, ROBERT OTTOKAR (1871 - 1970)	100-1800	F,L
LINDSAY, R.A. (1888 -)	100-1000	L
LINDSAY, THOMAS CORWIN (1845 - 1907)	300-3000	I.,F
LINFORD, CHARLES (1846 - 1897)	400-2500	L
LINGLE, BENJAMIN (20TH C)	*100-600	L
LINSON, CORWIN KNAPP (1864 - 1934)	600-9500 +	L,I
LINTON, FRANK BENTON ASHLEY (1871 - 1944)	300-900	X (F)
LINTOTT, EDWARD BERNARD	*100-1500	
LINTOTT, EDWARD BERNARD (1875 - 1951)	300-5000	F,L,S
LIPPINCOTT, WILLIAM HENRY	*14000	
LIPPINCOTT, WILLIAM HENRY (1849 - 1920)	400-19000	F,L,I
LIPSKY, PAT (1941 -)	500-2500	X
LITTLE, A.P. (19TH C)	100-1000	X (S)
LITTLE, ARTHUR (20TH C)	500-4500	X
LITTLE, JOHN WESLEY (1867 - 1923)	*100-850	L,M
LITTLE, NATHANIEL STANTON (1893 -)	500-4800	L,M
LITTLE, PHILIP	*100-1000	
LITTLE, PHILIP (1857 - 1942)	500-9000 +	M,L
LITTLEFIELD, WILLIAM HORACE (1902 - 1969)	100-2100	A
LITTLEWOOD, JOHN (19TH C)	100-600	X (G)
LITZINGER, DOROTHEA M. (1889 - 1925)	500-7500	L,S
LLOYD, SARA (20TH C)	450-3500	L,F
LOCHRIE, ELIZABETH DAVEY (1890 - 1976)	350-1500	X (F,G)
LOCK, F.W. (mid 19TH C)	*400-2500	L,F
LOCKE, W.R. (20TH C)	100-800	L
LOCKWOOD, JOHN WARD (1894 - 1963)	*100-1200	L
LOCKWOOD, WILTON (ROBERT) (1862 - 1914)	300-7000	F,S
LOEB, LOUIS (1866 - 1909)	150-13500	F,G,I
LOEBERS, ADRIAN (20TH C)	100-850	X (L)
LOEMANS, ALEXANDER FRANCOIS (19TH C)	400-6100	L

LOFTEN, RICHARD (20TH C)	100-600	X
LOGAN, FRANCES (20TH C)	200-1000	X (S)
LOGAN, MAURICE	*300-1200	
LOGAN, MAURICE (1886 - 1977)	300-9500	F,M,L
LOGAN, ROBERT FULTON (1889 - 1959)	500-4500	G,L
LOGAN, ROBERT HENRY (1874 - 1942)	500-5500	L,F
LOHREDL, G.S. (20TH C)	150-700	X
LONDONER, AMY (1878 -)	*100-600	G,F
LONE WOLF,	*600-12000	
LONE WOLF, (1882 - 1970)	1000-18000	X (F)
LONG, STANLEY M. (1892 - 1972)	*100-1000	F,G
LONGFELLOW, ERNEST WADSWORTH (1845 - 1921)	300-2000	L
LONGFELLOW, MARY KING (1852 - 1945)	*150-1500	L,M
LONGO, ROBERT (1923 -)	*2000-154000	A
LONGPRE, PAUL DE	*600-12000	
LONGPRE, PAUL DE (1855 - 1911)	600-15000	S
LONGPRE, RAOUL DE (19TH-20TH C)	500-36000	S
LOOMIS, (WILLIAM) ANDREW (1892 - 1959)	250-5200	I
LOOMIS, CHARLES RUSSELL (1857 - 1883)	*200-2800	M,L,F
LOOMIS, CHESTER R. (1852 - 1924)	400-3500	L,F
LOOMIS, JESSIE PARROTT (?)	*100-700	X (L)
LOOMIS, P.L. (early 20TH C)	100-300	X (S)
LOOMIS, W.H. (early 20TH C)	*300-1200	X (F)
LOOP, HENRY AUGUSTUS (1831 - 1895)	100-2000	F,L
LOOP, JEANETTE SHEPPERD H. (1840 - 1909)	100-1000	F
LOOP, JENNIE (19TH C)	400-1200	X (F)
LOPEZ, CARLOS (1935 -)	150-1600	X (F)
LOPEZ-LOZA, LUIS (1939 -)	700-2800	A
LORAN, EARLE (1905 -)	300-4000	L,M
LORENZ, RICHARD (1858 - 1915)	500-32000	G,F,L
LORING, FRANCIS WILLIAM (1838 - 1905)	300-1500	G,F,L
LORING, WILLIAM CUSHING (1879 -)	250-3000	F
LORSKI, BORIS LOVET (1894 - 1973)	*400-1200	X (F)
LOTHROP, GEORGE EDWIN (20TH C)	600-3000	X (A)

* Denotes watercolors, pastels, drawings, and/or mixed media

LOTICHIUS, ERNEST (late 19TH C)	400-2500	G,L,W
LOTT, E. (19TH C)	100-400	X (L)
LOTZ, MATILDA (1858 - 1923)	300-10000	X (W,M)
LOUDEN, NORMAN P. (1895 -)	50-800	F,L
LOUDERBACK, WALT S. (1887 - 1941)	700-8500	I
LOUGHEED, ROBERT ELMER (1910 - 1982)	800-35000	L,G,W,I
LOUIS, MORRIS (1912 - 1962)	10000-1100000	A
LOVE, GEORGE PATTERSON (1887 -)	*100-600	X (F)
LOVEJOY, RUPERT S. (1885 - 1975)	350-4000	L,M
LOVELL, KATHERINE ADAMS (1877 - 1965)	250-1200	L,F,S
LOVELL, TOM	*300-8000	
LOVELL, TOM (1909 -)	1500-125000	I,F,G
LOVEN, FRANK W. (1869 - 1941)	200-6000	L,I
LOVERIDGE, CHARLES (19TH C)	300-1800	L
LOVERIDGE, CLINTON (1824 - 1902)	800-10000+	L
LOVEWELL, ROMINER (1853 - 1932)	*300-1200	M,L,F
LOW, LAWRENCE GORDON (1912 -)	150-3500	F,S,I
LOW, MARY L.F. MACMONIES (1858 - 1946)	500-7500+	F
LOW, WILL HICOCK (1853 - 1932)	400-20000+	I
LOW, WILLIAM GILMAN (19TH - 20TH C)	500-3000	X (L,W)
LOWE, R. (19TH-20TH C)	100-400	X
LOWELL, MILTON H. (1848 - 1927)	100-1900	L
LOWELL, ORSON BYRON	*300-5800	
LOWELL, ORSON BYRON (1871 - 1956)	500-5000	I
LOWES, H.C. (19TH C)	200-800	X (W)
LOWING, M. (19TH C)	100-1000	L
LOWNES, ANNA (19TH C)	400-2500	X (S)
LOWRY, WILLIAM J. (19TH C)	100-700	L
LOZIER, AIMEE A. (20TH C)	100-600	F
LOZOWICK, LOUIS	*500-12500	
LOZOWICK, LOUIS (1892 - 1973)	1000-45000+	A
LUCAS, ALBERT PIKE (1862 - 1945)	350-10000	L
LUCE, L.W. (19TH C)	*100-500	L
LUCE, MOLLY (1896 -)	500-11000	G,F,L
LUCE, PERCIVAL DE (1847 - 1914)	250-1000	X (L)

LUCIONI, LUIGI (1900 - 1988)	1500-77000	L,S
LUDLOW, GABRIEL R. (1800 - 1838)	*24200	L
LUKENS, MARGARET (20TH C)	100-600	L,M
LUKS, GEORGE BENJAMIN	*500-25000	
LUKS, GEORGE BENJAMIN (1867 - 1933)	1500-2755000	G,F,L
LUM, BERTHA BOYNTON (1879 - 1954)	350-3500	F
LUMIS, HARRIET RANDALL (1870 - 1953)	500-25000	L,M
LUMLEY, ARTHUR (1837 - 1912)	300-2000	F,I
LUND, HAROLD (1904 -)	100-1200	X (M)
LUNDBERG, AUGUST FREDERICK (1878 - 1928)	150-40000	G,M
LUNDBORG, A.F. (20TH C)	100-900	X (L)
LUNDBORG, FLORENCE (1871 - 1949)	*150-850	X (I)
LUNDE, EMILY (1914 -)	1300	P
LUNDEAN, J. LOUIS (20TH C)	300-2000	X (W)
LUNDEBERG, HELEN (1908 -)	200-6100	M,G,F
LUNGREN, FERNAND HARVEY	*200-6000	
LUNGREN, FERNAND HARVEY (1857 - 1932)	*500-5500	L,I
LURIE, NANCY (NAN) (1934 -)	100-700	X (S)
LUSSIER, LOUIS O. (- 1884)	200-900	F
LUTKINS, MARGARET (20TH C)	100-500	L
LUTZ, DAN (1906 - 1978)	100-1500	G,L,A
LUX, THEODORE F. (1910 -)	300-2000	X (M)
LUYTIES, JAN VAN (19TH C)	100-800	L
LYFORD, PHILIP (1887 - 1950)	200-4200	F,L,I
LYMAN, JOSEPH (JR) (1843 - 1913)	500-3500	L
LYNCH, ROBERT (20TH C)	100-2000	L
LYNN, DAVID (20TH C)	100-700	L
LYONNEL, A. (19TH-20TH C)	100-700	L
LYRON, N.A. (19TH C)	200-1200	W

M

Artist	Prices	Subject
MAAR, DORA MARKOVIC (1909 -)	250-1200	X (L)
MACALLISTER, CARRIE R. (19TH-20TH C)	400-4000	L
MACAULIFFE, JAMES J. (1848 - 1921)	500-9500	G,M,L
MACCAMERON, ROBERT LEE (1866 - 1912)	500-15000	F,G
MACCARTHY, FRANK (1924 -)	*100-900	G,F,L
MACCAY, WILBUR (20TH C)	100-700	X (L)
MACCORD, CHARLES WILLIAM (1852 - 1923)	300-1200	L
MACCORD, ELIZABETH (19TH-20TH C)	100-600	X
MACCORD, MARY NICHOLENA (20TH C)	500-6500	X (L)
MACDONALD, HAROLD L. (1861 -)	100-1500	G,F
MACDONALD, JAMES EDWARD H. (1873 - 1932)	1000-125000	L
MACDONALD, L.W. (19TH-20TH C)	150-900	X (F)
MACDONALD-WRIGHT, STANTON	*500-8500	
MACDONALD-WRIGHT, STANTON (1890 - 1973)	600-40000+	A,F,S
MACDONALL, ANGUS P. (1876 - 1927)	*100-1800	F,G
MACDOUGALL, JOHN ALLAN (1843 -)	100-900	F
MACEWEN (MCEWEN), WALTER	*200-15000	
MACEWEN (MCEWEN), WALTER (1860 - 1943)	450-16000	G,F,L
MACFEE, S. (20TH C)	200-1400	M
MACGILVARY, NORWOOD HODGE (1874 - 1950)	300-7500	L,F
MACGINNIS, HENRY RYAN (1875 - 1962)	700-4500	F
MACHEFERT, ADRIAN C. (1881 -)	*100-500	L,F
MACHEN, WILLIAM HENRY (1832 - 1911)	350-2500	W,S
MACHESNEY, CLARA TAGGART (1860 -)	150-850	X (L)
MACHETANZ, FRED (1908 -)	900-18000	F,G
MACINNIS, CHARLES (19TH C)	300-1200	G,F
MACINTOSH, MARIAN T. (1871 - 1936)	300-2600	L
MACIVER, LOREN (1909 -)	1000-18000	A
MACKAY, EDWIN MURRAY (1869 - 1926)	600-8000	X (F)
MACKENDRICK, LILIAN (1906 -)	300-2500	X (F)
MACKENZIE, RODERICK D. (1865 - 1941)	600-13000	F,L
MACKNIGHT, DODGE (1860 - 1934)	*400-9500	L
MACKUBIN, FLORENCE (1866 - 1918)	*100-900	F,W
MACKY, ERIC S. (1880 - 1958)	200-2400	L,F

MACKY, CONSTANCE L.J. (1883 - 1961)	*100-800	L
MACLAUGHLIN, CHARLES J. (20TH C)	150-1500	F,L
MACLAUGHLIN, GERALD (20TH C)	200-1200	X
MACLEOD, WILLIAM (active 1840-65)	800-6500	L
MACMONNIES, FREDERICK WILLIAM (1863 - 1937)	1000-40000	G,F
MACMONNIES, MARY FAIRCHILD (1859 - 1946)	1000-18000	F
MACNALL, E. (20TH C)	100-600	S
MACNEAL, FREDERICK A. (early 20TH C)	*100-500	L
MACOMBER, MARY LIZZIE (1861 - 1916)	400-13500	F
MACRAE, ELMER LIVINGSTON	*200-3500	
MACRAE, ELMER LIVINGSTON (1875 - 1953)	500-46200	M,L,G,F
MACRAE, EMMA FORDYCE (1887 - 1974)	400-8800	F,S
MACRUM, GEORGE H. (20TH C)	500-8000	L,F
MACSOUD, NICHOLAS S. (1884 -)	100-850	L,F
MACY, WENDELL FERDINAND (1852 - 1902)	350-3000	L
MACY, WILLIAM STARBUCK (1853 - 1916)	400-5500	L,M,G
MADER, LOUIS (1842 - 1892)	2500-25000	P
MAENTEL, JACOB (1763 - 1863)	*2000-35000 +	P
MAGEE, JAMES C.	*100-600	
MAGEE, JAMES C. (1846 - 1924)	250-5000	L,M
MAHAFFEY, NOEL (1944 -)	1500-22000	X (G)
MAHER, KATE HEATH (1860 - 1946)	300-3200	L
MAHLON, BLAINE (20TH C)	*50-400	F
MAILLOT, VICTORIA (early 20TH C)	300-1500	X (S)
MAISON, MARY EDITH (1886 - 1954)	100-1700	L
MAJOR, B. (19TH-20TH C)	100-800	L
MAJOR, ERNEST LEE (1864 - 1950)	400-7500	F,L,S
MAKO, B. (1890 -)	100-1200	X
MALBONE, EDWARD GREENE (1777 - 1807)	1500-10000	F
MALCOLM, LLYOD R. (19TH C)	*150-900	X (M,L)
MALCOM, ELIZABETH (20TH C)	*100-500	X (F)
MALHERBE, WILLIAM (1884 - 1951)	300-6000	L,F,S
MALICOAT, PHILIP CECIL	*100-1600	
MALICOAT, PHILIP CECIL (1908 -)	700-3000	X (L)
MALONEY, LOUISE B. (20TH C)	200-1200	S

* Denotes watercolors, pastels, drawings, and/or mixed media

MAN-RAY, (Emmanuel Radinski)	*300-75000	
MAN-RAY, (Emmanuel Radinski) (1890 - 1976)	1500-325000+	A
MANGOLD, ROBERT	*1500-155000	
MANGOLD, ROBERT (1937 -)	3500-100000+	A
MANGRAVITE, PEPPINO (1896 -)	*400-3000	A,F
MANIATTY, STEPHEN GEORGE (1910 -)	100-1500	L,S
MANIGAULT, EDWARD M.(1887 - 1922)	500-18000	X
MANLEY, THOMAS R. (1853 - 1938)	100-1700	L
MANN, PARKER (1852 - 1918)	100-1800	L
MANNHEIM, JEAN (1863 -1945)	550-33000	L,F,M
MANNING, RUSSEL G. (- 1982)	*100-600	X (G)
MANOIR, IRVING K. (1891 - 1982)	150-950	L
MANZI, JEAN (19TH-20TH C)	200-1600	F
MAPES, JAMES J. (1806 - 1866)	200-1500	X (F)
MARATTA, HARDESTY GILLMORE (1864 -)	*200-1000	X (L,W)
MARBLE, JOHN NELSON (1855 - 1918)	100-650	L,F
MARBOEUF, V. (20TH C)	100-900	X (M)
MARCA-RELLI, CONRAD	*750-48000	
MARCA-RELLI, CONRAD (1913 -)	8000-88000	A
MARCHAND, JOHN NORVAL (1875 - 1921)	*300-4500	I
MARCHANT, EDWARD DALTON (1806 - 1887)	700-10000	F
MARCIUS-SIMONS, PINCKNEY (1867 - 1909)	500-50000	G,F
MARCY, WILLIAM (20TH C)	*100-300	X
MARDEN, BRICE	*5000-225000	
MARDEN, BRICE (1938 -)	10000-1100000	A
MARGESON, GILBERT TUCKER (1852 -)	100-1500	M
MARGO, BORIS (1902 -)	300-3600	A
MARGULIES, JOSEPH	*100-3200	
MARGULIES, JOSEPH (1896 - 1984)	400-3500	G,F,L,M
MARIA, WALTER DE (1935 -)	*500-13000	A
MARIN, JOHN	*100-44000	
MARIN, JOHN (1870 - 1953)	2500-82500+	A,M,L
MARINKO, GEORGE J. (1908 - 1989)	100-2400	X (F)
MARIS, WALTER DE (1877 -)	300-2000	X
MARK, GEORGE WASHINGTON (1795 - 1879)	800-10000	P

MARK, LOUIS (1867 - 1942)	100-1500	F
MARKHAM, CHARLES C. (1837 - 1907)	1000-10000	G,S
MARKHAM, KYRA (1891 - 1967)	300-22000	X (F)
MARKOS, LAJOS (1917 -)	500-10000	F,G
MARLATT, H. IRVING (1860 - 1929)	250-2200	M,L
MARPLE, WILLIAM L. (1827 - 1910)	500-4000	L
MARR, CARL RITTER VON (1858 - 1936)	200-12000	F
MARSCHNER, ARTHUR (1884 -)	100-500	L
MARSDEN, THEODORE (20TH C)	500-12000	W
MARSH, FELICIA MEYER (20TH C)	100-500	F,L
MARSH, FREDERICK DANA (1872 - 1961)	200-2200	F,G
MARSH, PEARL E. (20TH C)	*50-400	M,L
MARSH, REGINALD	*500-74500	
MARSH, REGINALD (1898 - 1954)	600-107000 +	G,F,I
MARSHALL, CLARK S. (19TH-20TH C)	100-900	L
MARSHALL, FRANK WARREN (1866 - 1930)	100-850	M,L
MARSHALL, MRS. MARY E. (19TH-20TH C)	150-1200	X (L)
MARSHALL, THOMAS W. (1850 - 1874)	500-4800	G,L
MARSHALL, WILLIAM EDGAR (1837 - 1906)	500-7500	F
MARTENET, MARJORIE D. (19TH-20TH C)	100-600	X
MARTENS, G. (early 19TH C)	100-850	X (F)
MARTIN, A. (19TH C)	100-1000	L
MARTIN, AGNES (1912 -)	*2500-460000	A
MARTIN, EMMA (19TH C)	*600-3800	X (F)
MARTIN, FLETCHER	*200-4000	
MARTIN, FLETCHER (1904 - 1979)	1200-61000	G,F
MARTIN, GILL (20TH C)	100-900	L
MARTIN, HELEN DOAK (19TH-20TH C)	100-600	L
MARTIN, HOMER DODGE (1836 - 1897)	500-25000 +	L
MARTIN, J. EDWARD B. (20TH C)	250-3300	X (L)
MARTIN, J.H. (19TH C)	150-950	X (L)
MARTIN, KEITH (20TH C)	*100-1150	X (G,F)
MARTIN, KNOX (1923 -)	400-5000	A
MARTIN, L.B. (19TH C)	400-2500	X (M)
MARTIN, NANCY (1906 -)	*50-500	F

* Denotes watercolors, pastels, drawings, and/or mixed media

MARTINEZ, JULIAN (1897 - 1943)	*300-2200	X (F)
MARTINEZ, XAVIER	*200-4000	
MARTINEZ, XAVIER (1869 - 1943)	800-8500	M,L,F
MARTINI, JOSEPH DE (1896 -)	*100-400	G,L
MARTINO, ANTONIO PIETRO (1902 - 1988)	400-14000	L
MARTINO, GIOVANNI (1908 -)	200-5000	M,L
MASON, ALICE TRUMBULL (1904 - 1971)	800-18000+	A
MASON, FRANK HENRY	*200-7700	
MASON, FRANK HENRY (1876 - 1965)	200-4300	L,G
MASON, GEORGE CHAMPLIN (1820 - 1894)	400-6500	L
MASON, GEORGE FREDERICK (1904 -)	*100-400	W,S
MASON, L.D. (19TH C)	100-900	X (L,W)
MASON, MAUD MARY (1867 - 1956)	200-3100	X (L,S)
MASON, ROY MARTELL (1886 - 1972)	*100-2100	X (G)
MASON, SANFORD (1798 - 1862)	500-3200	F
MASON, WILLIAM SANFORD (1824 - 1864)	800-6500	G,F
MASSEY, RAYMOND (20TH C)	300-2400	M
MASTERS, FRANK B. (1873 -)	*250-3000	I
MASTERS, WALTER (20TH C)	100-1000	F
MATHEUS, A. (19TH-20TH C)	100-700	L
MATHEWS, ARTHUR FRANK	*700-18000	
MATHEWS, ARTHUR FRANK (1860 - 1945)	1000-110000	F,G,L
MATHEWS, J. (early 19TH C)	2500-12000	P
MATHEWS, JOSEPH (1861 - 1893)	350-2800	X (F)
MATHEWSON, FRANK CONVERS (1862 - 1941)	200-3300	F,L,S
MATSON, VICTOR (1898 - 1972)	100-1200	L
MATTEI, ANTONIO (20TH C)	100-600	X (F)
MATTESON, TOMPKINS HARRISON (1813 - 1884)	600-9000+	G,F
MATTHEW, JACK (20TH C)	100-500	L
MATTHEWS, W.T. (19TH-20TH C)	100-500	X (F,S)
MATTSON, HENRY ELLIS (1887 - 1971)	100-1000	X (F,L)
MATULKA, JAN	*400-6500	
MATULKA, JAN (1890 - 1972)	1100-47000	A
MATZAL, LEOPOLD C. (1890 -)	150-850	F
MATZINGER, PHILIP F. (1860 - 1942)	300-2000	L

MAURER, ALFRED HENRY	*600-15000	
MAURER, ALFRED HENRY (1868 - 1932)	1200-190000	A,F,L
MAURER, LOUIS (1832 - 1932)	2500-100000	G,F,W
MAX, PETER	*200-1500	
MAX, PETER (B. 1937)	400-5000	A,F
MAXFIELD, CLARA (1879 - 1959)	*200-3500	S
MAXFIELD, JAMES E. (1848 -)	300-7500	L
MAXWELL, EDDA (19TH-20TH C)	400-4500	F
MAXWELL, PAUL (20TH C)	*100-500	X
MAY, J. (19TH-20TH C)	200-1000	L
MAYER, CONSTANT (1829 - 1911)	500-24000	G,F
MAYER, FRANK BLACKWELL (1827 - 1899)	400-30000	G,F
MAYER, PETER BELA (1887 - 1993)	500-20000	L,M
MAYFIELD, ROBERT B. (1869 - 1935)	100-800	X
MAYNARD, GEORGE WILLOUGHBY	*300-3500	
MAYNARD, GEORGE WILLOUGHBY (1843 - 1923)	300-9000	X (M,F)
MAYNARD, RICHARD FIELD (1875 -)	500-3500	X (F)
MAYNE, A. (19TH-20TH C)	50-300	M
MAYS, PAUL KIRTLAND (1887 - 1961)	200-2000	L
MAZZONOVICH, LAWRENCE (1872 - 1946)	500-12000	L
MCAFEE, ILA (1900 -)	100-800	L
MCAULIFFE, JAMES J. (1848 - 1921)	300-18000 +	G,M,L
MCBEY, JAMES (1883 - 1959)	*200-2000	L
MCCALL, CHARLES (20TH C)	200-1200	X (F)
MCCARTER, HENRY (1866 - 1942)	*100-2500	I,L
MCCARTHY, FRANK (1924 -)	1500-55000	I
MCCARTHY, HELEN K. (1884 - 1927)	100-1000	X (M)
MCCAY, WINSOR (1871 - 1934)	*2000-18000	I
MCCHESNEY, CLARA T. (early 20TH C)	*100-650	F,L
MCCHESNEY, ROBERT (1913 -)	100-900	A
MCCLELLAND, BARCLAY (1891 - 1943)	*100-500	X
MCCLOSKEY, JIM BURNS (1925 -)	400-3500	P,G
MCCLOSKEY, WILLIAM J. (1859 - 1941)	6000-165000 +	S
MCCOLLUM, ALLAN (20TH C)	500-3000	A
MCCOMAS, FRANCIS JOHN	*600-16500	

* Denotes watercolors, pastels, drawings, and/or mixed media

MCCOMAS, FRANCIS JOHN (1874 - 1938)	750-22000	L,M
MCCOMAS, GENE FRANCES (20TH C)	*100-500	F
MCCONNELL, GEORGE (1852 - 1929)	100-2200	M,L
MCCORD, CHARLES W. (1852 - 1923)	100-1500	L
MCCORD, GEORGE HERBERT	*250-1500	
MCCORD, GEORGE HERBERT (1848 - 1909)	400-11000	L,M
MCCOY, LAWRENCE R. (1888 -)	150-850	X (F)
MCCRACKEN, JOHN HARVEY (1934 -)	400-4700	A
MCCREA, SAMUEL HARKNESS (1867 -)	500-3500	L
MCCULLEN, A. (19TH C)	*350-2500	X (L)
MCCUTCHEON, JOHN T. (1870 -)	*100-500	I
MCDERMITT, WILLIAM T. (1884 -)	*100-700	L
MCDERMOTT, A. (20TH C)	100-800	X (L)
MCDERMOTT, J.R. (1919 - 1977)	100-1000	I
MCDONALD, MASON (1880 - 1961)	400-2500	X (M)
MCDONNOUGH, JAMES (19TH C)	100-800	X (F,G)
MCDORMAN, DONALD (20TH C)	400-8000	G
MCDOUGALL, J.A. JR (1843 -)	500-2500	X (G)
MCDOUGALL, JOHN ALEXANDER (1810 - 1894)	400-3500	F
MCDUFF, FREDERICK H. (1931 -)	600-8500	L,F
MCENTEE, JERVIS	*150-2000	
MCENTEE, JERVIS (1828 - 1891)	700-60000	L
MCENTEE, WILLIAM H. (1857 - 1919)	400-3500	F
MCEVOY, EUGENIE (20TH C)	100-600	X (L)
MCEWAN, WILLIAM (19TH C)	400-3500	X (L)
MCFARLAND, R. (early 19TH C)	700-6500	G,L
MCFARLANE, DUNCAN (19TH C)	7000-30000	M
MCFEE, HENRY LEE	*200-3000	
MCFEE, HENRY LEE (1886 - 1953)	500-22000	S,F,L
MCGARREL, JAMES (1930 -)	800-10000	A
MCGILL, ELOISE POLK (20TH C)	100-1200	F,L
MCGLYNN, THOMAS A. (1878 - 1966)	1500-14000	M,L
MCGRATH, CLARENCE (1938 -)	3000-12000	X
MCGRATH, JOHN (1880 - 1940)	100-900	L
MCGREW, RALPH BROWNELL	*900-10000	

MCGREW, RALPH BROWNELL (1916 -)	7000-55000	X (F)
MCGUINNESS, C.W. (early 19TH C)	*1000-5000	P
MCILHENNEY, CHARLES MORGAN (1858 - 1904)	300-7500	L,M
MCILWORTH, THOMAS (actice 1755-65)	400-1500	F
MCINTOSH, PLEASANT RAY (1897 -)	350-6100	L
MCINTOSH, ROBERT J. (20TH C)	100-800	X (F)
MCKAIN, BRUCE (1900 -)	350-2500	M,L
MCKAY, M.R. (19TH C)	150-1000	L
MCKENNEY, HENRIETTA F.(1825 - 1877)	400-2500	L
MCKEY, EDWARD MICHAEL (1877 - 1918)	150-2200	X
MCKILLOP, WILLIAM (20TH C)	400-2500	X (S)
MCKINLEY, HAZEL (20TH C)	*100-600	X
MCKNIGHT, THOMAS (20TH C)	300-6500	A
MCLANE, JEAN (see JEAN MCLANE JOHANSEN)		
MCLAUGHLIN, JOHN (1898 - 1976)	5000-20000	A
MCLAUGLIN, M. LOUISE (1847 - 1939)	*400-1500	F
MCLEAN, HOWARD (19TH-20TH C)	1200-18000	G,F
MCLEAN, RICHARD (1934 -)	5000-40000	A
MCLOUGHLIN, GREGORY (20TH C)	100-1600	X (S)
MCMANUS, GEORGE (1884 - 1954)	*150-1700	I
MCMANUS, JAMES GOODWIN (1882 -)	*100-2000	F
MCMEE, J.W. (19TH C)	2000-15000	G,F
MCMEIN, NEYSA (1890 - 1949)	*200-2000	I
MCNAIR, WILLIAM HUGH (1867 -)	100-650	L
MCNALTY, WILLIAM CHARLES (1889 -)	200-1200	X (L)
MCNEIL, WILLIAM (19TH C)	100-1000	F
MCNETT, W. BROWN (19TH-20TH C)	100-1400	L
MEAD, T. (19TH C)	100-700	X (F)
MEADE, WILLIAM (20TH C)	200-1000	X
MEAKIN, LOUIS HENRY (1853 - 1917)	500-11000	L
MEARS, HENRIETTA DUNN (1877 -)	100-1100	M,L
MECHAU, FRANK (1904 - 1946)	500-3500	G,W,L
MEEKER, EDWIN JAMES (1853 - 1936)	*100-4000	F,L
MEEKER, JOSEPH RUSLING (1827 - 1889)	800-22000 +	L
MEEKS, EUGENE (1843 -)	350-4500	G

* Denotes watercolors, pastels, drawings, and/or mixed media

MEESER, LILLIAN BURK (1864 - 1942)	100-2200	L,S
MEGARGEE, LON (1883 - 1960)	350-2100	F,L
MEIGS, WALTER (1918 -)	100-1000	L
MEIRHANS, JOSEPH (1890 - 1981)	800-4500	A
MELBY, G. (19TH C)	300-1200	X (M)
MELCHER, GEORGE HENRY (1881 - 1975)	100-4000	L,M
MELCHERS, JULIUS GARI (1860 - 1932)	1000-87500	F,L
MELEGA, FRANK (1906 -)	100-500	X
MELLEN, MARY BLOOD (1817 -)	800-7500+	L,M
MELLON, ELEANOR (1894 - 1979)	200-1500	F,L
MELROSE, ANDREW W. (1836 - 1901)	800-30000+	L,M
MELTSNER, PAUL R. (1905 - 1966)	200-5000	F,L
MELTZER, ANNA ELKAN (1896 - 1974)	300-3600	X (F)
MELTZER, ARTHUR (1893 -)	400-12000	L,F
MENDENHALL, EMMA (1873 -)	*100-800	F,L
MENDENHALL, JACK (1937 -)	3000-18000	A
MENGER, EDWARD (1832 -)	400-2000	L
MENKES, SIGMUND JOSEPH (1896 - 1986)	300-9500	F,S
MENOCAL, RICHARD DE (20TH C)	100-800	X
MENTE, CHARLES (19TH-20TH C)	200-2000	X (I)
MENZLER-PEYTON, BERTHA S. (1871 - 1950)	400-6100	L,F
MERKIN, RICHARD (1938 -)	*200-1500	A
MERRIAM, JAMES A. (1880 - 1951)	100-1600	L
MERRILD, KNUD (1894 - 1954)	150-800	X (A)
MERRILL, FRANK THAYER (1848 -)	200-1500	I
MERRILL, ROBERT S. (1842 - 1924)	50-900	M
MERRITT, ANNA LEA (1844 - 1930)	500-3100	F
MERRITT, WARREN C. (1897 - 1968)	*100-800	L
MERSEREAU, PAUL (1868 -)	100-3000	L
MERSFELDER, JULES (1865 - 1937)	100-2200	L,G
MESCHES, ARNOLD (20TH C)	100-700	X (F)
MESSER, EDMUND CLARENCE (1842 - 1919)	300-1500	L,F
MESTROVIC, IVAN (1883 - 1962)	*100-850	F
METCALF, ARTHUR W. (1874 -)	*100-700	M
METCALF, CONGER (1914 -)	*100-1600	F

METCALF, ELIAB (1785 - 1834)	800-3500	F
METCALF, WILLARD LEROY	*400-6000	
METCALF, WILLARD LEROY (1858 - 1925)	2500-320000+	L,M,F,I
METEYARD, THOMAS BUFORD (1865 - 1928)	300-3500	L,I
METHVEN, H. WALLACE (1875 -)	400-2800	X (L)
METZ, GERRY MICHAEL (1943 -)	300-5000	G
MEUCCI, ANTHONY (early 19TH C)	400-1800	F
MEULI, ZAZA (1909 -)	100-600	M,L
MEURER, CHARLES ALFRED (1865 - 1955)	250-40700	F,S,L
MEUTTMAN, WILLIAM (19TH-20TH C)	*500-3500	X (L)
MEYER, CHRISTIAN (1838 - 1907)	500-4000	L,F
MEYER, ERNEST (1863 - 1961)	100-700	L
MEYER, ERNEST FREDERICK (1863 - 1961)	300-2000	L
MEYER, GWEN (20TH C)	100-700	X (S)
MEYER, HERBERT (1882 - 1960)	500-4800	G,L,S
MEYER, RICHARD MAX (late 19TH C)	400-3200	G,L
MEYER-KASSEL, HANS (20TH C)	*100-500	F
MEYEROWITZ, WILLIAM (1898 - 1981)	200-5000	L,M,S,F
MEYERS, HARRY MORSE (1886 - 1961)	400-2000	I
MEYERS, RALPH (1885 - 1948)	500-3500	L,F
MEYERS, ROBERT WILLIAM (1919 - 1970)	500-11000	L
MEZA, ENRIQUE (20TH C)	100-600	X (L)
MICEU, VIRGINIA (19TH C)	400-2000	L
MICHAELIS, H. VON (20TH C)	300-1000	X
MICHEEL, WILLIAM (- 1986)	100-900	X (L)
MIDDLETON, STANLEY GRANT (1852 -)	400-9000	F,L
MIELATZ, CHARLES F. W. (1864 - 1919)	200-1200	M
MIELZINER, JO (1901 - 1976)	*100-1500	I
MIERUM, GEORGE H. (20TH C)	800-4500	X (L)
MIFFLIN, JOHN HOUSTON (1807 - 1888)	400-3500	F
MIFFLIN, LLYOD (1846 - 1921)	400-3500	L
MIGNOT, LOUIS REMY (1831 - 1870)	1000-56000+	L,F
MIKUS, ELEANORE (1927 -)	100-800	A
MILARSKY, A. (20TH C)	150-900	L
MILBURN, JOHN (19TH C)	500-4500	P

* Denotes watercolors, pastels, drawings, and/or mixed media

MILBURN, OLIVER (1883 - 1934)	400-2000	X
MILDER, JAY	*100-800	
MILDER, JAY (1934 -)	200-8000	A
MILDWOFF, BEN (20TH C)	*100-500	X (L)
MILES, EUGENE (20TH C)	50-600	L
MILES, JOHN C. (19TH C)	100-850	F,G
MILES, S.S. (19TH C)	300-1500	L
MILLAR, ADDISON THOMAS (1860 - 1913)	500-33000	F,G,L,S
MILLAR, JAMES (18TH C)	500-25000	F
MILLER, A.R. (20TH C)	100-500	A
MILLER, ALFRED JACOB	*350-125000	
MILLER, ALFRED JACOB (1810 - 1874)	650-200000	L,F
MILLER, BARSE	*100-1500	
MILLER, BARSE (1904 - 1973)	200-3500	L
MILLER, CHARLES HENRY (1842 - 1922)	200-10000	M,L
MILLER, EVYLENA NUNN (1888 - 1966)	100-5000	X (L)
MILLER, FRANCIS H. (1885 - 1930)	400-9500	F,L,S
MILLER, HENRY (1897 - 1980)	*300-2000 +	X (F,L)
MILLER, HERMAN (20TH C)	*100-400	X (L)
MILLER, J.C. (20TH C)	100-600	L
MILLER, JOHN PAUL (20TH C)	*100-1500	X (L)
MILLER, KENNETH HAYES (1876 - 1952)	300-12000	F,G,S,L
MILLER, LAURA (20TH C)	100-600	X (F)
MILLER, LESTER W. (1848 - 1931)	50-400	L
MILLER, MARGUERITE C. (20TH C)	100-600	X (F)
MILLER, MELVIN (1937 -)	250-1500	L,G
MILLER, MILFRED BUNTING (1892 - 1964)	1000-15000	F
MILLER, PHIL (20TH C)	*100-600	X (M)
MILLER, RALPH DAVISON (1858 - 1945)	200-3500	L
MILLER, RICHARD EDWARD (1875 - 1943)	4000-352000+	F,S,L
MILLER, THOMAS OXLEY (1854 - 1909)	200-1500	L
MILLER, WILLIAM RICKARBY	*600-7000	
MILLER, WILLIAM RICKARBY (1818 - 1893)	1000-40000	L,F,M,S
MILLER-URY, ADOLPH (1882 -)	200-1000	X (S)
MILLESON, ROYAL HILL (1849 -)	100-7000	L

MILLET, CLARENCE (1897 - 1959)	600-7000	L
MILLET, FRANCIS DAVIS	*500-6500	
MILLET, FRANCIS DAVIS (1846 - 1912)	1000-65000	F,M,I
MILLET, GERALDINE REED (19TH-20TH C)	250-1800	F
MILLETT, G. VAN (1864 -)	100-2500	F,G,L
MILLROSE, G. (19TH C)	100-800	L
MILONE, G. (19TH C)	300-4000	L,F
MINAMOTO, KANAME (20TH C)	100-800	F
MINNEGERODE, MARIETTA (19TH C)	*100-800	X (F)
MINNELLI, VINCENTE (1910 -)	*300-1500	I
MINOR, ANNE ROGERS (1864 -)	150-1200	L
MINOR, ROBERT CRANNELL (1840 - 1904)	300-6600	L
MIRA, ALFRED S. (20TH C)	300-18000	X (L)
MITCHELL, ALFRED R. (1888 - 1972)	350-19000	L,F,M
MITCHELL, ARTHUR (1864 -)	150-1200	L
MITCHELL, ARTHUR R. (1889 - 1977)	700-8500	L,F
MITCHELL, BRUCE (1908 - 1963)	*100-850	L
MITCHELL, C.T. (19TH-20TH C)	100-400	L
MITCHELL, CHARLES DAVID (1887 - 1940)	100-900	X (M)
MITCHELL, E.T. (19TH C)	200-1200	L
MITCHELL, GEORGE BERTRAND (1872 - 1966)	300-5500	L,F
MITCHELL, GLEN	*300-3500	
MITCHELL, GLEN (1894 - 1972)	300-3500	X (L)
MITCHELL, JAMES III (20TH C)	*200-1500	M
MITCHELL, JOAN	*400-22000	
MITCHELL, JOAN (1926 - 1992)	5000-506000	A
MITCHELL, JOHN CAMPBELL (1862 - 1922)	250-1800	L
MITCHELL, THOMAS JOHN (1875 - 1940)	200-1800	L
MIZEN, FREDERICK KIMBALL (1888 - 1964)	400-3600	I,F
MOCHARANAK, MARY (20TH C)	100-500	X (F,L)
MODRA, THEODORE B. (1873 - 1930)	*100-2800	W,L
MOELLER, LOUIS CHARLES (1855 - 1930)	2500-60000	G,F
MOESSEL, JULIUS (1871 - 1959)	3000-12000	A,F,L
MOFFETT, ROSS E. (1888 - 1971)	100-4950	X (L,I)
MOHLERS, R.H. (19TH C)	100-900	X (L,F)

* Denotes watercolors, pastels, drawings, and/or mixed media

MOHOLY-NAGY, LAZLO	*1000-250000	
MOHOLY-NAGY, LAZLO (1895 - 1946)	2000-123000	A
MOHRMANN, JOHN HENRY (1857 - 1916)	1000-5500	M
MOLARSKY, ABRAM	*150-2100	
MOLARSKY, ABRAM (1883 - 1951)	100-1000	X (L)
MOLARSKY, MAURICE (1885 - 1950)	400-6500	F,S
MOLARSKY, MAURICE (1885 - 1950)	800-5000	A
MOLDOBAN, SACHA (20TH C)	100-1500	X (L)
MOLINA, VALENTIN (1880 -)	400-1500	X
MOLINARY, ANDREAS (1847 - 1915)	700-5000	X (L)
MONEGAR, CLARENCE BOYCE (20TH C)	*100-500	L,G
MONKS, JOHN AUSTIN SANDS	*100-600	
MONKS, JOHN AUSTIN SANDS (1850 - 1917)	250-1900	W,L
MONSEN, G. (19TH C)	100-600	X (M)
MONTAGUE, FARLEIGH L. (19TH C)	100-800	L
MONTALANT, JULIUS O. (active 1850-60)	300-2000	L
MONTGOMERY, ALFRED (1857 - 1922)	400-6100	G,S,L
MONTGOMERY, S.N. (19TH C)	300-3000	L
MONTGOMERY, T. (19TH-20TH C)	*100-600	X (M)
MONTRICHARD, RAYMOND D. (1887 - 1937)	100-1400	S
MOON, CARL (1878 - 1948)	400-5500	X (F)
MOOR, C.H. (20TH C)	*100-800	L
MOORE, ABEL BUEL (19TH C)	400-1500	F
MOORE, BENSON BOND (1882 - 1974)	200-3500	L
MOORE, BRETT F. (20TH C)	400-5000	L
MOORE, EDWIN AUGUSTUS (1858 - 1928)	1000-6500	X (S)
MOORE, FRANK MONTAGUE (1877 - 1967)	300-10000	L,M
MOORE, GUERNSEY (1874 - 1925)	*500-3500	X (F)
MOORE, H.W. (19TH C)	150-1200	X (L)
MOORE, HARRY HUMPHREY	*350-21000	
MOORE, HARRY HUMPHREY (1844 - 1926)	1500-22000	F,M
MOORE, HERBERT (20TH C)	300-4000	X (F)
MOORE, JACOB BAILY (1815 - 1893)	*500-2500	F
MOORE, JAMES HENRY (1854 - 1913)	*100-600	X (L)
MOORE, JOHN (1941 -)	*300-1500	S

MOORE, NELSON AUGUSTUS (1824 - 1902)	250-11000	L,F
MOORE, R. H. (20TH C)	100-500	L
MOORE, W.J. (19TH C)	250-1100	X (M)
MOORE-PARK, CARLTON (1877 -)	250-3000	X (F)
MORA, FRANCIS LUIS	*200-9500	
MORA, FRANCIS LUIS (1874 - 1960)	500-31000	F,L,I
MORALES, ARMANDO	*1500-6000	
MORALES, ARMANDO (1927 -)	600-48000	A
MORAN, ANNETTE (19TH C)	500-4000	X (G)
MORAN, EDWARD (1819 - 1878)	800-72000 +	M,G,F
MORAN, EDWARD PERCY (1862 - 1935)	250-15000	F,G,L
MORAN, H. MARCUS (19TH C)	400-5500	L
MORAN, LEON (JOHN LEON)	*200-2200	
MORAN, LEON (JOHN LEON) (1864 - 1941)	450-9000	F,G,L
MORAN, PAUL NIMMO (1864 - 1907)	500-6000	F,G
MORAN, PETER (1841 - 1914)	700-35000	W,L
MORAN, THOMAS	*1000-190000	
MORAN, THOMAS (1837 - 1926)	1500-950000 +	L,M
MORAN, VICTOR (19TH C)	150-1000	X (G)
MORATZ, FRANK (20TH C)	100-500	X (F)
MORGAN, ANNIE LAURIE (19TH C?)	400-2000	X (S)
MORGAN, HOWARD (20TH C)	100-2000	L
MORGAN, JANE (1832 - 1898)	300-2000	G
MORGAN, MARY DENEALE	*100-3600	
MORGAN, MARY DENEALE (1868 - 1948)	350-9500	M,L
MORGAN, PATRICK (1904 -)	100-800	X (S)
MORGAN, RANDALL (1920 -)	300-1000	L,F
MORGAN, SISTER GERTRUDE (1900 - 1980)	200-3500	P
MORGAN, T. (19TH-20TH C)	*100-600	X (L)
MORGAN, THEODORE J. (1872 - 1947)	300-1500	L,S
MORGAN, WALLACE (1873 - 1948)	*100-900	I
MORGAN, WILLIAM (1826 - 1900)	400-7500	F,G
MORGENTHALER, CHARLES A. (1893 -)	100-600	F
MORLEY, MALCOLM	*1500-60000	
MORLEY, MALCOLM (1931 -)	2500-319000 +	A

* Denotes watercolors, pastels, drawings, and/or mixed media

MORO, PAUL (20TH C)	300-1800	L,S
MORONI, F. (early 20TH C)	100-750	F
MORRELL, EDITH WHITCOMB (19TH C)	100-750	X (M)
MORRELL, WAYNE BEAM (1923 -)	200-2000	L,M
MORRIS, A. (19TH-20TH C)	200-900	L
MORRIS, ANDREW (active 1845-55)	400-1500	F
MORRIS, C.D. (19TH-20TH C)	350-2000	L
MORRIS, CARL (20TH C)	200-1200	A
MORRIS, GEORGE (20TH C)	100-600	L
MORRIS, GEORGE FORD (1873 - 1960)	600-3000	X (F)
MORRIS, GEORGE L.K. (1905 - 1975)	1500-40000	A
MORRIS, JOHN FLOYD (20TH C)	100-9500	L
MORRIS, KYLE (1918 - 1979)	1000-7500	A
MORRIS, NATHALIE (19TH-20TH C)	300-900	X (F)
MORRIS, ROBERT (1931 -)	*500-65000	A
MORRISON, DAVID (1885 - 1934)	*100-850	X (M,S)
MORRO, SYDNE (20TH C)	*100-500	L
MORSE, EDWARD LIND (1857 - 1923)	400-1500	X (L,G)
MORSE, GEORGE FREDERICK (1834 - 1926)	200-2000	L,M
MORSE, GEORGE R. (19TH C)	100-600	L
MORSE, HENRY DUTTON (1826 - 1888)	400-6500	W
MORSE, I.B. (20TH C)	200-800	L
MORSE, J.B. (active 1875 - 1890)	100-1500	L
MORSE, MARY MINNS (1859 -)	*100-800	X (L)
MORSE, SAMUEL FINLEY BREESE (1791 - 1872)	800-35000+	F,M
MORSE, VERNON JAY (1898 - 1965)	250-3100	L
MORSE, W. (19TH C)	100-1000	X (L)
MORTON, CHRISTINA (20TH C)	100-800	X (F)
MORTON, WILLIAM E. (1843 - 1916)	500-5000	L
MORVILLER, JOSEPH (active 1855-70)	450-10000	L
MOSER, FRANK H. (1886 - 1964)	*100-2400	X (L)
MOSER, JAMES HENRY (1854 - 1913)	400-4800	F,L
MOSERT, ZOE (20TH C)	*400-1500	X (F)
MOSES, ("GRANDMA") (1860 - 1961)	1500-200500	P
MOSES, ED (1926 -)	*700-28000	A

MOSES, FORREST K. (1893 - 1974)	300-3500	P
MOSES, THOMAS G. (1856 - 1934)	100-750	L
MOSES, THOMAS PALMER (19TH C)	*100-700	X (L)
MOSES, WALTER FARRINGTON (1874 - 1947)	100-1500	L
MOSLER, GUSTAVE H. (1875 - 1906)	100-1500	G,L
MOSLER, HENRY (1841 - 1920)	300-22000	F,G
MOSLER, JOHN HENRY (19TH C)	*100-800	X (L)
MOSS, R.F. (1898 - 1954)	300-1500	L
MOSTEL, ZERO (20TH C)	100-1200	X (F)
MOTE, MARCUS (1817 - 1890)	2000-20000	F,L
MOTHERWELL, ROBERT	*1500-150000	
MOTHERWELL, ROBERT (1915 - 1991)	3000-1100000	A
MOTTET, JEANIE GALLUP (1864 - 1934)	400-4000	F
MOULTON, FRANK B. (1847 -)	150-1200	L,S
MOUNT, EVILINA (19TH C)	500-2500	L
MOUNT, NINA (1837 - 1920)	300-4500	X (L)
MOUNT, SHEPARD ALONZO (1804 - 1868)	750-18000	F,L,W
MOUNT, WILLIAM SIDNEY (1807 - 1868)	4000-900000	G,F,L,S
MOUNTFORT, ARNOLD (1873 - 1942)	300-12000	F
MOWBRAY, HENRY SIDDONS (1858 - 1928)	1000-78000	F
MOYERS, WILLIAM (1916 -)	400-5200	X
MOYLAN, LLOYD (1893 -)	500-3500	F,L
MOZERT, ZOE (20TH C)	*300-5000	F
MUE, MAURICE AUGUSTE DEL (1875 - 1955)	100-1200	L
MUELLER, ALEXANDER (1872 - 1935)	300-8500	F,L
MUHLENFELD, S.L.R.(active 1895-1905)	500-8500	M
MUIR, EMILY (1904 -)	*200-1200	G,F,L
MULERTT, CAREL EUGENE	*250-1500	
MULERTT, CAREL EUGENE (1869 - 1915)	600-3500	F,L
MULHAUPT, FREDERICK JOHN (1871 - 1938)	750-26500	M,L,F,S
MULLER, DANIEL (1888 - 1977)	300-1800	X (I,L)
MULLER, HEINRICH (1823 - 1853)	700-6500 +	L
MULLER, JAN	*400-6500	
MULLER, JAN (1922 - 1958)	600-20000	F,L
MULLER, KARL (19TH C)	*100-400 +	X

* Denotes watercolors, pastels, drawings, and/or mixed media

MULLER-URY, ADOLF FELIX (1862 -)	100-3500	F,L,S
MULLICAN, LEE (1919 -)	100-800	A
MULLIGAN, C.L.(20TH C)	100-600	X (F)
MUMFORD, ROBERT T. (19TH-20TH C)	100-400	L
MUNGER, GILBERT DAVIS (1837 - 1903)	600-9500	L,F
MUNN, PAUL SANDBY (1773 - 1845)	*300-2500	G,L
MUNRO, JANET (1949 -)	4675	P
MUNROE, ALBERT F. (19TH-20TH C)	300-3000	X (S)
MUNSON, H. (19TH C)	100-800	L
MUNSON, KNUTE (20TH C)	*150-750	F,L
MURA, FRANK (1861 -)	300-3000	X (L)
MURCH, WALTER TANDY (1907 - 1967)	1200-53000	A,S
MURPHY, ADAH CLIFFORD (early 20TH C)	200-1000	X (F,I)
MURPHY, C.A. (early 20TH C)	100-300	L
MURPHY, CHRISTOPHER JR (1902 - 1973)	200-3000	L,F,G
MURPHY, CHRISTOPHER P.H. (1869 - 1939)	200-2500	F,L
MURPHY, HERMAN DUDLEY	*100-7000	
MURPHY, HERMAN DUDLEY (1867 - 1945)	400-18000	S,L
MURPHY, JOHN FRANCIS	*300-7000	
MURPHY, JOHN FRANCIS (1853 - 1921)	600-16500 +	L
MURRAY, ELIZABETH	*100-21000	
MURRAY, ELIZABETH (1940 -)	4000-126500	A
MURRAY, ELIZABETH HEAPHY (1815 - 1882)	*2850	G
MURRAY, F. RICHARDSON (20TH C)	*3500	S
MURRAY, GEORGE (1822 -)	200-1100	L
MURRY, J.E. (19TH C)	200-1500	X (S)
MUSGRAVE, ARTHUR (1880-)	150-900	L
MUSGRAVE, HELEN G. (1890 -)	100-500	X
MUSGRAVE, INNOCK (19TH C)	100-600	X (F)
MUSGRAVE, SYLVESTER (19TH C)	400-5000	F
MUSS-ARNOLT, GUSTAV (1858 - 1927)	500-8000	W
MYERS, FRANK H. (1899 - 1956)	400-6600	M,L,S,F
MYERS, IRWIN O. (1888-)	*100-500	X (L)
MYERS, JEROME	*150-7500	
MYERS, JEROME (1867 - 1940)	600-35000	G,F

MYERS, MARY (1878 -)	*50-600	L,F
MYGATT, ROBERTSON K. (1861-1919)	100-4000	L

N

Artist	Prices	Subject
NADELMAN, ELIE (1885 - 1946)	*400-6500	A,F
NADHERNY, E.V. (20TH C)	100-1200	I
NAGEL, HERMAN F. (1876 -)	350-1500	X (W)
NAGLER, EDITH KROGER VAN (1895 - 1978)	100-2500	F,I
NAGLER, FRED A. (1891 - 1983)	*100-500	X (F)
NAGY, ERNEST DE (1906 - 1944)	50-600	L
NAHL, CHARLES CHRISTIAN (1818 - 1878)	1500-100000	G,F,L,W
NAHL, H.W. ARTHUR (1833 - 1889)	500-3500	X (S)
NAHL, VIRGIL THEODORE (1876 - 1930)	400-4500	I,L,F
NAILOR, GEROLD (1917 - 1952)	*100-4500	X (F)
NAKAGAWA, HIROMI (20TH C)	100-800	X (L)
NAKIAN, REUBEN (1897 - 1986)	*500-3600	A
NANGERONI, CARLO (1922 -)	250-1000	A
NANKIVELL, FRANK A. (1869 - 1959)	300-8500	L
NARJOT, ERNEST (1827 - 1898)	600-22000	L,F
NASH, WILLARD AYER	*200-2000	
NASH, WILLARD AYER (1898 - 1943)	2000-33000	L,F,S
NASON, GERTRUDE (1890 - 1968)	250-1500 +	X (S)
NAST, THOMAS	*200-21000	
NAST, THOMAS (1840 - 1902)	1800-60000	I
NATKIN, ROBERT	*900-6000	
NATKIN, ROBERT (1930 -)	500-30000	A
NATTI, HENRY VAN (1876 - 1962)	400-3500	X
NAUMAN, BRUCE (1941 -)	*10000-410000	A
NEAGLE, JOHN (1796 - 1865)	500-7500	F
NEAL, DAVID DALHOFF (1838 - 1915)	1000-4500	F
NEALE, A. (19TH-20TH C)	100-500	X (M)
NEAVES, DOROTHY P. (20TH C)	*150-650	X (S)

NEEDHAN, D. (19TH-20TH C)	100-2000	L
NEEL, ALICE (1901 - 1984)	500-12000	A,S,F
NEHLIG, VICTOR (1830 - 1910)	700-6500	F,G,L
NEILL, FRANCIS ISABEL (1871 -)	100-1000	L
NEILSON, RAYMOND PERRY R.(1881 - 1964)	600-22000	G,F
NEIMAN, LEROY	*350-12000	
NEIMAN, LEROY (1925 -)	750-40000	A
NELAN, CHARLES (1854 - 1904)	*100-750	X (I)
NELKE, ALEXANDER (19TH-20TH C)	100-500	L,M
NELL, MISS TONY (20TH C)	*100-850	X (I)
NELLE, ANTHONY (19TH-20TH C)	*1200-3500	I
NELSON, A. PATRICK (20TH C)	*100-600	I
NELSON, EDWARD D. (- 1871)	1200-6500	L
NELSON, ERNEST BRUCE (1888 - 1952)	800-18000	L,M
NELSON, GEORGE LAURENCE (1887 - 1978)	250-9000	F,L
NELSON, J. (late 19TH C)	300-1200	X (G)
NELSON, JOHN G.(19TH C)	100-700	L
NELSON, RALPH LEWIS (1885 -)	100-500	X (L)
NELSON, WILLIAM (1861 - 1920)	*100-4800	F,G,L
NEMETHY, ALBERT (19TH-20TH C)	300-4500	G,L,M
NEMETHY, GEORGE (20TH C)	450-3500	M
NEMETHY, H. (20TH C)	*150-400	L
NESBITT, LOWELL	*100-1800	
NESBITT, LOWELL (1933 -)	500-25000	A
NESBITT, ROBERT H. (19TH-20TH C)	200-1500	L
NESBITT, VICTOR (20TH C)	200-1500	I
NESEMANN, ENNO (1861 -)	100-1500	L
NETTLETON, WALTER (1861 - 1936)	300-3100	L
NEUFELD, WOLDEMAR (1909 -)	300-2500	L,I
NEUHAUS, KARL EUGEN (1879 - 1963)	*100-3200	L
NEUMAN, ROBERT S. (1926 -)	150-850	X (L)
NEUMANN, ROBERT VON (1888 - 1976)	100-2500	G,F
NEUVILLE, BARONESS HYDE DE (1779 - 1849)	*500-5000	F,G
NEVELSON, LOUISE (1900 - 1988)	*900-121000	A,F
NEWBERRY, JOHN STRONG (1822 - 1892)	*100-900	I,F

* Denotes watercolors, pastels, drawings, and/or mixed media   259

NEWELL, GEORGE GLENN (1870 - 1947)	300-3500	W,L
NEWELL, HUGH	*100-900	
NEWELL, HUGH (1830 - 1915)	700-26500+	G,F,L
NEWELL, IDA H. (20TH C)	100-500	X (F)
NEWELL, PETER SHEAF (1862 - 1924)	*100-1800	I
NEWHALL, HARRIOT B. (1874 - 1940)	*300-1500	G
NEWHAM, JOHN DEEING (19TH-20TH C)	300-1200	X (L)
NEWMAN, BARNETT	*20000-330000	
NEWMAN, BARNETT (1905 - 1970)	20000-1800000	A
NEWMAN, CARL (1858 - 1932)	300-2000	F,L
NEWMAN, GEORGE A. (1875 - 1949)	100-1500	L
NEWMAN, HENRY RODERICK (1833 - 1918)	*500-72000	S,L
NEWMAN, ROBERT LOFTIN (1827 - 1912)	500-8000	F
NEWMAN, S. (19TH C)	*700-7000	X
NEWMAN, WILLIE BETTY (1864 -)	100-900	F,L
NEWTON, A.PARKER (20TH C)	200-1200	X (M,L)
NEWTON, GILBERT STUART (1794 - 1835)	300-6000	G,F
NEY, LLOYD (1893 -)	*150-700	X (A)
NEYLAND, HARRY (1877 - 1958)	600-20000	F,L,M
NIBLETT, GARY (1943 -)	2500-35000	L,F
NICHOLAS, GRACE (19TH C)	100-600	P
NICHOLAS, P. (19TH C)	100-500	L,F
NICHOLAS, THOMAS A.(20TH C)	*1200-15000	S,L,M
NICHOLLS, RHODA HOLMES	*500-4800	
NICHOLLS, RHODA HOLMES (1854 - 1930)	200-1500	F,G
NICHOLS, BURR H. (1848 - 1915)	250-5500+	G,F,L
NICHOLS, CELESTE BRUFF (active 1885-1910)	200-1000	X (S)
NICHOLS, DALE WILLIAM	*500-3800	
NICHOLS, DALE WILLIAM (1904 -)	400-25000	L,G,F
NICHOLS, H.D. (19TH C)	*100-750	L
NICHOLS, HENRY HOBART (1869 - 1962)	300-15000	L,M
NICHOLS, HUBLEY (19TH C)	350-2500	X (M)
NICHOLS, SPENCER BAIRD (1875 - 1950)	400-5000	F,L
NICHOLSON, CHARLES W. (1886 - 1965)	100-1000	L,S
NICHOLSON, EDWARD HORACE (1901 - 1966)	250-6000	M,F,L

* Denotes watercolors, pastels, drawings, and/or mixed media

NICHOLSON, GEORGE WASHINGTON (1832 - 1912)	400-12000	L,F
NICHOLSON, LILLIE MAE (1884 - 1964)	250-3500	M,L
NICOLL, JAMES CRAIG (1846 - 1918)	300-10000	M
NICOLL, NICOL (1923 -)	*200-1200	X (G)
NICOLS, AUDLEY DEAN (20TH C)	400-2000	L
NIELSEN, PETER (20TH C)	15400	L
NIEMEYER, JOHN HENRY (1839 - 1932)	400-6200 +	F
NILES, GEORGE E. (1837 - 1898)	200-1200	X (G)
NIRO, ROBERT DE (1922 -)	400-1800	X (S)
NISBET, ROBERT H.	*100-800	
NISBET, ROBERT H. (1879 - 1961)	300-5500 +	L,F
NOBLE, JOHN (1874 - 1935)	750-4800	M,F
NOBLE, THOMAS SATTERWHITE (1835 - 1907)	400-9500	F
NOGUCHI, ISAMU	*2500-286000	
NOGUCHI, ISAMU (1904 - 1988)	1000-90000	L,F
NOHEIMER, MATHIAS (20TH C)	400-3500	A
NOLAN, E.B. (19TH-20TH C)	*100-500	X (L)
NOLAND, KENNETH (1924 -)	10000-500000 +	A,L
NOLF, JOHN THOMAS (1872 - 1950)	100-1200	I
NOLF, THEODORE E. (20TH C)	100-600	X (L)
NOLL, CHARLES (20TH C)	*100-500	M
NOONAN, JAMES (20TH C)	*100-400	L
NORBERG, C. ALBERT (1895 -)	250-1500	L,F
NORDELL, CARL JOHAN DAVID (1885 -)	300-7500 +	F,L,S
NORDELL, EMMA PARKER (20TH C)	150-1200	X (F)
NORDELL, POLLY (19TH-20TH C)	*100-600	F
NORDFELDT, BROR JULIUS OLSSON	*450-5500	
NORDFELDT, BROR JULIUS OLSSON (1878 - 1955)	500-33000	L,G,F,S
NORDHAUSEN, AUGUST HENRY (1901 -)	150-2900	F
NORDSTROM, CARL HAROLD (1876 - 1934)	200-2500	M,L
NORFOLK, WALTER (19TH-20TH C)	100-500	X
NORMAN, MABEL (20TH C)	100-400	X (G)
NORRIS, S. WALTER	*100-400	
NORRIS, S. WALTER (1868 -)	200-1500	X (L)
NORSE, STANSBURY (19TH C)	150-800	L

* Denotes watercolors, pastels, drawings, and/or mixed media   261

NORTH, NOAH (1809 - 1880)	2000-15000+	P
NORTHCOTE, JAMES (1822 - 1904)	250-8000	F,L,M
NORTON, L.D. (19TH-20TH C)	100-900	X (L,M)
NORTON, WILLIAM EDWARD	*200-3100	
NORTON, WILLIAM EDWARD (1843 - 1916)	100-25000	M,L
NORTWICK, EVAN (20TH C)	100-400	X (F,G)
NOTT, RAYMOND (1888 - 1948)	*100-1800	L
NOURSE, ELIZABETH	*1500-45000	
NOURSE, ELIZABETH (1859 - 1938)	2500-82500	F
NOVAK, LOUIS (1903 - 1983)	*100-750	L,M
NOVROS, DAVID (1941-)	400-25500	A
NOWAK, FRANZ (1885 - 1973)	*500-3500	S
NOYES, BERTHA (1876 - 1966)	150-850	X (F)
NOYES, GEORGE LOFTUS (1864 - 1951)	350-28000	L
NUDERSCHER, FRANK B. (1880 - 1959)	400-9000	F,L,I
NUHLER, AUGUSTUS W. (- 1920)	*100-600	X (M)
NUNAMAKER, KENNETH R. (1890 - 1957)	900-38500	L
NUNN, FREDERICK (1879 - 1959)	50-600	
NURSTRUM, C. (20TH C)	*100-600	X (M)
NUYTTENS, JOSEF PIERRE (1880 - 1960)	*100-700	X (F)
NYE, EDGAR H.(1879 - 1943)	200-4000	L
NYE, MOSES (19TH C)	200-1200	X (M)

O

Artist	Prices	Subject
O'DONOVAN, WILLIAM RUDOLPH (1844 - 1920)	*150-600	L
O'GRADY, DONN (20TH C)	300-1200	X
O'HAGEN, JOHN L. (20TH C)	100-500	X
O'HARA, ELIOT (1890 - 1969)	*200-1000	L
O'HIGGINS, PABLO	*200-2000	
O'HIGGINS, PABLO (1904 -)	500-12500	X (F)
O'KEEFFE, GEORGIA	*1500-605000	

* Denotes watercolors, pastels, drawings, and/or mixed media

O'KEEFFE, GEORGIA (1887 - 1986)	8000-1650000+	A
O'KELLEY, MATTIE LOU (1908 -)	3500-21000	P
O'KELLY, ALOYSIUS (1853 - 1892)	600-20000	F,L
O'LEARY, ANGELA (1879 - 1921)	*200-1500	L
O'LEARY, GALBRAITH (20TH C)	400-2000	L
O'NEAL, J. (20TH C)	150-850	X (L)
O'NEILL, ROSE CECIL (1875 - 1944)	*400-6600	I
O'SHEA, JOHN (1876-1956)	300-12000	L,M
O'SHEA, KAREN (20TH C)	100-600	X (S)
O'SULLIVAN, PAUL F. (20TH C)	*300-900	X (M)
OAKES, WILBUR (1876 -)	150-3000	X (M)
OAKLEY, THORNTON	*100-3000	
OAKLEY, THORNTON (1881 - 1953)	400-10000	I
OAKLEY, VIOLET (1874 - 1961)	*100-1900	F,S,I
OATES, MERRITT L.C. (19TH-20TH C)	100-300	X (F)
OBATA, CHUIRA (20TH C)	*100-500	X (L)
OBERTEUFFER, GEORGE (1878 - 1940)	800-25000	L,M
OCHTMAN, LEONARD (1854 - 1934)	700-14000+	L
OCHTMAN, MINA FUNDA (1862 - 1924)	200-4200	X (L)
ODDIE, WALTER M. (1808 - 1865)	500-6000	L
OELSHIG, AUGUSTA (20TH C)	300-1500	A
OERTEL, JOHANNES A. S. (1823 - 1909)	1000-31000	G,F
OF, GEORGE F. (1876 -)	500-6500	L,S
OGDEN, FREDERICK D. (19TH C)	400-1500	L,I
OGDEN, J. WILLIAM (19TH C)	100-700	L
OGLE, MARK (20TH C)	100-1200	L
OGLIVIE, JOHN CLINTON (1838 - 1900)	600-18000	L,M
OKADA, KENZO (1902 -)	2000-64000+	A
OKAMURA, ARTHUR (1932 -)	350-6500	A
OLDENBURG, CLAES THURE (1929 -)	*1000-88000	A
OLDFIELD, OTIS (1890 - 1969)	600-30000	F,L,M
OLESEN, OLAF (1837 -)	500-4000	L
OLINSKY, IVAN GREGOREVITCH (1878 - 1962)	1000-36000+	F
OLINSKY, TOSCA (1909 -)	200-2000	X (S)
OLITSKI, JULES (1922 - 1964)	2000-355000	A

OLIVEIRA, NATHAN	*500-20000	
OLIVEIRA, NATHAN (1928 -)	1000-40000	A
OLIVER, DAVID (20TH C)	100-500	X (L,F)
OLIVER, FREDERICK WE. (1876 - 1963)	100-2000	M,S
OLIVER, JEAN NUTTING (1883 -)	100-1000	X (F)
OLIVER, SANDI (20TH C)	500-4500	M,F
OLIVER, THOMAS CLARKSON (1827 - 1893)	400-11000	M
OLSEN, HENRY (1902 - 1983)	200-1000	L,M,S
OLSEN, HERB (1905 - 1973)	*100-650	L
OLSON, CARL GUSTAF THEODORE (1875 -)	100-500	L
OLSON, JOSEPH OLAF	*100-1200	
OLSON, JOSEPH OLAF (1894 - 1979)	125-5500	L,F
ONDERDONK, JULIAN (1882 - 1922)	600-23100	L
ONGLY, W. (19TH C)	150-900	L,F
ONTHANK, NAHUM B. (1823 - 1888)	200-2500	F
OPERTI, ALBERT JASPER (1852 - 1922)	*350-2500	M
OPPENHEIM, DENNIS A. (1938 -)	*800-14500	A
OPPER, JOHN (1908 -)	*200-2500	A
ORCULL, A.C. (late 19TH C)	100-500	L
ORD, JOSEPH BAYAS (1805 - 1865)	2000-18000	F,S
ORDWAY, ALFRED T. (1819 - 1897)	100-1800	L
ORGAN, MARJORIE	*100-300	
ORGAN, MARJORIE (1886 - 1931)	200-3500	I
ORMSBY, DOROTHY (19TH-20TH C)	400-1800	L,F
ORR, ALFRED EVERITT (1886 -)	*100-500	L,I
ORR, ELLIOT (1904 -)	100-900	X (F)
OSBURN, SALLY (20TH C)	*100-650	F
OSCAR, CHARLES	*200-1800	
OSCAR, CHARLES (20TH C)	200-900	X (F)
OSHIVER, HARRY JAMES (1888 -)	200-1500	X (S)
OSSORIO, ALFONSO ANGEL	*400-13000	
OSSORIO, ALFONSO ANGEL (1916 -)	26400	A
OSTHAUS, EDMUND HENRY	*500-16000	
OSTHAUS, EDMUND HENRY (1858 - 1928)	500-40000	W
OSTRANDER,WILLIAM CHESEBOURGH (B.1858)	*350-1200	X (L)

* Denotes watercolors, pastels, drawings, and/or mixed media

OSTROWSKY, SAM (1885 -)	100-1200	F,S
OSVER, ARTHUR (1912 -)	100-1000	X
OTIS, BASS (1784 - 1861)	800-9100	F
OTIS, GEORGE DEMONT	*200-1500	
OTIS, GEORGE DEMONT (1877 - 1962)	650-30500	L,M
OTTE, WILLIAM LOUIS	*100-2100	
OTTE, WILLIAM LOUIS (1871-1951)	400-14000	L,M
OTTINGER, GEORGE MORTON (1833 - 1917)	800-18000	G
OUREN, KARL (1882 - 1943)	200-3600	L
OVEREND, WILLIAM HEYSMAN (1851 - 1898)	500-6500	M,I
OWEN, BILL (1942 -)	6500-35000	G,F,L
OWEN, CARLOS J. (19TH C)	*100-500	X (L)
OWEN, FRANK EDWARD (1907 -)	400-2000	A
OWEN, GEORGE (active 1855-75)	400-3500	G,F
OWEN, JOEL (20TH C)	*100-600	L
OWEN, ROBERT EMMETT (1878 - 1957)	600-10000+	L
OWLES, ALFRED (1896 -)	*150-900	S

P

Artist	Prices	Subject
PAALEN, ALICE (20TH C)	*150-750	A
PACE, STEPHEN (1918 -)	500-5000	A
PACH, WALTER (1883 - 1958)	400-2500	X (F)
PACKARD, MABEL (19TH-20TH C)	500-2500	X (L)
PADDOCK, ETHEL LOUISE (1887 -)	*100-950	G,F,M
PAGE, EDWARD A. (1850 - 1928)	100-2400	M,G,L
PAGE, ELIZABETH AMIE (1908 -)	100-1800	L
PAGE, JOSEPHINE A. (20TH C)	100-1200	L
PAGE, MARIE DANFORTH (1869 - 1940)	900-18000	F
PAGE, WALTER GILMAN (1862 - 1934)	450-18000	F,L,M,S
PAGE, WILLIAM	*400-10000+	
PAGE, WILLIAM (1811 - 1885)	1000-18000+	F,L,G,M

PAGES, JULES EUGENE (1867 - 1946)	700-20000	L,F,G
PAGINTON, (19TH-20TH C)	200-1800	L
PAIL, EDOUARD (1851 - 1916)	300-4300	L
PAIN, WILLIAM BOWYER (1856 - 1930)	*100-700	L
PAINE, GEORGE S. (19TH C)	*100-700	L
PAINE, H.H. (19TH C)	1500-6000	P
PAINE, SUSANNAH (1792 - 1862)	1000-7500	F,L
PAIRPOINT, NELLIE M. (19TH-20TH C)	100-750	L,W
PALFRIES, J. (19TH C)	100-600	X (L)
PALLADIN, DANIEL (or "CHETHLATE") (1929 - 1984)	500-3000	A
PALMER, ADELAIDE (1851 - 1928)	400-2500	S
PALMER, ERASTUS DOW (1817 - 1904)	*100-300	F
PALMER, PAULINE (1865 - 1938)	250-5000+	L,F
PALMER, SAMUEL (1805 - 1881)	*100-21000+	L (W)
PALMER, WALTER LAUNT	*500-15000	
PALMER, WALTER LAUNT (1854 - 1932)	900-33000+	L,F,M
PALMER, WILLIAM C.	*100-1500	
PALMER, WILLIAM C. (1906 - 1987)	1000-6600	X (L,I)
PALMORE, THOMAS DALE (1940 -)	150-1500	X (S)
PALUMBO, ALPHONSO (1890 -)	200-5500	L
PANCOAST, MORRIS HALL (1877 - 1963)	150-10000	L,I
PANSING, FRED (1844 - 1916)	1000-35000+	M,L
PAPE, ERIC (1870 - 1938)	800-20000	L,F,S
PAPPAS, JOHN L. (1898 -)	100-300	X (L)
PAPPE, CARL (20TH C)	100-500	L
PARADISE, JOHN (1783 - 1833)	200-3000	P
PARADISE, PHILLIP (1905 -)	*250-1800	X (M)
PARCELL, MALCOLM S. (1896 -)	500-3500	L,G
PARIS, WALTER (1842 - 1906)	*150-9000	L
PARISEN, WILLIAM DE (1800 - 1832)	100-850	F
PARISH, BETTY W. (1910 -)	*50-300	M
PARISH, JANE (19TH C)	800-3000	S
PARK, DAVID	*800-18000	
PARK, DAVID (1911 - 1960)	1000-110000	A

* Denotes watercolors, pastels, drawings, and/or mixed media

PARK, ROSWELL (1807 - 1869)	*5000-25000	X (L)
PARKER, CHARLES STEWART (1860 - 1930)	200-2000	L,M,F
PARKER, CUSHMAN (1882 - 1940)	800-2500	I
PARKER, EDGAR (1840 - 1892)	800-6000	L,F
PARKER, JOHN ADAMS (1829 - 1905)	400-4500	L
PARKER, JOHN F. (1884 -)	100-800	X (S)
PARKER, KAY PETERSON (20TH C)	*100-500	X
PARKER, LAWTON S. (1868 - 1954)	2000-80000 +	F,L
PARKER, PAUL (1905 -)	100-700	X (S)
PARKER, RAYMOND (1922 - 1990)	500-7500	A
PARKER, S. PERKINS (1862 - 1942)	200-2000	M,L
PARKHURST, H. (20TH C)	100-900	X (G)
PARKINGTON, J. (19TH C)	100-750	L
PARKS, JAMES DALLAS (1907 -)	500-5000	X (F)
PARRISH, CLARA WAEVER (- 1925)	*150-850	L,F
PARRISH, DAVID BUCHANAN (1939 -)	2000-14500	A
PARRISH, MAXFIELD FREDERICK	*200-45000	
PARRISH, MAXFIELD FREDERICK (1870 - 1966)	1500-242000	I
PARRISH, STEVEN WINDSOR (1846 - 1938)	250-5500	L
PARROT, A. (19TH C)	100-500	L
PARROTT, WILLIAM SAMUEL (1844 - 1915)	500-6500	L
PARSHALL, DEWITT	*100-800	
PARSHALL, DEWITT (1864 - 1956)	200-1800	L,M
PARSHALL, DOUGLAS EWELL (1899 -)	400-4200	L
PARSONS, A. (19TH C)	150-1200	X (L,M)
PARSONS, BETTY B. (1900 - 1982)	*100-2200	L
PARSONS, CHARLES (1821 - 1910)	400-3500	M,G
PARSONS, M.A. (19TH C)	*800-2500	L
PARSONS, MARION RANDALL (1880 - 1953)	300-4000	L,F
PARSONS, ORRIN SHELDON (1866 - 1943)	1200-32000	L
PARSONS, PHILLIP B. (1896 - 1977)	100-1500	L
PARSONS, THEOPHILUS (1876 - 1934)	100-900	L,F
PARTEE, MCCULLOUGH (20TH C)	*200-1000	X (F)
PARTINGTON, RICHARD LANGTRY	*200-4000	
PARTINGTON, RICHARD LANGTRY (1868 - 1929)	400-7200	L,M

PARTON, ARTHUR B.(1842 - 1914)	450-18000	L
PARTON, ERNEST (1845 - 1933)	500-7000	L
PARTON, HENRY WOODRIDGE (1858 - 1933)	600-4500	F,L
PARTON, HULDA (19TH-20TH C)	100-500	X (L)
PARTRIDGE, WILLIAM H. (1858 -)	100-1200	L
PASCIN, JULES	*700-60000	
PASCIN, JULES (1885 - 1930)	2500-515000	A,F
PASKELL, WILLIAM FREDERICK	*100-900	
PASKELL, WILLIAM FREDERICK (1866 - 1951)	250-1500+	L,M
PASPAYNE, GEORGE F. (20TH C)	*300-700	M,L
PATECKY, ALBERT (20TH C)	100-800	L,F
PATTEN, MARION (1889 - 1941)	100-900	M,L
PATTERSON, AMBROSE McCARTHY (1877 - 1930)	400-11000	L
PATTERSON, CHARLES ROBERT (1878 - 1958)	400-8500	M
PATTERSON, HOWARD ASHMAN (1891 -)	100-2500	L,F
PATTERSON, MARGARET JORDAN (1867 - 1950)	*200-3100	I,L
PATTERSON, ROBERT (1898 - 1981)	100-800	I
PATTISON, JAMES WILLIAM (1844 - 1915)	600-4500	L,F
PATTON, KATHERINE (19TH-20TH C)	300-1500	X (M,L)
PATTY, WILLIAM ARTHUR (1889 - 1961)	100-1500	X (M)
PAUL, JEREMIAH (- 1830)	2000-65000	G,F
PAULI, RICHARD (1855 - 1892)	300-1500	L
PAULL, GRACE (1898 -)	*100-500	G,F
PAULSON, O. (19TH C)	400-4500	L
PAULUS, FRANCIS PETRUS (1862 - 1933)	200-4000	G,L,S
PAUS, HERBERT ANDREW (1880 - 1946)	*200-4000	I
PAVIL, ELIE ANATOLE (1873 - 1948)	500-16000	L,F
PAXSON, EDGAR SAMUEL	*300-35000	
PAXSON, EDGAR SAMUEL (1852 - 1919)	600-70000	F,G,I
PAXSON, ETHEL EASTON (1885 - 1982)	150-3000	L,F,I
PAXTON, ELIZABETH V.O. (1877 - 1971)	500-8500	X (L,F)
PAXTON, JOHN (19TH-20TH C)	500-6000	F
PAXTON, WILLIAM A. (19TH-20TH C)	200-1200	L
PAXTON, WILLIAM MCGREGOR	*150-39000	
PAXTON, WILLIAM MCGREGOR (1869 - 1941)	100-350000	F,L,S,W

* Denotes watercolors, pastels, drawings, and/or mixed media

PAYNE, EDGAR ALWIN (1882 - 1947)	800-74000	L,M,S
PAYNE, ELSIE PALMER	*1400-2800	
PAYNE, ELSIE PALMER (1884 - 1971)	600-2500	M,L,F
PAYNE, GEORGE S. (1860 - 1938)	*200-900	X (S)
PAYNE, HILMA M. (20TH C)	250-1000	L
PAYZANT, CHARLES (1898 - 1980)	*300-2500	L
PAYZANT, CLAUDE L. (20TH C)	100-900	M,L
PEABODY, RUTH EATON (1898 - 1967)	200-4500	X (L)
PEAKE, CHANNING (1910 -)	*100-700	X (F)
PEALE, CHARLES WILLSON (1741 - 1827)	3500-????+	F
PEALE, HARRIET CANY (1800 - 1869)	600-7500+	F,S
PEALE, JAMES (1749 - 1831)	1500-375000	S,F,L,M
PEALE, MARY JANE (1826 - 1902)	700-12100	S,F
PEALE, RAPHAELLE (1774 - 1825)	8000-500000	S,F
PEALE, REMBRANDT (1778 - 1860)	2000-380000+	F
PEALE, RUBENS (1784 - 1865)	700-10000	S,W
PEALE, SARAH MIRIAM	*100-900	
PEALE, SARAH MIRIAM (1800 - 1885)	750-43000	F,S
PEALE, TITIAN RAMSEY	*700-35000	
PEALE, TITIAN RAMSEY (1799 - 1885)	1000-40000	I,W,L
PEALLZOR, ESTELLE (20TH C)	50-400	L
PEARCE, CHARLES SPRAGUE (1851 - 1914)	150-70000+	F
PEARCE, EDGAR LEWIS (1885 -)	200-6000	X (F)
PEARCE, WILLIAM HOUGHTON SPRAGUE (19TH-20TH C)	100-1800	L,M
PEARL, MOSES P. (20TH C)	250-1800	L
PEARLSTEIN, PHILIP	*500-20000	
PEARLSTEIN, PHILIP (1924 -)	2500-58000	A,F
PEARSON, CORNELIUS (1805 - 1891)	*200-2100	L
PEARSON, HENRY (1914 -)	200-1000	X (A)
PEARSON, JAMES (1900 -)	100-500	X
PEARSON, MARGUERITE STUBER (1898 - 1978)	100-29000	F,M,S
PEARSON, ROBERT (- 1891)	500-3500	X (M)
PEASE, G.M. (19TH C)	200-1500	X (L)
PEASLEE, MARGUERITE ELLIOTT (20TH C)	*100-600	L,S

PEBBLES, FRANK MARION (1839 - 1928)	200-2500	F,L,M
PECK, CHARLES E. (1827 - 1900)	150-1800	L
PECK, HENRY JARVIS (1880 - 1964)	200-1200	I
PECK, SHELDON (1797 - 1868)	5000-100000	P
PECKHAM, (DEACON) ROBERT	*300-1200	
PECKHAM, (DEACON) ROBERT (1785 - 1877)	1200-55000	F
PECKHAM, LEWIS (1788 - 1822)	500-6000	F
PEDERSON, ROBERT HOLM (1906 -)	200-1200	X (M)
PEELE, JOHN THOMAS (1822 - 1897)	400-18000	G,F,W
PEETERS, E. (19TH C)	200-1200	S
PEIRCE, H. WINTHROP (1850 - 1935)	300-4500	F,L,I
PEIRCE, WALDO (1884 - 1970)	300-9000	G,S,F
PEIXOTTO, ERNEST CLIFFORD (1869 - 1940)	250-3500	I,L
PEIXOTTO, FLORIAN (19TH C)	300-3300	X (L)
PELL, ELLA FERRIS (1846 -)	400-2000	X (F,I)
PELL, J. (19TH-20TH C)	200-1500	L
PELLAGALE, W.E. (19TH C)	100-650	L,F
PELS, ALBERT (1910 -)	100-3500	F
PELTON, AGNES	*100-2100	
PELTON, AGNES (1881 - 1961)	100-7500 +	F,L
PENE DU BOIS, GUY	*100-5000	
PENE DU BOIS, GUY (1884 - 1958)	3000-105000	G,F
PENFIELD, EDWARD (1866 - 1925)	*200-3500	I
PENFOLD, FRANK C. (19TH-20TH C)	800-10000	F
PENNELL, HARRY (early 20TH C)	250-3500	L
PENNELL, JOSEPH	*100-6500	
PENNELL, JOSEPH (1860 - 1926)	*100-14500	I
PENNEY, FREDERICK D. (1900 - 1988)	150-1600	L
PENNIMANN, JOHN RITTO (1782 - 1841)	2500-30000	G,F
PENNINGTON, HARPER (1854 - 1920)	500-7500	F
PENNOYER, ALBERT SHELDON (1888 - 1957)	200-5000	L,F
PENT, ROSE MARIE (- 1954)	100-600	L
PEPPER, BEVERLY (1924 -)	*500-3500	A
PEPPER, CHARLES HOVEY (1864 - 1950)	*100-1100	L
PERBANDT, CARL VON (1832 - 1911)	300-11000	L

* Denotes watercolors, pastels, drawings, and/or mixed media

PERCEVAL, DON (1908 - 1979)	*6050	F
PERCIVAL, EDWIN (1793 -)	400-1000	F
PERCONI, D.F. (20TH C)	400-2000	X (G)
PERCY, LORAN (20TH C)	100-500	L
PEREIRA, IRENE RICE	*100-5000	
PEREIRA, IRENE RICE (1901 - 1971)	400-10500	A
PERELLI, ACHILLE (1822 - 1891)	400-3000	S,W
PERILLO, GREGORY (1929 -)	400-9000	F,G
PERKINS, D.H. (20TH C)	*100-700	X (L)
PERKINS, GRANVILLE	*200-2800	
PERKINS, GRANVILLE (1830 - 1895)	100-20000	L,M,I
PERKINS, RUTH HUNTER (1911 -)	300-4000	P
PERKINS, SARAH	*500-3000	
PERKINS, SARAH (1771 - 1831)	1000-20000	P (F)
PERLAR, L. (19TH C)	300-1500	X
PERLE, F. (early 20TH C)	100-850	X (M)
PERRAULT, JOSEPH (20TH C)	100-300	X (M)
PERREIRA, JOAN (20TH C)	100-700	A
PERRINE, VAN DEARING (1869 - 1955)	900-5000	A
PERRY, CLARA FAIRFIELD (- 1941)	200-1000	L
PERRY, CLARA GREENLEAF (1871 - 1960)	100-4000	L,G
PERRY, ENOCH WOOD	*500-6000	
PERRY, ENOCH WOOD (1831 - 1915)	200-48000	F,G,L
PERRY, F.C. (19TH C)	100-700	L
PERRY, LILLA CABOT (1848 - 1933)	400-35200	F,L
PERRY, WILLIAM C. (20TH C)	100-1400	X
PERSSON, FRITIOF (20TH C)	100-600	L
PERU, ALTO (18TH C)	1500-8000+	F
PESCE, GIRLO (20TH C)	100-800	X (M)
PETERDI, GABOR (1915 -)	*100-700	A
PETERIS, J.H. (20TH C)	100-700	X (M)
PETERS, CARL WILLIAM (1897 - 1988)	300-5000	L,M
PETERS, CHARLES ROLLO (1862 - 1928)	450-18000	L,M
PETERSEN, CARL (1885 -)	150-900	L
PETERSEN, EINAR (1885 - 1986)	1980	L

PETERSEN, K. GUNNOR (1905 - 1985)	*50-400	F,L
PETERSEN, L. (19TH C)	1000-4500	M
PETERSEN, THOMAS (20TH C)	300-1200	X (M)
PETERSON, JANE	*500-18000 +	
PETERSON, JANE (1876 - 1965)	200-126500	M,F,L,S
PETERSON, ROLAND (1926 -)	150-8000	X
PETICOLAS, ARTHUR EDWARD (1793 - 1853)	3000-18000	L
PETICOLAS, PHILIP A. (1760 - 1843)	150-900	F
PETO, JOHN FREDERICK (1854 - 1907)	4000-420000 +	S
PETROFF, GILMER (1913 -)	*200-800	X (F)
PETRUS, P. (19TH-20TH C)	100-800	X (L)
PETRY, VICTOR (1903 -)	200-3000	X (S)
PETRYN, ANDREW (20TH C)	100-1500	X (I)
PETTET, WILLIAM (1942 -)	300-5000	A
PETTIBONE, RICHARD (1938 -)	150-950	X
PETTY, GEORGE (20TH C)	*300-7500	I
PETTY, JOHN (20TH C)	*100-450	L
PEW, GERTRUDE (20TH C)	*100-1200	X (F)
PEYRAUD, FRANK C. (1858 - 1948)	300-5000	L,F
PEYSTER, EVA DE (early 19TH C)	*400-1000	P
PFEIFFER, FRITZ (1889 - 1960)	500-4500	X
PFEIFFER, HEINRICH R. (1874 - 1960)	100-2100	M,L
PHARES, FRANK (20TH C)	100-600	I
PHELAN, CHARLES T. (1840 -)	200-1500	W,L
PHELAN, HAROLD LEE (1881 -)	100-800	L
PHELPS, EDITH CATLIN (1875 - 1961)	100-5600	F,L
PHELPS, HELEN W. (1864 - 1944)	50-500	F
PHELPS, WILLIAM PRESTON (1848 - 1923)	300-7000	L,G
PHILBRICK, OTIS (1888 - 1973)	300-2000	X (S,F)
PHILIP, FREDERICK WILLIAM (1814 - 1841)	400-3500	F,S
PHILIPP, ROBERT (1895 - 1981)	100-21000	F,G,M,S
PHILIPPOTEAUX, PAUL D. (1846 -)	700-5500	G,F,L
PHILIPS, FRANK ALBERT (19TH C)	400-3500	X
PHILLIPS, AARON FRANCIS (1848 - 1899)	300-1500	L,F
PHILLIPS, AMMI (1788 - 1865)	2700-250000 +	P

* Denotes watercolors, pastels, drawings, and/or mixed media

PHILLIPS, BERT GREER (1868 - 1956)	1000-70000	F,L,S,I
PHILLIPS, C. (mid 19TH C)	100-800	X (S)
PHILLIPS, C.E. (19TH C)	100-1000	L
PHILLIPS, COLES	*500-12000	
PHILLIPS, COLES (1880 - 1927)	800-10000	I
PHILLIPS, GORDON (1927 -)	400-18700	G,F
PHILLIPS, JOHN CAMPBELL (1873 - 1949)	100-3300	F,L
PHILLIPS, MARJORIE (1895 -)	150-3000	G,F,S
PHILLIPS, R. (20TH C)	200-1000	X (S)
PHILLIPS, S. GEORGE (- 1965)	350-9400	L,F
PHILLIPS, WALTER JOSEPH (1884 - 1963)	*800-8500	L
PHIPPEN, GEORGE (1916 - 1966)	3000-60000	I,L,F
PIAZZONI, GOTTARDO (1872 - 1945)	300-5000	L
PICKARD, C.G. (20TH C)	100-800	L
PICKETT, JOSEPH (1848 - 1918)	2000-35000	P
PICKNELL, GEORGE W. (1864 - 1943)	200-1700	L
PICKNELL, WILLIAM LAMB (1854 - 1897)	700-50000	F,L
PIENE, OTTO (1928 -)	800-18000+	A
PIENKOWSKI, JONI (20TH C)	300-1200	X
PIERCE, CHARLES FRANKLIN (1844 - 1920)	100-5000	L,W
PIERCE, WALDO	300-3500	
PIERCE, WALDO (1884 - 1970)	400-5000+	F,S
PIERCEY, A. (20TH C)	100-500	X
PIERSON, ALDEN (1874 - 1921)	600-4500	X (L)
PIG, ROBERT (20TH C)	100-700	X (M)
PIKE, MARION HEWLETT (1914 -)	300-1200	X (S)
PILES, L.M. (late 19TH C)	300-2500	L
PILLSBURY, FRANKLIN C. (20TH C)	100-500	X (F)
PINE, GERI (1914 -)	200-1500	X (F)
PINE, ROBERT EDGE (1742 - 1788)	1000-10000	F
PINE, THEODORE E. (1828 - 1905)	250-5000	F
PINNEY, EUNICE (1770 - 1849)	*500-12000	P
PIPPIN, HORACE (1888 - 1946)	7500-165000+	P
PITMAN, J. (early 20TH C)	100-500	L,F
PITTMAN, HOBSON (1898 - 1972)	200-5000	S (I)

PITZ, HENRY CLARENCE (1895 - 1976)	150-2500	I,L
PLATT, CHARLES ADAMS (1861 - 1933)	350-6800	M,G,F
PLATT, MARTHA A. (19TH-20TH C)	200-1000	X (S)
PLEASONTON, RUTH (20TH C)	100-500	X (F)
PLEGER, E. (20TH C)	100-400	X (L,W)
PLEISSNER, OGDEN MINTON	*700-52000	
PLEISSNER, OGDEN MINTON (1905 - 1983)	1500-55000	G,L
PLETCHER, GERRY (20TH C)	*100-600	X
PLETKA, (20TH C)	100-600	F,L
PLIMPTON, W.E. (early 20TH C)	100-1100	X (L)
PLUMB, HENRY GRANT (1847 - 1936)	*400-3000	X (F)
PLUMMER, EDWIN (1802 - 1880)	*3000-5000+	P
PLUMMER, ETHEL (19TH C)	*100-500	L
PLUMMER, WILLIAM H. (19TH-20TH C)	200-10000	M,L
PODCHERNIKOFF, ALEXIS M. (1886 - 1933)	300-7700	L,F
POEHLMANN, THEO (20TH C)	100-500	X (F)
POGANY, "WILLY" (1882 - 1955)	*150-1200	F,I
POHL, EDWARD H. (19TH-20TH C)	200-1200	L
POHL, HUGO DAVID (1878 - 1960)	200-2000	I,F
POINCY, PAUL (1833 - 1909)	700-7500	G,F
POINDEXTER, JAMES THOMAS (1832 - 1891)	800-3500	F
POLINSKIE, KENNETH (20TH C)	*100-400	X
POLK, ANITA (19TH C)	400-1000	X (F)
POLK, CHARLES PEALE (1767 - 1822)	2000-110000	F,G
POLLACK, MARK A. (20TH C)	100-600	X (S)
POLLOCK, CHARLES CECIL (1902 - 1988)	700-5000	L
POLLOCK, JACKSON	*4500-600000+	
POLLOCK, JACKSON (1912 - 1956)	7500-5720000+	A
POLLOCK, JAMES ARLIN (1898 - 1949)	100-1500	L
POND, DANA (1880 - 1962)	100-4100	F,L
POND, MABEL E. DICKINSON (early 20TH C)	100-700	X (L)
PONSEN, TUNIS (1891 - 1968)	250-3500	F,M
POOLE, E. ABRAM (1883 - 1961)	200-4800	L,F
POOLE, EARL LINCOLN (1891 - 1934)	*100-600	W,I
POOLE, EUGENE ALONZO (1841 - 1912)	6050	S

* Denotes watercolors, pastels, drawings, and/or mixed media

POONS, LARRY (1937 -)	2000-176000	A
POOR, ANN (1887 - 1970)	100-250	X (F)
POOR, HENRY VARNUM	*100-750	
POOR, HENRY VARNUM (1888 - 1970)	300-4800	L,S
POORE, HARRY (19TH C)	200-1200	X
POORE, HENRY RANKIN (1859 - 1940)	300-8500	L,G,W
POPE, ALEXANDER (1849 - 1924)	500-20000+	S,W,F
POPE, ARTHUR (1880 -)	*100-600	X (L)
POPE, JOHN (1820 - 1886)	100-2000	L,G,F
POPE, THOMAS BENJAMIN (- 1891)	300-3000	L,G,S
PORAY, STANISLAUS P. (1888 - 1948)	150-1800	S
PORIN, T. (19TH C)	100-600	X (M)
PORTER, CHARLES EATON (1850 - 1923)	200-15100	S
PORTER, DAVID (1780 - 1843)	2000-18000	M
PORTER, E. (19TH-20TH C)	100-400	X (M)
PORTER, FAIRFIELD	*600-30000	
PORTER, FAIRFIELD (1907 - 1975)	2000-285000	L,M,F
PORTER, KATHERINE (1941 -)	1000-33000	A
PORTER, MARY KING (1865 - 1930)	*100-600	X (F,L)
PORTER, R.W. (19TH-20TH C)	*100-600	X (L)
PORTER, RUFUS (1792 - 1884)	2500-60000+	P
PORTER, S.R. (19TH C)	300-1200	L
PORTER, V.F. (20TH C)	200-1000	X (M)
PORTINOFF, ALEXANDER (1887 - 1949)	*100-500	X (L)
PORTZLINE, FRANCIS (1800 - 1847)	*1000-9000	X
POSEN, STEPHEN (1939 -)	3500-42000	A
POSSNER, HUGO A.(20TH C)	100-600	X
POST, CHARLES JOHNSON (1873 -)	300-1500	X (L,I)
POST, EDWARD C. (active 1850-60)	600-7000	L
POST, GEORGE BOOTH (1906 -)	*100-1100	L
POST, WILLIAM MERRITT (1856 - 1935)	100-6800	L
POTTER, EDNA (20TH C)	100-750	L
POTTER, HARRY SPAFFORD (1870 -)	100-850	L,I
POTTER, LOUIS MCCLELLAN (1873 - 1912)	600-27500	G,F
POTTER, MARY HELEN (1862 - 1950)	100-1300	L,S

POTTER, WILLIAM J. (1883 - 1964)	200-2000	F,L,M
POTTHAST, EDWARD HENRY	*300-30000	
POTTHAST, EDWARD HENRY (1857 - 1927)	600-255000	G,F,L
POTTS, WILLIAM SHERMAN (1867 - 1927)	100-900	F
POULSON, M.B. (19TH C)	300-3000	X (M)
POUSETTE-DART, NATHANIEL J. (1886 - 1965)	*100-600	X (F)
POUSETTE-DART, RICHARD (1916 -)	7100-99000	A
POWELL, ACE	*200-3500	
POWELL, ACE (1912 - 1978)	700-6500	F
POWELL, ARTHUR JAMES EMERY (1864 - 1956)	250-8000	L
POWELL, LUCIEN WHITING	*100-3500	
POWELL, LUCIEN WHITING (1846 - 1930)	200-5500	L,M
POWELL, M. (- 1711)	700-3500	F
POWER, JAMES P. (19TH C)	100-600	G,L
POWERS, A.G. (active 1845-65)	1500-6500	F
POWERS, AMANDA (active 1835)	3000-66000	P (F)
POWERS, ASAHEL LYNDE (1813 - 1843)	2500-20000	P
POWERS, MARION KIRKPATRICK (20TH C)	100-3500	F
POWIS, PAUL (19TH-20TH C)	300-2500	X (S,L)
POZZATTI, RUDY (1926 -)	100-600	X
PRATHER, WILLIAM E. (19TH-20TH C)	100-750	X (S)
PRATT, A.M. (19TH C)	300-1500	X (L)
PRATT, BALDWIN (1903 -)	100-900	L
PRATT, CATHERINE (19TH C)	300-1200	X (S)
PRATT, HENRY CHEEVER (1803 - 1880)	1000-5000	F,L,M
PRATT, JOHN F. (20TH C)	100-600	X (F)
PRATT, MATTHEW (1734 - 1805)	5000-25000	F
PRATT, ROBERT M. (1811 - 1888)	700-25000	G,F,S
PRELLWITZ, HENRY (1865 - 1940)	200-1800	M,L
PRENDERGAST, CHARLES E. (1868 - 1948)	*800-53000	L,F
PRENDERGAST, MAURICE BRAZIL	*550-1870000	
PRENDERGAST, MAURICE BRAZIL (1859 - 1924)	4000-1815000	A,L,F
PRENTICE, GILBERT M. (20TH C)	100-400	M
PRENTICE, LEVI WELLS (1851 - 1935)	100-41000 +	S,L
PRENTISS, LILLIAN (20TH C)	100-700	X (G)

* Denotes watercolors, pastels, drawings, and/or mixed media

PRESCOTT, F.R. (early 19TH C)	100-700	X (L)
PRESSER, JOSEF (1907- 1967)	*100-600	X
PRESTON, JESSE GOODWIN (1880 -)	100-900	L
PRESTON, MAY WILSON	*250-2500	
PRESTON, MAY WILSON (1873 - 1949)	200-18000	F,I
PRESTON, WILLIAM (20TH C)	*150-1000	X
PRESTOPINO, GREGORIO (1907 - 1984)	500-14000	F
PREUSSER, ROBERTS O. (1919 -)	300-9000	A
PREVOST, EUGENE (20TH C)	400-1500	X (S)
PREY, JUAN DE' (20TH C?)	*100-600	X (L)
PRICE, ALAN (20TH C)	150-5200	L
PRICE, CLAYTON S. (1874 - 1950)	1500-18000	F,G
PRICE, GARRETT (1896 - 1979)	*150-900	F,S
PRICE, L.A. (19TH-20TH C)	200-800	X (W)
PRICE, M. ELIZABETH (1875 - 1960)	100-900	X (L,M)
PRICE, NORMAN MILLS (1877 - 1951)	*100-2500	I
PRICE, WILLIAM HENRY (1864 - 1940)	100-1600	L,F
PRIEBE, KARL (1914 -)	*100-2000	F,G
PRIESTMAN, BERTRAM WALTER (1868 - 1951)	100-2300	M,L
PRINCE, L.E. (late 19TH C)	100-750	L
PRINCE, WILLIAM MEAD (1893 - 1951)	200-1000	I
PRINGLE, JAMES FULTON (1788 - 1847)	2500-12000	M
PRIOR, WILLIAM MATTHEW (1806 - 1873)	500-77000 +	P
PRITCHARD, GEORGE THOMPSON (1878 - 1962)	300-4400	L,M,G,F
PRITCHARD, J. AMBROSE (1858 - 1905)	300-2000	L
PRITCHARD, ZARAH H. (20TH C)	*100-500	L
PROBST, JOACHIM (1913 -)	100-900	X
PROBST, THORWALD A. (1886 - 1948)	100-6600	L,I
PROCTOR, ALEXANDER PHIMISTER (1862 - 1950)	*100-2500	W,F,L
PROCTOR, BURT (1901 - 1980)	500-12000	X (F)
PROHASKA, JOSEPH (20TH C)	150-1000	L
PROHASKA, RAYMOND (1901 - 1981)	200-1500	I
PROOM, AL (1933 -)	100-2800	X (S)
PROPER, IDA SEDGWICK (1876 - 1957)	1000-32000	F,L
PROUDFOOT, WILLIAM A. (20TH C)	150-900	L

PUDOR, HEINRICH (19TH C)	400-2000	F
PUMMIL, ROBERT (1936 -)	1000-10000	G,F
PURDY, ALBERT J.(1835 - 1909)	150-6500+	F
PURDY, DONALD ROY (1924 -)	100-5000	F,L,S
PURDY, ROBERT (20TH C)	100-600	X (S)
PURWIN, SIGMUND (20TH C)	100-500	X
PUSHMAN, HOVSEP T. (1877 - 1966)	800-29000	F,S
PUTHUFF, HANSON DUVALL (1875 - 1972)	500-17000	L
PUTMAN, DONALD (1927 -)	500-4500	F
PYLE, HOWARD	*500-13500	
PYLE, HOWARD (1853 - 1911)	1700-66000	I

Q

Artist	Prices	Subject
QUARTERLY, CHARLES (19TH C)	250-1800	L
QUARTLEY, ARTHUR (1839 - 1886)	450-9800	M
QUICK, ISRAEL (19TH-20TH C)	100-400	X (F)
QUIDOR, JOHN (1801 - 1881)	200-175000	F,L
QUIGLEY, EDWARD B. (1895 - 1968)	500-6000	G,F,L
QUINCY, EDMUND (1903 -)	200-7200	L,M
QUINLAN, WILL J. (1877 -)	250-1200	M,L
QUINN, EDMOND T. (1868 - 1926)	200-1000	F
QUINN, JAMES P. (1870 - 1951)	50-600	X (F)
QUIRT, WALTER (1902 - 1968)	300-3000	A

R

* Denotes watercolors, pastels, drawings, and/or mixed media

Artist	Prices	Subject
RAAB, GEORGE (1866 - 1943)	*100-300	L
RABES, MAX (1868 - 1944)	900-38500	F,G
RABORG, BENJAMIN (1871 - 1918)	100-800	L
RACHMIEL, JEAN (1871 -)	150-1800	X (L)
RACKOW, LEO (1901 -)	*200-1200	X
RADENKOVITCH, YOVAN (1903 -)	50-250	X (S)
RAFFAEL, JOSEPH	*600-9000	
RAFFAEL, JOSEPH (1933 -)	1200-55000	A
RAGAN, LESLIE D. (1897 -)	100-2500	I
RAHMING, NORRIS (1886 -)	*50-500	L
RAIN, CHARLES WHEEDON (1911 -)	100-2900	X (S)
RALEIGH, CHARLES SIDNEY (1830 - 1925)	2500-35000	P (M)
RALEIGH, HENRY PATRICK (1880 - 1945)	*175-1500	I,F,M
RAMAGE, JOHN (1748 - 1802)	700-6000	F
RAMESCH, E. (19TH C)	100-900	X (F)
RAMME, H. (early 20TH C)	150-850	X (F)
RAMOS, MEL	*1200-44000	
RAMOS, MEL (1935 -)	2500-187000	A
RAMSDELL, FRED WINTHROP (1865 - 1915)	300-2500	L,F
RAMSEY, MILNE (1846 - 1915)	550-35000	S,L
RAND, ELLEN G. EMMET (1876 - 1941)	*100-700	X (F)
RAND, HENRY ASBURY (1886 -)	250-1400	L
RANDALL, RUTH H. (1896 -)	*50-350	L
RANDELL, ASA GRANT (1869 -)	*250-1500	L
RANDOLPH, JOHN (19TH-20TH C)	200-1200	X (W)
RANDOLPH, LEE FRITZ (1880 - 1956)	300-2000	L,F
RANGER, HENRY WARD	*125-6000	
RANGER, HENRY WARD (1858 - 1916)	600-25000	L
RANN, VOLLIAN BURR (1897 - 1956)	150-1000	X (F)
RANNEY, WILLIAM TYLEE (1813 - 1857)	8000-300000 +	G,F
RANSOM, ALEXANDER (19TH C)	300-1500	L,F
RANSOM, CAROLINE L. ORMES (1838 - 1910)	400-3500	L,S,F
RAPHAEL, JOSEPH (1872 - 1950)	100-27000	L,F,S
RAPP, J. (19TH-20TH C)	200-1200 +	X (L)

* Denotes watercolors, pastels, drawings, and/or mixed media   279

RAQUERE, THOMAS J. (20TH C)	*100-700	X (L)
RARPHARO, J. (20TH C)	100-600	X (W,L)
RASCH, GUSTAV (1836 - 1906)	250-2000	F
RASCHEN, HENRY (1856 - 1937)	700-60000	G,F,L
RASER, J. HEYL (1924 - 1901)	600-10000	L
RASKIN, JOSEPH (1897 - 1981)	400-6200	F,L
RASMUSSEN, JOHN (1828 - 1895)	1000-52250	X (L)
RATNER, JOHN RYKOFF (1934 -)	500-6000	X (A)
RATTNER, ABRAHAM (1895 - 1978)	300-18000	A
RATTRAY, ALEXANDER WELLWOOD (1849 - 1902)	300-2800	L,F
RAUGHT, JOHN WILLARD (1957 - 1931)	300-1000	X (L)
RAULAND, ORLAND (20TH C)	400-4500	X (M)
RAUSCHENBERG, ROBERT	*1500-5750000	
RAUSCHENBERG, ROBERT (1925 -)	5500-1760000	A
RAVLIN, GRACE (1885 - 1956)	600-5000	G,F
RAWSON, ALBERT LEIGHTON (1829 - 1902)	400-3500	L
RAWSON, CARL W. (1884 - 1970)	100-900	L,F
RAY, MAN (1890 - 1976)	1100-148500	A
RAY, RUTH (- 1977)	100-2000	A
RAYMOND, GRACE RUSSELL (1877 -)	100-900	X (M)
REA, LOUIS EDWARD (1868 - 1927)	300-1700	L
READ, JAMES B. (1803 - 1870)	500-2500	F
READ, RALPH (20TH C)	150-700	X (L)
READ, THOMAS BUCHANAN (1822 - 1872)	200-4800	F
REAM, CARDUCIUS PLANTAGENET (1837 - 1917)	800-12000	S
REAM, MORSTON CONSTANTINE (1840 - 1898)	600-15000	S
REASER, WILBUR AARON	*150-1800	
REASER, WILBUR AARON (1860 - 1942)	150-5000	M,L,F
REBAY, HILLA	*450-4000	
REBAY, HILLA (1890 - 1967)	1500-16000	A
RECKHARD, GARDNER ARNOLD (1858 - 1908)	150-4000	S,L,F
RECKLESS, STANLEY L. (1892 -)	37500	A
REDDIE, MACIVOR (20TH C)	150-1200	L,M
REDEIN, ALEX (1912 - 1965)	100-800	X (F)
REDELIUS, F.H. (20TH C)	100-1500	X (S)

REDFIELD, EDWARD WILLIS (1869 - 1965)	500-138000	L,M
REDIN, CARL (1892 - 1944)	500-5000	L
REDMAN, B. (19TH-20TH C)	700-3000	M
REDMOND, CHARLES (19TH C)	100-500	X (G)
REDMOND, GRANVILLE (1871 - 1935)	250-45000+	L,M,S
REDMOND, JOHN J. (19TH C)	150-1200	F,L
REDMOND, MARGARET (1867 - 1948)	300-4500	F,S
REDWOOD, ALLEN CARTER	*400-5000	
REDWOOD, ALLEN CARTER (1844 - 1922)	800-7500	F,G,I
REED, ALICE (20TH C)	100-300	S
REED, EARL H. (1863 -)	600-3000	L,W
REED, ETHEL (1876 -)	*200-1200	F
REED, MARJORIE (1915 -)	150-2800	G,F
REED, PETER FISHE (1817 - 1887)	200-1000	L,F
REEDER, DICKSON (20TH C)	*100-500	X
REEDY, LEONARD HOWARD	*250-2000	I
REEDY, LEONARD HOWARD (1899 - 1956)	500-4500	I
REESE, BERNARD (JR) (19TH-20TH C)	150-850	X (F)
REGAN, GREGORY T. (20TH C)	100-400	L
REHDER, JULIUS CHRISTIAN (1861 - 1955)	100-7500	M,L
REHN, FRANK KNOX MORTON	*150-1500	
REHN, FRANK KNOX MORTON (1848 - 1914)	150-3000+	M,L
REICHARDT, FERDINAND (1819 - 1895)	1000-17000	L
REICHARST, T. (19TH C)	500-6000	L
REICHMAN, FRED (1925 -)	100-850	X (W)
REID, J.B. (20TH C)	*200-1000	L,F
REID, JAMES (1907 -)	100-850	X (M)
REID, JEAN A. (1882 -)	*50-600	L,F
REID, JOHN T. (19TH C)	200-2000	X (F)
REID, PATTY (20TH C)	*100-1500	F,L
REID, ROBERT LOUIS	*200-38000	
REID, ROBERT LOUIS (1862 - 1929)	1000-198000+	F,L
REID, VICTOR E. (20TH C)	100-700	X (M)
REIFFEL, CHARLES (1862 - 1942)	450-15000+	L
REILLY, FRANK JOSEPH (1906 - 1967)	300-6500	I

REIMERS, JOHANNES (20TH C)	*100-500	L
REINDEL, EDNA (1900 -)	800-4000	X (S)
REINDEL, WILLIAM G. (1871-1948)	100-1000	L,M
REINEZ, S.A. (19TH C)	*100-400	G,F
REINHARDT, AD	*1500-25000	
REINHARDT, AD (1913 - 1967)	5000-450000	A
REINHARDT, SIEGFRIED GERHARD (1925 -)	100-6000	A
REINHART, BENJAMIN FRANKLIN (1829 - 1885)	1000-20000	G,F,L
REINHART, CHARLES STANLEY (1844 - 1896)	*200-1500	I
REINHART, STEUART 1897 -)	150-1200	X (F)
REISMAN, PHILIP (1906 -)	7000	X (G,F)
REISS, FRITZ WINOLD (1886 - 1953)	*300-18000	F
REISS, H. (19TH-20TH C)	150-1000	X (G)
REISS, LIONEL S. (1894 -)	*100-600	X
REITER, CHRISTIAN (1864 -)	300-1500	F
RELYEA. CHARLES M. (1863 -)	100-900	L,I
REMENICK, SEYMOUR (1923 -)	100-2000	A
REMINGTON, FREDERIC SACKRIDER	*1100-175000	
REMINGTON, FREDERIC SACKRIDER (1861 - 1909)	6000-825000+	G,F
REMINGTON, S.J. (19TH C)	400-2500	L
REMISOFF, NICOLAI (1887 -)	*100-1300	I,F,L
REMSEN, IRA "REM" (1876-1928)	44000	M
RENOUARD, GEORGE (1884 - 1954)	100-2500	F,M,L
RENSHAW, ALICE (19TH C)	*100-500	X (F)
RESNICK, MILTON (1917 -)	1400-132000	A
RETTIG, JOHN (1860 - 1932)	100-2100	F,L
RETTIG, MARTIN (20TH C)	100-1200	X (S,F)
REULANDT, LE GRANDE de (19TH C)	1000-15000+	M
REUSSWIG, WILLIAM	*300-4000	
REUSSWIG, WILLIAM (1902 - 1978)	400-9000	I,G,F
REUTERDAHL, HENRY	*300-3500	
REUTERDAHL, HENRY (1871 - 1925)	250-6000	M,I
REYNARD, GRANT TYSON (1887 - 1967)	*100-1500	I
REYNOLDS, FREDERICK T. (1882 -)	400-5000	G,F,L
REYNOLDS, J.F. (19TH-20TH C)	100-600	X (S,M)

REYNOLDS, JAMES (1926 -)	1500-60000	X (G)
REYNOLDS, W.S. (19TH-20TH C)	700-10000+	S
REYNOLDS, WELLINGTON JARED (1866 -)	*500-6500	F,M
RHEAD, LOUIS JOHN (1857 - 1926)	*200-5000	X (I,F)
RHONE, P. (19TH C)	100-500	L
RIBA, PAUL (1912 - 1977)	200-3500	L,S
RIBAK, LOUIS (1902 - 1980)	500-7500	G,F
RIBCOWSKY, DEY DE (1880 - 1936)	300-5000	L,M,F
RICCI, ULYSSES A. (1888 - 1960)	100-600	X (F,L)
RICCIARDI, CAESARE (1892 -)	100-900	L,S,F
RICE, G.S. (late 19TH C)	500-5000	F
RICE, HENRY W. (1853 - 1934)	*100-900	M,L,G
RICE, WILLIAM CLARKE (1875 - 1928)	150-950	F,I
RICE, WILLIAM MORTON JACKSON (1854 - 1922)	500-3000	S,F
RICE-PEREIRA, IRENE	*100-5000	
RICE-PEREIRA, IRENE (1901 - 1971)	400-7500	A
RICH, JOHN HUBBARD (1876 - 1954)	900-34000	F,S
RICHARDS, ELLA E. (19TH-20TH C)	150-2000	X (G)
RICHARDS, FREDERICK DEBOURG (1822 - 1903)	200-24000	L,M
RICHARDS, JOHN (1935 -)	100-650	X (F)
RICHARDS, THOMAS ADDISON (1820 - 1900)	550-25000	L,F,S,I
RICHARDS, WILLIAM TROST	*100-42000	
RICHARDS, WILLIAM TROST (1833 - 1905)	100-190000+	M,L,S,F
RICHARDSON, ALLAN (early 20TH C)	500-3500	X (F)
RICHARDSON, FRANCIS HENRY (1859 - 1934)	250-4000	M,L,F
RICHARDSON, HARRY L. (20TH C)	*100-500	X
RICHARDSON, JOHN (20TH C)	150-900	X (F)
RICHARDSON, LOUIS H. (1853 - 1923)	100-4200	L,M
RICHARDSON, MARGARET FOSTER (1881-)	700-6500	F
RICHARDSON, MARY CURTIS (1848 - 1931)	300-9500	F
RICHARDSON, MARY NEAL (1859 - 1937)	100-1000	X (F)
RICHARDSON, THEODORE J.	*250-1800	
RICHARDSON, THEODORE J. (1855 - 1914)	200-3500	L
RICHARDSON, VOLNEY A. (20TH C)	150-2700	X (S)
RICHARDT, FERDINAND J.(1819 - 1895)	900-17000	L

RICHENBURG, ROBERT B. (1917 -)	500-6500	A
RICHERT, CHARLES HENRY	*100-500	
RICHERT, CHARLES HENRY (1880 - 1974)	100-1300	L,M
RICHES, WILLIAM J. (late 19TH C)	.100-600	X (F)
RICHMOND, AGNES M. (1870 - 1964)	300-15000	F
RICHTER, HANS (1888 - 1975)	*500-2000	A
RICHTER, HENRY L. (1870 - 1960)	100-900	L
RICKARDS, F. (early 19TH C)	600-3000	F
RICKLE, T. (early 19TH C)	400-2000	X (L)
RICKMAN, PHILIP (1891 - 1982)	*400-9500	W
RICKS, DOUGLAS (20TH C)	1000-6500	L,G
RIDDEL, JAMES (- 1928)	*100-700	X
RIDER, ARTHUR GROVER (1886 - 1975)	800-35000	M,L
RIDER, HENRY ORNE (1860 -)	100-1200	L
RIECKE, GEORGE A.E. (1848 - 1924)	250-3500	L,W
RIECKE, JOHANN GEORGE L.(1817 - 1898)	300-2500	L,G,W
RIESENBERG, SIDNEY (1885 - 1962)	300-3500	I
RIFKA, JUDY (20TH C)	*1500-7500	A
RIFKIN, LOUIS (19TH C)	100-500	X (L)
RIGGS, ROBERT (1896 - 1970)	700-25000	G,F,I
RILEY, KENNETH (1919 -)	700-60000	I
RILEY, MARY G. (1883 - 1939)	100-600	X (L)
RILEY, NICHOLAS F. (1900 - 1944)	*200-1500	I,F
RIMMER, WILLIAM (1816 - 1879)	2500-60000	G,F,L
RINCK, ADOLPH D. (active 1835-60)	200-800	F
RING, ALICE BLAIR (1869 -)	300-7000	F,L
RION, HANNA (1875 - 1924)	300-1200	L,M
RIPLEY, AIDEN LASSELL	*100-19000	
RIPLEY, AIDEN LASSELL (1896 - 1969)	250-38500+	W,L,F
RIPLEY, LUCY PERKINS (19TH-20TH C)	200-1200	X (F,A)
RISING, C.P. (early 20TH C)	*100-850	L
RITMAN, LOUIS (1889 - 1963)	700-420000+	F
RITSCHEL, WILLIAM P.	*100-3000	
RITSCHEL, WILLIAM P. (1864 - 1949)	550-82500	M,L,S
RITTENBERG, HENRY R. (1879 - 1969)	100-5500	S,F

RITTER, ALONZO W. (1898 -)	100-400	X (F)
RITTER, HENRY (1816 - 1853)	1000-6000	G,F
RITTER, PAUL (1829 - 1907)	450-9000	L
RIVERS, GEORGIE THURSTON (1878 -)	*100-400	X (F,L)
RIVERS, LARRY	*1000-87500	
RIVERS, LARRY (1923 -)	5000-470000	A
RIX, JULIAN WALGRIDGE (1850 - 1903)	500-16500	L,M
ROBBINS, ELLEN (1828 - 1905)	*300-4200	S
ROBBINS, H. (20TH C)	100-600	X (S)
ROBBINS, HORACE WOLCOTT (1842 - 1904)	700-26500	L
ROBBINS, RAIS A. (20TH C)	300-2000	X
ROBERTI, ROMOLO (1896 -)	*100-400	X (G)
ROBERTS, BLANCHE GILROY (1871 -)	100-900	L
ROBERTS, ELIZABETH W.	*150-900	
ROBERTS, ELIZABETH W. (1871 - 1927)	600-18000	X (M)
ROBERTS, MORTON (1927 - 1964)	800-15000	I
ROBERTS, NATHAN B. (19TH C)	600-3500	F
ROBERTS, VIRGINIA (20TH C)	100-600	X (M)
ROBERTSON, ANNA MARY (see "MOSES")		
ROBERTSON, ANNE L. (1844 - 1933)	600-45000	G,F
ROBERTSON, ARCHIBALD (1765 - 1835)	*450-3500	F
ROBERTSON, FREDERICK E. (1878 - 1953)	100-1000	X (L)
ROBERTSON, ROBERT (20TH C)	150-750	I
ROBINS, LOUISA (1898 -)	*100-600	X (F)
ROBINSON, ALEXANDER (1867 - 1940)	*100-3200	M,L
ROBINSON, BOARDMAN (1876 - 1952)	*100-2500	I
ROBINSON, CHARLES DORMAN (1847 - 1933)	100-14000	L,M
ROBINSON, DAVID (20TH C)	*50-400	L
ROBINSON, FLORENCE VINCENT (1874 - 1937)	*200-3000	L,F
ROBINSON, GLADYS LLOYD (20TH C)	100-750	X (S)
ROBINSON, HAL (1875 - 1933)	200-4500	L
ROBINSON, MRS. A.K. (19TH C)	200-1000	X (W)
ROBINSON, THEODORE (1852 - 1896)	4500-375000 +	L,F
ROBINSON, THOMAS (1835 - 1888)	200-4000	L,G,W
ROBINSON, WILLIAM S.	*150-1500	

ROBINSON, WILLIAM S. (1861 - 1945)	400-14500	F,L,M
ROBINSON, WILLIAM T. (1852 -)	150-3300	L,G,M
ROBUS, HUGO	*500-7500	
ROBUS, HUGO (1885 - 1964)	1000-40000	A
ROCKENSCHAUB, GERWALD (20TH C)	1000-4000	A
ROCKLINE, VERA (1896 - 1934)	600-7000	F
ROCKMORE, NOEL DAVIS (1928 -)	300-2500	X
ROCKWELL, AUGUSTUS (19TH C)	400-3500	L,F
ROCKWELL, CLEVELAND	*300-5000	
ROCKWELL, CLEVELAND (1837 - 1907)	800-40000+	M,L
ROCKWELL, FREDERIC (20TH C)	100-900	F,A
ROCKWELL, NORMAN	*1000-50000	
ROCKWELL, NORMAN (1894 - 1978)	4000-264000	I
RODGERS, RUTH EASTMAN (20TH C)	*100-1600	F,G
RODNEY, H.C. (19TH C)	500-5000	X (G)
RODRIGUEZ, A.C. (19TH C)	100-1000	L
ROE, CLARENCE (1909 -)	100-700	L
ROE, NICHOLAS (19TH C)	250-3000	L
ROEDING, FRANCES (1910 -)	300-1200	X (F)
ROESEN, SEVERIN (1815 - 1872)	8000-250000	S
ROGER, CHARLES A. (1866 - 1907)	100-1500	L,F
ROGERS, FRANKLIN WHITING (1854 -)	400-13200	W,L
ROGERS, GRETCHEN W. (1881 - 1967)	400-5000	F
ROGERS, NATHANIEL (1788 - 1844)	400-2000	F
ROGERS, S.D. (19TH C)	300-3500	L
ROGERS, WILLIAM (19TH-20TH C)	100-700	X (M)
ROGERS, WILLIAM ALLEN (1854 - 1931)	*300-2000	I
ROHDE, H. (20TH C)	100-600	L,W
ROHLAND, PAUL (20TH C)	100-400	X (S)
ROHN, RAY (1888 - 1935)	850-300	X (G)
ROHOWSKY, MEYERS (1900 - 1974)	350-1500	X
ROHRHIRSCH, RICHARD (1833 - 1892)	400-2800	X (S)
ROLFE, EDMUND (19TH-20TH C)	350-1800	S
ROLLE, AUGUST H.O. (1875 - 1941)	250-9100	L,M
ROLLINS, WARREN E. (1861 - 1962)	500-27500	F,L

ROLSHOVEN, JULIUS (1858 - 1930)	500-16500	F,L
ROMANO, UMBERTO	*100-500	
ROMANO, UMBERTO (1905 -)	200-8800	F
ROMANOVSKY, DIMITRI (20TH C)	150-2500	X
ROMANSKI, HARRY (1861 -)	200-1200	X (L)
RONDEL, FREDERICK (1826 - 1892)	600-15000+	G,L
RONEY, HAROLD ARTHUR (1899 -)	200-2500	X (L)
ROOS, PETER (1850 -)	100-2900	L
ROOSEVELT, S. MONTGOMERY (1863 - 1929)	*100-600	X (F)
ROPES, JOSEPH (1812 - 1885)	400-2100	L
RORPHURO, J. (20TH C)	100-500	X (F)
ROSAR, M. (19TH C)	100-900	L
ROSAS, CHARLES (20TH C)	200-1500	L
ROSATI, JAMES (1912 - 1988)	*100-900	A
ROSE, ANTHONY LEWIS DE (1803 - 1836)	350-1200	F
ROSE, GUY (1867 - 1925)	1000-100000+	L
ROSE, HERMAN (1909 -)	450-5000	L
ROSE, HORACE L. (19TH-20TH C)	100-600	X (L)
ROSE, IVER	*100-500	
ROSE, IVER (1899 - 1972)	200-2400	G,F
ROSE, W. (- 1938)	300-1800	X
ROSELAND, HARRY (1868 - 1950)	1500-230000+	G,F
ROSEN, CHARLES (1878 - 1950)	700-35200	L
ROSEN, ERNEST T. (1877 - 1926)	150-1000	X (F)
ROSEN, STEPHEN (19TH C)	100-400	F,L
ROSENBAUM, RICHARD (19TH C)	*100-850	X (G,I)
ROSENBERG, HENRY MORTIKAR (1858 - 1947)	150-1000	X (F)
ROSENBERG, JAMES N. (1874 - 1970)	300-1500	L
ROSENBERRY, O.W. (20TH C)	*100-600	X
ROSENBORG, RALPH M. (1913 -)	100-600	X (A,L)
ROSENKRANZ, CLARENCE C. (19TH-20TH C)	200-1000	L
ROSENQUIST, JAMES	*2000-88000	
ROSENQUIST, JAMES (1933 -)	5000-440000+	A
ROSENTHAL, ALBERT (1863 - 1939)	200-15500	F
ROSENTHAL, DORIS (1889 - 1971)	100-750	G,F,L

ROSENTHAL, MAX (1833 - 1918)	300-1500	F,M
ROSENTHAL, TOBY EDWARD (1849 - 1917)	700-25000	F,G
ROSENWEY, PAUL (20TH C)	100-800	L,M
ROSNER, CHARLES (1894 - 1975)	*150-500	M
ROSS, ALEX (1909 - 1990)	*200-1500	I
ROSS, CARRIE (20TH C)	200-1200	X (F,L)
ROSS, CHANDLER R. (20TH C)	400-2500	S
ROSS, DENMAN WALDO (1853 - 1935)	400-1500	L
ROSS, GORDON (20TH C)	*100-600	X (G)
ROSS, HARRY LEITH (1886 - 1973)	1000-6500	L,M
ROSS, LILLI (20TH C)	100-300	X
ROSS, SANFORD (20TH C)	*100-600	X (L)
ROSSEAU, PERCIVAL LEONARD (1859 - 1937)	350-44000	W,L
ROSSER, C. (20TH C)	100-800	X (F,G)
ROSSITER, THOMAS PRITCHARD (1818 - 1871)	900-9500	G,F,L,M
ROTCH, BENJAMIN SMITH (1817 - 1882)	400-2000	L
ROTENBERG, HAROLD (1905 -)	100-1200	X (L)
ROTERS, CARL G.(20TH C)	*100-600	L
ROTH, ERNEST DAVID	*100-550	
ROTH, ERNEST DAVID (1879 - 1964)	250-3500	L,M
ROTHBORT, SAMUEL (1882 - 1971)	200-7200	L
ROTHENBERG, SUSAN (1945 -)	*20000-550000	A
ROTHERMEL, PETER FREDERICK (1817 - 1895)	300-8000	F
ROTHKO, MARK	*2500-231000	
ROTHKO, MARK (1903 - 1970)	20000-3630000	A
ROTHSTEIN, E. (1907 -)	100-400	X (G)
ROUILLION, M.W. (19TH-20TH C)	100-900	X (L)
ROULAND, ORLANDO (1871 - 1945)	200-7300	M,L
ROUSSEAU, HELEN HOFFMAN (1898 -)	*5500	L,M
ROUSSEFF, W. VLADMIR (1890 - 1934)	100-850	X (L)
ROUX, A. (19TH C)	100-900	L
ROUZEE, W. (19TH C)	100-600	L,M
ROWE, J. STAPLES (1856 - 1905)	*100-350	X (F)
ROY, FRANK (20TH C)	100-800	L
ROYCE, WOODFORD (1902 -)	150-1800	X (L,S)

* Denotes watercolors, pastels, drawings, and/or mixed media

RUBEN, RICHARD (1925 -)	150-800	A
RUBINS, HARRY W. (1865 - 1934)	100-900	X
RUCKER, ROBERT (20TH C)	200-1600	X (L)
RUDD, N. (19TH C)	2800	X (M)
RUDELL, PETER EDWARD (1854 - 1899)	150-1500	L
RUDOLPH, ERNEST (19TH-20TH C)	400-2000	X (L)
RUFF, BEATRICE (20TH C)	100-650	X (L)
RUGE, CARL (20TH C)	*250-1000	X
RUGGLES, ELIZA E. (19TH C)	*150-950	X (L)
RUIZ, B. YAMERO (?)	200-2500	L,G,F
RUMMELL, RICHARD (1848 - 1924)	*350-3800	M
RUNGIUS, CARL	*500-15000	
RUNGIUS, CARL (1869 - 1959)	1000-80000	W,L
RUSALL, J.L. (19TH C)	100-500	L
RUSCHA, EDWARD	*600-82500	
RUSCHA, EDWARD (1937 -)	2500-300000	A
RUSH, OLIVE	*100-650	
RUSH, OLIVE (1873 - 1966)	100-1500	X (A)
RUSS, C.B. (active 1880-1920)	350-2500	L
RUSSELL, ALFRED (20TH C)	100-500	L,F
RUSSELL, BENJAMIN (1804 - 1885)	*750-7500	M
RUSSELL, CHARLES MARION	*2500-210000	
RUSSELL, CHARLES MARION (1864 - 1926)	15000-530000+	G,F,I
RUSSELL, EDWARD JOHN (1832 - 1906)	*400-3600	M,F
RUSSELL, EDWIN (19TH C)	200-900	F
RUSSELL, GEORGE D. (19TH C)	*100-500	L
RUSSELL, GRACE L. (20TH C)	100-500	X (M)
RUSSELL, HILDA (20TH C)	100-800	X
RUSSELL, MORGAN (1886 - 1953)	650-176000	A,S
RUSSELL, MOSES B. (1810 - 1884)	150-1000	L,F
RUSSELL, WALTER (1871 - 1963)	400-77000	F,M,I
RUSSELL, WILLIAM GEORGE (1860 -)	*100-850	X (M)
RUTHERFORD, HARRY (19TH C)	300-2500	F,L
RUTLEDGE, JANE (20TH C)	100-500	X (L)
RUTTAN, C.E. (20TH C)	100-800	X

RUTTER, W. B. (19TH C)	100-1000	L
RYAN, ANNE (1889 - 1954)	*600-9500	A
RYAN, TOM	*2500-40000	
RYAN, TOM (1922 -)	3500-50000	I
RYDEN, HENNING (1869 - 1939)	250-3000	F,M,L
RYDER, ALBERT PINKHAM (1847 - 1917)	3500-????	F,L,M
RYDER, CHAUNCEY FOSTER (1868 - 1949)	300-35000	L,F
RYDER, HENRY ORNE (19TH C)	200-1200	L,M
RYDER, JACK VAN (1898 - 1968)	300-1800	L
RYDER, PLATT POWELL (1821 - 1896)	100-15000	G,F
RYDER, WORTH (1884 - 1960)	*150-600	L,F
RYLAND, ROBERT KNIGHT (1873 - 1951)	200-8500	F,I
RYMAN, ROBERT	*3000-45000	
RYMAN, ROBERT (1930 -)	8000-2300000	A
RYNERSON, BEULAH (20TH C)	100-700	X

S

Artist	Prices	Subject
SABELA, H.J. (19TH-20TH C)	200-1000	X (S)
SACCARO, JOHN	*7700	L
SACCARO, JOHN (1913-1981)	4875	L
SACCO, LUCA (1858 - 1912)	300-3000	G,F,L
SACKLARIAN, STEPHEN (1899 -)	7000-55000	A
SACKS, JOSEPH (1887 - 1974)	300-3250	L
SACKS, WALTER T. (1895 -)	*100-800	L
SADONA, MATTEO (1881 - 1964)	*150-1200	X (L)
SAGE, KAY (1898 - 1963)	1200-25000	A
SAGER, HERMAN (20TH C)	100-600	L
SAINT-PHALLE, NIKI DE (1930 -)	*600-35000	A
SALEMME, ATTILIO (1911 - 1955)	1500-10500	A
SALINAS, PORFIRIO (1910 - 1972)	800-25000	L
SALING, PAUL E. (1876 - 1936)	100-1800	L

SALLA, SALVATORE (20TH C)	200-1200	X (L)
SALLE, DAVID	*350-60000	
SALLE, DAVID (1952 -)	2000-100000	A
SALMON, ROBERT (1775 - 1842)	3500-127000	M,L
SALT, JOHN (1937 -)	4000-47000	A
SALTONSTALL, ELIZABETH (1900 -)	100-500	X
SALTZMAN, LINDA B. (1903 -)	200-800	A
SALVI, EDWARD (20TH C)	200-1200	A
SALZMANN, E. (19TH C)	500-1800	X (L)
SAMARAS, LUCAS (1936 -)	*1500-80000	A
SAMBROOK, RUSSELL (20TH C)	200-1500	X (G)
SAMMONS, CARL (1886 - 1968)	150-4500	L,M
SAMMONS, FREDERICK H. C.(1853 - 1917)	400-2000	X (S)
SAMPLE, PAUL STARRETT	*300-3500	
SAMPLE, PAUL STARRETT (1896 - 1974)	450-20000	G,L,M,I
SAMPSON, ALDEN (1853 -)	*100-500	L
SAMUELS, IRVING K. (20TH C)	*100-600	X (L)
SANBORN, PERCY (1849 - 1929)	700-10000	M
SAND, MAXIMILEN E. (19TH C)	*100-1000	X (F)
SAND, PERCY TSISETE (1918 -)	*100-300	X (F)
SANDER, LUDWIG (1906 - 1975)	750-5500	A
SANDER, TOM	*200-1800	
SANDER, TOM (20TH C)	400-3600	W
SANDERSON, CHARLES WESLEY (1838 - 1905)	*100-450	L
SANDHAM, HENRY (1842 - 1912)	*100-1100	L
SANDORHAZL, W.B. (19TH C)	400-2500	L
SANDZEN, SVEN BIRGER (1871 - 1954)	200-7500	L
SANFORD, GEORGE T. (active 1840-50)	*800-4500	M
SANFORD, WALTER (1915 -)	100-2000	L,F
SANGER, JOSEPH (20TH C)	150-600	X (G)
SANGER, WILLIAM (1875 -)	*100-600	X (F)
SANTORO, JOSEPH L. (20TH C)	*50-700	L
SANTRY, DANIEL (1858 - 1915)	200-2500	L
SARG, TONY (1882 - 1942)	*100-1100	I
SARGEANT, GENEVE RIXFORD (1868 - 1957)	100-1800	L,F

SARGENT, HENRY (1770 - 1845)	3000-25000	G,F
SARGENT, JOHN SINGER	*600-135000+	
SARGENT, JOHN SINGER (1856 - 1925)	3000-1485000+	F,L
SARGENT, PAUL TURNER (1880 - 1946)	700-12000	X (L)
SARGENT, RICHARD (1911 - 1978)	*100-7000	I
SARGENT, WALTER (1868 - 1927)	200-11000	L
SARISKY, MICHAEL (1906 -)	100-850	F,S
SARKISIAN, SARKIS	*50-100	
SARKISIAN, SARKIS (1909 - 1977)	200-1600	F,S
SARNOFF, ARTHUR (20TH C)	*100-1700	X
SARRAZIN, LOUISE (20TH C)	*100-600	X
SARTAIN, WILLIAM (1843 - 1924)	200-3300	L
SARTELLE, HERBERT (20TH C)	100-700	L
SASLOW, HERBERT (1920 -)	200-1000	X (S)
SATTERLEE, WALTER	*100-1200	
SATTERLEE, WALTER (1844 - 1908)	400-3500	G,F
SAUER, WILLIAM (20TH C)	200-1000	L,F
SAUERWEIN, FRANK PETER	*650-2500	
SAUERWEIN, FRANK PETER (1871 - 1910)	1000-10000	L,G,F
SAUL, PETER	*300-12500	
SAUL, PETER (1934 -)	700-25000	A
SAUNDERS, H. WENDEROTH (20TH C)	100-1000	X (L)
SAUNDERS, NORMAN (1906 - 1988)	300-2000	I
SAURA, ANTONIO (1930 -)	3000-140000	A
SAVAGE, EUGENE FRANCIS (1883 - 1978)	1000-40000+	A,G,F,L
SAVAGE, R.A. (19TH C)	200-18700	X (F)
SAVITSKY, JACK	*100-725	
SAVITSKY, JACK (1910 - 1991)	350-4000	P
SAWTELLE, ELIZABETH A. (20TH C)	200-1200	X (S)
SAWTELLE, MARY BERKELEY (1872 -)	500-9000	X
SAWYER, HELEN ALTON (1900 -)	300-3000	L,S
SAWYER, W.B. (20TH C)	250-1500	L
SAWYER, WELLS M. (1863 - 1960)	100-2000	M,L
SAWYERS, MARTHA (1902 - 1988)	*300-5000	A
SAYER, RAYMOND (19TH-20TH C)	100-800	M,L

* Denotes watercolors, pastels, drawings, and/or mixed media

SAYRE, FRED GRAYSON (1879 - 1939)	400-6500+	L
SAYRES, S.T. (19TH C)	100-700	X (L)
SCALELLA, JULES (1895 -)	100-2500	X (L)
SCHABELITZ, RUDOLPH F.(1884 - 1959)	100-3000	G,I
SCHAEFFER, MEAD (1898 - 1980)	100-12000	I
SCHAETTE, LOUIS (- 1917)	200-2000	F
SCHAFER, FREDERICK F.(1839 - 1927)	200-8800	L
SCHALDACH, WILLIAM J.	*100-1500	
SCHALDACH, WILLIAM J. (1896 - 1982)	400-2500	W
SCHAMBERG, MORTON L.	*1200-9000	
SCHAMBERG, MORTON L.(1881 - 1918)	2500-70000+	A
SCHANKER, LOUIS	*100-4500	
SCHANKER, LOUIS (1903 - 1981)	700-13200	A
SCHANS, S.V.D. (19TH C)	3000-25000	F
SCHARY, SAUL (1904 - 1978)	100-2800	L,F
SCHARY, SUSAN (20TH C)	100-600	X (F)
SCHATER, F. (19TH C)	500-4000	X (L,F)
SCHATTENSTEIN, NIKOL (1877 - 1954)	400-5000+	F
SCHELL, FRANCIS H. (1834 - 1909)	*100-3000	I
SCHELL, FREDERICK B. (1838 - 1905)	*400-5000	M
SCHENCK, PENELOPE JOSEPHINE (1883 -)	*200-1500	L,F
SCHEUERLE, JOE (1873 - 1948)	*350-2800	F
SCHIAVO, A.J. (20TH C)	*100-500	X (F)
SCHILLE, ALICE	*500-6500	
SCHILLE, ALICE (1869 - 1955)	500-8000	X (F)
SCHINDLER, A. ZENO (1815 - 1880)	*700-4500	L,F
SCHLAIKJER, JES WILLIAM (1897 -)	400-4500	F,L
SCHLECT, RICHARD (20TH C)	100-600	L
SCHLEETER, HOWARD BEHLING (1903 - 1976)	100-750	X (L)
SCHLEGEL, FRIDOLIN (19TH C)	400-1200	F
SCHLEMM, BETTY LOU (1934 -)	*100-500	M
SCHLEMMER, FERDINAND L. (1893 - 1947)	100-800	X (L)
SCHLENIER, T.M. (1820 - 1880)	200-1200	L
SCHMEDTGEN, WILLIAM HERMAN (1862 - 1936)	*150-900	I
SCHMID, RICHARD ALLAN (1934 -)	150-9000	L,F

SCHMIDT, CARL (1885-1969)	400-10000	L,M,S,F,G
SCHMIDT, CHRISTAIN F.(18TH-19TH C)	400-3500	G,F,L
SCHMIDT, J.W. (20TH C)	450-2500	M
SCHMIDT, JAY (1929 -)	400-3500	X (G)
SCHMIDT, KARL	*200-4700	
SCHMIDT, KARL (1890 - 1962)	200-8250	L,M
SCHMIDT, M.A. (20TH C)	100-1000	X (L)
SCHMITT, ALBERT FELIX (1873 -)	300-1500	X (S)
SCHMITT, CARL (1889 -)	200-3500	S,L
SCHMITT, PAUL A. (1893 -)	100-900	L
SCHNAKENBERG, HENRY (1892 - 1970)	100-5500	W,L,S
SCHNEIDAU, CHRISTIAN VON (1893 - 1976)	100-5000	F,L,M,S
SCHNEIDER, ARTHUR (1866 - 1942)	100-700	L,I
SCHNEIDER, FRANK (1935 -)	100-1200	X (M)
SCHNEIDER, GERARD (1896 - 1986)	2500-97000	A
SCHNEIDER, OTTO HENRY (1865 - 1950)	500-22000	L,M
SCHNEIDER, SUSAN HAYWARD (1876 -)	100-900	X (L)
SCHNEIDER, THEOPHOLE (1872 -)	100-400	X
SCHNEIDER, WILLIAM G. (1863 - 1912)	*200-1500	X (F)
SCHOEN, CELESTE (20TH C)	100-500	F
SCHOEN, EUGENE (1880 - 1957)	200-3000	X (F)
SCHOFIELD, WALTER ELMER (1867 - 1944)	1000-55000	L,M
SCHOLDER, FRITZ (1937 -)	1000-35000	A
SCHONZEIT, BEN (1942 -)	2000-25000	A
SCHOONOVER, FRANK EARLE (1877 - 1972)	600-35000	I
SCHOTT, MAX (19TH-20TH C)	700-3500	X (F)
SCHOTTLE, MARK (20TH C)	100-850	X
SCHRAG, KARL (1912 -)	*300-3500	A
SCHRAM, ABRAHAM J. (1897 -)	100-900	L,M
SCHREIBER, GEORGES	*150-7000	
SCHREIBER, GEORGES (1904 - 1977)	500-6800	G,M,I
SCHREYVOGEL, CHARLES (1861 - 1912)	350-200000	G,F,L
SCHUBERT, ORLANDO V. (1844 - 1928)	*100-400	L
SCHUCKER, JAMES W.	*100-500	
SCHUCKER, JAMES W. (1903 - 1990)	100-900	X (F)

SCHUELER, JON R. (1916-)	100-1000	A
SCHUESSLER, MARY (20TH C)	100-700	X (L)
SCHULTE, ANTOINETTE (1897 - 1981)	100-850	X (S)
SCHULTZ, CARL (19TH C)	*400-2500	F
SCHULTZ, GEORGE F. (1869 -)	100-4000	F,L,M
SCHULTZ, ROBERT E. (1928 - 1978)	400-7500	X
SCHULZ, CHARLES (1922 -)	*150-5000	X
SCHULZ, TONY (19TH C)	100-750	L
SCHUMACHER, CHARLES J. (19TH C)	250-1500	L
SCHUMACHER, WILLIAM E. (1870 - 1931)	400-4500	L,M
SCHUSSELE, CHRISTIAN	*400-2500	
SCHUSSELE, CHRISTIAN (1824 - 1879)	600-20000	G,F,L
SCHUSTER, DONNA N.	*100-1500	
SCHUSTER, DONNA N. (1883 - 1953)	350-9000	F,L
SCHUYLER, REMINGTON (1884 - 1955)	250-3500	F,G
SCHWAB, EDITH F. (1862 - 1924)	*50-400	L
SCHWABE, HENRY AUGUST (1843 - 1916)	200-1500	F
SCHWACHA, GEORGE (1908 -)	100-1500	L
SCHWARTZ, A.W. (20TH C)	300-1200	L,M
SCHWARTZ, ANDREW THOMAS (1867 - 1942)	150-22000	L,M
SCHWARTZ, DANIEL (1929 -)	200-1500	I
SCHWARTZ, DAVIS F.	*100-800	
SCHWARTZ, DAVIS F. (1879 - 1969)	150-3500	L
SCHWARTZ, WILLIAM S. (1896 - 1977)	100-10000	G,F
SCHWEIDER, ARTHUR (1884 -)	100-700	X (M)
SCHWINN, BARBARA E. (1907 -)	*100-700	I
SCIOCCHETTI, L. (20TH C)	100-600	X (L)
SCIVER, PEARL A. VAN (1896 -)	250-1500	L,S
SCOFIELD, K.M. (19TH C)	100-400	X (L)
SCOFIELD, WILLIAM BACON (1864 - 1930)	300-1800	L
SCOTT, CHARLES T. (1876 -)	400-2500	L,F
SCOTT, EDITH A. (1877 - 1978)	300-4000	F
SCOTT, EDWIN (19TH-20TH C)	500-4500	X (L)
SCOTT, EMILY MARIA SPAFORD (1832 - 1915)	*200-1500	S
SCOTT, FRANK EDWIN (1863 - 1929)	400-4500	G,F

SCOTT, GERALDINE A. (1900 -)	150-1200	L
SCOTT, HOWARD (1902 - 1983)	200-1500	I
SCOTT, JOHN WHITE ALLEN (1815 - 1907)	300-12100	L,M,F
SCOTT, JULIAN (1846 - 1901)	500-8500+	F,L
SCOTT, THOMAS J. (19TH C)	200-900	X (W)
SCOTT, WILLIAM EDOUARD (1884 -)	150-2500	X
SCOTT, WILLIAM J. (1879 - 1940)	*400-2500	F
SCREYER, C.H. (19TH-20TH C)	150-950	L
SCUDDER, JAMES LONG (1836 - 1881)	350-4500	X (L,S)
SEAGER, EDWARD (1809 - 1886)	*50-1100	L
SEARLE, ALICE T. (1869 -)	300-2000	X (S)
SEARLE, HELEN R. (1830 - 1889)	1000-20000	S
SEARS, CARRIE (19TH C)	100-900	L,M
SEARS, TABER (1870 - 1950)	*150-2400	L
SEAVEY, E. LEONE (19TH C)	250-1800	X
SEAVEY, GEORGE W. (1841 - 1916)	350-4000	X (S)
SEBOLA, CAROL (1939 -)	*100-600	L
SECOR, DAVID PELL (1824 - 1909)	100-450	X (M)
SECUNDA, ARTHUR (20TH C)	300-1500	L,F
SEERY, JOHN (1941 -)	300-7500	A
SEGAL, GEORGE (1924 -)	*900-528000	A
SEGALMAN, RICHARD (20TH C)	*150-600	X (F)
SEIBERT, J.O. (19TH-20TH C)	100-500	X (F)
SEIDEL, A. (19TH C)	*100-500	X(S)
SEIFERT, PAUL A. (1840 - 1921)	*4000-26000	L
SELDEN, DIXIE (20TH C)	200-1000	L
SELDEN, HENRY BILL (1886 - 1934)	150-2500	L,F
SELF, COLIN (1941 -)	*400-2000	F
SELIGER, CHARLES (1926 -)	100-1000	A
SELINGER, EMILY (1854 -)	400-1800	S
SELINGER, JEAN PAUL (1850 - 1909)	200-4500	F,M,S
SELLAER, VINCENT (20TH C)	*400-7500	F
SELLERS, ANNA (1824 - 1905)	700-3500	X (S)
SELTZER, OLAF CARL (1877 - 1957)	*1400-88000	G,F
SELTZER, WILLIAM S. (20TH C)	500-5000	F

* Denotes watercolors, pastels, drawings, and/or mixed media

SELZER, F. (19TH-20TH C)	200-1200	F,L
SEMON, JOHN (- 1917)	100-1600	L
SENAT, PROSPER LOUIS (1852 - 1925)	200-7200	M,L
SENDAK, MAURICE (1928 -)	*100-9000	I
SENNHAUSER, JOHN (1907 - 1978)	*400-3500	A
SENSEMAN, RAPHAEL (1870 - 1965)	*100-500	X (L)
SEPESHKY, ZOLTAN L. (1898 - 1934)	150-10000	F,S,L
SERGER, FREDERICK B. (1889 - 1965)	100-850	X (F)
SERISAWA, SUEO (1910 -)	350-2000	L
SERRA, RICHARD	*1200-66000	
SERRA, RICHARD (1939 -)	4000-65000	A
SERRA-BADUE, DANIEL (1914 -)	400-2000	X
SERRES, JOHN THOMAS (1759 - 1825)	200-17400	L,M
SESSIONS, JAMES (1882 - 1962)	*150-4700	L,F,M
SETHER, GULBRAND (early 20TH C)	*100-1000	L
SEVERN, ARTHUR (?)	*100-350	X (M)
SEWARD, JAMES (20TH C)	100-900	X (F)
SEWELL, AMANDA BREWSTER (1859 - 1926)	400-4500	F
SEWELL, AMOS (1901 - 1983)	250-1500	I
SEWELL, ROBERT VAN VORST (1860 - 1924)	200-5000	F,L
SEXTON, FREDERICK LESTER (1889 -)	100-3600	L,I,F,S
SEYFFERT, LEOPOLD (1887 - 1956)	300-4600	F,S
SEYMOUR, RUTH (20TH C)	100-600	L,S
SHACKENBERG, HENRY E. (19TH C)	150-900	X (L)
SHACKLETON, CHARLES (- 1920)	250-1000	X (L)
SHADE, WILLIAM AUGUST (1848 - 1890)	800-4500	F,G
SHAFER, S. P. (19TH C?)	200-1500	X (S)
SHAHN, BEN	*350-65000	
SHAHN, BEN (1898 - 1969)	3500-150000	A,I
SHALLENBERGER, MARTIN C. (1912 -)	*100-650	M
SHANNON, JAMES JEBUSA (1862 - 1923)	800-30000	F
SHAPLEIGH, FRANK HENRY (1842 - 1906)	350-18000	L,M
SHARP, JAMES CLEMENT (1818 - 1897)	2000-35000	X (S)
SHARP, JOSEPH HENRY	*150-20000	
SHARP, JOSEPH HENRY (1859 - 1953)	150-125000	F,I

SHARP, LOUIS HOVEY (1875 - 1946)	100-4500	L,F
SHARP, WILLIAM ALEXANDER (1864-1944)	*100-2500	L
SHARP, WILLIAM (active 1840-90)	800-8000	G,I
SHARPLES, FELIX THOMAS (1786 -)	*500-5000	F
SHARPLES, JAMES (1751 - 1811)	*6500-30000	F
SHATTUCK, AARON DRAPER	*200-2800	
SHATTUCK, AARON DRAPER (1832 - 1928)	500-12000	L,F,W
SHATTUCK, WILLIAM R. (1895 - 1962)	100-700	X (F)
SHAW, CHARLES GREEN (1892 - 1974)	500-25000	A
SHAW, G. (19TH C)	800-6500	L
SHAW, JOSHUA (1777 - 1860)	3500-75000	L,F,S,W
SHAW, SUSAN M. (19TH C)	600-2500	X (S)
SHAW, SYDNEY DALE (1879 - 1946)	100-4500	X (L)
SHAW,GLEN (1891 -)	100-900	X (M)
SHAYLOR, H.W. (19TH C)	*100-400	M
SHEARER, CHRISTOPHER H. (1840 - 1926)	200-5200	L,F,M
SHEARER, VICTOR (1872 - 1951)	200-1500	L
SHEBLE, H. (20TH C)	*300-2500	F
SHEELER, CHARLES	*600-55000 +	
SHEELER, CHARLES (1883 - 1965)	3500-400000 +	A,L
SHEETS, MILLARD	*1500-28000	
SHEETS, MILLARD (1907 - 1989)	2000-36000	A,L
SHEETS, NAN (1889 - 1976)	150-3000	L,M
SHEFFER, GLEN C. (1881 - 1948)	100-3200	F,M
SHEFFERS, PETER W. (1894 - 1949)	200-1500	X
SHEFFIELD, ISAAC (1798 - 1845)	6000-45000	P (F)
SHELDON, CHARLES (1894 - 1961)	*50-400	X (F)
SHELTON, ALPHONSE J. (1905 - 1976)	300-3000	M,L
SHELTON, WILLIAM H. (1840 - 1912)	100-900	F,G
SHEPHARD, CLARENCE E. (1869 - 1949)	100-1500	L,F
SHEPHERD, J. CLINTON (1888 - 1975)	100-2500	F,G
SHEPLEY, ANNIE B. (19TH C)	350-2000	X (F)
SHEPPARD, JOSEPH SHERLY (1930 -)	150-2200	X (F)
SHEPPARD, WARREN (1858 - 1937)	500-19500	M
SHEPPARD, WILLIAM LUDLOW (1833 - 1912)	*400-5300	F,G,I

* Denotes watercolors, pastels, drawings, and/or mixed media

SHERMUND, BARBARA (20TH C)	*100-1500	X (F)
SHERRY, WILLIAM G.	*100-600	
SHERRY, WILLIAM G.(1914 -)	300-3000	L
SHERWOOD, MARY CLARE (1868 - 1943)	1500-7500	L,F
SHERWOOD, WALTER (19TH-20TH C)	350-2000	L,F
SHERWOOD, WILLIAM ANDERSON (1875 - 1951)	100-5800	L
SHIELDS, THOMAS W. (1850 - 1920)	600-8000	X
SHIKLER, AARON (1922 -)	500-9500	F
SHILLING, ALEXANDER (1859 -)	150-2000	L
SHINN, EVERETT	*600-250000 +	
SHINN, EVERETT (1876 - 1953)	2500-125000	G,F,I
SHIRK, JEANETTE C. (19TH-20TH C)	*100-900	X
SHIRLAW, WALTER	*100-2000	
SHIRLAW, WALTER (1838 - 1909)	200-7000+	F,G,I
SHITE, JULIA (20TH C)	*200-1000	X (F)
SHIVELY, DOUGLAS (1896 -)	150-1500	L
SHOKLER, HARRY (1895 - 1978)	200-2300	X (L)
SHOOK, NEVIL (20TH C)	100-600	X
SHOOK, WILLIS (20TH C)	100-400	X (L)
SHOPE, SHORTY (1900 -)	500-8500	X (F)
SHOTWELL, HELEN H, (1908 -)	200-2000	F
SHOUP, CHARLES (20TH C)	2000-6500	X (S)
SHOVE, JOHN J. (19TH C)	*700-3500	X
SHRADER, EDWIN ROSCOE (1879 - 1960)	350-1200	X (I)
SHRIVER, CRANE (late 19TH C)	300-1500	X
SHUCKER, JAMES W. (19TH-20TH C)	100-500	X (F)
SHULL, DELLA (19TH-20TH C)	300-1800	F
SHULTZ, ADOLPH ROBERT (1869 - 1963)	150-3200	L,S
SHURTLEFF, ROSWELL MORSE (1838 - 1915)	300-2800	L,M,I
SHUSTER, WILLIAM HOWARD (1893 - 1969)	400-3600	L,F
SHUTE, R.W. and S.A.(circa 1803 - 1836)	*3000-45000	P
SIBBEL, SUSANNA (active 1800-15)	*2000-8500	P
SIEBEL, FRED (20TH C)	*150-750	X (G)
SIEBERT, EDWARD S. (1856 - 1944)	300-20000	L,F,M
SIEGFRIED, EDWIN C. (1889 - 1955)	*100-2500	L

SIEGRIEST, LUNDY (19TH-20TH C)	*200-1200	F,L
SIENKIEWICZ, CASIMIRE A. (1890 - 1974)	100-1500	L,M
SIES, WALTER (19TH C)	400-2500	L,F
SIEVAN, MAURICE (1898 -)	100-900	X (L)
SIGLING, GEORGE ADAM (19TH-20TH C)	300-1500	F
SILLSBY, CLIFFORD (1896 -)	100-600	X (S)
SILVA, FRANCIS AUGUSTUS	*1500-77000	
SILVA, FRANCIS AUGUSTUS (1835 - 1886)	2500-184000	M,L
SILVA, WILLIAM POSEY (1859 - 1948)	250-6100	L,M
SIMKHOVITCH, SIMKA (1893 - 1949)	100-5000	F,G,L
SIMMONS, EDWARD EMERSON (1852 - 1931)	200-66000	G,F,L
SIMON, HOWARD (1903 - 1979)	100-850	I
SIMON, MOLLY (1890 -)	100-800	X (G)
SIMONI, MARY BELL E. (1897 - 1986)	900-4200	L,S,W
SIMPSON, CHARLES (1885 - 1938)	100-7200	X (G)
SIMPSON, JAMES ALEXANDER (1775 - 1848)	800-3500	F
SIMROCK, E. (19TH C)	200-3000	G,F
SIMS, F. (19TH C)	300-1800	F,L
SINCLAIR, GERRIT VAN W. (1890 - 1955)	100-1200	G,L
SINCLAIR, IRVING (20TH C)	100-7000	X (M,L)
SINDALL, H.S. (19TH C)	400-6000	L
SINGER, CLYDE J.	*100-2000	
SINGER, CLYDE J. (1908 -)	500-10000	G
SINGER, WILLIAM HENRY (JR)	*500-8500	
SINGER, WILLIAM HENRY (JR) (1868 - 1943)	200-6100	L
SIPORIN, MITCHELL (1910 -)	*100-900	F,I
SISSON, FREDERICK RHODES (1893 - 1962)	*100-1300	L
SISSON, LAURENCE P.	*200-1800	
SISSON, LAURENCE P. (1928 -)	250-4700	L,M
SITZMAN, EDWARD R. (1874 -)	200-4000	L
SKEELE, HANNAH BROWN (1829 - 1901)	400-1200	F
SKELTON, LESLIE JAMES (1848 - 1929)	300-4500	L
SKIDMORE, THORNTON (1884 -)	600-4500	I,L
SKILLING, WILLIAM (20TH C)	500-6000	X (W)
SKINNER, CHARLES (19TH C)	*200-900	I,F

* Denotes watercolors, pastels, drawings, and/or mixed media

SKIRVING, JOHN (active 1835-65)	300-1800	M
SKLAR, DOROTHY (20TH C)	*100-800	G,F,L
SKOU, SIGURD	*100-1800	
SKOU, SIGURD (1878 - 1929)	600-7200	A,M,L
SKYNNER, THOMAS (early 19TH C)	2500-60000+	P (F)
SLADE, CALEB ARNOLD (1882 - 1961)	250-2500	L,F
SLADE, CONRAD (1871 - 1949)	150-900	X
SLAFTER, THEODORE S. (late 19TH C)	100-700	L
SLAYTON, M.E. (1901 -)	300-4000	X (L)
SLOAN, JOHN	*600-7800	
SLOAN, JOHN (1871 - 1951)	700-210000	G,F,I
SLOAN, SAMUEL (1815 - 1884)	*350-3000	F
SLOANE, ERIC (1910 - 1985)	1000-37000	L,W,I
SLOANE, MARIAN P. (- 1955)	100-2500	L
SLOMAN, JOSEPH (1883 -)	150-750	I
SLOUN, FRANK J. VAN	*100-2000	
SLOUN, FRANK J. VAN (1879 - 1938)	500-11000	F,L,G
SLUSSER, JEAN PAUL (1886 -)	500-6500	L,S
SMALL, ARTHUR (20TH C)	500-4000	M
SMALL, FRANK O. (1860 -)	800-7000	X (F)
SMALL, RENA (1902 - 1987)	100-600	M,L
SMEDLEY, WILL LARYMORE (1871 - 1958)	100-900	X (L,I)
SMEDLEY, WILLIAM THOMAS	*500-10000	
SMEDLEY, WILLIAM THOMAS (1858 - 1920)	800-20000	F,I
SMIBERT, JOHN (1688 - 1751)	2000-35000	F
SMILEY, HOWARD P. (20TH C)	*100-450	L
SMILLIE, GEORGE HENRY	*100-4000	
SMILLIE, GEORGE HENRY (1840 - 1921)	300-15000	L
SMILLIE, HELEN SHELDON J. (1854 - 1926)	400-2500	X (F,L)
SMILLIE, JAMES (1807 - 1885)	700-3000	F,L
SMILLIE, JAMES DAVID	*250-8500	
SMILLIE, JAMES DAVID (1833 - 1909)	400-21000	L,I
SMITH, ALBERT (1862 - 1940)	100-800	L
SMITH, ALFRED E. (1863 - 1955)	400-16000	L,S,I
SMITH, ANITA MILLER (1893 -)	300-2500	L

SMITH, ARCHIBALD CARY (1837 - 1911)	2500-22000	M
SMITH, BISSELL PHELPS (1892 -)	100-800	M,L
SMITH, CALVIN RAE (1850 - 1918)	600-3500	X (F)
SMITH, CHARLES L.A.	*100-2300	
SMITH, CHARLES L.A. (1871 - 1937)	150-1800	L,M
SMITH, CHARLES WILLIAM (1893 -)	300-1800	I
SMITH, CHARLOTTE H. (20TH C)	100-650	X (L)
SMITH, CHRISTOPHER JOHN (1891 - 1943)	200-3200	L,F,M,S
SMITH, DAN (1865 - 1934)	*200-1200	I
SMITH, DAVID	*1000-20000	
SMITH, DAVID (1906 - 1965)	10000-750000 +	A
SMITH, DE COST (1864 - 1939)	900-8500 +	F,I
SMITH, DUNCAN (1877 - 1934)	100-900	X (F)
SMITH, EDWARD GREGORY (1880 - 1961)	300-3500	L
SMITH, ELLA TANNER (1877 - 1918)	100-900	L
SMITH, ELMER BOYD (1860 - 1943)	800-21000	F,I
SMITH, ERIK JOHAN (20TH C)	*100-750	L
SMITH, ERNEST B. (1866 - 1951)	100-6600	M,L
SMITH, FRANCIS HOPKINSON	*600-35000 +	
SMITH, FRANCIS HOPKINSON (1838 - 1915)	800-10000	L
SMITH, FRANK HILL (1841 - 1904)	400-2000	F,L
SMITH, FRANK VINING	*400-2000	
SMITH, FRANK VINING (1879 - 1967)	400-6500	M
SMITH, FREDERICK CARL	*100-900	
SMITH, FREDERICK CARL (1868 - 1955)	250-2800	L,F
SMITH, GEAN (1851 - 1928)	250-10000	W,F,G
SMITH, HARRY C. (20TH C)	100-600	L
SMITH, HARRY KNOX (1879 - 1934)	*100-1500	F
SMITH, HASSEL W. (1915 -)	500-12100	A
SMITH, HENRY PEMBER	*200-3500	
SMITH, HENRY PEMBER (1854 - 1907)	400-10000	L,M
SMITH, HENRY S. (early 19TH C)	*400-3000	M
SMITH, HOPE (1879 -)	300-1800	L
SMITH, HOUGHTON C.(19TH-20TH C)	150-950	L
SMITH, HOWARD EVERETT (1885 - 1970)	400-8500	I,F,L

* Denotes watercolors, pastels, drawings, and/or mixed media

SMITH, JACK WILKINSON (1873 - 1949)	250-18000+	L,M
SMITH, JEROME HOWARD (1861 - 1941)	100-1400	X (L)
SMITH, JESSIE WILLCOX (1863 - 1935)	600-28000	I
SMITH, JOHN FRANCIS (1868 - 1941)	250-3000	L,M
SMITH, JOHN RUBENS (1775 - 1849)	500-6500	L,M,F
SMITH, JOSEPH B. (1798 - 1876)	2500-12000+	M
SMITH, JOSEPH LINDON	*250-5800	
SMITH, JOSEPH LINDON (1863 - 1950)	200-16500	F,L
SMITH, LANGDON (1870 - 1959)	*150-850	F,L
SMITH, LAWRENCE BEALL (1909 -)	2000-35000	F,G
SMITH, LEON POLK	*350-3000	
SMITH, LEON POLK (1906 -)	1000-44000	A
SMITH, LETTA CRAPO (1862 - 1921)	400-3500+	L,S
SMITH, LILLIAN GERTRUDE (19TH-20TH C)	*300-1000	L
SMITH, LOWELL ELLSWORTH (1924 -)	*3000-20000	L,F,G
SMITH, MAE (19TH C)	100-800	X (S)
SMITH, MARY (1842 - 1878)	600-12000	W,L,S
SMITH, MORTIMER L. (late 19TH C)	500-15000	L,M
SMITH, OLIVER (1896 -)	*450-2000	X (F)
SMITH, OLIVER PHELPS (1867 - 1953)	*300-2500	L
SMITH, PAUL WILLIAMSON (- 1949)	150-900	L,S
SMITH, ROSAMOND LOMBARD (20TH C)	700-29000	F
SMITH, ROYAL BREWSTER (1801 - 1849)	4000-22000+	P,F
SMITH, RUFUS WAY (1900 -)	300-1200	L
SMITH, RUSSELL (1812 - 1896)	300-8800	L,M,F
SMITH, THOMAS LOCHLAN (1835 - 1884)	500-4500	G,L
SMITH, WALTER GRANVILLE	*150-5300	
SMITH, WALTER GRANVILLE (1870 - 1938)	350-35000	L,F,I
SMITH, WUANITA (1866 -)	*100-900	I
SMITH, XANTHUS RUSSELL (1839 - 1929)	500-40000	M,L,F
SMITHSON, ROBERT (1938 - 1973)	*3500-26000	A
SMUKLER, BARBARA (20TH C)	*100-650	A
SMUTNY, JOSEPH (1855 - 1903)	300-1200	X (F)
SMYTHE, EUGENE LESLIE (1857 - 1932)	150-2000	L,G
SMYTHE, SAMUEL G. (1891 -)	200-1000	I

SNELGROVE, WALTER (1924 -)	300-3100	A
SNELL, HENRY BAYLEY (1858 - 1943)	400-6600	M,L
SNELL, IDA (19TH C)	400-2500	X (S)
SNIDOW, GORDON	*2500-45000	
SNIDOW, GORDON (1936 -)	10000-55000	G,F
SNOW, EDWARD TAYLOR (1844 - 1913)	800-9500	X (S)
SNOW, P. (19TH C)	100-900	X (S)
SNOWE, FRANK (19TH-20TH C)	100-1000	L
SNYDER, BLADEN TASKER (1864 - 1923)	150-2500	L
SNYDER, CLARENCE (1873 -)	*100-450	X (L)
SNYDER, JOAN (1940 -)	*800-25000	A
SNYDER, WESLEY (20TH C)	*100-500	
SNYDER, WILLIAM HENRY (1829 - 1910)	700-8000	G,L
SOBLE, JOHN JACOB (20TH C)	600-4800	X (L,F)
SODERSTON, LEON (20TH C)	100-850	L
SOELEN, THEODORE VAN (1890 - 1964)	450-6000	L,F
SOGLOW, OTTO (1900 - 1975)	*100-850	X (I)
SOHIER, ALICE RUGGLES (1880 -)	400-10000	F
SOLDIER, ANDREW STANDING (20TH C)	100-600	X (F)
SOLING, PAUL (20TH C)	300-1200	L
SOLMAN, JOSEPH (1909 -)	700-5000	A
SOLOMON, HARRY (1873 -)	350-1200	X (F)
SOLOMON, HYDE (1911 -)	200-2500	A
SOMERBY, LORENZO (early 19TH C)	1200-5000	L
SOMMER, CARL A. (1839 - 1921)	400-3800	L
SOMMER, CHARLES A. (1829 - 1894)	450-3000	L
SOMMER, ELVA A. (19TH-20TH C)	100-600	L
SOMMER, OTTO (19TH C)	750-40000	W,L
SOMMER, WILLIAM	*150-4600	
SOMMER, WILLIAM (1867 - 1949)	250-6800	L,F
SONN, ALBERT H. (1869 - 1936)	*150-1200	X (F)
SONNTAG, WILLIAM LOUIS (JR.)(1870 - 1898)	*350-10000+	L,F
SONNTAG, WILLIAM LOUIS (SR.)	*500-5000	
SONNTAG, WILLIAM LOUIS (SR.)(1822 - 1900)	1000-40000+	L
SOREN, JOHN JOHNSTON (- 1889)	400-4500	M,L

* Denotes watercolors, pastels, drawings, and/or mixed media

SOTTER, GEORGE WILLIAM (1879 - 1953)	1000-40000	L,M
SOULAGES, PIERRE (1919 -)	2500-357000	A
SOULE, CARLETON (1911 -)	150-850	M,L
SOULEN, HENRY JAMES (1888 - 1965)	400-8500	I
SOUTER, JOHN BULLOCK (1890 - 1972)	500-3100	F,L
SOUTHWARD, GEORGE (1803 - 1876)	300-4500	L,S,F
SOYER, ISAAC (20TH C)	300-8800+	G,L
SOYER, MOSES	*200-3500	
SOYER, MOSES (1899 - 1974)	400-20000	F
SOYER, RAPHAEL	*500-5000	
SOYER, RAPHAEL (1899 - 1987)	1100-95000+	F
SPACKMAN, CYRIL SAUNDERS (1887 - 1963)	400-3500	X (F,L)
SPADER, WILLIAM EDGAR (1875 -)	200-1000	F,I
SPAHR, JOHN (20TH C)	150-800	X (L)
SPANDORF, LILLY (20TH C)	*75-450	L,M
SPANG, FREDERICK (1834 - 1891)	100-900	X (F)
SPANGENBERG, GEORGE (1907 - 1954)	850-1800	L,M,P,S
SPARHAWK-JONES, ELIZABETH (1885 -)	500-8500	F
SPARKS, ARTHUR WATSON (1870 - 1919)	350-4500	L,F
SPARKS, WILLIAM (1862 - 1937)	350-14000	L,M,F
SPAT, GABRIEL (1890 - 1967)	700-6000+	G,F
SPAULDING, HENRY PLYMPTON (1868 -)	*100-750	M,L
SPEAR, ARTHUR PRINCE (1879 - 1959)	400-7500	F,L
SPEAR, THOMAS TRUMAN (1803 - 1882)	300-2000	F
SPEER, WILLIAM W. (1877 -)	100-900	L
SPEICHER, EUGENE EDWARD (1883 - 1962)	600-18000	F,L,S
SPEIGHT, FRANCIS (1896 - 1989)	250-3100	L
SPELMAN, JOHN A. (1880 - 1941)	100-2200	L
SPENCER, ASA (1805 - 1847)	100-1200	X (L)
SPENCER, FREDERICK R. (1806 - 1875)	300-4200+	F,G
SPENCER, HOWARD BONNELL (1888 - 1967)	400-4000	L,M
SPENCER, JOHN C. (1870 - 1946)	500-3500	S,W
SPENCER, LILLY MARTIN (1822 - 1902)	300-32000+	F,S
SPENCER, MARGARET FULTON (1882 -)	150-900	S
SPENCER, NILES (1893 - 1952)	2000-48000	A,L

* Denotes watercolors, pastels, drawings, and/or mixed media   305

SPENCER, ROBERT S. (1879 - 1931)	1200-52000+	G,L,M
SPICUZZA, FRANCESCO J.	*100-2000	
SPICUZZA, FRANCESCO J. (1883 - 1962)	100-3000	F,M,L,S
SPIEGAL, A. (20TH C)	200-900	X
SPIERS, HARRY	*100-650	
SPIERS, HARRY (1869 - 1947)	250-1500	L,F
SPIRO, EUGENE	*195-700	
SPIRO, EUGENE (1874 - 1972)	200-10200	L
SPRAGUE, CURTISS (19TH C)	*100-600	L
SPRINCHORN, CARL	*150-2500+	
SPRINCHORN, CARL (1887 - 1971)	500-5000	A,L
SPRINGER, CHARLES HENRY (1857 - 1920)	100-800	M
SPRUANCE, BENTON MURDOCH (1904 - 1967)	*400-2000	X (L)
SQUINT-EYE, (active 1880-90)	*150-800	X
SQUIRE, E.P. (19TH C)	500-3000	X (L)
SQUIRE, MAUD H. (early 20TH C)	150-800	F,L
SRULL, DONALD (20TH C)	100-500	X
STABLER, ? (1871 - 1943)	150-650	X (L)
STACEY, ANNA LEE (1871 - 1943)	250-6100	L
STACEY, JOHN FRANKLIN (1859 - 1941)	100-10000	L
STAGER, B. (19TH-20TH C)	100-600	X (L)
STAHL, BENJAMIN ALBERT (1910 - 1987)	200-7500	I
STAHLEY, JOSEPH (20TH C)	100-600	X (F)
STAHR, PAUL C. (1883 - 1953)	400-6000	I
STAIGER, PAUL (1941 -)	600-5000	A
STAIGG, RICHARD MORRELL (1817 - 1881)	400-3500	G,F,L
STAMOS, THEODOROS	*1000-18000	
STAMOS, THEODOROS (1922 -)	1100-130000+	A
STANCLIFF, J.W. (1814 - 1879)	500-5500	M,L
STANCZAK, JULIAN (1928 -)	700-9000	A
STANDING, WILLIAM (1904 - 1951)	400-8500	G,F
STANGE, EMILE (1863 - 1943)	200-2000	L,F
STANLAWS, PENRHYN (1877 - 1957)	400-8000	I
STANLEY, CHARLES ST.GEORGE (active 1870-80)	*200-800	F
STANLEY, JANE C. (1863 -)	*100-700	L

STANLEY, JOHN MIX (1814 - 1872)	2500-57500	F,L
STANLEY, ROBERT (BOB) (1932 -)	400-1000	A
STANTON, GEORGE CURTIN (1885 -)	200-1200	L,F
STANTON, JOHN A. (1857 - 1929)	150-1700	X (F)
STANWOOD, FRANKLIN (1856 - 1888)	350-8500	L,M,S
STAPPEN, BARBARA VAN (20TH C)	100-450	X (L)
STARE, GRETA E. (19TH-20TH C)	100-700	X (S)
STARK, OTTO (1859 - 1926)	500-18000	F,L,I
STARKWEATHER, WILLIAM E. B. (1879 - 1969)	150-10000	L,F
STARR, SIDNEY (1857 - 1925)	*250-3000	X (F)
STARRETT, WILLIAM K. (20TH C)	*100-500	I
STAUFFER, E. (20TH C)	100-500	F,L
STEARNS, JUNIUS BRUTUS (1810 - 1885)	1500-30000 +	G,F,L
STEBBINS, ROLAND STEWART (1883 - 1974)	300-2700	X (G)
STEELE, THEODORE CLEMENT (1847 - 1926)	700-19000	L,F
STEELE, THOMAS SEDGWICK (1845 - 1903)	300-5000	S
STEELE, ZULMA (1881 - 1979)	200-3000	X (L,M)
STEENE, WILLIAM (1888 - 1965)	200-4000	F
STEENKS, GUY L. (19TH-20TH C)	200-1800	X (L)
STEFAN, ROSS (20TH C)	600-10000	X (G,F)
STEICHEN, EDWARD J. (1879 - 1973)	1500-35000	L
STEIG, WILLIAM (1907 -)	*100-700	I
STEIN, LEO (19TH-20TH C)	200-950	L
STEIN, WALTER (1924 -)	*100-600	X
STEINBERG, SAUL (1914 -)	*100-110000 +	A
STELLA, FRANK	*5000-1320000	
STELLA, FRANK (1936 -)	6000-540000 +	A
STELLA, JOSEPH	*600-25000	
STELLA, JOSEPH (1880 - 1946)	2500-500000 +	L,S,F
STELLE, MARIAN WILLIAMS (1916 -)	250-1500	M
STENGEL, G.L. (1872 - 1937)	200-1200	X (L)
STEPHAN, GARY	*500-4500	
STEPHAN, GARY (1942 -)	1000-18000	A
STEPHENS, ALICE BARBER (1858 - 1932)	*300-4000	I
STEPHENS, ANSON R. (19TH C)	100-600	X

STERN, J. (19TH C)	300-1200	X (G)
STERNE, HEDDA (1916 -)	800-7500	A
STERNE, MAURICE	*100-7500	
STERNE, MAURICE (1878 - 1957)	550-14000	A,L
STERNER, ALBERT EDWARD	*100-5500	
STERNER, ALBERT EDWARD (1863 - 1946)	300-5000	F,S,L,I
STERNER, HERALD (20TH C)	300-1500	M
STERRIS, JEROME L. (19TH-20TH C)	100-700	X (L)
STETSON, CHARLES WALTER (1858 - 1911)	400-6200	F,L,S
STETTHEIMER, FLORINE	*800-60000	
STETTHEIMER, FLORINE (1871 - 1944)	110000	A,S
STEVENS, JOHN CALVIN (1855 -)	250-4400	X (L,F)
STEVENS, VERA (1867-1950)	150-1200	F
STEVENS, WILLIAM CHARLES (1854 - 1917)	150-1000	L
STEVENS, WILLIAM LESTER	*150-2000	
STEVENS, WILLIAM LESTER (1888 - 1969)	600-8500 +	L,M,S
STEVENSON, ALFRED (19TH C)	300-1000	L,F
STEVER, JOSEPHINE (19TH C)	200-1000	X (L)
STEWARD, JOSEPH (1753 - 1822)	5000-40000	P
STEWARD, SETH W. (19TH-20TH C)	400-4500	L,S
STEWART, JAMES LAWSON	*400-3000	
STEWART, JAMES LAWSON (1855 - 1919)	700-35000	F
STEWART, JEANETTE (1867 -)	250-1200	X (L,F)
STEWART, JULIUS LEBLANC	*400-18000	
STEWART, JULIUS LEBLANC (1855 - 1919)	3000-187000 +	F,G
STEWART, MALCOLM (1829 - 1916)	300-1200	X (F)
STEWART, RON (20TH C)	*200-2600	X (L,F)
STICK, FRANK (1884 - 1966)	300-3300	L,G
STICKROTH, HENRY I. (- 1922)	100-1000	X (F)
STILL, CLYFFORD (1904 - 1980)	10000-1100000 +	A
STILLMAN, WILLIAM JAMES (1828 - 1901)	150-1200	L
STIMSON, JOHN WARD (1850 - 1930)	200-1200	F,I
STINSON, CHARLES (20TH C)	100-700	X (L)
STITES, JOHN RANDOLPH (1836 -)	300-2500	G,L,F
STITT, HERBERT D. (1880 -)	400-3500	X (L)

* Denotes watercolors, pastels, drawings, and/or mixed media

STIX, MARGUERITE (20TH C)	150-650	X(F)
STOBIE, CHARLES (1854 - 1931)	400-7200	F,G
STOCK, ERNEST (20TH C)	100-2000	X (L)
STOCK, FRANK (20TH C)	300-1000	X
STOCK, JOSEPH WHITING (1815 - 1855)	5000-86000	P
STODDARD, ALICE KENT (1893 - 1976)	800-25000	F
STODDARD, FREDERICK LINCOLN (1861 - 1940)	350-2500	F,L,I
STOKES, FRANK WILBERT (1854 - 1927)	300-2000	X (L)
STOLL, JOHN THEODORE E. (1889 -)	150-1500	F,L,I
STOLTENBERG, HANS J. (1870 - 1963)	100-1210	L
STONER, HARRY A. (1880 -)	100-750	I
STOOPS, HERBERT MORTON (1888 - 1948)	900-30000	I
STORER, CHARLES (1817 - 1907)	200-3100	L,M,S
STORRS, JOHN BRADLEY	*600-5000	
STORRS, JOHN BRADLEY (1885 - 1956)	3500-10000	A
STORY, GEORGE HENRY (1835 - 1923)	1200-22000	F,G
STORY, JULIAN RUSSEL (1857 - 1919)	400-7500	F
STOTT, W.R.S. (20TH C)	400-8000	F,L
STRAIN, DANIEL (active 1865-90)	300-2000	F
STRANG, RAY C. (1893 - 1957)	500-7000	I
STRAUS, F. (19TH C)	300-1500	L
STRAUS, MEYER (1831 - 1905)	500-7500 +	L,M
STRAUSS, CARL SUMNER (1873 -)	600-3500	X (L)
STRAYER, PAUL (1885 - 1981)	300-3000	I,F
STREATOR, HAROLD A. (1861 - 1926)	400-2000	L
STREET, FRANK (1893 - 1944)	250-3600	I,L,F
STREET, ROBERT (1796 - 1865)	400-30000	L,F
STRISIK, PAUL (1918 -)	*400-5000	L,M
STROBEL, OSCAR (1891 -)	100-900	X (L)
STROH, EARL (1924 -)	800-3000	A
STRONG, ELIZABETH (1855 - 1941)	450-10000	F,L,S
STRONG, JOSEPH D. (1852 - 1900)	400-4800	L,F
STRONG, RAY S. (1905 -)	150-900	L
STROUD, IDA WEELS (1869 -)	*400-2500	M,L
STRUCK, HERMAN (1887 - 1954)	300-3600	L,G

STUART, ALEXANDER CHARLES (1831 - 1898)	400-5500	M
STUART, GILBERT (1755 - 1828)	1500-97500+	F
STUART, JAMES EVERETT (1852 - 1941)	300-6500	L
STUART, JANE (1812 - 1888)	1500-12100	F
STUBBS, WILLIAM PIERCE (1842 - 1909)	1000-10000	M,G
STUBER, DEDRICK BRANDES (1878 - 1954)	350-8300	L,M
STUECKMANN, FREDERICK C. (20TH C)	600-2500	X (F)
STUEMPFIG, WALTER (1914 - 1970)	300-19000	L,S,M,F
STULL, HENRY (1851 - 1913)	500-21000+	W
STURGIS, KATHERINE (1904 -)	150-1500	X (F)
STURTEVANT, HELENA (1872 - 1946)	300-25000	L,M
SULLIVAN, DENIS (19TH C)	*100-600	X (G)
SULLIVAN, EDMUND J. (20TH C)	*100-650	I
SULLIVANT, THOMAS STARLING (1854 - 1926)	*100-1000	I
SULLY, ALFRED (1820 - 1879)	400-3800	F
SULLY, JANE COOPER (1807 - 1877)	350-1500	X (F)
SULLY, THOMAS	*700-18000	
SULLY, THOMAS (1783 - 1872)	1000-143000	F
SULTAN, DONALD	*9000-25000	
SULTAN, DONALD (1951 -)	3000-27500	A
SUMMA, EMILY B. (1875 -)	150-2000	L
SUMMERS, IVAN (1889 - 1964)	100-1700	L
SUMMERS, ROBERT (1940 -)	3500-18000	G,F,L
SUNDBLOM, HADDON HUBBARD (1899 - 1976)	600-27500	I
SUPLIN, ANN (19TH C)	150-850	P
SURBER, PAUL (20TH C)	*200-900	X (L,F)
SURENDORF, CHARLES FREDERICK (1906 - 1979)	*100-500	L,F,G
SUTER, E.V. (19TH-20TH C)	*100-700	X (F)
SUTTER, SAMUEL (1888 -)	100-1500	L
SUTTERLIN, CHARLES (20TH C)	100-700	L
SUTTON, RUTH H. (1898 - 1960)	100-600	L
SUTTON (JR), HARRY (1897 - 1984)	300-6600	L,F,S
SUTZ, ROBERT	*300-2500	
SUTZ, ROBERT (19TH-20TH C)	1000-8500	F
SUYDAM, HENRY (1817 - 1865)	800-3500	L

* Denotes watercolors, pastels, drawings, and/or mixed media

SUYDAM, JAMES AUGUSTUS (1819 - 1865)	1000-15000+	M,L
SUZUKI, JAMES HIROSHI (1933 -)	150-3500	A
SVENDSEN, SVEND (1864 - 1915)	200-3100	L,F,M
SVOBODA, VINCENT A. (1877 - 1961)	*100-700	X (L,F)
SWAIN, C. (19TH-20TH C)	*100-700	L,G
SWAN, EMMA LEVINIA (1853 - 1927)	100-1200	X(S)
SWAN, S.W. (19TH-20TH C)	*150-850	X(L)
SWANSON, GLORIA (1899 - 1983)	200-1200	L,F,S
SWANSON, JACK (1927 -)	400-3500	G,F
SWANSON, RAY (1937 -)	4500-30000	F,G
SWEENEY, S.C. (1876 -)	100-800	X (M)
SWEET, CHARLES A. (20TH C)	300-1500	X (L)
SWEET, F.H. (active 1880 - 1895)	100-600	X (L)
SWEET, GEORGE (1876 -)	300-1200	G,L
SWERINGEN, RON VAN (20TH C)	300-1800	F,G,L
SWETT, WILLIAM OTIS (JR) (1859 - 1938)	100-900	L,W
SWIFT, C. A. (20TH C)	*100-400	L,G,F
SWIFT, CLEMENT NYE (1846 - 1918)	400-6000	M,G,W,L
SWIFT, IVAN (1873 - 1945)	200-1200	L
SWINNERTON, JAMES GUILFORD (1875 - 1974)	400-18000	L
SWOPE, DAVID (18TH C)	*500-3500	F
SWOPE, KATE F. (19TH-20TH C)	250-1700	F,L
SWORD, JAMES BRADE (1839 - 1915)	300-18000	G,L,M,F
SWORDS, CRAMER (20TH C)	100-800	X (S)
SYARTO, RON (20TH C)	100-700	X
SYKES, ANNIE G. (20TH C)	*100-600	X (S)
SYLVESTER, FREDERICK OAKES (1869 - 1915)	300-10000	L
SYLVESTER, H. M. (19TH-20TH C)	100-800	L,M
SYLVESTER, HARRY ELLIOTT (1860 - 1921)	100-900	L
SYMMERS, AGNES (1889 -)	300-2000	X (L)
SYMONS, GEORGE GARDNER (1863 - 1930)	500-53000	L
SYNDER, BLADEN TASKER (1864 - 1923)	150-3500	F,L
SZANTO, A. KAROLY L. (20TH C)	*300-1500	X (G)
SZYK, ARTHUR (1894 - 1951)	*500-4500	I

T

Artist	Prices	Subject
TABACHNICK, ANNE (20TH C)	50-400	X (S)
TABER, W. (19TH-20TH C)	200-3300	X (F,I)
TACK, AUGUSTUS VINCENT	*100-7200	
TACK, AUGUSTUS VINCENT (1870 - 1949)	4000-220000	A,F
TAGGART, JOHN G. (active 1845-65)	150-1000	X (F)
TAGGART, LUCY M. (19TH-20TH C)	300-2000	X (L,F)
TAHY, JANOS DE (1865 - 1928)	100-800	X (F)
TAIT, ARTHUR FITZWILLIAM (1819 - 1905)	1500-250000 +	F,G,W
TAIT, JOHN R. (1834 - 1909)	150-1500	L,W
TAL, ADAM (20TH C)	*200-1200	L,W
TALBOT, HENRY S. (19TH C)	400-2000	M
TALBOT, JESSE (1806 - 1879)	600-18000	F,L
TALCOTT, ALLEN BUTLER (1867 - 1908)	300-3000	X (L)
TALLANT, RICHARD H. (1853 - 1934)	300-2500	L
TAM, REUBEN (1916 -)	400-2200	X
TANAKA, YASUSHI (1886 -)	400-3500	F,G,S
TANBERG, LILLIAN F. (20TH C)	100-700	X
TANGUY, YVES	*600-209000	
TANGUY, YVES (1900 - 1955)	3000-506000	A
TANNER, HENRY OSSAWA (1859 - 1937)	2000-30000 +	G,L,F,W
TANNING, DOROTHEA	*250-8700	
TANNING, DOROTHEA (1912 -)	1000-40000	A
TANT, CHARLES DU (20TH C)	300-2000	X (F)
TARBELL, EDMUND CHARLES	*250-6500	
TARBELL, EDMUND CHARLES (1862 - 1938)	4000-350000 ·↰	F,G,S
TATE, GAYLE B. (1944 -)	800-5000	X (S)
TAUBES, FREDERICK (1900 - 1981)	350-4000	F,L,S
TAUSZKY, DAVID ANTHONY (1878 - 1972)	250-1800	F
TAVE, DO (19TH-20TH C)	300-1500	X (F)
TAVERNIER, JULES	*100-2300	
TAVERNIER, JULES (1844 - 1899)	1200-66000	L,S
TAYLOR, ANNA HEYWARD (1879 -)	*100-600	X (F)

* Denotes watercolors, pastels, drawings, and/or mixed media

TAYLOR, BERTHA FANNING (1918 - 1980)	*150-1200	F
TAYLOR, CHARLES JAY (1855 - 1929)	250-1800	I
TAYLOR, E. (19TH C)	100-700	L
TAYLOR, EDGAR J. (1862 -)	100-1000	I
TAYLOR, FARWELL M. (1905 -)	*100-450	L
TAYLOR, FRANK H. (19TH-20TH C)	*100-1800	L
TAYLOR, HENRY FITCH (1853 - 1925)	400-4000	X (L)
TAYLOR, JAY C. (19TH C)	100-750	L
TAYLOR, JOHN W. (1897 -)	*100-1600	L
TAYLOR, M.A. (early 19TH C)	500-3500	G,L
TAYLOR, RALPH (1896 -)	1000-18000	F
TAYLOR, WALTER (20TH C)	*100-700	F
TAYLOR, WILLIAM FRANCIS (1883 - 1934)	300-1500	X (L,I)
TAYLOR, WILLIAM LADD (1854 - 1926)	*150-1800	I,M,L
TCHACBASOC, NAHUM (20TH C)	200-1000	X (F)
TCHELITCHEW, PAVEL	*200-22000	
TCHELITCHEW, PAVEL (1898 - 1957)	400-35000	A
TEAGUE, DONALD (1897 -)	*500-40000	I,F,L
TEATER, ARCHIE B. (20TH C)	100-650	X (L,G)
TEED, DOUGLAS ARTHUR (1864 - 1929)	250-5000	F,G,L,S
TEICHMAN, SABINA (1905 - 1983)	300-5000	X (F)
TEPPER, SAUL	*200-2800	
TEPPER, SAUL (1899 - 1987)	200-5200	I,F
TERAOKA, MASAMI	*100-2800	
TERAOKA, MASAMI (20TH C)	100-1000	X (L,F)
TERELAK, JOHN (20TH C)	250-4000	M
TERPNING, HOWARD A. (1927 -)	2500-150000	F,I
TERRY, JOSEPH ALFRED (1872 - 1939)	200-2300	G,L,S
TESAR, JOSEPH (19TH-20TH C)	200-1800	X (M)
TESTAGUZZA, GINO (20TH C)	100-700	X (F)
THAL, SAM	*100-600	
THAL, SAM (1903 - 1964)	300-1000	X (F,M)
THALINGER, E. OSCAR (1885 -)	100-2100	L,M,S
THATCHER, EARL (19TH-20TH C)	*100-500	X (F)
THAYER, ABBOTT HANDERSON (1849 - 1921)	750-40000	F,L,W

THAYER, ALBERT R. (19TH-20TH C)	300-2500	L,F
THAYER, SANFORD (20TH C)	300-3000	X (L,F)
THAYER, W.G. (19TH-20TH C)	100-500	X
THEIL, E. DU (20TH C)	100-300	X (L)
THEMMEN, CHARLES (19TH C)	300-1800	L
THEOBALD, ELISABETH STUTEVANT (1876 -)	100-850	L
THEOBALD, SAMUEL (JR) (19HT - 20TH C)	300-1400	X (L)
THERIAT, CHARLES JAMES (1860 -)	400-4200	F
THEROUX, CAROL (20TH C)	*100-600	F
THEUS, JEREMIAH (1719 - 1774)	2000-25000	P
THEVENAZ, PAUL (20TH C)	*100-600	X (S,F)
THIEBAUD, WAYNE	*1500-143000	
THIEBAUD, WAYNE (1920 -)	5000-495000 +	A
THIEME, ANTHONY	*300-2500	
THIEME, ANTHONY (1888 - 1954)	1000-45000	M,L
THOM, JAMES CRAWFORD (1835 - 1898)	450-6000	G,F,L
THOMAS, A. (19TH-20TH C)	400-3500	L
THOMAS, ALICE BLAIR (20TH C)	100-850	X (L)
THOMAS, BYRON (1902 -)	400-2000	X (L)
THOMAS, CHARLES H. (19TH C)	*800-7000	M,F
THOMAS, DANIEL (19TH C)	*100-450	M
THOMAS, GROSVENOR (1856 - 1923)	100-1400	L,F,S
THOMAS, PAUL K.M. (1875 -)	150-1000	L
THOMAS, REYNOLDS (20TH C)	*100-600	X (F)
THOMAS, RICHARD D. (20TH C)	100-850	G,L
THOMAS, STEPHEN SEYMOUR (1868 - 1956)	300-12000	F,L,M
THOMASON, FRED T. (20TH C)	200-1000	X (G)
THOMPSON, (ALFRED)WORDSWORTH (1840 - 1896)	400-44000	M,G,F,L
THOMPSON, BOB	*400-4500	
THOMPSON, BOB (1937 - 1966)	1200-18000	A
THOMPSON, C.A. (19TH C)	700-6000	G,L
THOMPSON, CEPHAS GIOVANNI (1809 - 1888)	200-8500	G,F,L
THOMPSON, CHARLES A. (active 1850-60)	250-950	X (L,G)
THOMPSON, ELISE (19TH C)	100-750	X(G)

* Denotes watercolors, pastels, drawings, and/or mixed media

THOMPSON, ELOISE REID (20TH C)	*100–650	X (S)
THOMPSON, FREDERICK LOUIS (1868 -)	200-5000	M,L
THOMPSON, GEORGE ALBERT	*100–650	
THOMPSON, GEORGE ALBERT (1868 - 1938)	300-5500	L,M
THOMPSON, HARRY IVES (1840 - 1906)	800-4500	F,L
THOMPSON, J. HARRY (19TH-20TH C)	100-650	X (L)
THOMPSON, JEROME B. (1814 - 1886)	250-62000	L,G,F
THOMPSON, LESLIE P. (1880 - 1963)	450-12000+	F,L,S
THOMPSON, MALCOLM (1901 -)	50-450	L
THOMPSON, RODNEY (1878 -)	*100–450	I
THOMPSON, WALTER W. (1881 - 1948)	200-1800	L
THOMPSON, WILLIAM JOHN (1771 - 1845)	500-8000	G,F
THOMPSON-PRITCHARD, E. (20TH C)	150-850	X (L)
THOMSON, HENRY GRINNELL (1850 - 1939)	500-27500	X (L)
THOMSON, TOM (1877 - 1917)	1000-32000	L,W
THON, WILLIAM	*100-750	
THON, WILLIAM (1906 -)	350-1800	L
THONY, EDUARD (1866 - 1950)	*300-3100	G,F,L
THONY, GUSTAV (1888 - 1949)	1000-8500	L
THORN, JAMES CRAWFORD (1835 - 1898)	350-1500	F,L
THORNE, ANNA LOUISE (1878 -)	*100-750	X (F)
THORNE, DIANA (1895 -)	250-1500	X (W)
THORNE, S.A. (early 19TH C)	*600-2000	L
THORTON, CHARLES H. (19TH C)	100-850	L
THOURON, HENRY J. (1851 - 1915)	600-6500	G
THRASHER, LESLIE (1889 - 1936)	300-4000	F,I
THULSTRUP, THURE DE	*250-1800	
THULSTRUP, THURE DE (1849 - 1930)	700-6000	F,M,I
THURBER, JAMES (1894 - 1961)	*200-3500	X (I)
THURN, ERNEST (1889 -)	100-800	X (S)
THURSTON, JOHN K. (1865 - 1955)	*100-800	M
TICE, CHARLES WINFIELD (1810 - 1870)	1000-6500	L,F,S
TIETJANS, M.H. (20TH C)	150-900	X (F)
TIFFANY, LOUIS COMFORT	*800-55000	
TIFFANY, LOUIS COMFORT (1848 - 1933)	700-61000	F,L,M

* Denotes watercolors, pastels, drawings, and/or mixed media   315

TILTON, JOHN ROLLIN (1828 - 1888)	300-3300	L
TILYARD, PHILLIP (1785 - 1830)	500-25000	F
TIMMINS, HARRY LAVERNE (1887 - 1963)	200-1500	I
TIMMONS, EDWARD J. FINLEY (1882 - 1960)	200-2000	L
TINDALL, KARL (1892 -)	*100-500	L
TING, WALASSE	*300-2400 +	
TING, WALASSE (1929 -)	600-8700	A
TINGLEY, FRANK FOSTER (20TH C)	*200-850	X
TINKLER, BARRIE KEITH (1935 -)	500-5000	A,L,F
TINSLEY, F. (19TH-20TH C)	100-600	X (F)
TIRELL, PAUL (20TH C)	200-800	F,L
TIRRELL, G. (19TH C)	2000-8500	M
TITCOMB, MARY BRADISH	*300-2000	
TITCOMB, MARY BRADISH (1856 - 1927)	1500-33000	F,I
TITCOMBE, WILLIAM HENRY (1824 - 1888)	400-3000	L,F
TITLE, CHRISTIAN (20TH C)	100-3300	L
TITLOW, HARRIET WOODFIN (20TH C)	300-1500	X (F)
TITTLE, WALTER ERNEST (1883 - 1960)	*100-1900	L,F,I
TOBEY, ALTON (20TH C)	*100-500	X
TOBEY, MARK	*300-55000	
TOBEY, MARK (1890 - 1976)	900-69000	A,F
TODAHL, JOHN O. (1884 -)	100-800	X (M)
TODD, CHARLES S. (1885 -)	*400-1000	X (W)
TODD, HENRY STANLEY (1871 -)	150-750	F
TOFT, P. (19TH C)	*150-850	L
TOJETTI, DOMENICO (1806 - 1892)	400-6600 +	F
TOJETTI, EDUARDO (1852 - 1930)	100-2200	W,F
TOJETTI, EDWARD (19TH C)	100-800	X (F)
TOJETTI, M. (19TH C)	100-700	X (F)
TOJETTI, VIRGILIO (1849 - 1901)	300-8500	F
TOLEGIAN, MANUEL J. (20TH C)	200-1200	F,L
TOLMAN, STACY (1860 - 1935)	200-4500	L,M
TOMANECK, JOSEF (1889 -)	100-12700	F
TOMLIN, BRADLEY WALKER	*500-15000	
TOMLIN, BRADLEY WALKER (1899 - 1953)	2500-165000 +	A,I

TOMPKINS, FRANK HECTOR (1847 - 1922)	600-10000+	F
TONEY, ANTHONY (1913 -)	100-750	X
TONK, ERNEST (1889 -)	850-6500	X (G)
TOOKER, GEORGE	*3000-25000	
TOOKER, GEORGE (1920 -)	10000-400000	G,F
TOPCHEVSKY, MORRIS (1899 - 1947)	150-2000	L
TOPPAN, CHARLES (1796 - 1874)	200-900	X
TOPPING, JAMES (1879 - 1949)	150-5000	L
TORAN, ALPHONSE T. (1898 -)	100-800	X (S,F)
TORLAKSON, JAMES	*200-2800	
TORLAKSON, JAMES (1951 -)	400-4500	X
TORREY, ELLIOT BOUTON (1867 - 1949)	300-4300	F,G,L,M
TORREY, GEORGE BURROUGHS (1863 - 1942)	100-1200	M,F
TOSSEY, VERNE (20TH C)	200-1300	I
TOUSSAINT, RAYMOND (1875 - 1939)	*100-400	X (F)
TOWLE, H. LEDYARD (1890 - 1973)	*200-3500	X (G,F)
TOWNSEND, ERNEST (1893 - 1945)	350-5000	F,L,I
TOWNSEND, HARRY EVERETT (1879 - 1941)	250-2500	I
TOWNSEND, LEE (1895 - 1965)	100-900	G,F
TOWNSHEND, A.A. (19TH C)	*100-400	X (S)
TOWNSHEND, H.R. (early 20TH C)	100-500	X (L)
TOWNSLEY, CHANNEL PICKERING (1867 - 1921)	1000-7500	L,F,S
TRACY, CHARLES (1881 - 1955)	*100-700	X
TRACY, JOHN M. (1844 - 1893)	700-27500+	G,W
TRATMAN, ROBERT (20TH C)	100-900	X (F,L)
TRAVER, GEORGE A.	*200-1500	
TRAVER, GEORGE A. (1864 - 1928)	350-4000	M,L,G
TRAVER, MARION GRAY (1892 -)	100-1000	L
TRAVIS, PAUL BOUGH	*250-2000	
TRAVIS, PAUL BOUGH (1891 - 1975)	300-3500	A
TREAT, ASA (19TH C)	700-3000	X (S)
TREBILCOCK, PAUL (1902 - 1981)	200-6600	F
TREDUPP, CHARLES (19TH-20TH C)	100-850	M
TREDUPP, G. (19TH C)	200-1000	X (M)
TREIDLER, ADOLPH (1886 - 1981)	*100-850	I

TRENT, VICTOR PEDRETTI (1891 -)	100-850	L
TREVILLE, DE (20TH C)	100-500	X (L)
TRIBE, GEORGE T. (19TH-20TH C)	100-600	X (L)
TRIESTE, JOANSOVITCH (19TH C)	400-2500	M
TRIGGS, JAMES M. (20TH C)	100-400	M
TRISCOTT, SAMUEL PETER ROLT (1846 - 1925)	*150-1500	M,L
TROCCOLI, GIOVANNI B. (1882 - 1940)	400-5000	F
TRONE, NETTIE (20TH C)	100-400	X (L)
TROTT, BENJAMIN (1770 - 1843)	400-3500	F
TROTTER, NEWBOLD HOUGH	*100-500	
TROTTER, NEWBOLD HOUGH (1827 - 1898)	350-7000 +	W,L
TROUBETZKOY, PIERRE (1864 - 1936)	600-8800	F
TROUSSER, L. (19TH C)	*500-3000	X
TROVA, ERNEST	*600-3000	
TROVA, ERNEST (1927 -)	1200-22000	A
TROYE, EDWARD (1808 - 1874)	2500-60000	W
TRUE, DOROTHY (20TH C)	400-2000	X (A)
TRUESDELL, GAYLORD SANGSTON (1850 - 1899)	400-13000	W,F,L
TRUEX, VAN DAY (20TH C)	*100-500	L
TRUITT, ANNE (1921 -)	600-5000	A
TRUMBULL, EDWARD (early 20TH C)	*150-1300	X (I)
TRUMBULL, JOHN (1756 - 1843)	2500-100000 +	F,L
TRYON, DWIGHT WILLIAM (1849 - 1925)	500-55000 +	L
TSCHACBASOV, NAHUM (1899 -)	100-1300	X (F)
TSCHADY, HERBERT BOLIVAR (1874 - 1946)	100-1500	L,F,I
TSCHUDI, RUDOLF (1855 - 1953)	300-1500	X (F,G)
TUBBY, J.T. (20TH C)	*150-850	X
TUCKER, A.P. (19TH-20TH C)	*100-1000	M,L
TUCKER, ALLEN (1866 - 1939)	600-21000	L,F
TUCKER, MARY B. (active 1838-48)	*350-6000 +	P (F)
TUDGAY, FREDERICK (active 1850-75)	8000-36000	M
TUDOR, ROBERT M. (19TH C)	800-6500 +	G,F
TUPPER, ALEXANDER GARFIELD (1885 -)	100-900	L,M
TURNBULL, GRACE H. (1880 - 1976)	200-1000	L,F,S
TURNBULL, JAMES B. (1909 - 1976)	400-3000	X (F)

* Denotes watercolors, pastels, drawings, and/or mixed media

TURNER, A.L. (19TH C)	100-700	X (L,M)
TURNER, CHARLES H. (1848 - 1908)	200-7200	L,F,M
TURNER, CHARLES YARDLEY (1850 - 1919)	500-9500	G,F,L
TURNER, HARRIET FRENCH (1886 - 1967)	100-400	X
TURNER, HELEN MARIA (1858 - 1958)	1500-38000	F,L
TURNER, ROSS STERLING (1847 - 1915)	*200-2000	M,L
TURNEY, WINTHROP D. (1884 - 1965)	100-850	X
TURTLE, ARNOLD E. (1892 - 1954)	50-500	L,F,S
TUTTLE, RICHARD	*1000-53000	
TUTTLE, RICHARD (1941 -)	1500-44000	A
TWACHTMAN, JOHN HENRY	*500-20000	
TWACHTMAN, JOHN HENRY (1853 - 1902)	5000-470000+	L
TWACHTMAN, JULIAN ALDEN (1935 -)	200-900	X (L)
TWARDOWICZ, STANLEY (1917 -)	300-1200	A
TWINING, YVONNE (1907 -)	400-9500	L,G,F
TWOHY, JULIUS (20TH C)	100-500	X (F)
TWOMBLY, CY	*4500-1800000+	
TWOMBLY, CY (1929 -)	2500-2145000	A
TWORKOV, JACK	*500-14000	
TWORKOV, JACK (1900 - 1982)	5000-71500	A
TYLER, BAYARD HENRY (1855 - 1931)	300-6500	L,F
TYLER, HATTIE (20TH C)	150-950	X (W)
TYLER, JAMES GALE (1855 - 1931)	500-25000+	M,I
TYNG, GRISWOLD (1883 -)	*300-2800	I
TYSON, CARROLL SARGENT	*100-1400	
TYSON, CARROLL SARGENT (JR) (1878 - 1956)	500-6500	M,L

U

Artist	Prices	Subject
UFER, WALTER (1876 - 1936)	1000-375000	F,L
UHL, S. JEROME (1842 - 1916)	250-2500	L,F
UHLE, BERNHARD (1847 - 1930)	100-2000	F
ULLMAN, EUGENE PAUL (1877 - 1953)	200-5000	F,L,M
ULLMAN, PAUL (1906 - 1944)	200-1500	X (L)
ULP, CLIFFORD (1885 - 1957)	300-1000	F,L
ULREICH, EDUARD (20TH C)	100-800	X
ULRICH, CHARLES FREDERIC (1858 - 1908)	2500-250000	F,L
UNDERWOOD, CLARENCE (1871 - 1929)	*100-1200	X (F)
UPJOHN, ANNA MILO (20TH C)	*100-900	F
URBAN, JOSEPH (1872 - 1933)	*200-2500	I
URSULESCU, MIHAI (1913 -)	100-900	X (F)
URWICK, WALTER C. (1864 - 1943)	400-3000	F,L
USHER, RUBY W. (20TH C)	*100-450	X (F)
UTZ, THORNTON	*100-700	
UTZ, THORNTON (1914 -)	300-3500	I

V

Artist	Prices	Subject
VACHELL, ARTHUR H. (1864 -)	100-900	F,M
VAGO, SANDOR (1887 -)	100-2500	F,L
VAIL, EUGENE LAURENT (1857 - 1934)	300-6600 +	M,F
VAILLANT, LOUIS D. (1875 -)	100-900	F
VALENCIA, MANUEL (1856 - 1935)	200-6100	L
VALENCIA, RAMONA (20TH C)	200-1200	X (L)
VALENKAMPH, THEODORE V.C.(1868 - 1924)	300-4200	M,L
VALENSTEIN, ALICE (1904 -)	*100-600	X (L)
VALENTIEN, ALBERT R. (1862 - 1925)	100-900	S,L,F
VALENTINE, FRANCIS BARKER (1897 -)	300-1200	X (F)
VALLEE, JEAN FRANCOIS DE (18TH - 19TH C)	2000-6500	F
VAN BEEST, ALBERT (1820 - 1860)	800-7500 +	M

* Denotes watercolors, pastels, drawings, and/or mixed media

VAN BUREN, RAEBURN L. (1891 - 1987)	*100-750	I
VAN ELTEN, HENDRICK D.K. (1829 - 1904)	500-11000	L
VAN INGEN, HENRY A. (1833 - 1898)	500-4800	L,W
VAN LAER, ALEXANDER T.	*150-1000	
VAN LAER, ALEXANDER T. (1857 - 1920)	300-2500	L,M
VAN MILLETT, GEORGE (1864 -)	100-2500	F,G
VAN SCRIVEN, PEARL A. (1896 -)	100-850	X (S)
VAN SOELEN, THEODORE (1890 - 1964)	450-6500	L,F
VAN STAPPEN, BARBARA (20TH C)	100-500	X (L)
VAN VEEN, PIETER J.L. (1875 - 1961)	350-7000	F,L,M,S
VANARDEN, GEORGE (19TH C)	300-2500	X (W)
VANDERHOOF, CHARLES A. (- 1918)	*50-1200	L
VARADY, FREDERIC (1908 -)	*100-1400	I
VARGAS, ALBERTO (1896 -)	4000-18000	I
VARIAN, GEORGE EDMUND (1865 - 1923)	300-2000	I,F
VARRIALE, W. STELLA (1927 -)	500-3000	X
VASILIEF, NICHOLAS IVANOVITCH (1892 - 1970)	200-3100	F,M,S
VAUGHAN, CHARLES A. (active 1845-60)	200-800	F
VAWTER, JOHN WILLIAM (1871 -)	100-900	L,I
VEDDER, ELIHU	*200-24500	
VEDDER, ELIHU (1836 - 1923)	100-55000	F,I
VEEN, PIETER J.L. VAN (1875 - 1961)	350-7000	F,L,M
VEENFLIET, RICHARD (19TH C)	*100-1200	X (L,G)
VEER, MARY VAN DE (1865 -)	*150-900	F,S
VER BECK, FRANK (1858 - 1933)	*200-1200	I
VERNER, ELIZABETH O'NEILL (1883 -)	*250-5200	F
VERNON, ARTHUE G. (- 1919)	*100-500	L
VERNON, WILLIAM HENRY (1820 - 1909)	*100-500	X (W,L)
VERY, MARJORIE (20TH C)	*100-700	L,M
VETTER, CORNELIA COWLES (1881 -)	100-300	X (L,S)
VEZIN, CHARLES (1858 - 1942)	500-6500	L
VEZIN, FREDERICK (1859 -)	300-5000	X
VIANDEN, HEINRICH (1814 - 1899)	300-2500	L
VIAVANT, GEORGE L. (1872 - 1925)	*400-4000	W,L
VICENTE, ESTEBAN	*500-5500	

VICENTE, ESTEBAN (1904 -)	850-25000	A
VICKERY, ROBERT REMSEN (1926 -)	1000-18000	F
VIGIL, VELOY (1931 -)	400-3000	X (F)
VIGNARI, JOHN T. (20TH C)	100-600	X (M)
VILLA, HERNANDO GONZALLO (1881 - 1952)	200-3000	F,L
VILLA, THEODORE B. (20TH C)	*500-4500	X
VILLACRES, CESAR A. (20TH C)	1000-5500	F,L
VINCENT, HARRY AIKEN	*250-1800	
VINCENT, HARRY AIKEN (1864 - 1931)	250-12100	M,L,F
VINGOE, FRANK (19TH C)	100-700	L
VINTON, FREDERIC PORTER (1846 - 1911)	500-7800	L,F
VIVIAN, CALTHEA (1857 - 1943)	100-1100	X
VOELCKER, RUDOLPH A. (1873 -)	200-1000	X (L)
VOGT, ADOLF (1843 - 1871)	200-2500	L,F
VOGT, FRITZ G. (1890 - 1900)	*250-8500	P
VOGT, LOUIS CHARLES	*100-1000 +	
VOGT, LOUIS CHARLES (1864 - 1939)	400-5000	L,M
VOLK, DOUGLAS (1856 - 1935)	400-9000	L,F
VOLKERT, EDWARD CHARLES (1871 - 1935)	500-5800	G,F,W
VOLKMAR, CHARLES (1809 - 1890/95)	250-3000	L,F
VOLL, F. USHER DE (1873 - 1941)	*100-800	L,F
VOLLMER, GRACE L. (1884 - 1977)	150-1200	X (S)
VOLLMERING, JOSEPH (1810 - 1887)	500-18000	L
VON PERBANDT, CARL (1832 - 1911)	400-4500	L
VON SCHMIDT, HAROLD (1893 - 1982)	900-50000	I,G
VONDROUS, JOHN C. (1884 -)	100-900	X (I)
VONNOH, ROBERT WILLIAM (1858 - 1933)	1500-61000	L,F
VOORHEES, CLARK GREENWOOD (1871 - 1933)	400-9000 +	L
VOS, HUBERT	*300-1800 +	
VOS, HUBERT (1855 - 1935)	400-3500	S,F,G
VOS, IZAAK DE (20TH C)	100-600	L
VOSS, FRANK B. (20TH C)	8500	X
VOSS, FRANKLIN B. (1880 - 1953)	1500-14000	W,F
VREELAND, ANDERSON (19TH-20TH C)	300-2000	X (M)
VREELAND, FRANCIS VAN (1879 -)	*200-800	F,L

* Denotes watercolors, pastels, drawings, and/or mixed media

VREY, TOM (19TH C)	100-700	X (G)
VUKOVIC, MARKO (20TH C)	200-1000	X (S)
VYTLACIL, VACLAV	*300-2500	
VYTLACIL, VACLAV (1892 - 1984)	150-5000	A,L

W

Artist	Prices	Subject
WACHTEL, ELMER (1864 - 1929)	500-28000	L
WACHTEL, MARION KAVANAGH	*1100-66000	
WACHTEL, MARION KAVANAGH (1875 - 1954)	1000-50000	L,F
WACKERMANN, HERBERT (1945 -)	500-3000	F
WADE, C.T. (20TH C)	100-700	X (M)
WADE, PEARL S. (19TH-20TH C)	100-1000	L
WADHAM, WILLIAM JOSEPH (1863 - 1950)	*150-1200	L
WADLER, R.C. (20TH C)	150-700	L
WADSWORTH, ADELAIDE E. (1844 - 1928)	100-900	L,M
WADSWORTH, FRANK RUSSELL (1874 - 1905)	300-2500	L,F
WADSWORTH, WEDWORTH (1846 - 1927)	*100-1000	L,I
WAGNER, A.P. (20TH C)	100-600	L
WAGNER, BLANCHE COLLET (1873 - 1958)	300-1200	X
WAGNER, EDWARD (19TH-20TH C)	200-1200	X (L)
WAGNER, FRED	*100-800	
WAGNER, FRED (1864 - 1940)	100-6500	L
WAGNER, JACOB (1852 - 1898)	500-8800	F,L
WAGNER, JOSEF DE (20TH C)	100-500	X (F)
WAGONER, HARRY B. (1889 - 1950)	200-3500	L
WAGUE, J.R. (19TH C)	100-700	X (L)
WAITE, A.A. (19TH C)	150-850	X (F)
WAITE, EMILY BURLING (1887 - ca.1962)	600-4500	X (F)
WAITT, MARION MARTHA P.(19TH C)	300-1500	L
WALCOTT, HARRY M. (1870 - 1944)	*24200-159500	G
WALDEGG, T. (20TH C)	100-700	L

WALDEN, LIONEL (1861 - 1933)	500-5000	M,G
WALDMAN, PAUL (1936 -)	600-5000	A
WALDO, HOWARD (19TH C)	*100-450	M,L
WALDO, J. FRANK (active 1870-80)	300-1200	L
WALDO, SAMUEL LOVETT (1783 - 1861)	400-5500+	F,M
WALES, GEORGE CANNING (1868 -)	*100-800	X (M)
WALES, J. (19TH C)	400-4500	X
WALES, NATHANIEL F. (active 1800-15)	2000-8500	F
WALES, ORLANDO G. (1865 - 1933)	300-2000	X (S)
WALES, SUSAN MAKEPIECE LARKIN (1839 - 1927)	*100-600	L,M
WALKER, CHARLES ALVAH (1848 - 1920)	300-3500	L
WALKER, DUGALD S. (1865 - 1937)	*100-800	I
WALKER, FRANCIS S. (1872 - 1916)	400-2500	L
WALKER, HAROLD (1890 -)	100-900	L
WALKER, HENRY OLIVER (1843 - 1929)	250-3000	F,L,S
WALKER, INEZ NATHANIEL (1911 - 1979)	*400-1500	P
WALKER, J. EDWARD (20TH C)	100-850	L
WALKER, JAMES (1819 - 1889)	2000-35000	G,F,L
WALKER, JAMES S. (early 20TH C)	*100-300	L
WALKER, JESSE JENKINS (19TH C)	100-800	L
WALKER, WILLIAM AIKEN	*500-5000	
WALKER, WILLIAM AIKEN (1838 - 1921)	1500-99000	G,F,M,S
WALKLEY, DAVID BIRDSEY (1849 - 1934)	300-2800+	F,L
WALKOWITZ, ABRAHAM	*250-3500	
WALKOWITZ, ABRAHAM (1880 - 1965)	600-22000	A,F
WALL, A. BRYAN (1872 - 1937)	300-6400	X (F)
WALL, ALFRED S. (1825 - 1896)	350-4000+	L
WALL, HERMAN C. (1875 -)	300-1500	X (F)
WALL, W.C. (19TH C)	6600	X (S)
WALL, WILLIAM ALLEN	*200-2800+	
WALL, WILLIAM ALLEN (1801 - 1885)	400-3000	F,L,M
WALL, WILLIAM ARCHIBALD (1828 - 1875)	300-1500	F,L
WALL, WILLIAM GUY (1792 - 1864)	600-18000	L
WALLACE, DAVID (20TH C)	*100-1000	F,G
WALLACE, FREDERICK ELLWOOD (1893 - 1958)	50-2300	F,S

* Denotes watercolors, pastels, drawings, and/or mixed media

WALLACE, LILLIE T. (20TH C)	300-1500	X (M,L)
WALLER, FRANK (1842 - 1923)	200-5000	F,L,M
WALLIN, CARL E. (1879 -)	100-3800	F,A,L
WALLINGER, CECIL A. (19TH C)	100-300	X (L)
WALLIS, FRANK (- 1934)	300-1000	X (L)
WALROND, E.M. (20TH C)	100-1000	L
WALSON, BONNIE (20TH C)	100-600	X (F)
WALTENSPERGER, CHARLES E. (1871 - 1931)	250-4100	M,F
WALTER, CHRISTIAN J. (1872 - 1938)	300-5000	L
WALTER, L. (19TH C)	300-1500	X (M)
WALTER, MARTHA (1876 - 1976)	600-44000	F,L
WALTER, WILLIAM FRANCIS (1904 -)	100-800	L
WALTERS, EMILE (1893 -)	400-5000	L
WALTERS, H. (19TH C)	100-600	X (L)
WALTERS, JOSEPHINE (- 1883)	500-3000	L
WALTERS, RAY (20TH C)	100-500	L
WALTHER, CHARLES H. (1879 - 1938)	150-4400	L
WALTMAN, HARRY FRANKLIN (1871 - 1951)	200-1800	F,L
WALTON, HENRY (1804 - 1865)	*1500-10000	P
WALTON, WILLIAM (1843 - 1915)	200-4000	L,S
WANDESFORDE, JUAN B. (1817 - 1902)	500-4800	G,L,F,I
WANSTREET, C. (20TH C)	100-500	M,L
WARD, C.M. (19TH-20TH C)	100-700	G,F
WARD, CHARLES (1900 -)	200-1900	X (L)
WARD, CHARLES CALEB	*1000-7500	
WARD, CHARLES CALEB (1831 - 1896)	1500-31000	G,F,L
WARD, EDGAR MELVILLE (1839 - 1915)	100-7500	G,L
WARD, EDMUND F. (1892 -)	500-6500	I
WARD, ELLEN (19TH C)	100-900	X (L)
WARD, HAROLD MORSE (1889 - 1973)	100-700	L
WARE, THOMAS (19TH C)	800-5500	P
WARHOL, ANDY	*1000-4070000	
WARHOL, ANDY (1928 - 1988)	5000-4070000	A
WARNER, EARL A. (1883 -)	*100-500	M,L
WARNER, EVERETT LONGLEY (1877 - 1963)	800-12000	L,F

WARNER, JUSTINE A. (20TH C)	100-700	M,L
WARNER, NELL WALKER (1891 - 1970)	200-4500	M,S,F
WARREN, A. COOLIDGE (1819 - 1904)	400-2500	S
WARREN, ALONZO (19TH-20TH C)	200-1000	X (L)
WARREN, ANDREW W. (- 1873)	600-10000	M,L
WARREN, CONSTANCE WHITNEY (1888 - 1948)	*100-700	F
WARREN, EMILY (19TH C)	100-700	X (M,L)
WARREN, HAROLD BROADFIELD (1859 - 1934)	*150-2500	F,M,L
WARREN, J. C. (19TH C)	300-1200	X (W)
WARREN, MELVIN CHARLES	*4000-24000	
WARREN, MELVIN CHARLES (1920 -)	15000-150000	F,G
WARREN, WESLEY (20TH C)	100-500	X (M)
WARSHAW, HOWARD (1920 -)	900-3000	A
WARSHAWSKY, ABEL GEORGE (1873 - 1959)	500-15500+	L,F
WARSHAWSKY, ALEXANDER (1887 - 1962)	200-1500	L,F
WARTHEIN, LEE R. (20TH C)	100-800	X (F)
WASHBURN, CADWALLADER (1866 - 1965)	200-1500	X (F)
WASHBURN, JESSIE M. (20TH C)	100-600	X (L)
WASHES, J. (19TH-20TH C)	*100-500	X (S)
WASHINGTON, ELIZABETH F.	*300-1000	
WASHINGTON, ELIZABETH F. (1871 - 1953)	100-1700	L
WASSON, GEORGE SAVARY (1855 - 1926)	100-1250	M,L
WATERHOUSE, M.S. (19TH C)	150-1000	F
WATERMAN, MARCUS A. (1834 - 1914)	400-4800	F,L
WATERS, GEORGE W. (1832 - 1912)	300-3500	L,F
WATERS, SUSAN C. (1823 - 1900)	1000-45000+	P,F,L,W
WATKINS, CATHERINE W. (20TH C)	250-1500	L
WATKINS, FRANKLIN CHENAULT (1894 - 1972)	300-10000	G,F,L
WATKINS, SUSAN (1875 - 1913)	200-2500	F
WATKINS, WILLIAM (19TH C)	400-2000	F
WATROUS, HARRY WILLSON (1857 - 1940)	300-45000	F,I,S
WATSON, A. FRANCIS (19TH C)	100-600	X (L)
WATSON, AMELIA MONTAGUE (1856 - 1934)	*200-950	M,L,I
WATSON, DAWSON (1864 - 1939)	300-7500	L
WATSON, EDGAR MELVILLE (1877 - 1956)	100-500	X (L)

* Denotes watercolors, pastels, drawings, and/or mixed media

WATSON, EDITH SARAH (1861 -)	*100-300	X (L)
WATSON, ELIZABETH VILA T.(- 1934)	100-850	F
WATSON, HENRY SUMNER (1868 - 1933)	300-2000	I,W
WATSON, HOMER RANSFORD (1855 - 1936)	400-7500	L
WATSON, JESSIE N. (1870 - 1963)	*75-500	L
WATSON, NAN (1876 - 1966)	100-1200	S
WATSON, ROBERT (20TH C)	100-2300	F,G
WATSON, WALTER (19TH-20TH C)	200-1800	L
WATSON, WILLIAM R. (19TH-20TH C)	100-600	L
WATTS, PETER (20TH C)	100-600	X
WATTS, WILLIAM CLOTHIER (1869 - 1961)	*100-2000	L
WAUD, ALFRED R. (1828 - 1891)	*200-6100	I,M
WAUGH, COULTON	*100-900	
WAUGH, COULTON (1896 - 1973)	200-900	I
WAUGH, FREDERICK JUDD (1861 - 1940)	300-40000	M,F,S
WAUGH, IDA (- 1919)	300-4000	G,F
WAUGH, SAMUEL BELL (1814 - 1885)	350-4000	L,F
WAY, ANDREW JOHN HENRY (1826 - 1888)	500-19000+	S,L,F
WAY, EDNA (20TH C)	*100-700	M,L
WEAVER, JAY (20TH C)	450-2500	G,I
WEBB, A.C. (1888 -)	300-2000	F,I
WEBBER, CHARLES T. (1825 - 1911)	300-6500+	F,L
WEBBER, F. WILLIAM (19TH-20TH C)	150-1000	L
WEBBER, WESLEY (1839 - 1914)	250-8000	M,L,I
WEBER, C. PHILIP (1849 -)	400-8800	L
WEBER, CARL	*100-3200	
WEBER, CARL (1850 - 1921)	400-17500	L,W
WEBER, CARL T. (19TH-20TH C)	100-500	X
WEBER, E.R. (20TH C)	100-700	X (S)
WEBER, F. WILLIAM (20TH C)	100-900	L,M
WEBER, FREDERICK (19TH C)	*200-1600	X (F)
WEBER, FREDERICK T. (1883 - 1956)	100-950	X (M)
WEBER, MAX	*300-53000	
WEBER, MAX (1881 - 1961)	500-99000	A,F
WEBER, OTIS S.	*100-600	

WEBER, OTIS S. (late 19TH C)	200-4800	M
WEBER, PAUL	*100-2600	
WEBER, PAUL (1823 - 1916)	350-38500	L,F,W
WEBER, PHILIPP (1849 - 1921)	500-9500	L
WEBSTER, EDWIN AMBROSE (1869 - 1935)	300-7700	F,M
WEBSTER, W.M. (20TH C)	100-600	X (F)
WEDEPHOL, THEODOR (1863 - 1923)	*100-800	X (L,M)
WEEDEN, ELEANOR REVERE (1898 -)	100-1000	I
WEEKES, A. (19TH C)	300-1800	X (G)
WEEKS, EDWIN LORD (1849 - 1903)	1000-110000 +	F,L
WEEKS, JAMES (1922 -)	3500-18000	A,L
WEGER, MARIE (1882 - 1980)	100-3600	X (S)
WEIGAND, GUSTAVE A.(1870 - 1957)	200-3600	L
WEINBERG, EMILIE SIEVERT (20TH C)	150-850	X (L)
WEINREICH, AGNES (1873 - 1946)	200-3300	X (L)
WEIR, JOHN FERGUSON (1841 - 1926)	900-48000	L,S,F
WEIR, JULIAN ALDEN	*500-43000	
WEIR, JULIAN ALDEN (1852 - 1919)	750-440000	F,L,S
WEIR, ROBERT WALTER	*100-2900	
WEIR, ROBERT WALTER (1803 - 1889)	600-88000	G,F,L,I
WEIS, JOHN ELLSWORTH (1892 -)	300-4200	F,L
WEISER, MARY E. (19TH-20TH C)	100-600	X (S)
WEISMAN, WILLIAM H. (19TH-20TH C)	150-1500	M,L
WEISS, BERNARD J. (20TH C)	100-600	X (L)
WEISS, MARY L. (early 20TH C)	100-600	X (S)
WEISS, S.A. (early 20TH C)	100-3100	X
WELBECK, G.A. (19TH-20TH C)	150-950	X (L,F)
WELCH, JACK	*100-650	
WELCH, JACK (1905 -)	500-4000	I
WELCH, LUDMILLA P. (19TH-20TH C)	300-2500	L,W
WELCH, MABEL R. (- 1959)	150-1000	X (F)
WELCH, THADDEUS	*150-2000	
WELCH, THADDEUS (1844 - 1919)	200-15000	L,F
WELDON, CHARLES DATER (1844 - 1935)	1000-8500	I
WELDON, H.A. (19TH-20TH C)	150-850	L

WELLER, CARL F. (1853 - 1920)	*100-500	X (L)
WELLINGTON, J.(19TH-20TH C)	100-900	L
WELLIVER, NEIL (1929 -)	3000-38500	A
WELLS, BENJAMIN B. (1856 - 1923)	400-3500	X (F)
WELLS, BETTY (20TH C)	*100-800	X
WELLS, C.H. (19TH C)	*150-600	L
WELLS, LYNTON (1940 -)	350-20000	A
WELLS, NEWTON ALONZO (1852 -)	300-1500	L,S
WELLS, WILLIAM L.	*100-650	
WELLS, WILLIAM L. (1890 -)	100-1800	I,L
WELS, CHARLES (20TH C)	*100-500	X (F)
WELSH, WILLIAM P. (1889 -)	*200-1200	X (I,F)
WENBAN, SION LONGLEY	*100-1900	
WENBAN, SION LONGLEY (1848 - 1897)	300-2000	L
WENCK, PAUL (1892 -)	200-1500	L,I
WENDEL, THEODORE (1857 - 1932)	800-45000	L,M
WENDEROTH, AUGUSTUS (1825 -)	400-4500	F,W,L
WENDEROTH, FREDERICK A. (19TH-20TH C)	300-1800	X (S)
WENDT, WILLIAM (1865 - 1946)	500-55000+	L,F
WENGENROTH, STOW (1906 - 1978)	*300-1800	L,M
WENGER, JOHN	*100-600	
WENGER, JOHN (1887 -)	300-5500	X (F)
WENTWORTH, DANIEL F. (1850 - 1934)	400-2500	L
WENTWORTH, R. (19TH C)	300-1500	L
WENZELL, ALBERT BECK	*100-9000	
WENZELL, ALBERT BECK (1864 - 1917)	100-5000	I
WERNER-BEHN, HANS (early 20TH C)	100-600	X
WERTINFIELD, JOSEPH (20TH C)	100-350	X (F)
WESCOTT, PAUL (1904 - 1970)	300-2500	X (L,M)
WESLEY, JOHN (1928 -)	300-2500	A
WESSEL, HERMAN H. (1878 - 1969)	400-5000	M,F
WESSELMANN, TOM	*2500-462000	
WESSELMANN, TOM (1931 -)	2000-528000	A
WESSELS, GLENN (1895 - 1982)	*1540	L
WESSON, ROBERT (1902 - 1967)	200-2800	L

WEST, BENJAMIN	*400-20000+	
WEST, BENJAMIN (1738 - 1820)	600-37500	F,G,L
WEST, LEVON FAIRCHILD (1900 - 1968)	*200-2100	F
WEST, PETER B. (1833 - 1913)	300-2000	G,W,L
WEST, RAPHAEL LAMARR (1769 - 1850)	*350-7200	F,I,L
WEST, T. (19TH C)	100-600	X (L)
WEST, WILLIAM EDWARD (1788 - 1857)	400-2500	F,M
WESTERMANN, HORACE CLIFFORD (1922 - 1981)	*500-132000	A
WESTHCILOFF, CONSTANTIN (20TH C)	250-2500	X (L)
WESTON, MORRIS (19TH-20TH C)	100-500	X (L)
WETHERBEE, GEORGE FAULKNER (1851 - 1920)	500-7500	F,L
WETHERBY, ISAAC AUGUSTUS (1819 - 1904)	800-6000	P
WETHERILL, ELISHA KENT KANE (1874 - 1929)	600-18000	M,W,L,F
WEYDEN, HARRY VAN DER (1868 -)	350-8800	L
WEYL, MAX (1837 - 1914)	450-5500+	L
WHEATON, FRANCIS (1849 -)	*100-4800	L
WHEELER, CHARLES ARTHUR (1881 - 1977)	150-4500	X (F)
WHEELER, CLIFTON (1883 - 1953)	300-3500	F
WHEELER, WILLLIAM R. (1832 - 1894)	250-4000	F
WHEELOCK, MERRILL GREENE (1822 - 1866)	*200-1200	M,L
WHEELOCK, WALTER W. (early 19TH C)	250-950	F
WHEELOCK, WARREN (1880 - 1960)	150-1500	F,L
WHELAN, THOMAS (20TH C)	150-950	X (L)
WHISTLER, JAMES ABBOTT MCNEIL	*1500-100000+	
WHISTLER, JAMES ABBOTT MCNEIL (1834 - 1903)	5000-2600000	L,F
WHITAKER, CHARLES W. (20TH C)	150-800	X (L)
WHITAKER, GEORGE WILLIAM	*300-1900	
WHITAKER, GEORGE WILLIAM (1841 - 1916)	400-5000	M,S,L,F
WHITAKER, WILLIAM	*400-4000	
WHITAKER, WILLIAM (1943 -)	800-9500	X (F)
WHITCOMB, JON	*200-800	
WHITCOMB, JON (1906 - 1988)	200-4500	I
WHITE, CHARLES (1918 - 1980)	*800-6000	F
WHITE, CHARLES HENRY (1878 -)	600-3500	X (L,F)
WHITE, CLARENCE SCOTT (1872 -)	300-3000	L,M

WHITE, EDITH (1855 - 1946)	300-5500	S
WHITE, EDWIN D.(1817 - 1877)	200-10000	F,G
WHITE, H. WADE (20TH C)	100-750	L,I
WHITE, HENRY COOKE	*100-1500	
WHITE, HENRY COOKE (1861 - 1952)	200-2500	L
WHITE, NONA L. (1859 -)	*100-500	L
WHITE, ORRIN AUGUSTINE	*150-1100	
WHITE, ORRIN AUGUSTINE (1883 - 1969)	400-9000	L
WHITE, THOMAS GILBERT (1877 - 1939)	100-5500	L,F
WHITEHEAD, WALTER (1874 - 1956)	300-1000	L
WHITEHORNE, JAMES A. (1803 - 1888)	300-1500	F
WHITEMAN, SAMUEL EDWIN (1860 - 1922)	200-1200	L
WHITESIDE, FRANK REED (1866 - 1929)	200-2100	L,M
WHITING, HENRY H. (19TH C)	400-4000	L
WHITING, HENRY W. (19TH C)	150-3500	L
WHITING, LILLIAN V. (20TH C)	100-700	X
WHITMAN, A.M. (19TH-20TH C)	*100-800	X (L)
WHITMAN, EDWIN (20TH C)	100-700	X (G)
WHITMORE, M. COBURN (1913 -)	500-8000	I
WHITMORE, WILLIAM R. (19TH-20TH C)	100-800	X (L)
WHITNEY, E. S. (19TH C)	100-750	L,M
WHITON, H.W. (19TH C)	100-700	L
WHITTAKER, JOHN BARNARD (1836 - 1926)	400-5500	F,L
WHITTEKER, LILIAN (20TH C)	500-4500	L
WHITTEMORE, LILLIAN (19TH C)	*100-500	X (S)
WHITTEMORE, WILLIAM JOHN (1860 - 1955)	500-7000	F,M,L
WHITTREDGE, THOMAS WORTHINGTON (1820 - 1910)	2000-450000+	L,M
WHORF, JOHN	*350-33000	
WHORF, JOHN (1903 - 1959)	800-23100	F,M,L
WICKEY, HARRY (1892 -)	*100-600	X (F)
WICKS, HEPPLE (19TH-20TH C)	100-7200	L
WIDFORSS, GUNNAR MAURITZ (1879 - 1934)	*300-17000	L,F
WIDNER, G.O. (19TH C)	800-6000	L
WIEGAND, CHARMION VON	*300-1500	

WIEGAND, CHARMION VON (1899 -)	400-17600	A
WIEGAND, GUSTAVE ADOLPH (1870 - 1957)	400-6200	L
WIEGHORST, OLAF CARL	*300-9000	
WIEGHORST, OLAF CARL (1899 - 1988)	4000-80000	F,G,W
WIES, W. (19TH-20TH C)	100-600	X (L)
WIESSLER, WILLIAM (1887 -)	100-900	X (S)
WIGGINS, (JOHN) CARLETON (1848 - 1932)	200-12100+	L
WIGGINS, GUY CARLETON (1883 - 1962)	500-48000	L,M
WIGGINS, SIDNEY MILLER (1883 - 1940)	150-950	X (L,M)
WIGHT, MOSES (1827 - 1895)	300-6000+	G,F
WIGLE, ARCHIE PALMER (20TH C)	50-500	M,L,S
WILATCH, MICHA (1910 -)	300-2000	X (L)
WILBUR, THEODORE E. (19TH C)	150-750	X (L)
WILCOX, FRANK NELSON (1887 -)	*250-4000	L,F
WILCOX, RAY D. (1883 -)	100-1200	M
WILCOX (WILLCOX), WILLIAM (1831 -)	200-800	L
WILDE, JOHN (1919 -)	2000-18000	F
WILDE (WILD), HAMILTON GIBBS (1827 - 1884)	200-1500	F,G,L
WILDER, ARTHUR B.	*150-750	
WILDER, ARTHUR B. (1857 - 1949)	300-3000	L
WILDER, F. H. (active 1845-50)	400-1500	F
WILDER, FRANKLIN (19TH C)	*2000-8500	P
WILDHABER, PAUL (20TH C)	75-750	L
WILES, IRVING RAMSAY	*300-28600+	
WILES, IRVING RAMSAY (1861 - 1948)	200-99000	G,F,M,I
WILES, LEMUEL MAYNARD (1826 - 1905)	500-15000	L
WILES, M. (20TH C)	100-600	X (S)
WILEY, WILLIAM T.	*800-15000	
WILEY, WILLIAM T. (1937 -)	1000-36000	A
WILFORD, LORAN FREDERICK	*100-650	
WILFORD, LORAN FREDERICK (1893 - 1972)	250-2500	F,I
WILFRED, LEMUEL (20TH C)	300-800	X (L)
WILGUS, WILLIAM JOHN (1819-1853)	2000-25000+	F
WILKIE, ROBERT D. (1828 - 1903)	500-16000	G,L,S,W
WILKINSON, J. WALTER (1892 -)	100-850	X (F)

WILL, JOHN M. AUGUST (1834 - 1910)	*100-1200	F,L
WILLARD, ARCHIBALD M. (1836 - 1918)	300-5500+	F,L
WILLEY, PHILO "CHIEF" (1886 - 1980)	500-5000	P
WILLIAMS, CHARLES DAVID (1875 - 1954)	*200-1500	I
WILLIAMS, EDWARD K. (1870 -)	350-2400	L
WILLIAMS, FLORENCE W. (- 1953)	300-4600	M,F,L
WILLIAMS, FREDERICK BALLARD (1871 - 1956)	200-8000	F,G,L
WILLIAMS, FREDERICK DICKENSON (1829 - 1915)	250-6050+	F,L
WILLIAMS, GEORGE ALFRED (1875 - 1932)	*100-1500	F
WILLIAMS, HENRY (1787 - 1830)	300-2800	F
WILLIAMS, ISAAC L. (1817 - 1895)	300-3000	F,L
WILLIAMS, J.F. (19TH C)	100-850	X (M)
WILLIAMS, JOHN SCOTT (1877 -)	*100-1000	L,I
WILLIAMS, M.C. (19TH C)	100-1000	G
WILLIAMS, MARY BELLE (1873 - 1943)	200-3100	L,F,S
WILLIAMS, MARY R. (1857 - 1907)	400-4500	F
WILLIAMS, MAY (20TH C)	*150-600	X (L,F)
WILLIAMS, MICAH	*1000-20000	
WILLIAMS, MICAH (active 1815-30)	1000-19800+	P
WILLIAMS, MILDRED EMERSON (1892 -)	150-3200	X (F)
WILLIAMS, PAUL A. (1934 -)	500-12000	F,L
WILLIAMS, PAULINE BLISS (1888 - 1962)	300-3200	X (L)
WILLIAMS, ROBERT F. (20TH C)	150-1000	X (L)
WILLIAMS, VIRGIL (1830 - 1886)	300-5500+	G,F,L
WILLIAMS, WILLIAM (c.1710 - 1790)	600-18000	F,L
WILLIAMS, WILLIAM JOSEPH (1759 - 1823)	500-4500	F
WILLIAMSON, CHARTERS (1856 -)	250-1200	L
WILLIAMSON, JOHN (1826 - 1885)	500-13000	L,F,S
WILLIS, ALBERT PAUL (1867 - 1944)	150-1500	L
WILLIS, EDMUND A.(VAN) (1808 - 1899)	300-4000	G,L,W
WILLIS, THOMAS (1850 - 1912)	*750-5000	M
WILLIS, W.L. (19TH-20TH C)	100-600	X (M)
WILLISON, T.J. (20TH C)	100-700	L
WILLSON, B. (19TH C)	200-1200	L
WILLSON, JAMES MALLERY (1890 -)	100-900	X (L,M)

WILLSON, MARY ANN (active 1810-30)	*1000-7500	P
WILMARTH, CHRISTOPHER (1943 -)	400-2000	X
WILMARTH, LEMUEL EVERETT (1835 - 1918)	700-18000	G,F,S
WILSON, ALEXANDER (1766 - 1818)	100-1000	X (S)
WILSON, CHARLES THELLER (1855 - 1920)	150-1000	L,F
WILSON, DONALD ROLLER (1938 -)	500-47000	F,I
WILSON, DOUGLAS (19TH C)	200-1000	X
WILSON, GAHAN (20TH C)	*100-1000	X (F)
WILSON, HENRY MITTON (1873 - 1923)	100-600	X (L)
WILSON, HARRIET (20TH C)	*100-600	X (S)
WILSON, JAMES (19TH C)	1000-6500	L
WILSON, JANE (1924 -)	700-20000	A
WILSON, MORTIMER (1906 -)	400-5200	I
WILSON, RAY (1906 - 1972)	100-600	L
WILSON, ROBERT BURNS (1851 - 1916)	*250-850	L
WILSON, SOLOMON (1894 - 1974)	100-3100	X (L,M)
WILSON, T. (19TH C)	100-650	L
WILTZ, ARNOLD (1889 - 1937)	200-1000	L
WIMAR, CHARLES (1828 - 1863)	5000-75000	F,M,W,L
WINDFORSS, GUNNAR (1879 - 1934)	*5000-10000	L
WINGERT, EDWARD OSWALD (1864 - 1934)	100-1600	X (L)
WINNER, WILLIAM E. (1815 - 1883)	1000-26000	G,F
WINSLOW, HENRY (1874 -)	400-3500	X (L,M)
WINSOR, HELEN A. (19TH C)	300-1800	X
WINTER, ALICE BEACH (1877 - 1970)	400-3500	F,I
WINTER, ANDREW (1893 - 1958)	400-11000 +	M,L
WINTER, CHARLES ALLEN (1869 - 1942)	200-8500	F,L,I
WINTERS, TERRY	*66000-30250	
WINTERS, TERRY (1949 -)	110000-135000	X
WISBY, JACK (1870-1940)	300-2000	L,M
WISTEHUFF, REVERE F. (1900 - 1971)	400-3500	I
WITHERSTINE, DONALD FREDERICK (1896 -)	200-1200	L
WITHROW, EVELYN ALMOND (1858 - 1928)	200-3000	F,L
WITKOWSKI, KARL	*300-2500	
WITKOWSKI, KARL (1860 - 1910)	1000-20000	G

* Denotes watercolors, pastels, drawings, and/or mixed media

WITKOWSKI, KARL (1860 - 1910)	1000-20000	G
WITT, JOHN H. (1840 - 1901)	600-18000	F,L
WITTER, E.S. (20TH C)	100-850	L
WIX, HENRY OTTO (1866 - 1922)	*150-950	L
WOELFLE, ARTHUR WILLIAM (1873 - 1936)	200-3500+	M,L,F,S
WOELFLE, WILLIAM (20TH C)	100-600	S
WOHL, MILLIE (20TH C)	250-2400	A
WOLCOTT, HAROLD (20TH C)	300-2800	X (F,L)
WOLCOTT, JOHN GILMORE (1891 -)	100-900	X (F)
WOLCOTT, ROGER A. (20TH C)	150-850	F
WOLCOTT, ROGER H. (20TH C)	150-800	X (L)
WOLF, BEN (20TH C)	100-450	X (F)
WOLF, CHAS. H. (early 19TH C)	10000-40000	P
WOLF, F.H. (20TH C)	200-800	X (S)
WOLF, GEORG (1882 - 1962)	500-7500	G,W,F,L
WOLF, GUSTAVE (1863 - 1935)	300-3500	X (M)
WOLF, HENRY (1852 - 1916)	150-650	L,F,S
WOLF, LONE	*600-3500	
WOLF, LONE (1882 - 1965)	1000-18000	F,L
WOLF, WALLACE L. DE (1854 - 1930)	250-1800	L
WOLFE, BYRON (1904 - 1973)	*1000-8500	X (F)
WOLFE, JACK (20TH C)	200-1500	A
WOLFE, WAYNE (20TH C)	5000-30000	X (L)
WOLFF, B. (20TH C)	100-400	X (L)
WOLFF, GUSTAV (1863 - 1934)	300-3000	L,M
WOLINS, JOSEPH (19TH-20TH C)	150-1200	L,M
WOLLASTON, JOHN (active 1735-70)	2000-18000	F
WONNER, PAUL JOHN (1924 -)	*500-4500+	X
WOOD, A.M. (19TH C)	100-850	X (L)
WOOD, ALEXANDER (19TH-20TH C)	300-6500	F,L
WOOD, DOROTHY MACHADO (20TH C)	100-600	L
WOOD, GEORGE ALBERT (1845 - 1910)	300-3500	L
WOOD, GEORGE BACON JR (1832 - 1910)	300-3500+	L,G
WOOD, GRANT	*700-325000	
WOOD, GRANT (1892 - 1942)	1500-1375000	F,L,G,W

WOOD, HOWARD (1922 -)	150-850	A
WOOD, HUNTER (1908 -)	400-3000	M,F
WOOD, J. OGDEN (1851 - 1912)	150-4500	L,W
WOOD, JAMES LONGACRE (1863 - 1938)	1000-20000	F
WOOD, JULIA S. (1890 -)	100-700	L
WOOD, ROBERT (1889 - 1979)	700-15000	L,M,F
WOOD, ROBERT E. (1926 - 1977)	600-8500+	L
WOOD, STANLEY L. (1860 - 1940)	500-5000	X (I,F)
WOOD, THOMAS WATERMAN	*2000-45000+	
WOOD, THOMAS WATERMAN (1823 - 1903)	700-121000	G,F
WOOD, VIRGINIA HARGRAVES	*100-750	X (F)
WOOD, WILLIAM R.C. (1875 - 1915)	300-2600	L
WOOD, WORDEN	*250-1100	
WOOD, WORDEN (active 1912- 1937)	500-3000	M,I
WOODBURN, STEPHEN (20TH C)	150-2000	X
WOODBURY, CHARLES HERBERT (1864 - 1940)	700-82500	F,M,L
WOODBURY, MARCIA OAKES (1865 - 1913)	250-2000	F
WOODCOCK, HARTWELL L. (1853 - 1929)	*100-1600	M,L
WOODLEIGH, ALMA (AC. 1880 - 1890)	100-2100	L,F
WOODRACH, KARL L. (20TH C)	*100-350	X (M)
WOODRUFF, DANIEL F. (20TH C)	*500-2500	L
WOODRUFF, G.L. (19TH C)	300-1000	X (S)
WOODRUFF, JOHN KELLOGG (1879 - 1956)	*100-500	X (L)
WOODSIDE, JOHN ARCHIBALD (1781 - 1852)	1000-42000+	P
WOODSON, MAX R. (20TH C)	100-500	X (F,L)
WOODVILLE, RICHARD CATON (1825 - 1856)	2000-75000	G
WOODWARD, ELLSWORTH (1861 - 1939)	*250-6600	G,M,I
WOODWARD, HILDEGARD H. (19TH-20TH C)	*200-700	X (L)
WOODWARD, LAURA (19TH C)	100-2100	X (S)
WOODWARD, MABEL MAY	*100-2000	
WOODWARD, MABEL MAY (1877 - 1945)	600-27500	F,M,L,S
WOODWARD, ROBERT STRONG (1885 - 1960)	400-3500	L
WOODWARD, STANLEY WINGATE (1890 - 1970)	100-3500	M,I
WOODWARD, WILLIAM	*300-4500	
WOODWARD, WILLIAM (1859 - 1939)	400-5000	G,F

WOOLF, SAMUEL JOHNSON (1880 - 1948)	100-6000	L,F
WOOLFE, MICHAEL A. (1837 - 1899)	*100-850	I
WOOLRYCH, F. HUMPHRY W.	*100-800	
WOOLRYCH, F. HUMPHRY W. (1868 -)	100-2000	F,L,S,I
WOOSTER, AUSTIN C. (19TH C)	350-26000	S,L
WORDEN, J. (20TH C)	100-300	X (F)
WORES, THEODORE (1860 - 1939)	50-12000+	F,M,I
WORTH, THOMAS	*200-1200	
WORTH, THOMAS (1834 - 1917)	500-4500	G,L
WRENN, CHARLES LEWIS (1880 - 1952)	100-1500	F,I
WRIGHT, CHARLES H. MONCRIEF (1870 - 1939)	500-6000	L,F,I
WRIGHT, CHARLES LENOX (1876 -)	400-3800	X (L,I)
WRIGHT, EMMA R. (20TH C)	100-600	M,L
WRIGHT, FRANK LLOYD (1869 - 1959)	*800-176000	I
WRIGHT, GEORGE FREDERICK (1828 - 1881)	100-1500	L,F
WRIGHT, GEORGE HAND	*300-3500	
WRIGHT, GEORGE HAND (1872 - 1951)	800-8600	I,G,F
WRIGHT, GEORGE W. (1834 - 1934)	1800-45000	G,F
WRIGHT, JAMES COUPER (1906 - 1969)	*100-900	S
WRIGHT, JAMES HENRY (1813 - 1883)	500-6500	L,M,F,S
WRIGHT, JAMES W. (20TH C)	100-650	X (L)
WRIGHT, R. STEPHENS (1903 -)	100-2400	L,M
WRIGHT, RUFUS (1832 - 1895)	500-4500	F,L,S
WUERMER, CARL (1900 - 1983)	1500-18000+	L
WUERPEL, EDMUND HENRY (1866 - 1958)	200-1000	X (L)
WUIRT, WALTER (20TH C)	400-2000	A
WUST, ALEXANDER	*100-2000	
WUST, ALEXANDER (1837 - 1876)	1000-14000	L,M,F
WUST, CHRISTOFFEL (1801 - 1853)	600-4500	F
WYAND, D.E. (19TH-20TH C)	*100-600	G,F
WYANT, ALEXANDER HELWIG	*400-7000	
WYANT, ALEXANDER HELWIG (1836 - 1892)	800-60000	L
WYCKOFF, J.H. (19TH C)	100-1100	X
WYDEVELD, ARNOUD (active 1855-65)	500-14000	S,W
WYETH, ANDREW	*300-319000	

WYETH, ANDREW (1917 -)	20000-385000+	L,W,F
WYETH, JAMES (1946 -)	*1500-53000	L
WYETH, NEWELL CONVERS (1882 - 1945)	2000-77000+	I,L
WYGANT, BOB (1927 -)	1500-12000	X
WYLIE, ROBERT (1839 - 1877)	500-7500 +	G
WYMAN, F.A. (19TH C)	1000-7500+	L,F

X

Artist	Prices	Subject
XCERON, JEAN (1890 - 1967)	1000-15500	A

Y

Artist	Prices	Subject
YAEGER, EDGAR (1904 -)	100-600	X
YALE, LEROY (1841 - 1906)	200-1000	X
YARD, SYDNEY JANIS (1855 - 1909)	*200-7200	L
YARROW, WILLIAM HENRY KEMBLE (1891- 1941)	*200-1200	L,M
YATES, CULLEN (1866 - 1945)	400-19000	M,L,S
YATES, ELIZABETH (1888 -)	150-900	X (S)
YATES, WILLIAM HENRY (1848 - 1934)	300-6000	F,L,S
YATRIDES, GEORGE (20TH C)	400-6000	G,F
YEATS, AGNES (20TH C)	*100-600	L
YECKLEY, NORMAN (19TH C - 20TH C)	100-10000	X (L)
YELLAND, RAYMOND DABB (1848 - 1900)	400-25000+	L,M
YENNAD, ADUASHA (20TH C)	100-600	X (M)
YENS, KARL (JULIUS HEINRICH) (1868 - 1945)	400-25000+	F,I,L
YEWELL, GEORGE HENRY (1830 - 1923)	500-15000	G,F
YOAKUM, JOSEPH E (1886 - 1973)	*400-6500	X
YOHN, FREDERICK COFFAY (1875 - 1933)	300-4500	I

* Denotes watercolors, pastels, drawings, and/or mixed media

YONG, JOE DE	*100-2500	
YONG, JOE DE (1894 - 1975)	500-5000	G,F
YORKE, MIGNON (20TH C)	*100-600	I
YORKE, WILLIAM G. (1817 - 1883)	5000-25000	M
YORKE, WILLIAM H. (1847 - 1921)	5000-25000	M
YOUENS, CLEMEMT T. (19TH-20TH C)	200-800	X (L)
YOUNG, AUGUST (1839 - 1913)	700-5000	G,F
YOUNG, B.S. (late 19TH C)	800-5000	X (M)
YOUNG, BARBARA (1920 -)	100-650	F
YOUNG, CHARLES MORRIS	*300-2500	
YOUNG, CHARLES MORRIS (1869 - 1964)	1000-9500	M,L
YOUNG, CLIFF (20TH C)	100-1500	F
YOUNG, EDWARD (1823 - 1882)	200-2000	L,M
YOUNG, FRED GRANT (19TH-20TH C)	100-700	X (S)
YOUNG, HARVEY OTIS	*300-1800	
YOUNG, HARVEY OTIS (1840 - 1901)	400-12000	L,F,W
YOUNG, JAMES HARVEY (1830 - 1918)	400-3000	F
YOUNG, JOE DE (1894 - 1975)	200-1500	F
YOUNG, MABEL (20TH C)	350-1800	X (L)
YOUNG, MAHONRI MACKINTOSH	*100-1700	
YOUNG, MAHONRI MACKINTOSH (1877 - 1957)	300-5000	F,L
YOUNG, OSCAR VAN (1906 -)	300-1500	X
YOUNG, PETER (20TH C)	800-15000	A
YOUNG, WILLIAM (1874 -)	800-10000	L
YOUNG, WILLIAM S. (active 1850-70)	300-8500	L
YOUNG-HUNTER, JOHN (1874 - 1955)	300-3500	L,F
YOUNGERMAN, JACK	*400-11000	
YOUNGERMAN, JACK (1926 -)	800-11000	A
YUAN, SI CHEN (1912-1974)	200-4000	M,L,F
YUTZLER, ARLINGTON (20TH C)	100-450	X (L)

Z

Artist	Prices	Subject
ZAJAC, JACK (1929 -)	400-2500	A
ZAKANITCH, ROBERT S. (1935 -)	4000-20000	A
ZAKHAROV, FEODOR (1882 - 1935)	200-1200	X (M)
ZANDT, THOMAS KIRBY VAN (ac. 1814 - 1886)	400-4000	W
ZANDT, WILLIAM T. VAN (19TH C)	500-7000	F,W
ZANG, JOHN J. (19TH C)	600-5500	F,L
ZANSTZINGER, M.G. (20TH C)	*75-400	X (W)
ZANTHO, DARIN (20TH C)	100-700	X
ZEIGLER, LEE W. (1868 -)	*200-1000	I
ZELDIS, MALCAH (1931 -)	500-7500	P
ZELLINSKY, C.L. (19TH C)	400-9500	W,F
ZELTNER, WILLIAM (19TH C)	*250-1200	X (F)
ZEMSKY, JESSICA (20TH C)	*300-2700	X (F,L)
ZETTEL, JOSEPHINE (20TH C)	*100-600	M,S
ZIEGLER, EUSTACE PAUL (1881 - 1969)	900-42000	L,F
ZIEGLER, NELLIE (20TH C)	400-5000	L,M
ZIMMELE, MARGARET SCULLY (1872 -)	150-950	L,I
ZIMMERMAN, CARL (19TH-20TH C)	100-1700	L,M
ZIMMERMAN, FREDERICK A.(1886 - 1974)	150-3600	L
ZIMMERMAN, JOSEPH (1923 -)	100-1000	L
ZIMMERMAN, MASON W. (1861 -)	*150-900	X (L)
ZIMMERMAN, PAUL (1921 -)	100-600	X (F)
ZIMMERMAN, RENE (1904 -)	100-4000	X (G,L)
ZIMMERMAN, WILLIAM (20TH C)	*150-650	X (W)
ZION, BEN (20TH C)	100-600	X (S)
ZIROLI, NICOLA VICTOR (1908 -)	300-3000	X (F)
ZISKIND, A. (20TH C)	200-1000	F
ZOGBAUM, RUFUS FAIRCHILD	*400-2500	
ZOGBAUM, RUFUS FAIRCHILD (1849 - 1925)	600-6500	I,F,M
ZOGBAUM, WILFRED M.(1915 - 1965)	900-6000	A
ZOLAN, DONALD J. (20TH C)	100-7000	M,F
ZORACH, MARGUERITE T. (1887 - 1968)	600-29000	A,L,F,S
ZORACH, WILLIAM	*400-12100	
ZORACH, WILLIAM (1887 - 1966)	1000-70000	A,L

340   * Denotes watercolors, pastels, drawings, and/or mixed media

ZORNES, JAMES MILFORD	*200-6600	
ZORNES, JAMES MILFORD (1908 -)	250-4800	L,M
ZORTHIAN, JIRAYR H. (1912 -)	*150-900	X (I)
ZOX, LARRY (1936 -)	800-8500	A
ZUANICH, FRANK (20TH C)	100-900	L
ZUBER, J. (19TH C)	500-2000	X (S)
ZUCCARELLI, FRANK EDWARD (20TH C)	100-700	X (F)
ZUCKER, JOSEPH (1941 -)	*400-18000	A
ZUILL, ABIE LUELLA (1856 - 1921)	300-2500	S,L
ZWAAN, CORNELIS CHRISTIAN	*100-500	
ZWAAN, CORNELIS CHRISTIAN (1882 - 1964)	100-5500	F,L,S
ZWERLING, LISA (20TH C)	100-600	X

RECORD PRICES

The following prices are record *auction* prices realized - as of 08/30/93 - for each of the respective artists, and are isolated here because they are far above the "typical" price range for each artist. Within the alphabetical listing of artists, which make up the largest portion of this *Guide*, the price range for each of these artists will be followed by a "+" to indicate that you should refer to the list below for further information. [*note*: Most prices include a 10%-15% buyers premium, and a "*" preceding a price indicates the work was a watercolor, pastel, or mixed media.]

ARTISTS	RECORD	SUBJ	DATE
AHL, HENRY H.	11,000	L	5/88
ALBRIGHT, ADAM EMORY	63,800	G	3/90
ALEXANDER, JOHN W.	517,000	F	5/88
ALLSTON, WASHINGTON	200,600	F	12/81
AMES, EZRA	99,000	F	1/86
ANSHUTZ, THOMAS POLLOCK	*60,500	F	12/87
ANSHUTZ, THOMAS POLLOCK	1,540,000	G	5/88
APPEL, CHARLES P.	9,350	L	3/86
APPELTON, GEORGE WASHINGTON	28,600	P	10/87
ARIOLA, FORTUNATO	27,500	L	12/88
ARTSCHWAGER, RICHARD	990,000	A	11/89
BAKER, WILLIAM BLISS	34,500	M	6/81
BARBIER, GEORGES	23,000	F	9/90
BARLOW, MYRON	38,500	F	6/90
BASCOM, RUTH H.	(pair) *35,000	P(F)	12/86
BAUM, CHARLES	16,500	S	5/86
BAZIOTES, WILLIAM	385,000	A	5/90
BEAUX, CECILIA	363,000	F	12/92

BELKNAP, ZEBAKIAH	82,500	P(F)	12/90?
BELL, EDWARD AUGUSTE	13,200	F	1/89
BELLOWS, GEORGE W.	*220,000	F	5/89
BELLOWS, GEORGE W.	1,430,000	F	5/88
BENSON, EUGENE	20,900	G	11/85
BENSON, FRANK W.	583,000	G	5/90
BENTON, THOMAS HART	1,540,000	G	12/89
BERNEKER, LOUIS F.	24,200	F	12/89
BICKNELL, FRANK A.	24,200	L	11/88
BIERSTADT, ALBERT	2,640,000	L(W)	5/89
BIRNEY, WILLIAM VERPLANCK	27,500	G	5/86
BISHOP, RICHARD E.	13,750	W	4/89
BISPHAM, HENRY COLLINS	16,500	W	12/88
BISTTRAM, EMILE J.	52,800	A	12/89
BLACK, OLIVE PARKER	11,000	L	3/90
BLUEMNER, OSCAR	396,000	A	5/87
BLUHM, NORMAN	46,000	A	2/90
BLUM, ROBERT FREDERICK	473,000	F	6/82
BLUM, ROBERT FREDERICK	*104,000	F	12/82
BONHAM, HORACE	28,600	G	5/90
BORG, CARLO	41,250	L	3/90
BOSTON, JOSEPH H.	45,100	F	1/89
BOUGUEREAU, E. J. G.	81,400	F	2/87
BRECKENRIDGE, HUGH HENRY	65,000	?	5/91
BREDIN, RAY SLOAN	35,200	F	5/86
BREWSTER Jr, JOHN	852,500	P(F)	1/88
BRICHER, ALFRED THOMPSON	*176,000	M	12/87
BROOKE, RICHARD NORRIS	12,100	L	6/88
BROWN, BENJAMIN C.	26,400	L	4/89
BROWN, GEORGE LORING	49,500	L	5/90
BROWN, HARRISON B.	11,000	L	5/86
BROWN, JOHN APPLETON	28,600	L	3/85
BROWN, JOHN GEORGE	270,000	G	11/90
BROWN, WILLIAM MASON	50,600	L	5/86
BROWNE, MATILDA	30,800	F	12/93

BRUSH, GEORGE DEFOREST	242,000	F	12/92
BUEHR, KARL ALBERT	20,900	L	9/84
BUNDY, HORACE	16,500	F	10/87
BURLIUK, DAVID	275,000	G	11/88
BURPEE, WILLIAM PARTRIDGE	23,100	L	11/89
BURTON, CHARLES	*35,200	P	12/90?
CADMUS, PAUL	154,000	F	12/89
CADY, HARRISON	36,800	I	5/93
CALIFANO, JOHN	36,000	G	12/85
CARBEE, SCOTT CLIFTON	10,450	F	11/86
CARISS, HENRY T.	6,325	G	4/84
CARLSON, JOHN FABIAN	41,800	L	5/90
CARTER, CLARENCE HOLBROOK	38,500	G	11/89
CASILEAR, JOHN WILLIAM	39,600	L	11/89
CASSATT, MARY S.	*4,510,000	F	5/88
CATLIN, GEORGE	539,000	F	11/89
CAVALLON, GIORGIO	99,000	A	11/89
CHAMBERS, THOMAS	88,000	P(M)	1/87
CHANDLER, JOSEPH GOODHUE	40,700	P	10/88
CHAPMAN, CARLTON THEODORE	22,000	M	12/89
CHASE, WILLIAM MERRITT	*2,200,000	F	12/88
CHIARIACKA, ERNEST	11,000	L	12/86
CHITTENDEN, ALICE BROWN	27,500	S	10/87
CHRISTY, HOWARD CHANDLER	115,500	I	5/88
CHURCH, FREDERIC EDWIN	8,250,000	M	5/89
CHURCHILL, W.W.	23,000	G	11/88
CLARK, WALTER APPLETON	11,500	L	12/87
CLAVE, ANTONI	241,700	A	10/90
COALE, GRIFFITH BAILY	26,400	L	5/87
COATES, EDMUND C.	47,500	F	7/84
COLE, THOMAS	1,045,000	L	5/88
COLEMAN, CHARLES CARYL	170,500	S	10/84
COPELAND, CHARLES	12,100	L	4/88
COUTTS, GORDON	8,800	F	6/81
CROPSEY, JASPER F.	660,000	L	4/81

CURRY, JOHN STUEART	82,500	G	12/88
DABO, LEON	39,600	M	5/88
DAHLAGER, JULES	13,200	L	5/89
DALEE, JUSTUS	(pair) *6,500	P	10/88
DARRAH, ANN SOPHIA T.	6,600	S	10/84
DAVIS, WARREN B.	*39,600	F	12/88
DAVIS, WARREN B.	17,600	F	5/88
DECKER, JOSEPH	759,000	S	11/89
DEHAAS, M. F. H.	55,000	M	?/90
DEMING, EDWARD WILLARD	33,000	G	4/82
DESSAR, LOUIS PAUL	12,650	F	1/80
DEVOLL, F. USHER	30,000	L	12/89
DEWING, THOMAS WILMER	594,000	F	3/88
DICKINSON, PRESTON	374,000	A(S)	12/87
DINE, JIM	*825,000	A	5/89
DINE, JIM	660,000	A	11/89
DIXON, L. MAYNARD	192,500	L	6/88
DOVE, ARTHUR G.	484,000	A	12/87
DUFNER, EDWARD	220,000	L	11/89
DUNNING, ROBERT SPEAR	286,000	S	12/85
DURRIE, GEORGE HENRY	385,000	L	5/89
DYER, URIAH N.	30,800	?	?
EAKINS, THOMAS	*3,520,000	G	5/90
EDWARDS, GEORGE WHARTON	28,600	L	4/88
EMMET, LYDIA FIELD	50,600	F	4/87
ENNEKING, JOHN JOSEPH	121,000	L	6/83
EVERGOOD, PHILIP	38,500	A(F)	12/87
FASSETT, TRUMAN E.	14,300	L	5/88
FEININGER, LYONEL	806,000	A	10/90
FERY, JOHN	8,167	L	10/85
FIELD, ERASTUS SALISBURY	66,000	P(F)	10/85
FINCK, HAZEL	20,000	L	5/91
FISKE, GERTRUDE	52,800	L	12/88
FOSTER, BEN	9,500	L	9/78
FRANKENSTEIN, GODFREY NICHOLAS	16,500	L	12/86

FRERICHS, WILHELM C. A.	22,000	L	11/85
FRIESEKE, FREDERICK CARL	825,000	F	5/91?
GAMMELL, ROBERT HALE IVES	35,200	F	9/91
GAY, EDWARD	18,700	L	1/89
GAY, WALTER	70,400	G	12/87
GERRY, SAMUEL LANCASTER	16,500	L	7/82
GIFFORD, ROBERT SWAIN	17,000	L	5/91
GIFFORD, SANFORD ROBINSON	550,000	L	12/92
GILCHRIST, WILLIAM WALLACE	35,200	F	5/88
GLACKENS, WILLIAM	715,000	L	12/87
GLARNER, FRITZ	330,000	A	?/91
GOODWIN, (RICHARD) LABARRE	56,100	S	11/80
GRAHAM, JOHN D.	275,000	A	12/85
GRANT, FREDERIC M.	17,600	L(F)	12/86
GREACEN, EDMUND WILLIAM	88,000	F	12/87
GROPPER, WILLIAM	240,000	?	4/91
GROSZ, GEORGE	325,000	A	12/90
HABERLE, JOHN	517,000	S	5/87
HALE, PHILIP LESLIE	132,000	F	5/88
HALL, GEORGE HENRY	46,750	S	4/87
HALLETT, HENRICKS A.	7,700	M	12/86
HAMBLEN, STURTEVANT	104,500	P	?/91
HAMILTON, HAMILTON	30,800	F	9/92
HAMILTON, JAMES	21,500	M	12/79
HAMILTON, WILLIAM R.	12,650	F	5/86
HARTLEY, MARSDEN	1,155,000	A	12/92
HARVEY, GEORGE	203,500	L	5/88
HAVEN, FRANKLIN DE	7,150	L	4/85
HAWTHORNE, CHARLES W.	121,000	F	12/84
HAYS, WILLIAM JACOB (SR)	31,900	W	10/82
HEADE, MARTIN JOHNSON	1,925,000	L	12/87
HEALY, GEORGE P.A.	22,000	F	9/81
HENRI, ROBERT	462,000	L	5/87
HENRY, EDWARD LAMSON	275,000	G	7/80
HICKS, EDWARD	990,000	P	11/90

HICKS, THOMAS	297,000	F	12/87
HILER, HILAIRE	3,080	L	6/88
HILL, JOHN WILLIAM	*55,000	L	11/80
HILLS, LAURA COOMBS	*45,100	S	5/89
HINCKLEY, THOMAS HEWES	20,900	W	5/87
HOBBS, GEORGE THOMPSON	5,280	L	5/88
HOFFBAUER, CHARLES	50,600	G	5/88
HOFFBAUER, CHARLES	*9,350	F	5/86
HOFFMAN, CHARLES	126,500	P(L)	1/86
HOPKINS, MILTON WILLIAM	77,500	P	11/90
HORTON, WILLIAM SAMUEL	104,500	?	?
HUBACEK, WILLIAM	14,300	S	12/88
HUNT, THOMAS L.	35,750	M	2/90
HUTCHENS, FRANK T.	9,075	F	5/86
INNESS, GEORGE	935,000	L	5/89
INUKAI, KYOHEI	18,700	A	5/88
JACOBSEN, ANTONIO	60,984	M	6/85
JAMBOR, LOUIS	27,500	G	11/88
JARVIS, JOHN WESLEY	71,500	F	1/87
JOHANSEN, JEAN MACLANE	26,400	F	12/86
JOHNS, JASPER	15,500,000	A	11/88
JOHNSON, DAVID	165,000	S	5/89
JOHNOSN, FRANK TENNEY	385,000	G	12/92
JOHNSON, JOSHUA	660,000	P(F)	1/88
JONES, JOE	66,000	G	9/90
KAULA, WILLIAM J.	52,800	L	5/88
KELPE, PAUL	38,500	A	12/87
KENDALL, WILLIAM SERGEANT	46,750	F	5/86
KENNEDY, WILLIAM W.	38,500	P	1/84
KENSETT, JOHN FREDERICK	616,000	M	12/87
KEY, JOHN ROSS	35,200	L	1/81
KING, CHARLES BIRD	385,500	F	5/90
KITAJ, RONALD B.	385,000	A	5/87
KOERNER, HENRY	52,250	F	4/91
KOONING, WILLIAM DE	8,000,000	A	11/90

KOONING, WILLIAM DE	*1,210,000	A	5/83
KRIMMEL, JOHN LEWIS	308,000	G	12/83
KROLL, LEON	93,500	L	9/88
KRONBERG, LOUIS	25,300	F	11/86
KUHN, WALT	308,000	F	12/92
KUNIYOSKI, YASUO	616,000	S	12/87
LATHROP, WILLIAM LANGSON	18,700	L	12/88
LAURENCE, SYDNEY	187,000	L	8/88
LAWMAN, JASPER HOLMAN	52,800	L	4/88
LAWRIE, ALEXANDER	8,800	F	5/88
LAWSON, ERNEST	220,000	L	5/87
LEVINE, JACK	93,500	G	5/88
LEVY, ALEXANDER O.	20,900	F	5/88
LINSON, CORWIN KNAPP	42,900	L	3/88
LITTLE, PHILIP	13,200	L	5/87
LOVERIDGE, CLINTON	18,700	L	5/87
LOW, MARY L.F.(MacMONNIES)	17,600	F	12/81
LOW, WILL HICOK	45,100	I	5/88
LOZOWICK, LOUIS	203,000	A	12/87
MACDONALD-WRIGHT, STANTON	484,000	A	5/90
MAENTEL, JACOB	143,000	P	1/87
MAN-RAY	825,000	A	11/79
MANGOLD, ROBERT	176,000	A	5/88
MARSH, REGINALD	165,000	G	12/87
MARTIN, HOMER DODGE	33,000	L	5/86
MASON, ALICE TRUMBULL	22,000	A	12/87
MATTESON, TOMPKINS H.	21,000	G	8/90
MEEKER, JOSEPH R.	38,500	L	12/88
MELLON, MARY BLOOD	51,700	M	3/92
MELROSE, ANDREW W.	37,500	M	10/73
METCALF, WILLARD LEROY	638,000	L	5/88
MIGNOT, LOUIS REMY	82,500	L	7/87
MILLER, HENRY	7,700	F	6/88
MILLER, RICHARD E.	638,000	F	5/90
MORAN, EDWARD	156,500	M	12/93

MORAN, THOMAS	1,045,000	L	11/90
MORLEY, MALCOLM	506,000	A	?/90
MORSE, SAMUEL F.B.	57,200	F	12/88
MULLER, HEINRICH E.	25,300	L	5/84
MULLER, KARL	15,750	X	4/91
MURPHY, JOHN FRANCIS	19,800	L	9/81
McAULIFFE, JAMES J.	37,400	M	6/87
McCLOSKEY, WILLIAM JOHN	231,000	S	12/87
NASON, GERTRUDE	14,850	S	5/88
NEWELL, HUGH	27,500	G	5/81
NEWMAN, BARNETT	1,754,500	A	5/85
NICHOLS, BURR H.	17,600	L	5/88
NIEMEYER, JOHN HENRY	14,300	F	12/86
NISBET, ROBERT H.	22,000	L	12/88
NOLAND, KENNETH	2,035,000	A	11/89
NORDELL, CARL J.	11,000	F	6/82
NORTH, NOAH	39,600	P(F)	1/87
O'KEEFFE, GEORGIA	1,800,000	A	12/87
OCHTMAN, LEONARD	24,000	L	4/85
OKADA, KENZO	170,000	A	10/90
OLINSKY, IVAN G.	90,500	F	5/93
OWEN, ROBERT EMMETT	13,200	L	12/86
PAGE, WILLIAM	77,000	F	5/86
PALMER, PAULINE	45,100	L	10/87
PALMER, SAMUEL	50,700	L	11/90
PALMER, WALTER LAUNT	39,600	L	12/87
PANSING, FRED	44,000	M	9/86
PARKER, LAWTON S.	198,000	F	5/88
PASCIN, JULES	515,000	A	11/90
PASKELL, WILLIAM F.	2,500	L	2/85
PEALE, HARRIET CARY	80,000	F	5/91
PEALE, CHARLES WILLSON	451,000	F	3/86
PEALE, REMBRANDT	4,070,000	F	12/85
PEARCE, CHARLES SPRAGUE	247,500	F	6/81
PELTON, AGNES	27,500	L	5/88

PERU, ALTO	28,600	F	5/81
PETERSON, JANE	*30,800	F	5/85
PETO, JOHN FREDERICK	506,000	S	6/84
PHILLIPS, AMMI	682,000	P (F)	1/85
PIENE, OTTO	38,050	A	12/90
PIERCE, WALDO	7,260	M	3/86
PIPPIN, HORACE	385,000	P	12/87
PLUMMER, EDWIN	*9,900	P	10/88
POLLACK, JACKSON	11,550,000	A	5/89
POLLACK, JACKSON	*1,210,000	A	11/87
POPE, ALEXANDER	187,000	S	11/81
PRENTICE, LEVI WELLS	50,600	S	5/87
PRIOR, WILLIAM MATTHEW	82,500	P(F)	8/88
RANNEY, WILLIAM TYLEE	748,000	G	10/80
RAPP, J.	4,400	L	6/88
REDMOND, GRANVILLE	132,000	L	6/90
REHN, FRANK K.M.	4,950	M	11/84
REID, ROBERT LOUIS	341,000	L	12/88
REIFFEL, CHARLES	30,800	L	11/89
REINHARDT, AD	2,530,000	A	5/90
REMINGTON, FREDERIC S.	4,730,000	G	11/89
REULANDT, LE GRAND de	26,400	M	5/86
REYNOLDS, W.S.	17,600	S	5/86
RICHARDS, WILLIAM TROST	275,000	L	12/88
RIPLEY, AIDEN LASSELL	58,300	W	5/90
RITMAN, LOUIS	451,000	F	5/89
RITSCHEL, WILLIAM	66,000	M	3/88
ROBINSON, THEODORE	522,500	L(F)	12/86
ROCKWELL, CLEVELAND	52,500	M	11/87
RONDEL, FREDERICK	22,000	L	4/87
ROSE, GUY	126,000	L	12/88
ROSELAND, HARRY	253,000	F	11/90
ROSENQUIST, JAMES	2,090,000	A	11/86
ROTHKO, MARK	2,750,000	A	11/88
RUSSELL, CHARLES MARION	1,100,000	G	11/89

SARGENT, JOHN SINGER	1,430,000	F	5/86
SARGENT, JOHN SINGER	*192,000	F	8/86
SAVAGE, EUGENE FRANCIS	44,000	F	9/90
SAYRE, FRED GRAYSON	11,000	L	5/86
SCHAMBERG, MORTON LIVINGSTON	308,000	A	5/90
SCHATTENSTEIN, NIKOL	11,550	F	4/88
SCOTT, JULIAN	33,000	F	6/83
SHEELER, CHARLES	1,870,000	A (L)	6/83
SHEELER, CHARLES	*242,000	A	12/87
SHINN, EVERETT	*308,000	F	5/88
SHIRLAW, WALTER	16,500	F	6/85
SKYNNER, THOMAS	(pair) 107,250	P	10/86
SMITH, DAVID	990,000	A	5/87
SMITH, DECOST	14,300	G	12/86
SMITH, FRANCIS HOPKINSON	*46,200	L	5/89
SMITH, JACK WILKINSON	49,500	L	6/88
SMITH, JOSEPH B.	32,000	M	11/83
SMITH, LETTA CRAPO	16,500	F	12/88
SMITH, ROYAL BREWSTER	(pair) 41,800	F	10/87
SONNTAG, WILLIAM LOUIS (Jr)	*13,200	M	5/88
SONNTAG, WILLIAM LOUIS (Sr)	55,000	L	12/88
SOYER, ISAAC	26,400	G	12/88
SOYER, RAPHAEL	176,000	F	12/85
SPAT, GABRIEL	12,100	G	3/88
SPENCER, FREDERICK	12,100	F	4/88
SPENCER, LILLY MARTIN	99,000	F	12/83
SPENCER, ROBERT S.	99,000	G	5/90
SPRINCHORN, CARL	*15,400	A	4/85
STAMOS, THEODOROS	192,500	A	2/88
STEARNS, JULIUS BRUTUS	66,000	G	1/87
STEINBERG, SAUL	*154,000	A	11/83
STELLA, FRANK	5,060,000	A	11/89
STELLA, JOSEPH	2,200,000	A	12/86
STEVENS, WILLIAM LESTER	12,100	L	3/87
STEWART, JULIUS L.	847,000	F	11/90

STILL, CLYFFORD	2,400,000	A	11/92
STRAUS, MEYER	15,400	L	12/86
STUART, GILBERT	990,000	F	1/86
STULL, HENRY	77,000	W	6/85
SULLY, THOMAS	143,000	F	12/88
SUYDAM, JAMES A.	88,000	M	11/89
TAIT, ARTHUR F.	418,000	G	1/87
TANGUY, YVES	506,000	A	5/88
TANNER, HENRY OSSAWA	275,000	G	12/81
TARBELL, EDMUND CHARLES	442,500	F	5/93
THIEBAUD, WAYNE	605,000	A	2/88
THOMPSON, LESLIE P.	26,400	F	5/86
TING, WALASSE	*45,706	F	10/92
TOJETTI, DOMENICO	16,500	F	1/88
TOMLIN, BRADLEY	572,000	A	11/89
TOMPKINS, FRANK HECTOR	16,500	F	12/86
TRACY, JOHN M.	50,600	G	9/83
TROTTER, NEWBOLD H.	17,050	W	1/82
TRUMBULL, JOHN	286,000	F	1/86
TRYON, DWIGHT WILLIAM	71,500	L	2/88
TUCKER, MARY B.	*25,300	P	10/87
TUDOR, ROBERT M.	17,050	G	5/86
TWACHTMAN, JOHN HENRY	605,000	L	12/86
TWOMBLY, CY	*4,800,000	A	11/90
TYLER, JAMES GALE	32,500	M	9/80
VAIL, EUGENE LAURENT	10,450	M	5/88
VOGT, LOUIS CHARLES	*4,950	L	12/86
VOORHEES, CLARK G.	12,100	L	12/88
VOS, HUBERT	*13,200	X(S)	?92
WALDO, SAMUEL LOVETT	33,000	F	10/78
WALKLEY, DAVID B.	7,424	F	3/82
WALL, ALFRED S.	13,475	L	4/85
WARSHAWSKY, ABEL GEORGE	26,000	L	4/86
WATERS, SUSAN C.	92,950	P(F)	9/81
WAY, ANDREW J.H.	20,900	S	5/86

WEBBER, CHARLES T.	13,200	F	11/86
WEEKS, EDWIN LORD	242,000	G	2/89
WENDT, WILLIAM	70,400	L	3/88
WEST, BENJAMIN	*165,000	F	5/84
WEYL, MAX	9,900	L	3/86
WHISTLER, ABBOTT McNEIL	*154,000	F	12/85
WHITTREDGE, T. WORTHINGTON	1,870,000	L	5/89
WIGGINS, JOHN CARLETON	18,700	L	12/84
WIGHT, MOSES	13,200	G	1/88
WILES, IRVING RAMSEY	*46,750	F	5/88
WILGUS, WILLIAM JOHN	143,000	F	12/86
WILLARD, ARCHIBALD M.	150,000	G	11/80
WILLIAMS, FREDERICK D.	15,400	L	?
WILLIAMS, MICAH	22,000	P	6/86
WILLIAMS, VIRGIL	16,500	G	10/87
WINNER, WILLIAM E.	19,800	G	3/86
WINTER, ANDREW	18,700	M	5/87
WOELFLE, ARTHUR WILLIAM	9,350	L	12/80
WONNER, PAUL JOHN	30,800	S	2/88
WOOD, GEORGE BACON JR.	14,000	L	3/91
WOOD, ROBERT E.	17,000	L	3/84
WOOD, THOMAS WATERMAN	93,000	F	5/88
WOODSIDE, JOHN ARCHIBALD	286,000	P (L)	6/82
WOOLF, SAMUEL JOHNSON	60,500	?	?
WORES, THEODORE	19,800	L	5/87
WUERMER, CARL	23,100	L	5/84
WYETH, ANDREW	462,000	W	12/81
WYETH, NEWELL CONVERS	135,000	I	?/83
WYLIE, ROBERT	46,000	G	5/93
WYMAN, F.A.	41,800	L	1/84
YELLAND, RAYMOND DABB	55,000	L	3/92
YENS, KARL	37,400	F	12/87

APPENDIX

"On-Line" Database

For the serious art dealer,collector, appraiser, and auctioneer, the "on-line" database described below is essential. You go to your terminal, touch a few keys, and you quickly have access to the world's most complete coverage of international auction sales.

Artquest, a subscription computer service, was compiled by Richard Hislop, editor of *Art Sales Index* (ASI). This database contains the international sales results of the past 24 years. Presently on the database are the results from the sale of over one million paintings worldwide - the work of over 125,000 artists.

You can retrieve information in innumerable ways: by artist, title, size, medium, nationality, price (i.e., descending or ascending order), most recent sales, and much more. *Artquest* can also give you an analysis of each artist's auction record during the past 24 years, year by year. Information can be accessed in seconds; important when you are paying over $2.00 per minute for "connect" time. It is worth the expense, though, because you can glean information in seconds from *Artquest*, which you could not gather from guide books, after weeks of investigation.

I subscribe to *Artquest*, and wholeheartedly recommend it to any active art dealer, collector, appraiser, or auctioneer. Any novice to computers can learn to use *Artquest* successfully in a very short time. For more information call or write:

Artquest
Art Sales Index, Ltd.
1 Thames Street
Weybridge, Surrey KT13 8JG, UK

TELEPHONE: (0932) 856426
FAX: (0932) 842482

ART DEALERS

The following is a list of art dealers who have elected to advertise in this sixth edition. If you are a painting dealer and have an interest in placing an ad in the next edition, please call or write: **Currier Publications**, 241 Main Sreet, Stoneham, MA, 02180, tel: (800) 344-0760.

CALIFORNIA

K. Nathan Gallery
P.O. Box 344
La Jolla, CA 92038
(619) 459-3490

(Specializing in California Impressionist and American Folk Art)

CONNECTICUT

Gallery Forty Four
Rte 44 (opposite post office)
New Hartford, CT 06057
(203) 379-2083

(19th and 20th Century American Paintngs)

ILLINOIS

Summit Gallery
822 Dempter Street
Evanston, IL 60202
(708) 733-0330

(Fine American & European Paintings)

MAINE

Wiscasset Bay Gallery
Water Street, P.O.Box 309
Wiscasset, ME 04578
(207) 882-7682; 725-9735

(Buying 19th & 20th Century American and European Paintings; Special Interest in Maine and New England Artists.)

MASSACHUSETTS

Frank H. Hogan Fine Arts, Inc.
P.O.Box 1829
Orleans, MA 02653
(508) 255-2676

(please see Display Ad)

MINNESOTA

F.B.Horowitz Fine Art
830 Edgemoor Drive
Hopkins, MN 55305
(612) 935-2120/Fax:(612) 935-2129

(please see Display Ad)

NEW YORK

Green River Gallery
Boston Corners
RD 2, Box 130
Millerton, NY 12456
(518) 789-3311

(19th & 20th Century American
Art with Emphasis in Art of the
American West)

PENNSYLVANIA

Lagakos-Turak Gallery
132 South 17th Street
Philadelphia, PA 19103
(215) 735-4646

(19th & Early 20th Century
American Paintings)

VERMONT

Brady Galleries, Inc.
P.O.Box 9491
South Burlinton, VT 05407
(802) 475-2534

(please see Display Ad)

BIOGRAPHICAL RESOURCES

The following is a list of those dictionaries that deal specifically with American artists. The prices for these references may vary between $40 and $120.

- *19th Century Louisiana Painters and Paintings*, Martin and Margaret Wiesendanger

- *A Biographical Index of American Artists*, Smith

- *American Impressionism*, William H. Gerdts

- *American Women Artists 1830-1930*, The National Museum of Women in the Arts

- *American Women Artists From Early Indian Times To The Present*, Charlotte S. Rubinstein

- *Art and Artists of Indiana*, Mary Q. Burnet

- *Artists In California 1786-1940*, Edan Milton Hughes

- *Artists in Virginia Before 1900*, R. Lewis Wright

- *Artists of Early Michigan*, Arthur H. Gibson

- *Artists of the American West*, Doris Ostrander Dawdy

- *Artists of the Old West*, Ewers

- *Biographical Sketches of American Artists*, Helen R. Earle

- *California Artists 1935-1956*, Dewitt Clinton McCall

- *Contemporary Western Artists*, Harold Samuels

- *Dictionary of American Artists, Sculptors, and Engravers*, William Young

- *Dictionary of American Artists, Sculptors and Engravers*, Mantle Fielding, edited by Glenn B. Opitz

- *Dictionary of American Artists of the 19th & 20th Century*, Alice Coe McGlauflin

- *Dictionary of American Artists*, Alice McGlauflin

- *Dictionary of American Artists*, F. Levy

- *Dictionary of Contemporary American Artists*, Paul Cummings

- *Dictionary of Marine Artists*, E.R. Brewington

- *Dictionary of Women Artists*, Chris Pettey

- *Encyclopedia of American Art*, Milton Rugoff

- *Folk Artists Biographical Index*, George H. Meyer

- *Illustrated Biographical Encyclopedia of Artists of the American West*, Peggy and Harold Samuel

- *Index of Artists*, Daniel Trowbridge Mallett (2 vol)

- *Index to Artistic Biography*, Patricia P. Havlice

- *Masterworks of California Impressionism*, The Morton H. Fleisher collection

- *National Academy of Design Exhibition Record 1861-1900*, Maria Naylor (2 vol)

- *New Hampshire Scenery - A Dictionary of 19th Century Artists of New Hampshire Mountain Landscapes*, Catherine Campbell

- *Olana's Guide to American Artists* (2 vol.), Olana

- *Painters of the Humble Truth - Masterpieces of American Still Life*, William H. Gerdts

- *Plein Air Painters of California: The North*, Ruth Westphal

- *Plein Air Painters of California: The Southland*, Ruth Westphal

- *Provincetown Painters: 1890's to 1970's*, Everson Museum of Art

- *Publications in Southern California Art*, Nancy Moure (3 vol)

- *The Boston Athenaeum Art Exhibition Record 1827-1874*, R. Perkins and W. Gavin III

- *The Boston Painters 1900-1930*, Ives Gammel

- Appendix -

- *The Card Catalog of the Manuscript Collections of the Archives of American Art*, Scholarly Resources Inc. (10 vol)

- *The Classified Directory of Artists' Signatures, Symbols, & Monograms -American Artists*, H. H. Caplan

- *The Concise Dictionary of Artists' Signatures*, Radway Jackson

- *The Dictionary of Woman Artists (Born before 1900)*, Chris Petteys

- *The Illustrator in America 1880-1980*, Walt and Roger Reed

- *The New York Historical Society's Dictionary of Artists in America*, Groce and Wallace

- *The Society of Independent Artists*, Clark S. Marlor

- *Who Was Who in American Art*, Peter Hastings Falk

- *Who's Who in American Art*, Jaques Cattell Press

- *Women Artists in America*, Glenn B.Opitz

Olana Gallery
2 Carillon Road
Brewster, NY 10509
(914) 279-8077

(please see Display Ad)

Agencies

The leading resource, nationally, for biographical information is the National Museum of American Art, Washington, D.C. (a division of the Smithsonian Institution). It offers comprehensive details on American Paintings executed before the year 1914. Researchers can visit in person or make inquires through the mail. I have reproduced below the information available from the Smithsonian with regards to the Museum.

The *Inventory of American Paintings Executed Before 1914* is a computerized index listing over 230,000 records of paintings in public as well as private collections throughout the nation. Information is indexed by artist, owner, location, and subject matter. Complementing the descriptive indexes is an Image File of approximately 45,000 photographs and reproductions which are available for study in the inventory office.

The *Peter A. Juley and Son Collection* of approximately 127,000 photographic negatives documents works of art and artists. located in New York City and specializing in photography of fine arts, the Juley firm which was active from 1896 to 1975 produced many negatives of art historical significance. They recorded works of art now lost, destroyed, or altered in appearance. Preliminary computer indexing of the collection has been completed. Negatives will be made available in the NMAA Slide and Photograph Archives.

The *Smithsonian Art Index* was initiated in 1976 by the National Museum of American Art to identify and to record works of art - drawings, prints, paintings and sculpture - in Smithsonian divisions which were not part of the museum collection. The Index was designed as a research tool or directory to a vast amount of material that had been overlooked by or was largely unknown to scholars and the public. A total of 9,565 records representing 207,208 objects in the Smithsonian Institution is indexed by artist, division, donor/source, and subject.

The *Slide and Photograph Archives*, a facility for the visual documentation of American art, consists of approximately 60,000 35mm color slide and 200,000 photographs and negatives. Slides and photographs are available for research on the premises and a smaller collection of 12,000 slides is available for borrowing by the public.

The *Pre-1877 Art Exhibition Catalogue Index* is a computerized project to index information from over 700 rare catalogues of exhibitions which were held between 1790 and 1876 at art unions, museums, state fairs, auctions, commercial galleries, and lotteries in the United States and Canada. When completed, the Index will provide valuable information on individual artists, patrons, art organizations, media, and subject matter as well as on the histories of specific works of art that my no longer be extant.

The *Permanent Collection Data Base*, a computerized listing, provides information on the over 30,000 objects in the museum's permanent collection. The object records in the data base are indexed by artists, title, medium, department and other classifications.

THE ARCHIVES OF AMERICAN ART

The Archives of American Art which have seven offices nationwide, are another very important source of biographical material on American artists. The following are their locations and telephone numbers.

Boston, Massachusetts	(617) 565-8444
Detroit, Michigan	(313) 226-5744
Houston, Texas	(713) 526-1361
New York City	(212) 826-5722
San Francisco, California	(415) 556-2530
San Marino, California	(818) 405-7849
Washington, D.C.	(202) 357-2781(Headqtrs)

If you live in New York City, a wealth of art resources can be found in *The Frick Art Reference Library*, located at:

10 East 71st Street
New York, NY 10021

(212) 288-8700

Last, but not least, are the fine arts departments around the country in our major public libraries and museums.

APPRAISAL ORGANIZATIONS

If you have need of an art appraiser, be sure he or she is a member in good standing of one of the respected appraisal organizations, nationally. Here are your leading sources for qualified appraisers. Always ask for references.

The Appraisers Assoc.
of America (suite 2505)
60 E 42nd St
New York, NY 10165

(212) 867-9775

The American Society
of Appraisers
Box 17265
Washington, DC 20041

(703) 478-2228

The Art Dealers Association
575 Madison Avenue
New York, NY 10022

(212) 940-8590

The New England
Appraisers Assoc.
5 Gill Terrace
Ludlow, VT 05149

(802) 228-7444

The Intr'nl Society
of Appraisers
Box 280
River Forest, IL 60305

(312) 848-3340

United States Appr. Assoc.,Inc.
1041 Tower Road
Winnetka, IL 60093

(312) 446-3434

In addition to the list above, the *major* auction houses also provide appraisal services.

AUTHENTICATION SERVICES:

The Art Dealers Association will be helpful when you need an expert to authenticate a valuable work of art.

The International Foundation for Art Research (IFAR) provides an authentication service for valuable works of art. For more information on all their services, write or call:

IFAR
Executive Director
46 East 70th Street
New York, NY 10021

(212) 879-1780

PAINTING CONSERVATORS

Because of limitations of space, only a representative sample of conservators has been compiled from the United States. Only telephone numbers are given. Please remember, the simplest and safest approach to take in finding a competent conservator is to get a referral from a reputable art gallery or museum.

CALIFORNIA

Greaves, James L.	(213) 857-6161
Lohnert, Andrej	(909) 766-0361
Lorenz, Richard	(415) 929-1240
Minguillon, Emilio	(619) 726-4665

CONNECTICUT

Goring, Ruth Walker	(203) 572-8873
Hindermann, Andrea	(203) 535-2124
Kimball, David	(203) 653-5465
McElroy, Richard	(203) 928-6114

Art Restoration & Associates **(203) 387-4087**
Karen A. Lumpkin
   214 Derby Avenue
   Orange, CT 06477-1317
   Museum quality restorations. Trained in the conservation of paintings, frames, and fine art.

DISTRICT OF COLUMBIA

Page, Arthur H. IV	(202) 333-6269

FLORIDA

Putnam, Harold   (305) 567-5870

INDIANA

Phegley, Monica Radecki   (219) 287-0266

LOUISIANA

Bessor, Louise C.   (504) 241-2587

MARYLAND

Archer-Shee, Audrey Z.   (301) 822-0703
Caraher, Josepha   (301) 435-7275
Dennis, Alexandra   (301) 986-1296
Jones, Sian B.   (301) 433-0038
Klatzo, Cornelia   (301) 530-0880

MASSACHUSETTS

Abrams, Linda M.   (617) 272-8391
Bradley, Morton   (617) 643-6154
Brink, Elise   (617) 566-5252
Coren, Simon   (508) 394-1416

Peter Kostoulakos   **(508) 453-8888**
     15 Sayles Street
     Lowell, MA 01851
     Oil paintings cleaned and restored.

Peter Williams/Museum Services   **(617) 536-4092**
     30 Ipswich Street
     Boston, MA 02215
     (please see Display Ad)

MICHIGAN

Plaggemars, Howard O.   (616) 396-6607

MISSOURI

Larson, Sidney   (314) 445-2058

NEW HAMPSHIRE

Heritage Art Restoration   **(603) 942-5763**
   Rte 4 Box 104
   Northwood, NH 03261
   (please see Display Ad)

NEW JERSEY

Duff, Suzanne   (201) 228-9701
DeFlorio, Dante   (201) 744-2640

NEW MEXICO

Munzenrider, Claire   (505) 982-4300

NEW YORK

Bronold & Winnicke   (212) 982-3416
Farancz, Alan M.   (212) 563-5550
Katlan, Alexander   (718) 445-7458
Scott Jr., John C.   (212) 714-0620
Van Gelder, Mark E.   (607) 547-5585
VoorHees, Alan Lee   (607) 739-7898
West Lake Conservators, Ltd.   (315) 685-8534

PENNSYLVANIA

Bucks County Art &
   Antiques Company   **(215) 345-0892**
   246 West Ashland Street
   Doylestown, PA 18901
Restoration of oil paintings, frame repair and antique restoration.

RHODE ISLAND

Bosworth, David   (401) 789-1306

SOUTH CAROLINA

Newell, Virginia E.   (803) 254-1640

TEXAS

Kennedy, Ellen D.   (713) 520-1808
Rajer, Anton   (806) 655-7191
Van Slyke, Angelo   (713) 520-1808

VIRGINIA

Clover, Cecile   (804) 973-8126

WASHINGTON

Harrison, Alexander   (604) 732-5217

WISCONSIN

Rajer, Anton   (414) 457-3056

Museum Classics
5051 West Jefferson Blvd.
Los Angeles, CA 90016
(213) 731-7536

(please see Display Ad)

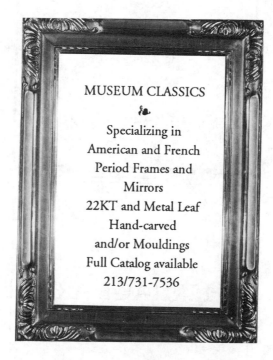

MUSEUM CLASSICS

Specializing in
American and French
Period Frames and
Mirrors
22KT and Metal Leaf
Hand-carved
and/or Mouldings
Full Catalog available
213/731-7536

PERIOD FRAMES

Below is a bibliography of titles pertaining to frame history.

Frame Bibliography

Adair, William. *Frames in America, 1700-1900: Survey of Fabrication, Technique and Style*, The American Institute of Architects Foundation, 1983.

Brettell, Richard R. and Starling, Steven. *The Art of the Edge: European Frames 1300 - 1900*. Art Institute of Chicago, IL, 1986

Grimm, Claus. *The Book of Picture Frames*. Abaris Books, NY, 1981

Grimm, Claus. *Alte Bilderrahmen*. Munich: Georg D.W. Callwey, 1978.

Heydenryk, Henry. *The Art and History of Frames.. An Inquiry into the Enhancement of paintings*. New York: James H. Heineman, 1963.

Jones, Harvey L. *Mathews. Masterpieces of the California Decorative Style*. Santa Barbara and Salt Lake City: Peregrine Smith, 1980.

Mitchell, Paul. *Italian Picture Frames 1500-1825: A Brief Survey*. Furniture History: The Journal of the Furniture History Society 20 (1984), pp. 18-47.

Maryanski, Richard A.. *Antique Picture Frame Guide*. Cedar Forest, NY, 1973.

Van Hoist, Niels. *Creators, Collectors, and Connoisseurs*. London: Thames and Hudson, 1967.

Wilner, Eli. *The Art of the Frame: American Frames of the Arts and Crafts Period*. Eli Wilner & Co. (catalog), NY, 1988

ART SERVICES

This section is new to the Sixth Edition. If you feel your business is unique to the art field, and you would like to advertise here, please call 1-800-344-0760. The following is our first advertiser for this new section:

The Gold Leaf
3537 East Palm Lane
Phoenix, AZ 85008
(602) 224-9274

Full line of gilded, hand lettered title plates on hardwood.

MOVING & STORAGE COMPANIES

This is a new section to the appendix. If you provide a service which would be appropriately advertised in this new section, please call 1-800-344-0760.

TCI
37 Elm Street #8
Westfield, NJ 07090
(800) 752-7002 (voice line)
(908) 789-7002 (fax line)

Additional References

PAINTING CONSERVATION:

- *The Care of Pictures*, George L. Stout

- *The Cleaning of Pictures*, Helmut Ruhemann

- *Conservation and Scientific Analysis of Paintings*, Madelaine Hours

- *The Restorer's Handbook of Easel Painting*, Gilberte Emile-Male

- *A Handbook on the Care of Paintings*, Caroline K. Keck

AID IN DATING PAINTINGS:

- *Antique Picture Frame Guide*, Richard A. Maryanski

- *Book of Picture Frames*, Grimm

- *Frames in America, 1700-1900: Survey of Fabrication,*
- Technique and Style, William Adair

- *American Costume 1840-1920*, Worrell

- *Two Centuries of Costume in America 1620-1820*, Alice M. Earle

- *Costume and Fashion: A Concise History*, James Laver

- *Treasury of American Design*, Clarence P. Hornung

- *American Artists' Material Suppliers Directory - 19th Century*, Alexander W. Katlan

Important Notes

Important Notes

Important Notes

Important Notes